December 19, 2019

For Gordon –

In friendship &
with highest respect

The Twenty-Second Amendment and the Limits of Presidential Tenure

The Twenty-Second Amendment and the Limits of Presidential Tenure

A Tradition Restored

Martin B. Gold

LEXINGTON BOOKS
Lanham • Boulder • New York • London

Published by Lexington Books
An imprint of The Rowman & Littlefield Publishing Group, Inc.
4501 Forbes Boulevard, Suite 200, Lanham, Maryland 20706
www.rowman.com

6 Tinworth Street, London SE11 5AL, United Kingdom

British Library Cataloguing in Publication Information Available

Library of Congress Control Number: 2019950671

ISBN 978-1-4985-6266-9 (cloth: alk. paper)
ISBN 978-1-4985-6267-6 (electronic)

™ The paper used in this publication meets the minimum requirements of American National Standard for Information Sciences—Permanence of Paper for Printed Library Materials, ANSI/NISO Z39.48-1992.

Dedicated to the memory of Wendell L. Willkie, Presidential nominee, foreign policy visionary, American statesman

Contents

Acknowledgments

I express special gratitude to Allegra Han, who has assisted me throughout the preparation of this book. She has been instrumental in securing pertinent materials from congressional debates, committee proceedings, and related materials. During this process, she has been her customary patient and dependable self, and I have been able to rely on her research with high confidence.

Erika Dowell, Director and Curator of *Modern Books and Manuscripts* at the Lilly Library, Indiana University, was immensely helpful in assisting me with the Wendell Willkie papers, which are housed there. These materials are central to an understanding of the 1940 presidential campaign, which led to Franklin Roosevelt's third term and ultimately fueled determination in Congress and the states to put term limits in the Constitution. My thanks as well go to David Willkie, Mr. Willkie's grandson, who facilitated my access to these papers.

I appreciate the assistance of Melissa S. Mead, The John M. and Barbara Kiel University Archivist and Rochester Collections Librarian at the Rush Rhess Library, and Melinda Wallington, Senior Library Assistant, both at the University of Rochester. The university is the repository for the Thomas E. Dewey papers.

Heather Moore is the Photo Historian at the United States Senate. Her counterpart in the House of Representatives is Michelle Strizever. Both kindly provided vital access to congressional photo records. I appreciate the chance to work with them. Most of the photos used in this book came from these sources.

I am grateful to Shelley Husband, formerly Chief of Staff and General Counsel of the House Judiciary Committee. Activity in 1947 that resulted in the Twenty-second Amendment began in that committee. Ms. Husband assisted my research into the committee's proceedings.

Gratitude goes as well to Rita Lari, Deputy Staff Director of the Senate Judiciary Committee and to the committee's Librarian, Chuck Papirmeister. The Judiciary Committee was the center of Senate activity on the Twenty-second Amendment. Both of them were helpful in guiding me to relevant materials.

Senator Alexander Wiley of Wisconsin chaired the Senate Judiciary Committee in 1947. I acknowledge the assistance of Lee Grady, Reference Archivist at the Wisconsin Historical Society, as well as Gregory T. Smith, Director of Archival Investigations at History Piquette, LLC in Wisconsin. Mr. Smith rendered substantial support to me in reviewing Senator Wiley's papers, which are located at the University of Wisconsin.

I am grateful for technical assistance from Taylor Rose, who has helped at various stages in the production of this manuscript.

I express great thanks to three friends and partners at Lexington Books. They are Emily Roderick, Editor for Political Science, African Studies, and Legal Studies; Becca Rohde, Associate Acquisitions Editor, Criminology and Legal Studies; and Assistant Editor, Alison Keefner. Each has been thoughtful and patient throughout my preparation of this book.

My wife, Celeste Gold, has given me invaluable editorial advice on this work, as she has on every other book I have ever written. Because of her keen eye and good judgment, she has much improved this material. Celeste has long worked at the United States Senate, and maintains a very active and demanding schedule there. Nevertheless, she selflessly and lovingly devotes time to help me on my manuscripts. She is my friend and collaborator, always.

Martin B. Gold
Washington, DC
July, 2019

Preface

On January 20, 2017, Donald J. Trump took the oath of office as the 45th President of the United States. His predecessor, Barack Obama, was forced to retire after eight years in office. Although Obama might have run successfully again, he was constitutionally ineligible to do so. The Twenty-second Amendment, ratified more than sixty years earlier, imposed a two-term limitation.

Dwight D. Eisenhower was the first president subject to these restrictions, and left the White House in 1961 after two terms. His successor, John F. Kennedy, completed thirty-four months in office before assassination. Lyndon B. Johnson finished the last fourteen months of Kennedy's term and won a full term of his own in the 1964 election.

Under the Twenty-second Amendment, Johnson would have been eligible to seek another elected term in 1968. The Amendment accounts for service by a person who has "held the office of President or acted as President" for up to two years of a term to which someone else was elected. Had Johnson won reelection in 1968, and finished his second elected term, he would have been president for eight years and fourteen months, the longest presidency ever, except for Franklin Roosevelt's, which lasted twelve years and thirty-eight days.

Voters elected Richard Nixon in 1968 and 1972, but he resigned only nineteen months into his second term. Gerald Ford completed the remaining twenty-nine months, then ran for election in 1976 for a term of his own. Ford lost. Had he won, he could not have run again in 1980, because he served more than half of Nixon's unexpired term.

Jimmy Carter succeeded Ford, but Ronald Reagan defeated him in 1980. The country reelected Reagan in 1984. On January 20, 1989, he became the first president since Eisenhower to finish two full terms. The Twenty-second Amendment disqualified him from seeking a third.

George Herbert Walker Bush followed Reagan. In 1992, Bush lost reelection to Bill Clinton, who went on to serve two complete terms. Clinton left office on January 20, 2001, still youthful and vigorous. The Twenty-second Amendment forced his retirement.

George W. Bush followed Clinton and was president for eight years. The Amendment also mandated Bush's retirement in 2009. Obama succeeded him.

Since it became part of the Constitution in 1951, the Twenty-second Amendment has legally barred five presidents from seeking to extend their time in office. As such, it has had a highly consequential impact on American history. Without it, the durably popular Eisenhower may have triumphed in 1960 over Senator John F. Kennedy. Having survived impeachment proceedings, Bill Clinton enjoyed strong approval ratings as his second term wound down. He would well been well positioned to win reelection. So would have Barack Obama. Had Obama been able to seek a third term, he may have taken the oath in 2017, rather than Trump.

Before the Twenty-second Amendment, an unwritten rule served to limit presidential tenure It was known as the two-term tradition. George Washington appeared to start it, when he left office in 1797 after two terms. Thomas Jefferson soon reinforced it, with his retirement in 1809. The tradition held fast for a century and a half.

Franklin Roosevelt broke through in 1940, when he successfully sought a third term. However, he was not the first president to try. Several others contemplated trying to stay on the job, or to return to the White House after a hiatus.

Roosevelt's wins, in 1940 for a third term and in 1944 for a fourth, provoked a question. Could or should a venerable tradition ever be restored? The answer came in the words of the Twenty-second Amendment.

This book explains how and why the amendment came to be. The length of presidential terms, as well as the question of reeligibility for office, were thorny topics for delegates to the Constitutional Convention, which met in Philadelphia in 1787. The story of the Twenty-second Amendment really begins there, nearly two centuries before it was ratified.

Chapter 1

The Constitutional Convention (1787) and Its Aftermath

On February 21, 1787, the Articles of Confederation Congress, meeting in New York, resolved "that in the opinion of Congress, it is expedient that on the second Monday in May next, a convention of delegates, who shall have been appointed by the several states, be held at Philadelphia." Virginia was America's most populous state. Deeply frustrated by the experience of governance under the Articles, and skeptical of repairing the system through cosmetic reforms, it led agitation to convene such a gathering. As Professor Richard Beeman writes, "The men responsible for initiating the call for a constitutional convention, their hopes and fears shaped by the challenges and frustrations of fighting a long, costly war and of securing peace and public order at home, had come to believe that the continental government's lack of 'energy' posed an equally formidable threat to liberty."[1]

Proposed by the Second Continental Congress in 1777, the Articles had been in effect since 1781. State governments exercised true power within that structure, with minor delegations to the national government. Article II expressly provided, "Each state retains its sovereignty, freedom, and independence, and every power, jurisdiction, and right, which is not by this Confederation expressly delegated to the United States, in Congress assembled."

Under the Articles, someone elected from within the ranks of Congress itself performed necessary executive functions. Article IX stated that, "The United States in Congress assembled shall have authority to appoint a committee, to sit in the recess of Congress, to be denominated 'A Committee of the States', and to consist of one delegate from each State; and to appoint such other committees and civil officers as may be necessary for managing the general affairs of the United States under their direction—to appoint one of their members to preside, provided that no person be allowed to serve in the office of president more than one year in any term of three years."

These men were known as the president of the United States in Congress assembled. Between 1781 and 1789, ten individuals served in this capacity, none for more than one year.

Operating under the Articles had been difficult for the fledgling United States. In April 1787, James Madison of Virginia prepared a paper titled, "Vices of the Political System of the United States."[2] He accurately critiqued a system in which the country was unable to provide for the common defense, could not present a uniform face to foreign powers, had no effective way to regulate interstate commerce, could not raise revenues, and had no capacity to command state compliance with national policy. Compounding these issues, the national legislative body was weak, and there was no independent president and no national judiciary. The United States was unlikely to thrive under such arrangements. The country might fail to remain unified. Worse yet, it could be vulnerable to foreign exploitation.

From New York, where he was attending the Confederation Congress, Madison wrote an April 16, 1787, letter to George Washington, outlining problems with the Articles, and recommending improvements to strengthen national authority. One such reform involved establishing a presidency. "A National Executive must also be provided," Madison said.[3]

As preparations for the convention were underway, Benjamin Franklin of Pennsylvania corresponded with Thomas Jefferson, then the American Minister to France. On April 19, 1787, Franklin wrote, "Our federal constitution is generally thought defective, and a convention first proposed by Virginia and since recommended by Congress, is to assemble here next month to revise it and propose amendments. . . . If it does not do good it will do harm, as it will show that we have not wisdom enough among us to govern ourselves."[4]

Most members of the Confederation Congress approached the convention cautiously, some even suspiciously, because it had the potential to produce changes that would weaken the role and power of states.[5] Adjustments to the Articles were necessary, it was generally agreed, but at the same time, state sovereignty was a jealously protected principle. The Articles themselves expressly stated, "Each State retains its sovereignty, freedom, and independence, and every power, jurisdiction, and right, which is not by this Confederation expressly delegated to the United States, in Congress assembled."[6]

The call for the convention stipulated that delegates would recommend revisions to the Articles to submit to Congress. Any that Congress approved, would be submitted to the state legislatures. To become effective, any such amendments would need unanimous approval of all states.[7]

Delegates began to assemble at the Pennsylvania State House, now known as Independence Hall, on Monday, May 14, 1787, but they did no business until a quorum of seven states finally materialized more than a week later, on Friday, May 25. Rhode Island never sent representatives to Philadelphia, so as a practical matter, it was a convention of twelve states, no more than eleven of which attended at any one time.[8] Not all delegates were present to vote on each of the propositions the Convention decided; thus, in many important cases the votes of particular states went unrecorded. Although appointed by their states, some delegates simply never arrived in Philadelphia at all. Others, like New Hampshire's, arrived quite late, or like New York's, left early.[9]

On the Convention's opening day, delegates unanimously elected General George Washington to preside, and attended to additional housekeeping matters. Every state was entitled to one vote, regardless of its size. This was the voting arrangement observed in the Confederation Congress. It vexed the large states to carry this principle forward to the Convention, but they needed the cooperation of smaller states to amend or even to replace the Articles.[10] Each state voted as a unit, regardless of the size of its delegation.[11] An evenly divided delegation meant that a state's vote did not count, the equivalent of an abstention.

On May 28 a committee chaired by George Wythe of Virginia reported a set of rules, which the Convention adopted.[12] Further rules came the next day, among which was a provision, suggested by North Carolina's Richard D. Spaight, for "a motion to reconsider a matter which has previously been determined by a majority."[13] The essence of this crucial rule was that nothing the Convention decided was ever final until the entire constitution was final. As features of the constitution took shape, they affected issues previously determined. Decisions already taken might need reconsideration in light of other decisions subsequently made, and states unrecorded on a previous vote could make their opinions heard during reconsideration. Moreover, certain topics were inherently controversial, and delegates seeking a reasonable place to stand were able to rethink previous conclusions. The most significant use of reconsideration came with respect to the National Executive, as delegates repeatedly changed their minds on difficult issues that formation of the presidency entailed. They took some sixty votes on these questions.[14]

Virginia exercised early leadership in directing the Convention's work.[15] Abandoning the idea that the Convention would simply address amendments to the Articles of Confederation, the Virginians proposed an expansive new government structure.[16] On Tuesday, May 29, their Governor, Edmund Randolph, rose to present a series of fifteen resolutions, known as the Virginia Plan.[17]

In contrast to the Articles of Confederation, which provided for a unicameral legislature and had no independent executive, Virginia Resolution Seven mandated "that a National Executive be instituted; to be chosen by the National Legislature." Richard Beeman, who chronicled the Convention, noted how distinct Randolph's proposal was from the constitutional structure that eventually materialized. "The seventh resolution, as presented by

Randolph, was sharply at odds with two central ideas that would eventually emerge as defining characteristics of the American government: democracy and separation of powers. Not only was the selection of the Executive one step removed from the people at large, but, in proposing that the Congress be given the power to select the Executive, the Virginia Plan could have subordinated the President to Congress."[18] In effect, as Beeman notes, the arrangement would have been more like a parliamentary system, in which the legislature dominates and the executive function derives direction from that body.[19]

As originally presented, the Virginia Plan left open the term of service. However, to preserve for the executive a measure of independence, the Plan specified that he "be ineligible a second time."[20]

Beginning on May 30, after Randolph presented the Virginia Plan, delegates debated it in the Committee of the Whole, chaired by Nathaniel Gorham of Massachusetts.[21] They addressed Resolution Seven on Friday, June 1, endeavoring to set the length of the presidential term.[22]

James Wilson of Pennsylvania proposed that the executive serve for three years, with no barrier to reelection.[23] Charles Pinckney of South Carolina countered with a single seven-year term. Virginia's George Mason argued that longer service, coupled with a bar to reelection, would preserve the executive's independence. According to Madison's notes, "Mr. Mason was for seven years at least, and for prohibiting re-eligibility as the best expedient for both preventing the effect of a false complaisance on the side of the Legislature toward unfit characters; and a temptation on the side of the Executive to intrigue with the Legislature for a re-appointment."[24]

Gunning Bedford of Delaware worried about leaving the executive in office for that long. If such a president were inadequate, the country could be stuck with him. "An impeachment would be no cure for this evil, as an impeachment would reach misfeasance only, not incapacity."[25] Therefore, Bedford endorsed Wilson's idea of a three-year term, and added that the executive should be eligible for reelection two additional times, thus a maximum of nine years.

There was a vote on Pinckney's motion for seven years. Five states voted in favor, four opposed, and Massachusetts divided.[26] General Washington ruled that a majority had voted in the affirmative.

The following day, Saturday, June 2, debate on the executive resumed, this time related to the mechanism of election. Wilson wanted to remove the choice of president from Congress and replace it with election by popular vote.[27] Per Madison's notes, "Mr. Wilson repeated his arguments in favor of an election without intervention of the States. He supposed too that this mode would produce more confidence among the people in the first magistrate than an election by the national Legislature."[28]

Elbridge Gerry of Massachusetts rose in opposition. Like nearly all the Framers, Gerry mistrusted direct democracy.[29] "He was not clear that people ought to act directly even in the choice of electors, being too little informed of personal characters in large districts and liable to deceptions."[30] On a roll call, Wilson's popular vote motion was defeated soundly. Two states voted in the affirmative and ten opposed.[31]

Delegates next voted on the idea of electing the executive by the national legislature, for a seven-year term of service. They affirmed it eight to two.[32] Also by the same margin, delegates overwhelmingly agreed to make the executive ineligible for reelection after a seven-year term.[33]

Deliberations on the executive continued on June 4, but did not involve questions of election, term of years, and reeligibility. On that Monday, the delegates decided on a unitary executive, to whom they gave the power of veto, subject to override by a two-thirds vote of each House. The Committee of the Whole favorably reported these proposals, having reached apparent consensus on these points.[34]

On June 9, Gerry reopened the question of how to select the National Executive. He again voiced the concern that election by Congress would leave a president too dependent on the Legislative Branch. In Madison's notes, "If the appointment should be made by the National Legislature, it would lessen the independence of the Executive which ought to prevail, would give birth to intrigue and corruption between the Executive and Legislature previous to the election, and to partiality in the Executive afterwards to friends who promoted him."[35]

To foster greater Executive independence, Gerry proposed to have state governors choose the National Executive, with each state having voting power in relation to its strength in the Senate. At that point in the Convention, the concept that all states would have equal representation in the Senate was not yet settled. In fact, Gerry favored proportional voting, so larger states would have outsized influence in presidential selection. Gerry of Massachusetts represented such a state.

Edmund Randolph objected, principally because Gerry's proposal would subordinate the Executive to state interests. Doing that would undermine the principle of National Government primacy over the states, a core basis for the Virginia Plan. Exclaimed Randolph, "A National Executive thus chosen will not be likely to defend with firmness the National rights against state encroachments."[36] Delegates defeated the Gerry plan resoundingly. Nine opposed, including Massachusetts, none was in favor.[37]

On June 13, the Committee of the Whole favorably reported the Virginia Plan, as amended.

The matter of the National Executive arose again on Saturday, June 16, when William Paterson presented the New Jersey Plan, which came in the form of amendments to the Articles of Confederation.[38] At the time, New Jersey was relatively sparse in population. Alarmed by Virginia's effort to structure a bicameral legislature with proportional representation in both chambers, New Jersey countered with a unicameral legislature, in which each state would have equal representation. Doing so would follow the pattern in the Confederation Congress. New Jersey, and other small states, insisted on such arrangements because they were gravely concerned about suffering diluted voting power otherwise. Indeed, Delaware's legislature specifically instructed the state's delegates to agree only to a plan that would preserve equal representation for every state.[39]

New Jersey's approach differed from Virginia's in several major respects. Rather than promoting a wholesale overhaul, Paterson proposed several amendments to the Articles of Confederation. One of these amendments involved creation of an Executive Branch.

New Jersey recognized that the absence of an Executive was a weakness of the existing system, but it did not want to establish too powerful a presidency. Accordingly, Paterson proposed an Executive composed of multiple individuals, not just one person.[40] In this way, it was possible to create independent Executive power and, at the same time, to dilute it. Under the New Jersey Plan, the unicameral legislature would choose the Executives, none of whom would be eligible to be elected a second time. Paterson did not specify how long they would serve.

Debate on New Jersey's initiative consumed the next day, Saturday, June 16. James Wilson of Pennsylvania urged rejection of Paterson's proposal for multiple executives. "In order to control the legislative authority, you must divide it," said Wilson. "In order to control the Executive, you must unite it. One man will be more responsible than three."[41] The delegates did not dispose of the New Jersey Plan before they adjourned that day.

Delegates reconvened on Monday, June 18, to hear a proposal from New York's Alexander Hamilton that differed significantly from both the New Jersey and Virginia Plans.[42] Hamilton imagined a very strong National Government, headed by an Executive chosen by electors from each Congressional district, rather than by Congress itself. Far from limiting tenure, Hamilton proposed that the executive and senators serve indefinitely, subject to a standard of "good behavior."[43]

Hamilton scholar Henry Cabot Lodge, who would later represent Massachusetts in both the House and Senate,[44] noted that, "The republic of Hamilton was to be an aristocratic as distinguished from a democratic republic, and the power of the separate states was to be eventually crippled." Continued Lodge, "These provisions, although purely republican, came much nearer to the British model than any other by their recognition of classes and of the political rights of property, while by the treatment of the states a highly centralized national government was to supersede entirely the confederate form. Hamilton had seen that all the difficulties arose from the too great power of the states, and further, as he believed, from the democratic forms of their governments."[45]

The delegates would never vote on the Hamilton proposal.[46]

Resolution of the New Jersey Plan finally came on Tuesday, June 19. Sitting again in the Committee of the Whole, the delegates considered a motion by Rufus King of Massachusetts that the Committee of the Whole report its work on the Virginia Plan without further alteration. In effect, that meant preferring the Virginia Plan to the New Jersey alternative. King's motion carried seven to three, with one state divided, defeating the New Jersey Plan.[47]

For the next several weeks, the delegates set the National Executive aside and turned attention to the structure of Congress. Now that they had buried New Jersey's idea for a unicameral legislature, there remained outstanding questions about how to build out the Senate. While there was no significant dispute about apportioning the House of Representatives on the basis of population, there was rancorous disagreement over whether to apply proportionality or equality to representation in the Senate. The dispute deadlocked the Convention, threatened to derail it, preoccupied the delegates, and led on July 2 to formation of the first Committee of Eleven. Every State then attending would send one representative.[48]

To end the deadlock on representation, the first Committee of Eleven proposed the Connecticut Compromise, providing for equal representation of all states in the Senate, while money bills would originate in the proportionally-elected House of Representatives. The Framers approved this proposal on July 16. By that time, New York delegates other than Hamilton had left, New Hampshire's had not arrived, so only ten States decided the question. Through the narrowest of margins, five to four with one State divided, delegates resolved a matter that threatened to dissolve the convention.[49]

With that immense obstacle out of the way, the delegates returned to issues concerning the National Executive. However, the effect of adopting the Connecticut Compromise would not be restricted to its impact on the Legislative Branch. It also affected the way some large state representatives looked at how Congress related to the rest of the government. Madison was among those whose views were changing, as would soon become apparent.[50]

Large states had united behind proportional representation in both chambers. Under the Virginia Plan, the House was to elect the Senate and Congress would elect the president and appoint the judiciary. Thus, large States would influence the entire government through their domination of the House.[51] This concept provoked strenuous objection from the small states and could not ultimately carry a majority in the Convention. Once the Connecticut Compromise enshrined the principle of equal representation in the Senate, large states could not control the entire Congress, and through it, the whole of the government.

On Tuesday, July 17, the delegates turned again to the presidency. Unanimously, they reaffirmed a unitary executive. Thereafter, they addressed several motions related to executive election and tenure, casting around futilely for a durable consensus. By nine to one, they rejected a motion by Gouverneur Morris of New York to elect the president by popular vote.[52] Luther Martin of Maryland proposed electors appointed by State legislatures choose the president.[53] His motion was defeated eight to two.[54] After rejection of these alternatives, delegates unanimously reaffirmed election by the national legislature.

Then, William Houston of New Jersey, seconded by Roger Sherman of Connecticut, proposed to strike out the clause that barred reeligibility. Gouverneur Morris spoke in favor. According to Madison's notes, "Morris espoused the motion. The ineligibility proposed by the motion as it stood tended to destroy the great motive to good behavior, the hope of being rewarded by a re-appointment."[55] Although it had been an article of faith that election by Congress and denial of reeligibility were bound together, Houston's motion carried by a vote of six to four.[56] For the first time in the proceedings, delegates lifted the barrier to reeligibility.

James McClurg of Virginia moved to strike the seven-year term and replace it with tenure during good behavior. Mason dissented. As Madison captured Mason's argument, "It would be impossible to define the misbehavior in such a manner as to subject it to a proper trial; and perhaps still more impossible to compel so high an offender holding his office by such a tenure to submit to a trial. He considered an Executive during good behavior as a softer name only for an Executive for life. And that the next would be an easy step to a hereditary monarchy."[57] McClurg's motion lost by a vote of four to six.[58] A motion to delete the seven-year term was defeated four to six.[59]

Delegates had made important choices, but were not at peace with their handiwork. Before adjourning for the day, the delegates agreed that the question of reeligibility and related issues would soon be considered again. Such reconsideration occurred two days later, on Thursday, July 19.

Having temporarily reaffirmed election by Congress, the Convention remained open to alternatives. Several delegates floated the idea of a vote by electors chosen by state legislatures. To avoid piecemeal resolution of these subjects, Morris moved that the Convention reopen all issues related to election and reeligibility of the president. "It is necessary to take into one view all that relates to the establishment of the Executive, on the due formation of which must depend the efficacy and utility of the union among the present and future States."[60] Delegates approved his motion unanimously.

In debate, Morris reversed the presumption of Legislative supremacy that earlier dominated the Convention. The country required a national leader, not one subject to legislative domination or influenced by parochial interests or intrigues. "We must either renounce the blessings of the Union or provide an Executive with sufficient vigor to pervade every part of it . . . . One great object of the Executive is to control the Legislature. . . . It is necessary then that the Executive Magistrate should be the guardian of the people, even of the lower classes, against Legislative tyranny, against the great and the wealthy who in the course of things will necessarily compose the legislative body."[61]

Morris insisted that to strengthen the office, the convention must not term limit the president. He warned that the effects of restricting tenure would be malign. "It will destroy the great incitement to merit public esteem by taking away the hope of being rewarded with a reappointment. . . . The love of fame is the great spring to noble and illustrious actions. Shut the civil road to glory and he may be compelled to seek it by the sword." It might also foster self-dealing and corruption. "It will tempt him to make the most of the short space of time allotted him, to accumulate wealth and provide for his friends."[62]

When Morris concluded, Oliver Ellsworth of Connecticut proposed a two-part solution addressing the method of election. Part one was that a body of electors choose the National Executive. Temporarily discarding election by Congress, the delegates approved the motion six to three.[63] Part two was that State legislatures choose the electors. That passed eight to two.[64] The election link between the Legislature and the Executive was, for the time being, severed, thus eliminating the principal rationale for prohibiting reeligibility.[65] When Luther Martin followed with a motion to render the Executive ineligible anyway, delegates turned him down by a vote of eight to two.[66]

The next question involved how long the Executive might serve. Delegates had previously agreed to seven years. Having removed the barrier to reeligibility, they were ready for something a bit shorter. Ellsworth proposed a term of six years. It was approved nine to one.[67]

Having rethought the presidency and reassembled all the pieces, delegates adjourned. July 19, 1787, had been a busy, apparently consequential day. They had scrapped a plan for Congress to elect the Executive for a single, seven-year term and replaced it with one providing for choice by electors for a six-year term with no barriers to reelection.[68]

However, even the new accord proved fragile, reflecting the lack of comfort or true consensus on these issues. Electors would be men of considerable power. How to select and apportion them? Dissension festered. As David Brian Robertson notes in his chronicle of the Convention, "Electors seemed to solve the problem of executive selection, until the delegates faced the problem of choosing the electors and weighing the states' relative influence in the selection process."[69]

On the following Tuesday, July 24, these vexatious disagreements caused delegates to reconsider the wisdom of creating an Electoral College. On motion by New Jersey's William Houston, delegates reinstituted election by Congress. The motion carried seven to four.[70]

With this policy reversal in hand, Martin revived the case to ban reeligibility. Morris grew exasperated. "In order to get rid of the dependence of the Executive on the Legislature, the expedient of making him ineligible for a second time has been devised. This was as much as to say we should give him the benefit of experience, and then deprive ourselves of the use of it."[71] Not only did he oppose the barrier to reeligibility, Morris also disliked extending the length of a single term in order to provide independence. Lengthy tenure without periodic accountability was an invitation to despotism, he argued.

> Make him ineligible for a second time and prolong his duration even to 15 years, will he by any wonderful interposition of providence cease to be a man? No, he will be unwilling to quit his exaltation, and the road to his object through the Constitution will be shut; he will be in possession of the sword, a civil war will ensue, and the Commander of the victorious army on whichever side will be the despot of America.[72]

Morris believed that getting the presidency right was the Convention's most onerous task. In his notes, Madison described Morris' views. "It is the most difficult of all rightly to balance the Executive. Make him too weak, the Legislature will usurp his powers. Make him too strong, he will usurp the Legislature. He preferred a short period, a re-eligibility, but a different mode of election."[73]

Unable to reach a solution, the delegates concurred with Morris' suggestion to postpone the issue, and turned to other subjects.

Delegates continued to struggle. On Wednesday, July 25, Ellsworth proposed a melded process. In it, the Legislature would choose the Executive, who would be eligible for a second term. Electors chosen by State legislatures would determine if he would be reelected. Ellsworth's election system proved too complex and was defeated four to seven.[74]

Charles Pinckney of South Carolina proposed an alternative by which Congress would elect the executive for a six-year term, but no one could serve more than six years in any twelve-year period. Thus, a talented executive could return to office after sitting out a term. Mason endorsed this idea as a viable alternative. "It rendered the Executive as effectually independent after his first election, and opened the way at the same time for the advantage of his future services."[75]

However, Morris was resolute in rejecting any form of term limits. A gap in service would not cure problems of corruption and intrigue, he said, and dishonest men would find ways to work around the safeguards. "The man in office will look forward to a period at which he will become re-eligible. . . . Such is the nature of man . . . that although he knows his existence will be limited to a span, he takes measures as if he were to live forever."[76] Pinckney's motion to create the possibility of split terms was defeated five to six.[77]

After the Convention opened on Thursday, July 26, Mason reprised various approaches that delegates had taken to the presidency. He argued that the framework originally recommended in June by the Committee of the Whole was the best alternative after all. He moved restoration of election by Congress for a single seven-year term, without possibility of reelection.[78] Mason's motion carried seven to three.[79]

Morris asked for a vote on the package of all presidential provisions as they then stood. This would include the selection, term, and reeligibility provisions just voted, and also related questions addressed at different times. These matters included language on execution of the laws, power of appointment, impeachment, and compensation. The Convention approved the comprehensive resolution by six to three.[80] This vote is especially noteworthy because George Washington, acting in the temporary absence of Virginia delegate Edmund Randolph, voted in the negative. In so doing, Washington opposed rendering the National Executive ineligible to continue in office.[81]

The resolutions that the Convention had agreed to on this and other topics were referred to the Committee on Detail, which began work several days earlier.[82] The Committee was composed of five delegates, charged with converting the decisions already taken and fashioning them into a draft constitution. Under the chairmanship of South Carolina's John Rutledge, the Committee worked between July 27 and August 6. In the interim, the Convention stood adjourned. On Monday, August 6, it reconvened to receive the Committee's report.[83]

Section 1, Article X, of the Committee's proposal read: "The Executive Power of the United States shall be vested in a single person. His stile shall be 'The President of the United States of America;' and his title shall be 'His Excellency.' He shall hold his office during the term of seven years; but shall not be elected a second time."

Recommendations in hand, delegates labored on. Between August 6 and August 24, they refined provisions related to the Legislative Branch. Late on August 24, they finally turned to Article X.

Morris led the debate. Among all the delegates, he would be the Framer most responsible for shaping the presidential office. In proceedings on the 24th, Morris aggressively contested both election by Congress and inclusion of term limits. According to Madison, "He dwelt on the danger of rendering the Executive uninterested in maintaining the rights of his station as leading to Legislative tyranny. The Executive is interested in courting popularity in the Legislature by sacrificing his Executive rights; and then he can go into that body, after the expiration of his Executive Office and enjoy there the fruits of his policy." Morris insisted that the president and the Congress needed separation.[84]

Therefore, Morris moved to replace selection by Congress with selection by electors "chosen by the people of the several States." His motion failed five to six.[85] A proposal by Daniel Carroll of Maryland for direct election by the people was defeated two to nine, the third major defeat for this idea.[86] After the day's skirmishing, election by Congress still stood.

Through the week of August 27, delegates continued work on the Committee of Detail recommendations. It was clear that certain points persistently evaded consensus, especially as to the chief executive. According to constitutional scholar Charles Thach, these included not just the executive's term and his reeligibility, but also the division of power between the president and the Senate on the conduct of foreign affairs and the appointment of judges, the issue of succession in the case of vacancy, and the question of impeachment.[87] On Friday, August 31, Connecticut's Roger Sherman moved to refer these topics to another special committee, again composed of one delegate from each state. Known as the Committee on Postponed Matters,[88] it was also called the Brearly Committee, after its chairman, David Brearly of New Jersey. Madison served on it. Morris did as well, affording him the opportunity to shape what the committee would propose on the presidency. Within the Brearly Committee, John Dickinson of Delaware was Morris' main ally.[89]

On Tuesday, September 4, the Committee reported a series of proposals. Among them were recommendations about presidential election and tenure, in addition to others concerning presidential powers.

To effect a separation between the branches, the Committee recommended that electors appointed by State legislatures choose the president. The number of such electors would be equivalent to a State's representation in Congress.[90] The presidential term was to be four years, without restriction on reeligibility. The Committee also proposed creating the office of the vice president, elected in the same manner and also with a four-year term. The person receiving the highest number of electoral votes would become president, and the runner-up would be vice president.[91] If no one secured a majority of electoral votes, the Senate would choose the president and the vice president from among the top five vote getters. At the time, political parties did not exist, and the premise was that multiple candidates would run, dividing the electoral vote so that none would reach the majority. Therefore, delegates imagined that the choice would devolve upon Congress.[92]Assignment of this task to the "aristocratic" Senate wound up being exceedingly controversial, and did not survive.

Edmund Randolph and Charles Pinckney demanded to know why the Brearly Committee had opted to create a system of electors, set out a four-year term, and removed barriers to reelection.[93] The Convention had not generated these ideas. It had briefly adopted, but then discarded, election by electors. Most of the time, it had insisted upon ineligibility for reelection. Never had delegates even debated a four-year term.[94]

Morris led the response.[95] Foremost in the Committee's thinking was the separation of powers. Election by Congress would foster intrigue and factionalism, Morris alleged. Earlier in convention proceedings, delegates considered that making an executive ineligible for reelection would diminish these dangers, but the Committee disagreed. Better to arrange a system that established executive independence from the start, by never making a president dependent on Congress for his office.[96] The solution was to establish independent electors, Morris said, and to create a system that would promote their independence and prevent collusion between them. He added that because the electors would all vote on the same day, but at diverse places throughout the country, conspiracy between them was impossible. Thus, "the great evil of cabal was avoided," he stated.[97]

Presidential scholar Thomas Cronin writes, "It was an ingenious and original compromise. Everyone got something; large states got electoral votes based on their population; small states got an assurance of at least three electoral votes and a contingency procedure based on a one-state-one-vote principle. Those who feared a 'tyranny of the majority' got an indirect method of electing presidents. Those who feared the national legislature got a method in which the states could play a major role."[98]

At this stage, Edmund Wilson interjected, speaking to the immense difficulty the delegates had faced in resolving the issue. "This subject has greatly divided the House, and will also divide the people out of doors. It is in truth the most difficult of all on which we have had to decide. . . . It also clears the way for a discussion of the question of reeligibility on its own merits, which the former mode of election seemed to forbid."[99]

The Convention did not act further on the report that day, giving delegates time to digest it. Discussion resumed on Wednesday, September 5.

When it did, Pinckney addressed the Convention. He was uneasy about allowing electors to choose the executive. He worried about parochialism. The electors would be prominent within their States, Pinckney acknowledged, but he feared they would lack a national perspective. As a result, the electoral vote was likely to fracture, leaving no one with a majority, and forcing the Senate to resolve the issue. Delegates imagined this would happen on a regular basis.[100]

Pinckney considered this possibility toxic. Along with the proposal to permit reeligibility, the effect would be to produce a perpetual president, dominated by the Senate. "This change in the mode of election was meant to get rid of the ineligibility of the President for a second time, whereby he will become fixed for life under the auspices of the Senate," Pinckney complained.[101]

Pinckney's colleague from South Carolina, John Rutledge, was similarly incensed. He moved to revive election by the Legislative Branch, with a seven-year term and no reeligibility. However, the Convention was winding down, and delegates lacked the will to bring back election by Congress. Rutledge's motion failed two to eight, with one state divided.[102]

On Thursday, September 6, the delegates decided to fix one of the problems Pinckney addressed. It was the issue of election by the Senate, in the event of an Electoral College deadlock. On motion by Connecticut's Roger Sherman, delegates shifted the responsibility to the House.[103]

As well that day, Richard Spaight and Hugh Williamson of North Carolina moved to make the executive's term seven years instead of four. Their proposal lost by a vote of three to eight.[104] Undaunted, they proposed a six-year term. It failed two to nine.[105] What followed was a vote to affirm a term of four years. It passed ten to one.[106]

On Saturday, September 8, the delegates appointed a five-member Committee on Style to "arrange the articles which had been agreed to by the House."[107] William Samuel Johnson of Connecticut was chairman. The Committee reported on September 12. In proceedings on that day and on the next three days, the Convention adopted a handful of amendments. None affected presidential election and tenure.

On Monday, September 17, 1787, the engrossed constitution was read, and then all forty-one delegates in attendance, apart from George Mason, Edmund Randolph, and Elbridge Gerry signed their names to it.[108] With Rhode Island missing for the whole Convention, and most of the New York delegation absent since July 10, eleven states appeared at the signing.[109]

In his notes, Madison captured a poignant moment as the Convention was ending. It concerned Benjamin Franklin of Pennsylvania, the oldest delegate. "Whilst the last members were signing it, Doctor Franklin, looking toward the President's chair, at the back of which a rising sun happened to be painted, observed to a few members near him that painters had found it difficult to distinguish in their art a rising sun from a setting sun. I have," said he, "often in the course of the session and the vicissitudes of my hopes and fears, looked at that behind the President without being able to tell whether it was rising or setting; but now at length I have the happiness to know that it is a rising and not a setting sun."[110]

RATIFICATION OF THE CONSTITUTION

Meeting in New York, the Confederation Congress received the proposed constitution and submitted it to the states. Ratification was swift. Under the process established in Article Seven, special conventions were to be called in every state. Agreement by nine of the thirteen states was sufficient for the constitution to be established.[111] On December 7, 1787, Delaware became the first to ratify. The ninth state was New Hampshire, on June 28, 1788. Of the original states, Rhode Island was the last, doing so by a margin of 34–32 on May 29, 1790. In four other conventions, the vote was also tight, reflecting abundant anti-Federalist sentiment.[112] However, several state conventions ratified unanimously.[113] During ratification, there was no pattern of approval or dissension as between large and small states.[114]

In their conventions, seven states recommended amendments that they believed Congress should propose once it convened under the constitution. Many of these ideas concerned establishing a bill of rights. However, only three recommendations involved the presidential term limits issue that so troubled the Framers.[115]

Concluding its proceedings on June 27, 1788, Virginia proposed, "That no person shall be capable of being President of the United States for more than eight years in any term of sixteen years." North Carolina made the same recommendation. Although Alexander Hamilton argued strenuously against presidential term limits in *The Federalist Papers*, Number 72, New York followed on July 26, 1788, with a highly detailed list of proposed amendments, one of which stated, "That no Person shall be eligible to the Office of President of the United States a third time."[116]

Reflecting some of these recommendations, the first Congress, proposed twelve amendments to the constitution, but none involved the presidential term.[117]

NOTES

1. Richard Beeman, *Plain, Honest Men: The Making of the American Constitution* (New York: Random House Trade Paperbacks, 2009), p. 21.
2. James Madison, "Vices of the Political System of the United States," http://press-pubs.uchicago.edu/founders/documents/v1ch5s16.html.
3. From James Madison to George Washington April 16, 1787, founders.archives.gov.
4. Walter Isaacson, *Benjamin Franklin: An American Life* (New York: Simon & Schuster, 2003), p. 445.
5. "The most radical proponents of states' rights even refused to attend. 'I smell a rat,' declared Patrick Henry. Samuel Adams justified his own absence by saying, 'I stumble at the threshold. I meet with a national government instead of a federal union of sovereign states.'" Ibid., p. 448.
6. Article II. Articles of Confederation.
7. Article XIII provided, "Every State shall abide by the determination of the United States in Congress assembled, on all questions which by this confederation

are submitted to them. And the Articles of this Confederation shall be inviolably observed by every State, and the Union shall be perpetual; nor shall any alteration at any time hereafter be made in any of them; unless such alteration be agreed to in a Congress of the United States, and be afterwards confirmed by the legislatures of every State."

8. David O. Stewart, *The Summer of 1787: The Men Who Invented the Constitution* (New York: Simon & Schuster Paperbacks), 2007, p. 51.

9. John Langdon and Nicolas Gilman attended for New Hampshire but did not arrive until July 23, 1798. "Robert Yates and John Lansing Jr., both of New York, left the Convention on July 10, 1787. They believed that their instructions did not permit them to participate in creating a new constitution. Their departure had a significant effect. It left Alexander Hamilton as the sole deputy remaining from New York. Afterwards, Hamilton did not vote on questions before the Convention because he could not by himself represent New York's delegation. Accordingly, New York effectively had no formal voice in the proceedings after July 10." Gregory E. Maggs, "A Concise Guide to the Records of the Federal Constitutional Convention as a Source of the Original Meaning of the U.S. Constitution," *The George Washington Law Review*. Vol. 80, 1707 (2012), p. 9. Hamilton did, however, sign the constitution, the sole New Yorker to do so. The rule in question was adopted by the delegates on May 28, 1787, on motion of Virginia's George Wythe, and stated, "A House to do business shall consist of the Deputies of not less than seven states; and all questions shall be decided by the greater number of these which shall be fully represented." Madison, p. 19.

10. "The Pennsylvanians urged that per-state voting be abandoned, but the Virginians 'discountenanced and stifled' the suggestion, fearing it would 'beget fatal altercations between the large and small States.'" Stewart, p. 51.

11. For example, Pennsylvania named eight delegates, while New Hampshire named two.

12. John R. Vile, "The Critical Role of Committees at the U.S. Constitutional Convention of 1787," *The American Journal of Legal History*, Vol. 48, No. 2 (April 2006), pp. 147–176, 149–152. https://www.jstor.org/stable/25434790 (accessed October 14, 2018).

13. James Madison, *The Debates in the Federal Convention of 1787 Which Framed the Constitution of the United States of America* (Buffalo, New York: Prometheus Books, 1987), p. 21.

14. Thomas Cronin, *Inventing the American Presidency* (Lawrence, Kansas: University of Kansas Press, 1989), p. 65.

15. Madison recounted, "It occurred to [the Virginia delegates] that from the early and prominent part taken by that state in bringing about the Convention, some initiative step might be expected from them." Stewart, p. 37.

16. "The plan was largely Madison's handiwork, although Madison himself insisted that is was the result of a 'consultation among the deputies,' by which he meant the collection of Virginians and Pennsylvanians who had gathered in Philadelphia before the Convention." Beeman, p.87.

17. "Randolph's selection as the person to present the Virginia Plan was a great honor and had come to Randolph after a career of important honors. He had been

an aide to General Washington, a very successful lawyer, a judge, a member of the Virginia legislature, a member of Congress, the attorney general of Virginia, and now he was the governor of that large state. He was only 33 years old." Denis J. Hauptly, *A Convention of Delegates: The Creation of the Constitution* (New York: Antheum, 1987), p. 41.

18. Beeman, p. 90. The author goes on to say, "Over the course of the long summer to come, the delegates would tie themselves into knots trying to find a means by which to assure that only wise and knowledgeable people would participate in the selection of the Executive, while at the same time guaranteeing the Executive some measure of independence from Congress." Ibid.

19. Ibid., p. 128.

20. Madison, pp. 24–25.

21. "A Committee of the Whole is typically used by an assembly for initial drafting of documents because its more flexible rules facilitate discussion." Maggs, p. 12. See also Vile, pp. 153–156. When the present-day House of Representatives resolves itself into the Committee of the Whole, the speaker does not preside but appoints another member to do so. This exact concept applied during the Constitutional Convention. When delegates met in the Committee of the Whole, Gorham presided in lieu of General Washington.

22. "When sitting as the Committee of the Whole, the same delegates could assemble in the East Room and discuss the Virginia Plan but they could take no final actions. The Committee of the Whole could only make recommendations to the Convention, at which point exactly the same delegates would reconstitute themselves as the Convention to consider the recommendations they had made to themselves. The circular device which prevailed for the next two weeks, was designed to encourage open discussion." Stewart, pp. 53–54.

23. Madison, p. 40.

24. Ibid.

25. Ibid., pp. 41–42.

26. Votes in favor came from New York, New Jersey, Pennsylvania, Delaware, and Virginia. Opposed were Connecticut, North Carolina, South Carolina, and Georgia, even though the motion for seven years came from Pinckney of South Carolina. Massachusetts divided. New Hampshire did not vote.

27. "Wilson was the first delegate to realize that the only way to create a true separation of powers, to render the Congress and President independent of one another, and to ensure their legitimacy in the eyes of the people, was to insist on direct popular election of each." Beeman, p. 129.

28. Madison, p. 42.

29. "Nearly all of the delegates—with the notable exception of Wilson—believed that the sheer expanse of America would frustrate any effort to create an informed electorate." Beeman, p. 131.

30. Madison, p. 42. "A few of the delegates—among them Elbridge Gerry of Massachusetts and Pierce Butler of South Carolina—no doubt opposed Wilson's proposal because of their fundamental distrust of the inherent abilities of ordinary citizens to make a wise choice. But by far the greater number of delegates opposed it because of their fear that America's vast expanse would make it difficult for voters,

whatever their wisdom, to make an informed decision—that local rather than national decisions would guide citizens in their voting." Beeman, p. 232.

31. Pennsylvania and Maryland supported the motion. New Jersey and New Hampshire did not vote. All other states voted no. Rhode Island was unrepresented at the Convention.

32. All states voted for this system, with the exception of Pennsylvania and Maryland, who opposed it. New Hampshire and New Jersey did not vote.

33. Massachusetts, New York, Delaware, Maryland, Virginia, North Carolina, and South Carolina voted aye. Connecticut and Georgia were negative. Pennsylvania divided. New Hampshire and New Jersey did not vote.

34. The vote was seven to three for the unitary executive, with Massachusetts, Connecticut, Pennsylvania, Virginia, North Carolina, South Carolina, and Georgia in the affirmative, and New York, Maryland, and Delaware negative. New Hampshire and New Jersey did not vote. The veto and override passed by voice vote.

35. Madison, p. 79.

36. Ibid.

37. Delaware divided. North Carolina and New Hampshire did not vote.

38. Hauptly, p. 66.

39. Ibid., p. 53.

40. The Confederation Congress elected three persons from within its own ranks to perform executive functions, known as Presidents of the United States in Congress Assembled.

41. Madison, p. 109.

42. In his biography of Hamilton, then-newspaper editor Arthur Vandenberg notes, "General opinions divided between the 'Virginia Plan' and the 'New Jersey Plan.' The former contemplated a Union of the People; the latter a mere league of States. Hamilton was satisfied with neither." Arthur H. Vandenberg, *The Greatest American: Alexander Hamilton* (New York: G.P. Putnam's Sons, 1921), p. 117.

43. Madison, p. 119.

44. Henry Cabot Lodge was in the House of Representatives from 1887 to 1893 and was a senator from 1893 to his death in 1924.

45. Henry Cabot Lodge, *Alexander Hamilton* (New York: Houghton, Mifflin and Company, 1884).

46. "In passages that would torment him in the future, he came perilously close to demanding an American king. 'No good Executive could be established on Republican principles,' he assured the delegates. . . . Hamilton proposed that the Chief Executive serve for his entire life. Anticipating the objection that this would create a 'monarch' . . . he blithely observed that 'Monarch is an indefinite term' and that any executive would function like a monarch, even if only for a term of years." Stewart, p. 95. As well, unlike a monarch, the executive would be subject to impeachment. Cronin, p. 66. Vandenberg saw the Hamilton proposal as protecting fragile government institutions against the rule of the mob. "The most striking novelty which Hamilton proposed was the election by state electors of a Senate and a President who should serve for life unless removed for cause. The motif permeating this entire structure was a powerful, centralized federal authority resting upon selective suffrage.

His basic purposes were dual: first, to avoid 'any confederation leaving the states in possession of their sovereignty,' as Madison tells us in his 'Reports'; second, to avoid that mutability in the institutions of government which he feared would be unstabilizing in whatever degree lack of central power would permit. . . . He believed in safeguarding democracy against its own passions in order that the best elements of democracy might be successfully protected against those self-contained dangers which his superior knowledge of history and human kind warned him greatly to be feared." Vandenberg, pp. 117–118.

47. Massachusetts, Connecticut, Pennsylvania, Virginia, North Carolina, South Carolina, and Georgia voted aye; New York, New Jersey, and Delaware voted no. Maryland divided. New Hampshire did not vote.

48. Vile, pp. 156–158.

49. The vote was on accepting recommendations from the First Committee of Eleven, otherwise known as the Gerry Committee. Connecticut, New Jersey, Maryland, Delaware, and North Carolina were affirmative. Pennsylvania, Virginia, South Carolina, and Georgia were negative. Massachusetts divided. New York and New Hampshire did not vote.

50. Madison was a key participant in formulating the Virginia Plan. Hauptly, p. 49.

51. Of the Virginia Plan, David O. Stewart has written, "The government framed by the fifteen resolutions did not have the careful system of checks and balances which emerged by the end of the Convention. The Virginia Plan called for all power to flow from a single legislative body. The people would elect the 'first branch' of the legislature, which would control the entire government." Stewart, p. 53.

52. Madison quoted Morris, "If the people should elect, they will never fail to prefer some man of distinguished character, or services, some man . . . of continental reputation. If the Legislature elect, it will be the work of intrigue, or cabal, and of faction." Madison, p. 267. Pennsylvania was affirmative. All other voting states were negative. New York and New Hampshire did not vote.

53. The original "Electors" idea, offered by James Wilson on June 22, was to have the people choose electors and not state legislators.

54. Delaware and Maryland voted aye. The other voting states voted no. New York and New Hampshire did not vote.

55. Madison, p. 267.

56. Massachusetts, Connecticut, New Jersey, Pennsylvania, Maryland, and Georgia voted to strike the restriction. Delaware, Virginia, North Carolina, and South Carolina voted to uphold it. New York and New Hampshire did not vote.

57. Madison, p. 272.

58. New Jersey, Pennsylvania, Delaware, and Virginia were a yes. Massachusetts, Connecticut, Maryland, North Carolina, South Carolina, and Georgia were a no. New York and New Hampshire did not vote. "Those voting in favor of the proposal probably did so not because they actually wanted to give the President an indefinite term, but as a way of signaling their opposition to any scheme that would make the executive overly dependent on the legislature for his election and continuance in office." Beeman, p. 234.

59. Massachusetts, Pennsylvania, Delaware, and North Carolina voted yes. Connecticut, New Jersey, Maryland, Virginia, South Carolina, and Georgia voted no. New York and New Hampshire did not vote.

60. Max Farrand, *The Records of the Federal Convention of 1787*, Vol. II (New Haven: Yale University Press, 1911), p. 52.

61. Farrand, p.52.

62. Ibid., p. 53.

63. Connecticut, New Jersey, Pennsylvania, Delaware, Maryland, and Virginia voted aye. North Carolina, South Carolina, and Georgia opposed. Massachusetts divided. New York and New Hampshire did not vote.

64. South Carolina and Virginia opposed.

65. David K. Nichols, "Hamstringing the Electorate: The Twenty-second Amendment and Presidential Selection" in *Restoring the Presidency: Reconsidering the Twenty-second Amendment* (Washington, DC: The National Legal Center for the Public Interest, 1990), p. 47.

66. North Carolina and South Carolina voted in favor. The others opposed. Again, New York and New Hampshire did not vote.

67. Only Delaware dissented.

68. The next day, July 20, they agreed to a proposal by Gerry to allocate electors per state. Per Madison's suggestion it was made temporary, so as to allow for subsequent changes in population. In the initial case, Massachusetts, Pennsylvania, and Virginia would each get three electors, Connecticut, New York, New Jersey, Maryland, North Carolina, and South Carolina would get two, New Hampshire, Rhode Island, and Georgia would get one.

69. David Brian Robertson, *The Original Compromise: What the Constitution's Framers Were Really Thinking* (New York: Oxford University Press, 2013), p. 126. Ultimately, the apportionment of electors mirrored representation in Congress. "It allowed for the same kind of compromise between the large states and the small states that was reached on the question of representation in the legislature. . . . This gave the small states some additional weight in the choice of president, weight they would not have had with a direct popular election." Nichols, p. 46.

70. New Hampshire, Massachusetts, New Jersey, Delaware, North Carolina, South Carolina, and Georgia voted in the affirmative. Connecticut, Pennsylvania, Maryland, and Virginia voted in the negative. New York did not vote. New Hampshire's delegates, who missed earlier votes, arrived in Philadelphia on July 23.

71. Madison, p. 316.

72. Ibid.

73. Ibid.

74. New Hampshire, Connecticut, Pennsylvania, and Maryland were affirmative. Massachusetts, New Jersey, Delaware, Virginia, North Carolina, South Carolina, and Georgia were negative. New York did not vote.

75. Ibid., p. 321.

76. Ibid., p. 322.

77. New Hampshire, Massachusetts, North Carolina, South Carolina, and Georgia voted yes. Connecticut, New Jersey, Pennsylvania, Delaware, Maryland, and Virginia voted no. New York did not vote.

78. "When he rose as the first speaker on Thursday, July 26, George Mason intended to settle the Convention's meandering deliberations surrounding the Presidency. To Mason's way of thinking, the delegates had chased their tails on this issue for far too long. He meant for them to reaffirm the Virginia Plan's prescription that Congress should choose the President for a single term of seven years." Stewart, p. 151.

79. In the affirmative were New Hampshire, Maryland, New Jersey, Virginia, North Carolina, South Carolina, and Georgia. Opposed were Connecticut, Pennsylvania, and Delaware. Massachusetts and New York did not vote.

80. New Hampshire, Connecticut, New Jersey, North Carolina, South Carolina, and Georgia voted aye. Pennsylvania, Delaware, and Maryland voted no. Virginia divided (even though the provision had its roots in the Virginia Plan submitted on May 29). Massachusetts and New York did not vote.

81. As Presiding Officer, Washington had otherwise refrained from voting.

82. "On July 23, 1787, with the general structure of the government settled, the Full Convention created a 'Committee of Detail' to turn the plan into an initial draft of the Constitution." Maggs, p. 14.

83. David O. Stewart reports that the raw material with which the Committee worked amounted to nineteen resolutions, totaling 1200 words. The Committee report was three times longer, and included forty-one sections spread over twenty-three articles. While generally faithful to the decisions already taken, sometimes it reversed course. See Stewart, pp. 169–170. It also filled in blanks. "They added provisions that the Convention never discussed." Stewart, p. 165, and also pp. 172–174, for depiction of such provisions.

84. Madison, p. 463.

85. Connecticut, New Jersey, Pennsylvania, Delaware, and Virginia voted in the affirmative. New Hampshire, Massachusetts, Maryland, North Carolina, South Carolina, and Georgia voted in the negative. New York did not vote.

86. Pennsylvania and Delaware voted aye. The rest opposed. New York did not vote.

87. Charles Thach, *The Creation of the Presidency, 1775–1789: A study in constitutional history* (Baltimore: Johns Hopkins Press, 1923), p. 131.

88. As well, it was known as the Committee on Unfinished Parts.

89. Stewart, pp. 212–213. "According to testimony from John Dickinson, written fifteen years later, the committee had not had an easy time of it," notes Richard Beeman. Confronting the possibility that a majority of the group might endorse election by Congress, Dickinson objected. "He reminded his colleagues that the 'powers which we have agreed to vest in the President were so many and so great' that the people would never agree to a constitution containing such a provision 'unless they themselves would be more immediately concerned in [the President's] election.'" Beeman, p. 299. This intervention gave Morris an opening, and the two of them along with Madison shifted discussion to making the choice by electors. Ibid.

90. Small states had achieved a major victory when they secured equal representation in the composition of the Senate. Their disproportional position in Congress would have given them a step up in the choice of president, if that responsibility had been left to the Legislative Branch. When the Brearly Committee made the shift to

the elector system, the small states did not complain, because the effect had been to export the concept of disproportionality into the Electoral College. Thach, p. 134.

91. After the bitterly contentious 1800 electoral deadlock between Thomas Jefferson and Aaron Burr, the Twelfth Amendment revised this system. Under the Twelfth Amendment, separate electoral votes are cast for president and vice president. David Brian Robertson describes the 1800 conundrum. "Because electors could vote for two candidates for President and were pledged to party candidates for President and Vice President, two candidates received an identical number of Electoral College votes. . . . Because Jefferson and Burr tied, under the existing Constitution, the choice between the two Democratic-Republicans had to be decided by the House of Representatives. The ambitious Burr refused to defer to Jefferson. After much wrangling, the House of Representatives chose Jefferson." Robertson, pp. 131–132. On February 17, 1801, on the 36th ballot, the House broke the tie. Little more than two weeks remained prior to Inauguration Day. For the story of the 1800 election and its resolution, see John Ferling, "Thomas Jefferson, Aaron Burr, and the Election of 1800." *Smithsonian Magazine*, November 1, 2004.

92. Michael J. Klarman, *The Framers' Coup: The Making of the United States Constitution* (Oxford: Oxford University Press, 2018), p. 232.

93. During the Convention, Alexander Hamilton spoke of the benefits of an extended presidential term, certainly much longer than four years. Nevertheless, in *The Federalist Papers* Number 71, he defended the four-year concept. It was sufficient time, he said, to pursue a program without fear of removal by voters, but long and stable enough to allow them to assess his worthiness. Moreover, the time between elections was short enough to give the people recourse against bad leadership. "As on the one hand, a duration of four years will contribute to the firmness of the executive in a sufficient degree to render it a very valuable ingredient in the composition, so on the other, it is not long enough to justify any alarm for the public liberty." *The Federalist Papers*, No. 71 (New York: Mentor Books, 1961), pp. 434–435.

94. As Thomas Cronin notes, the Committee left no record of its deliberations. "Plainly, this was just one more of the artful compromises along disparate views that were the hallmark of this convention," Cronin states. Those who wanted independence from Congress got the Electoral College. That helped those who feared the loss of an experienced executive. They got reeligibility, which also heartened delegates who wanted a longer term. Those who favored a shorter term got four years, in lieu of six or seven. Cronin, pp. 68–69.

95. Vile, pp. 170–171.

96. Ibid., p. 509.

97. Ibid.

98. Thomas E. Cronin, in Judith A. Best, *The Choice of the People: Debating the Electoral College* (Lanham, Maryland: Rowman & Littlefield Publishers, Inc., 1996), p. x.

99. Ibid., p. 510. "Those 'merits' as the delegates saw them, ran both ways. Allowing for re-eligibility might lead to an excessive concentration of power in the hands of one, long-serving executive. On the other hand, the delegates were reluctant to impose term limits on an able executive who had gained the respect of the people." Beeman, p. 302.

100. "In most elections, the delegates thought, the electors, being 'strangers to the several candidates,' would winnow the field of candidates down to five; the Senate would then choose the President. 'Nineteen times in twenty,' George Mason predicted, the President would be chosen by the Senate.'" Stewart, p. 214.

101. Ibid., p. 514.

102. North Carolina and South Carolina supported the motion. All other states opposed it. New Hampshire divided. New York did not vote.

103. The vote was ten to one, with only Delaware opposed. In the House, each state would be entitled to one vote, regardless of the size of its delegation. Sherman's compromise removed the Senate from the choice of president, but the one-vote-per-state retained the degree of small state power that would have existed had the responsibility been left there. "This solution would trim Senate power while ensuring equal State influence in Presidential selection." Robertson, p. 130. Madison found the change salutary, because he thought the House, being larger body, was less susceptible to corruption. A further effect would be to lessen the aristocratic influence of the Senate." Klarman, p. 233. The Brearly Committee had also allowed the Senate to choose the vice president in the event no candidate secured an electoral vote majority. Sherman's compromise did not effected this recommendation.

104. New Hampshire, Virginia, and North Carolina voted aye. The other states voted no. New York did not vote.

105. North Carolina and South Carolina were affirmative. All others opposed. New York did not vote.

106. All states were in favor except for North Carolina. New York did not vote.

107. Madison, p. 538.

108. These delegates detailed their reasons for refusing to sign, but none mentioned as a basis for dissent the absence of presidential term limits. Timothy O. Howe, "The Third Term," *The North American Review*, Vol. 130, No. 279 (February 1880), p. 190.

109. Maggs, p. 16.

110. Madison, p. 583.

111. "The Ratification of the Conventions of nine States, shall be sufficient for the Establishment of this Constitution between the States so ratifying the Same."

112. Massachusetts, New Hampshire, Virginia, and New York all ratified by close votes, though not quite as narrowly as Rhode Island.

113. These were Delaware, New Jersey, and Georgia.

114. For dates of ratification, as well as approval margins, see "Dates of Ratification of the Constitution," www.teachingamericanhistory.org (accessed July 14, 2018).

115. "Of the several hundreds of amendments suggested during the years when the Constitution was being adopted and put into effect, only four dealt with the term and re-eligibility of the Executive." Charles R. Lingley, "Public Opinion and the Third Term Tradition." *Texas Review*, Vol. 1, No. 4 (April 1916), p. 309.

116. "Recommendatory Amendments from State Conventions," Center for the Study of the American Constitution," Department of History, University of Wisconsin-Madison, www.csac.history.wisc.edu (accessed July 14, 2018). Hamilton identified five problems with term limits. They were (1) the prospect of reelection was an

inducement to govern well; (2) inherent limits on tenure would invite corruption and avarice; (3) the country would be deprived of an experienced executive; (4) a person best suited to respond to an emergency might be barred from doing so; and (5) denying voters freedom of choice might weaken their faith in democratic systems. Hamilton disfavored any constitutional change that would force rotation in office or generate a permanent bar. *The Federalist Papers*, No. 72 (New York: Mentor Books, 1961), pp. 436–437.

117. By 1791, the states ratified proposed amendments three through ten. Amendment two, dealing with Congressional pay, was finally ratified two centuries later, in 1992, possible because Congress never put a time restriction on ratification. It became the Twenty-seventh Amendment. Amendment one, which limited the size of each Congressional district to no more than 50,000 persons, was never ratified.

Chapter 2

A Tradition of Self-Restraint Begins

Thomas Jefferson (1808)

The Framers' work was completed, but Thomas Jefferson was unhappy. In particular, he considered the absence of term limits to be a major failing. Serving as minister of France, he wrote to James Madison in December 1787 from Paris. "The second feature I dislike, and strongly dislike, is the abandonment, in every instance, of the principle of rotation in office."[1]

Jefferson expressed similar sentiments in correspondence with John Adams, then the U.S. Minister to England. "He may be reelected from four years to four years for life," said Jefferson. "Reason and experience prove to us that a chief magistrate, so continuable, is an officer for life. When one or two generations shall have proved that this is an office for life, it becomes on every succession worthy of intrigue, of bribery, of force, and even of foreign interference."[2]

To George Washington, he wrote, "I was much an enemy of monarchy before I came to Europe. I am ten thousand times more so since I have seen what they are. . . . I shall hope that before there is a danger of this change taking place in the office of President, the good sense and free spirit of our countrymen will make the change necessary to prevent it."[3]

Jefferson fretted that the near-universal acceptability of George Washington to serve as president would numb the public to the dangers inherent in unlimited tenure. "Our jealousy is only put to sleep by the unlimited confidence we all repose in the person to whom we all look as our president. After him, inferior characters may perhaps succeed and awaken us to the danger which his merit has led us into." Within several months, Jefferson further expressed, "The perpetual re-eligibility of the same President will probably not be cured during the life of George Washington. His merit has blinded our countrymen to the danger of making so important an officer re-eligible."[4]

Given his distaste for unlimited tenure, Jefferson originally favored a single seven-year term. By 1805, the midpoint in his presidency, he revised his views. Jefferson was concerned that such a term, even though not renewable, was too long to leave an inadequate president in office. Thus, he had come to believe that two four-year terms were preferable. As he put it in a letter that year, "there should be a peaceable way of withdrawing a man in midway who is doing wrong." With a single term, the only way to curtail a presidency would be impeachment, a harsh and blunt instrument. Having the capacity to turn out a president after four years through election was better. "The service for eight years with a power to remove at the end of the first four comes nearly to my principle as corrected by experience," concluded Jefferson.

Students of American history know that Washington voluntarily left the presidency at the end of two terms, so they assume that he was the father of the voluntary two-term tradition. While that is technically so, it also distorts history.[5] Washington did not philosophically object to continuing a chief executive in office if circumstances required it. In that respect, it is possible to conclude that Washington would not have objected to Franklin Roosevelt's third-term bid, given prevailing international conditions in 1940. However, Washington cared nothing about perpetuating himself for a third term in 1796. Exhausted by the burdens of public service, troubled and besieged by partisanship and factionalism,[6] and knowledgeable that his example would shape how people thought about the presidency, Washington insisted on retiring to Mount Vernon after his second term.[7]

In his September 17, 1796, Farewell Address, Washington explained, "The acceptance of, and continuance hitherto in, the office to which your suffrages have twice called me have been a uniform sacrifice of inclination to the opinion of duty and to a deference for what appeared to be your desire. I constantly hoped that it would have been much earlier in my power, consistently with motives which I was not at liberty to disregard, to return to that retirement from which I had been reluctantly drawn. The strength of my inclination to do this, previous to the last election, had even led to the preparation of an address to declare it to you; but mature reflection on the then perplexed and critical posture of our affairs with foreign nations, and the unanimous advice of persons entitled to my confidence, impelled me to abandon the idea."

"I rejoice that the state of your concerns, external as well as internal, no longer renders the pursuit of inclination incompatible with the sentiment of duty or propriety, and am persuaded, whatever partiality may be retained for my services, that, in the present circumstances of our country, you will not disapprove my determination to retire."

According to Professor Bruce Peabody, Washington hoped to gain relief from public service, secure his own honor and reputation,[8] and to strengthen the presidency. Firmly resolved, Washington left office and achieved all three. "In the process, Washington quelled fears about the executive office and facilitated a peaceful transition to the next Administration," wrote Peabody.[9]

John Adams was out after one term, following his reelection loss in 1800. Thus, Jefferson's presidency presented the first practical test of self-imposed term limits. Jefferson won a landslide victory in 1804 for a second term.[10] After his inauguration, the president announced that the new term would be his last.[11] In 1808, as he was concluding his second term in the White House, Jefferson was sixty-five years old. Apart from his unshakable commitment to the principle of rotation, he also worried about the burdens of advancing age. As Professor David Crockett of Trinity University has written, "Jefferson's twin concerns were with the potential for tyranny and the health and vitality of the chief executive. The concern about tyranny can be interpreted as a fear that the leadership function of the presidency would be corrupted in monarchical directions. The concern about health relates to the weakness any institution would experience when it is composed of one person who is not operating at full strength and capacity."[12]

During 1806 and 1807, seven state legislatures, beginning with Vermont's, had importuned him to run for reelection.[13] A year after receiving the Vermont letter, Jefferson responded.[14] In a December 10, 1807, reply to the Vermonters, he affirmed his deep-seated objection to a third term. "That I should lay down my charge at a proper period is as much a duty as to have borne it faithfully." Jefferson added that without written or, at least voluntary, term limits, the presidency could become tantamount to a monarchy. For the author of the Declaration of Independence, such would be a horrendous step backward. "If some termination to the services of the Chief Magistrate be not fixed by the Constitution, or supplied by practice, his office, nominally four years, will, in fact, become for life; and history shows how easily that degenerates into an inheritance." Jefferson wanted the exact opposite result. He concluded by proclaiming the virtues of rotation in office. "Believing that a representative government, responsible at short periods of election, is that which produces the greatest sum of happiness to mankind, I feel it is a duty to do no act which shall essentially impair that principle."[15]

Given this bedrock philosophy, and having the benefit of Washington's example, Jefferson was comfortable following suit and stepping down after his second term. In a letter to his supporters in Connecticut, he wrote, "Having myself highly approved the example of an illustrious predecessor in voluntarily retiring from a trust, which, if too long continued in the same hands, might become the subject of reasonable uneasiness and apprehension, I could not mistake my own duty when placed in a similar situation."[16]

Near the end of Jefferson's time in office, the United States was facing significant problems in its relationships with European powers. Some who petitioned Jefferson to continue in the presidency cited these travails to justify it. However, unlike Washington, Jefferson did not believe in exceptions to the two-term rule. As he was about to leave office, he wrote to one such petitioner, "I am sensible of the kindness of your rebuke on my determination to retire from office at a time when our country is laboring under difficulties truly great. But if the principle of rotation be a sound one, as I conscientiously believe it to be with respect to this office, no pretext should ever be permitted to dispense with it, because there will never be a time when real difficulties will not exist and furnish a plausible pretext for dispensation."[17]

Jefferson's position became the standard through the voluntary retirements of his immediate successors, James Madison (1809–1817) and James Monroe (1817–1825). Nearing the end of his life, Jefferson took great satisfaction in his legacy. Having despaired that the public would be insensible to problems generated by the absence of term limits, Jefferson noted that the first four presidents eligible for a third term all forsook it. "The example of four Presidents voluntarily retiring at the end of their eighth year and the progress of public opinion that the principle is salutary have given it in practice the force of precedent and usage; inasmuch that should a President consent to be a candidate for a third election, I trust he would be rejected on this demonstration of ambitious views."[18]

Four of the first five presidents had been Virginians. In 1824, this dominance ended. That year, Secretary of State John Quincy Adams defeated General Andrew Jackson, Speaker of the House Henry Clay, and Secretary of the Treasury William Crawford to become America's sixth chief executive. In the balloting, four candidates divided the popular vote, with Jackson securing a plurality but not a majority necessary to prevail in the Electoral College.[19] Therefore, the election would be decided in the House of Representatives. Under the Twelfth Amendment, the House was to choose between the top three electoral vote getters, with each state getting one vote, a majority of states being necessary for election.[20]

Speaker Clay hoped to be among the top three, believing that he had the strength in Congress to prevail in a vote of the House. Since he finished fourth in electoral votes, he decided to support Adams.[21] Clay's commitment was sufficient to give Adams a victory over Jackson and Crawford on February 9, 1825. Adams won 13 state delegations, a majority of the 24 states voting. Seven states went for Jackson, and four for Crawford. It was the first election in which the winner in the Electoral College differed from the winner of the popular vote.[22] The 1824 election was also the initial time in which popular voting represented the dominant method to choose electors.[23] The victory was the result of deal-making between Adams and Clay, in which Clay swung sufficient House support to elect Adams, who appointed Clay Secretary of State.

Five days after the House vote, "Clay accepted Adams's offer to become Secretary of State, the office from which presidents seemed to spring, further infuriating Jackson. . . . He became convinced that Clay had sold his votes to Adams in exchange for the Cabinet appointment, and Jackson's fury at this alleged 'corrupt bargain' never abated."[24]

Clay denied there was a *quid pro quo*. He had wanted the job, so he accepted it when offered, even though he knew criticism would follow. However, he did not anticipate the extent to which it would be condemned. He maintained he had been right to vote for Adams and to persuade others to follow suit, but with the passage of time, he realized he had made a mistake to take the appointment. "By doing so, I injured both him and myself, and I often painfully felt I had seriously impaired my own capacity of public usefulness."[25]

The outcome seriously embittered Jackson and his supporters. They denounced the deal as a "corrupt bargain," and vowed retaliation.[26] Their revenge came four years later, when Jackson trounced Adams in the 1828 election.[27]

Aged and ill, Jackson would retire after two terms, further fixing the custom into the country's political culture.[28] Although he ran for reelection in 1832, Jackson advocated from his first days in office that the Constitution should be changed to provide for one term of either four or six years. In his First Annual Message to Congress, Jackson promoted both that idea and, not surprisingly, abolition of the Electoral College.[29]

During his presidency, Jackson sent six messages to Congress calling for a constitutional amendment to create the single term. For example, in his Third Annual Message to Congress, dated December 6, 1831, Jackson stated, "I have heretofore recommended amendments of the Federal Constitution giving the election of President and Vice-President to the people and limiting the service of the former to a single term. So important do I consider these changes in our fundamental law that I cannot, in accordance with my sense of duty, omit to press them upon the consideration of a new Congress."[30] These ideas were subject to periodic debate on Capitol Hill, and between 1832 and 1842, nine states petitioned lawmakers for such a constitutional amendment.[31] However, Congress was never receptive, preferring to leave in place the original constitutional formula of a four-year term without restriction on reeligibility.

Jackson was a week shy of seventy when he left the White House. He had set up his own succession, promoting the successful campaign of his second term vice president, Martin Van Buren.[32] The end of Jackson's presidency in 1837 meant that five of the first seven presidents had finished two full terms. No other president would do so until Ulysses Grant completed his second term in 1877. In between, there were ten presidents who served fewer than two terms, and only one, Lincoln, who had even been reelected.[33]

Nevertheless, even in that era, the term limits' issue was very much alive. Carrying out the platform of the Whig Party, President William Henry Harrison (1841) endorsed a single six-year term.[34] President James Buchanan (1857–1861) and Andrew Johnson (1865–1869) did likewise. Each was in his first and only term. Congress took no action on any such recommendations.

NOTES

1. S. Hearings (1940), testimony of Dr. Young B. Smith, Dean of Columbia Law School, p. 324. In this, Jefferson was far from alone. His fellow Virginians, Edmund Randolph and George Mason, plus the state's Governor, Patrick Henry, were also upset about executive re-eligibility. Cronin, pp. 73–74.

2. Jon Meacham, *Thomas Jefferson: The Art of Power* (New York: Random House, 2012), p. 213. Adams did not share Jefferson's concern about monarchy. Adams was greatly satisfied with the Constitution, but for the absence of a Bill of Rights. However, as to the presidency, he was concerned that it was too weak, not too strong. Adams did not believe presidential appointments should be subject to Senate confirmation. As well, he would have preferred less frequent elections. "He was not so concerned about a president staying long in office . . . as he was about too frequent elections, which often brought out the worst in people and increased the chances of foreign influence." David McCullough, *John Adams* (New York: Simon & Schuster, 2001), p. 380.

3. Quoted in "The Third Term Tradition in American Politics (1927)," *Editorial Research Reports 1927* (Vol. 1), Washington, DC: CQ Press. http:/library.cqpress.com/cqresearcher/cqresrre1927031900 (accessed October 8, 2018).

4. Ibid. Professor David Crockett summarizes the core difference between Jefferson's insistence on term limits and Hamilton's abhorrence of them. "Where Jefferson is most concerned with tyranny and health, Hamilton is focused primarily on the desire for stability in the administration of government." David A. Crockett, "The Contemporary Presidency: 'An Excess of Refinement': Lame Duck Presidents in Constitutional and Historical Context," *Presidential Studies Quarterly*, Vol. 38, No. 4 (December 2008), pp. 707–721, 711. http://www.jstor.org/stable/41219711 (accessed October 12, 2018). See also, Thomas H. Neale, writing about delegates weighing the length of terms and related topic of reeligibility. "The delegates sought to balance the need for energy and stability in the executive (thus suggesting a term longer than the one or two years served by most state governors at the time), with the fear that a too-lengthy term would lead to excessive concentration of power. The question of re-eligibility was similarly influenced by fears of tyranny: would an infinitely re-electible presidency lead to dictatorship or monarchy?" Thomas H. Neale, "Presidential and Vice Presidential Terms and Tenure," Congressional Research Service, Report RS20827 (February 26, 2001), p. 1.

5. "While Washington's retirement in 1796 surely had some impact on the practice of presidents refusing to seek more than two terms, portraying him as the willful

founder of this custom is misleading." Bruce G. Peabody, "George Washington, Presidential Term Limits, and the Problem of Reluctant Leadership," *Presidential Studies Quarterly*, Vol. 31, No. 3 (September 2001), p. 442. http://www.jstor.org/stable/27552322.

6. "Washington's decision to retire was influenced not only by the attraction of his abandoned life in Mount Vernon, but by his growing aversion to (and exhaustion with) late-eighteenth century politics." Peabody, p. 444.

7. "Had he wished for a third nomination, he could have had it, and Gouverneur Morris is only one of many who strongly urged him to continue." Harold Laski, *The American Presidency: An Interpretation* (New York: Harper & Brothers Publishers, 1940), p. 65. Washington died on December 14, 1799, before he would have completed a third term.

8. Voluntarily relinquishing power was its own form of virtuous public service and burnished one's reputation. "In the Eighteenth Century Virginian society with which Washington was most familiar, the public exhibition of distinguished service and virtuous political behavior, especially disinterested commitment to the public good, ensured an individual's social standing." Peabody, p. 443.

9. Peabody, p. 441.

10. Jefferson won more than 70 percent of the vote against Federalist Charles Cotesworth Pinckney, and carried fifteen of seventeen states. "Easily elated, unwilling to forebode trouble, devoid of humor, and unable to see himself in any but the heroic light, President Jefferson basked in the sunshine of his popularity and power." Henry Adams, *History of the United States of America During the Administrations of Thomas Jefferson* (New York: Literary Classics of the United States, 1986), p. 438.

11. Adams, p. 685.

12. Crockett, p. 711. In an 1807 letter to the Vermont legislature, Jefferson stated, "Truth, also, requires me to add, that I am sensible of that decline which advancing years brings on; and feeling their physical, I ought not doubt their mental effect." Thomas Jefferson, "Letter to the Legislature of Vermont," December 10, 1807, www.teachingamericanhistory.org (accessed October 12, 2018).

13. Vermont's letter was dated November 5, 1806.

14. Charles Lingley, an early Twentieth Century scholar on the term limits tradition, believes this indicates that its acceptance was not yet well engrained in public opinion, in contrast to the president's well-defined views on the topic. "Even Jefferson had to admit that the absence of a restriction (had) 'scarcely excited an objection in America.'" Lingley, p. 309.

15. Adams, pp. 324–325. Jefferson sent similar letters to the New Jersey and Pennsylvania legislatures. Howe, p. 126.

16. Ibid., p. 325.

17. Ibid. Jefferson died in 1826.

18. Ibid.

19. In 1824, all four candidates had run from the Democratic-Republican Party. It was the end of the Era of Good Feelings. By 1828, the party had split, and Andrew Jackson, the Democrat opposed President John Quincy Adams, the National Republican. In any case, in 1824, Andrew Jackson got 99 electoral votes, John Quincy Adams

won 84, William Crawford received 41, and Henry Clay got 37. Jackson's total was inflated by the Three-fifths Clause in the Constitution, which enhanced Southern representation in Congress and the Electoral College because it allowed three-fifths of slaves to be counted for such purposes even though they could not vote. Fred Kaplan, *John Quincy Adams: American Visionary* (New York: HarperCollins Publishers, 2014), p. 389.

20. Ratification of the Twelfth Amendment was complete in 1804, replacing a system found in the original Constitution, in which the runner-up in the Electoral College would become the vice president. In pertinent part, the Twelfth Amendment provides, "The person having the greatest number of votes for President, shall be the President, if such number be a majority of the whole number of Electors appointed; and if no person have such majority, then from the persons having the highest numbers not exceeding three on the list of those voted for as President, the House of Representatives shall choose immediately, by ballot, the President. But in choosing the President, the votes shall be taken by states, the representation from each state having one vote."

21. H.W. Brands, *Heirs of the Founders* (New York: Doubleday, 2018), p. 111.

22. H.W. Brands, *Andrew Jackson: His Life and Times* (New York: Random House, 2005), pp. 383–388. In particular, he steered the Kentucky, Ohio, and Missouri delegations to Adams. Kaplan, p. 391. The president-elect was already considering Clay for a Cabinet appointment. Shortly after his election by the House, Adams proceeded to appoint Clay Secretary of State. Jackson denounced the maneuver as a "corrupt bargain." On Capitol Hill, Jackson supporters advocated for a constitutional amendment that would prevent the appointment of Members of Congress during their term of service or for two years thereafter. This retributive proposal went nowhere. Ibid., p. 391. In the popular vote, Jackson had beaten Adams by just over 12 points, from 43 percent to 31 percent.

23. In six states, the legislatures chose electors, as had been the earlier practice. In the remaining 18 states, electors were chosen by popular vote. Jackson needed 131 electoral votes for an absolute majority, but with the Electoral College divided among four candidates, he fell short with 99. Robert V. Remini, *The Life of Andrew Jackson* (New York: Harper & Row Publishers, 1988), pp. 150–151.

24. Jon Meacham, *American Lion: Andrew Jackson in the White House* (New York: Random House, 2009), pp. 44–45.

25. David S. Heidler and Jeanne T. Heidler, *Henry Clay: The Essential American* (New York: Random House, 2010), p. 185. Professing his innocence, Clay maintained that his decision to support Adams if he himself were eliminated had been made before the election, in October 1824, and that he had so informed friends. When supporters of Jackson and John C. Calhoun threatened violence if Clay were taken into the Cabinet, Clay asked for a congressional investigation as to whether a deal had been made. Witnesses did not come forward and the inquiry was dropped. Mary C. Hargreaves, "Adams, John Quincy," *Encyclopedia of the American Presidency*, Volume I (New York: Simon & Schuster, 1994), p. 21.

26. "The public announcement of Clay's decision came like a thunderclap," notes Robert Remini. "The west did not want John Quincy Adams. They had voted for Old Hickory. For Clay singlehandedly to overrule this judgment made a mockery

of representative government." Remini, p. 153. "And so began the longest, bitterest, ugliest campaign in American political history. Adams wasn't even inaugurated before Jackson's hometown paper, the Nashville Gazette, declared him a candidate for president in 1828." Brands, *Jackson*, p. 389.

27. In the 1824 election, the Democratic-Republican Party, which coalesced as an anti-Federalist force, and which had dominated American politics for a quarter century, finally broke apart. The Adams wing, which Jackson defeated on 1828, had become the National Party. It soon morphed into the Whigs. Jackson prevailed in 1828 and 1832, followed by his Vice President Martin Van Buren, in 1836, but 1840 saw the election of the first Whig President William Henry Harrison.

28. See Remini, pp. 327–336 for a discussion of Jackson's generally declining health. In his Farewell Address, Jackson referred to his declining condition, "My own race is nearly run; advanced age and failing health warn me that before long I must pass beyond the reach of human events and cease to feel the vicissitudes of human affairs." Meacham, *American Lion*, pp. 338–339.

29. "I would therefore recommend such an amendment of the Constitution as may remove all intermediate agency in the election of the President and Vice-President. The mode may be so regulated as to preserve to each state its present relative weight in the election, and a failure in the first attempt may be provided for by confining the second to a choice between the two highest candidates. In connection with such an amendment it would seem advisable to limit the service of the Chief Magistrate to a single term of either 4 or 6 years." Andrew Jackson, "First Annual Message, December 8, 1829," The American Presidency Project, www.presidency.ucsb.edu. (accessed October 13, 2018).

30. Andrew Jackson, Third Annual Message, December 6, 1831, The American Presidency Project, www.presidency.ucsb.edu. (accessed October 13, 2018).

31. Ames, p. 127.

32. Van Buren in 1836 and George H.W. Bush in 1988 have been the only two vice presidents in American history to run successfully for the presidency directly upon completion of service as vice president. Jackson proclaimed open neutrality as to his succession, but he boosted Van Buren when possible. Jackson's biographer, Jon Meacham, describes this professed disinterest as "unconvincing," and notes that, "Not even a full year into his Administration, Jackson was promoting Van Buren for president." Meacham, *American Lion,* p. 308. Of Jackson's efforts on Van Buren's behalf, H.W. Brands observes, "He was relieved to relinquish power, especially to one he trusted as much as he did Martin Van Buren. It didn't strike him as odd that he, as the champion of the people's right to choose their leaders, should essentially appoint his own successor." Brands, *Jackson,* pp. 529–530.

33. Van Buren (elected 1836) served one term, as did Polk (1844), Pierce (1852), and Buchanan (1856). Harrison (1840) died in office, meaning that he and his Vice President John Tyler had partial terms. The same situation prevailed for Zachary Taylor (1848) and his Vice President Millard Fillmore. Abraham Lincoln (1860 and 1864) served one full term and was elected a second time, but his death by assassination meant that the term commencing in 1865 was partial for him and for his Vice President Andrew Johnson.

34. Ames, p. 127.

Chapter 3

A Tradition Challenged

Ulysses S. Grant (1880)

The first meaningful challenge to the two-term tradition might have occurred in the 1876 election, when it was imaginable that President Ulysses S. Grant would seek a third term. Republican vulnerability animated this possibility. The 1874 mid-terms had badly disrupted the party's total dominance of Congress, in effect since the start of the Civil War. Democrats won ninety-three seats in the House, reassuming control of that chamber. They also gained nine seats in the Senate, weakening the Republican majority there. A combination of the economic upheaval associated with the Panic of 1873, scandals during the second Grant Administration, and the regaining of Democratic control over Southern political structures (the so-called "redeeming" of the South) were instrumental in this massive turnover.[1]

Talk of a third term for Grant roiled the mid-term election. Grant failed to renounce interest, stoking Democratic turnout in 1874.[2] As the *New York Herald* commented, "Grant, in his power and might . . . no longer aimed at the fame of Washington—a double term and a quiet retirement into private life—but believed that the country was actually willing to bestow upon him an honor that Washington put away—the honor of a third term. And although the traditions of our Constitution and of our political life revolted at this violation of a sacred precept, our strong-willed and stubborn President, with his complying followers, drove on and on, determined to win, by the sheer force of Executive power, this unusual recognition." *The Herald* continued, "It was against this principle that the people in the elections of last fall proclaimed a revolt."[3]

Republicans feared that the outcome of the mid-terms might foretell a return of Democrats to the White House.

Nonetheless, Grant remained the hero of the Civil War. Two decades after the war's conclusion, he retained much public affection in the country, even if his prestige suffered from scandals within his administration and recent electoral setbacks. Although Grant was, to a degree, damaged goods, some Republicans believed he was the strongest candidate the party could run.

The president had loyalists who embraced the idea of a third term. Among them were South Carolina Republicans, who in 1874, passed a resolution stating, "We pledge ourselves to the support of President Grant for a third term, assured that by doing so we shall preserve that peace and unity throughout the whole country so necessary to its prosperity." Some Republican newspapers around the country were prepared to go along. On May 7, 1875, a Missouri paper, *The Andrew County Republican* editorialized, "The Republican Party is not tired of President Grant; the people are not tired of him. There is nothing in our laws, or the spirit of our institutions, that forbid him for holding the office a third, a fourth, or more times, if the choice of the people falls on him. No precedent of the past condemns it; the wishes of our forefathers in regard to Washington, similarly situated, seem to approve."[4]

Very much in their camp was his wife, Julia.[5] But Grant himself was not convinced. While he was not personally implicated in the scandals, he knew they had marred his administration.[6] It was possible that his political future might be brighter if he stepped away for a while from the White House. Initially, Grant made no answer to the South Carolina Republicans or other like-minded people.[7]

Witnessing this upsurge for Grant, some other state Republican Parties were alarmed. On May 26, 1875, the Pennsylvania Republican Convention adopted a resolution insisting on "firm and unqualified adherence to the unwritten law of the Republic, which wisely, and under the sanction of the most venerable examples, limits the Presidential service to two terms." The resolution continued, "we the Republicans of Pennsylvania, in recognition of this law, are unalterably opposed to the election to the Presidency of any person for a third term."[8]

Finally, Grant responded. On May 27, 1875, he dispatched a letter to the Pennsylvania Republicans denying he wanted renomination.[9] Addressed to Harry White, president of the Pennsylvania Republican Convention, the letter said of a third term, "I do not want it any more than I did the first. I would not write or utter a word to change the will of the people in expressing and having their choice. . . . I am not, nor have I been, a candidate for re-nomination." However, Grant added to this disclaimer that the sole ironclad way of preventing a third-term candidacy would be "an amendment to the Constitution . . . the length of time or number of terms for which any one person shall be eligible for the office of President. Until such an amendment is adopted, the people cannot be restricted in their choice by resolutions, further that they are now restricted as to age, nativity, etc." And to establish that he, like Washington, was not personally hostile to the idea of a third term, Grant said, "It may happen, in the future of the country, that to change an Executive because he has been eight years in office, will prove unfortunate, if not disastrous."[10]

This observation created the impression, perhaps accurate, that Grant was hedging his bets, and opened him to severe criticism from his opponents. The Wilmington, Delaware, *Daily Gazette,* interpreted Grant's statement to say, "He will accept the nomination if tendered, with the accompanying assurance that the public good requires him to accept. This is as much as any President could say, and more than any other has ever said. It is an avowal that he sees nothing objectionable per se in the idea of a third term; that he does not regard it as opposed to our political traditions or the genius of our institutions, that he would be pleased to hold the office another term if the people desire it, and that he will construe his nomination by a Republican National Convention that they do desire it, and will accept the candidacy." The *Daily Gazette* was appalled. It implored, "The Republican Party must go straightforward in the line of duty so happily marked out by the Pennsylvania Convention, and respectfully, but firmly, disclaim all purpose of re-nominating General Grant."[11]

The *New York Sun* expressed similar disdain, describing Grant's letter as "cunning." Wrote the *Sun*, "When he says he does not want the third term. He carefully leaves the door open in the hope that, after all, it may be given to him; and he ingeniously argues the constitutional point that the people have a right to elect a man President as often as they wish."[12]

Before sending the letter to the Pennsylvanians, Grant read it to his cabinet, but did not seek their advice. Julia asked, "And why did you not read it to me?" The president responded, "Oh, I know you too well. It would never have gone if I had read it." Julia asked that Grant bring her the letter and read it then, but he replied that it was gone. "No, it is already posted; that is why I lingered in the hall to light my cigar, so the letter would be beyond recall." Julia was hurt. "Oh, Ulys, was that kind to me? Was it just to me?" But Grant responded, "I do not want to be here another four years. I do not think I could stand it. Don't bother about it, I beg of you." Julia was not assuaged. "I did feel deeply injured," she recalled."[13]

Because Grant's letter lacked finality, it did not put the issue to rest for many Republicans. Subsequently, eight state parties protested breaking the two-term tradition. For example, the New York Republican Convention declared "unalterable opposition to the election of any President for a third term." Massachusetts Republicans resolved, that "sound reason, as well as unbroken usage of the Republic, illustrated by the example of Washington, requires that the term of the Chief Magistrates of the United States should not exceed a second term." And the Ohio Republicans similarly resolved, "That the observance of Washington's example in retiring at the close of a second Presidential term will be in the future, as it has been in the past, regarded as a fundamental rule in the unwritten law of the Republic."[14]

Democrats could not be sure whether the president's prior disclaimer of interest in a third term would hold up if there were a convention draft. A June 12, 1875, editorial in the *Northern Ohio Journal* reflects that skepticism. It focused on Grant's remark about a constitutional amendment, and demanded a "decided and unequivocal expression from the people as will forever settled the question of a third term, not only for Mr. Grant, but also for all future occupants of the Presidential chair."[15]

Other Democrat-leaning papers were similarly disdainful. On June 16, 1875, the *Louisiana Democrat* reprinted in full an editorial from the *New York World*. The editorial seized upon Grant's constitutional amendment statement as signaling openness to a third term, and condemned "the egotism, the wrongheadedness, the contempt of law and public opinion, and the insatiable greed of its author."[16]

Congressional Democrats were much in tune with these views, wanting to stifle any draft-Grant momentum. Congress was out of session at the time when Grant sent his letter to the Pennsylvanians. However, when the Forty-fourth Congress convened on December 6, 1875, House Democrats moved swiftly and preemptively to end Grant's prospects. On December 14, the House agreed to a resolution by Representative William Springer (D-IL), declaring that a third-term bid would be contrary to the public interest. The resolution stated, "that in the opinion of this House, the precedent established by Washington and other Presidents of the United States in retiring from the presidential office after their second term has become by universal concurrence a part of our republican system of government, and that any departure from this time-honored custom would be unwise, unpatriotic, and fraught with peril to our free institutions."[17] By a vote of 234 to 18, it passed without debate. A heavy majority of Republicans also supported it.[18]

The bipartisan rebuke from the House via the Springer Resolution had its intended effect. As *Congressional Quarterly* has written, "Nothing more was heard of the third term after the adoption of this resolution."[19]

A decade after the Civil War, Reconstruction was essentially over. The antebellum political elite increasingly dominated southern states, which were again part of the Union. This ruling class replaced post-war Republican governments.[20] Jim Crow governments rapidly extinguished voting rights for African-Americans, then a reliable Republican electorate. In the parlance of former Confederates, the South had been "redeemed." Once this happened, Democrats could count on overwhelming popular vote majorities in that region, as well as monolithic support in the Electoral College.

In the 1876 election, Democratic Governor Samuel Tilden of New York beat Ohio Governor Rutherford B. Hayes by three percentage points in the popular vote. However, "redemption" of the South was not quite complete in Florida, Tennessee, and Louisiana. This circumstance generated disputed electoral counts from those states. How would a politically divided Congress respond? It was apparent that the Democratic-controlled House and the Republican-controlled Senate would not agree on which electoral counts to accept. Thus, at the end of January 1877, Congress established a fifteen-member commission, composed of five senators, five representatives, and five Supreme Court justices, to review the disputed outcomes. Republicans were able to secure an eight to seven majority, and by that exact margin in each disputed case, the commission recommended acceptance of the votes cast by Hayes electors. As a result, when Congress counted the electoral votes on March 1 and 2, 1877, Hayes prevailed over Tilden 185 to 184, notwithstanding efforts by some Democrats to protest the outcome.[21]

When he accepted the Republican nomination, Hayes had announced he would serve only one term.[22] He believed that such a self-limitation would advance the cause of patronage reform.[23] Inasmuch as the 1876 Republican platform was silent on term limits, Hayes acted on his own. The *New York Herald*, in a July 16, 1876, editorial, approved of his position. "Unfettered as he was by any advice from the Republican Party, General Hayes might have plausibly declined to step off its platform to ground which it was too cautious to occupy, and thus have kept his chances for a second term of office open for the future. But he saw there is something outside of platforms, and what the Convention was too timid to do for the party, he had the courage to do for himself."[24] Elected on this pledge. Hayes, in his Match 4, 1877, Inaugural Address, advocated a constitutional amendment limiting a president to one six-year term.[25]

With Hayes in the White House, Grant became a private citizen. He was 55 years old. Shortly thereafter, he and Julia made a highly publicized trip overseas, the first such journey ever taken by a president, sitting or former. Circumnavigating the globe, they traveled for two years and four months. In the fall of 1879, Grant again set foot in the United States, to enormous acclaim. His time out of office seemed to have done much to rehabilitate his reputation. Immensely favorable coverage of Grant's trip replaced publicity about scandals. A political revival seemed possible.[26]

Noting the vast political upside of his well-publicized travels, Grant's advisers wanted him to remain overseas. However, the Grants insisted on returning home, and landed in California to a tumultuous reception on September 20, 1879. According to press reports, "General Grant arrived at San Francisco Saturday from Japan, after his extended tour of the old world, which began in May 1877, and was received with elaborate and hearty demonstrations by great crowds of people belonging to that city and other towns of the state." The paper went on, "General Grant is looking extremely well, and expresses great satisfaction with the experiences of his trip, and surprise at the tremendous demonstration that greeted his arrival home."[27] Other press commentators took note. The *Boston Advertiser* editorialized, "General Grant returns to us a more mature and a wiser man than he set out. . . . No man has been so warmly welcomed in America as General Grant will be since Lafayette was here, more than half a century ago. No American has ever made the tour of the world amid honors so universal and elaborate. So it is that the distinguished citizen returns to us no ore as the politician and the party man, whose name once excited various divisions among the people, but as an illustrious American, whom all may wisely and consistently honor for his great services in the past, and for the credit with which he has represented the whole nation in all the civilized countries of the globe."[28]

John Sherman, who, as treasury secretary, was to contest the general for 1880 nomination, describes Americans' response to Grant's reception abroad. "General Grant returned from his voyage around the world, arriving in San Francisco in December 1879, and from that time until he reached Washington, his progress was a grand popular ovation. He had been received in every country through which he passed, especially in China and Japan, with all the honors that could be conferred upon a monarch."[29]

However, Grant's advisers have been right. Once he returned, the glory of his trip began to fade. It soon became clear that political bosses, if not Grant himself, had in mind to convert his revived popularity into an 1880 presidential candidacy. The icon was converted into a more ordinary politician,

Grant's Army adjutant, Adam Badeau, writes, "Everyone who knew anything about American politics could foresee an immense enthusiasm on this arrival, which, if it was developed opportunely, might sweep him into the presidency, while, if time were allowed for it to cool, all the opposition and efforts of rival candidates could, of course, be concentrated, and render even his re-nomination difficult. . . . Grant's stubbornness in returning had produced exactly the result his friends had foreseen. Time was given for the opposition to crystallize."[30]

Dissension came from figures such as Sherman and Senator James G. Blaine, each ambitious himself for the White House, among others. On December 22, 1879, the *New York Herald* published a comprehensive political analysis of Grant's situation. It wrote, "Secretary Sherman has always been opposed to a third term, and is now as strongly opposed to it as ever." Similarly, the Herald reported, "Mr. Blaine is himself a Presidential candidate, and has no intention of withdrawing." President Rutherford Hayes, himself voluntarily term-limited, was also cool to a Grant comeback. Of Hayes, the *Herald* stated, "the report that President Hayes favors or prefers the re-nomination of General Grant is equally and entirely false. . . . Nothing is more certain here that he does not look with favor on the re-nomination of General Grant." The *Herald* reported that at a recent meeting of the Republican National Committee, there was widespread anxiety that a Grant candidacy would doom the party in certain regions. "It is regarded as certain that with Grant as a candidate, the Republicans would lose Ohio, and his nomination would make Illinois and Wisconsin states, and make Indiana sure for the Democrats" But, why so? Some of the weakness might stem from a hangover from the scandals of Grant's two administrations. However, there was also a strong aversion among certain populations to the principle of a third-term candidacy. The *Herald* observed,

> Among close observers of political events, the general sentiment is that the opposition to the third term movement is so intense and profound among our foreign-born citizens and, especially, Germans . . . Mr. Richard Smith, of the *Cincinnati Gazette*, who has been here for several days . . . makes the important observation that the German Americans in Ohio are so hostile to a third term that if Grant were nominated, the would go off from the party in a body, and the state would be carried by the Democrats. This was not because they disliked Grant, but because of a strong prejudice against imperialism, in the direction of which they thought the third term pointed.[31]

These negative sentiments did not abate with time. At the end of May, 1880, a political correspondent for the Chicago Tribune reported from Ohio, "With a purpose of ascertaining the views of German voters on the third term and General Grant's candidacy, a large number of the leading citizens of German birth were called upon and requested to speak out their thoughts on this important subject. Those visited were all businessmen engaged in manufacture, merchants, and capitalists. Their expressions are pointed and forcible in every respect." The persons interviewed were Republicans.

A central Ohio sheriff, himself of German descent and also a Republican, elaborated on this sentiment. "Now they have got an idea that a third term means monarchy," said the sheriff, and that is so set in their heads that it is utterly useless to try to reason with them.[32]

It was not only men of such immigrant stock that were concerned. On May 22, 1880, little more than a week before the convention opened, the *Indianapolis Leader* wrote,

> The spontaneous sentiment of the rank and file of the Republicans in every state of the union is against the nomination of General Grant to a third term. It has been claimed that the colored people of the South are a unit for Grant. This, however, is disproved by the fact that from those states in which the machinery of the party is controlled by colored men, Grant has not a single solid delegation. . . . The election of any man to a third term would be a violation of an honored tradition of the country; a departure from a custom who maintenance thousands of conscientious Republicans, however much mistaken, believe essential to the perpetuation of the Republic.[33]

Although several presidents had been diplomats earlier in their careers,[34] no president had ever traveled abroad during or after his term. Grant's two years overseas transformed him into an international figure, well versed in both European and Asian politics. For Grant, the trip was utterly transformative, whetting his appetite another nomination.[35] Notes Badeau, "He had become a profound thinker and an international statesman during his travels. He had seen other countries, both the peoples and the rulers . . . his views were widened and his whole character changed; but at the same time his national feeling and his democratic preferences were intensified."[36]

Grant also had domestic political imperatives. He fretted about the effects of a Democratic comeback in reconstructed states. As Ron Chernow observes,

> Grant had worried about resurgent southern Democrats back home, ex-Confederates who had recaptured control of every state in the region and threatened to undo everything he had accomplished. . . . Grant regretted the rise of the South and deemed it his duty "to save the results of the war."[37]

The 1878 elections left Democrats in control of the House while returning them to a majority in the Senate. Within those numbers was a solid phalanx of Democrats in the reconstructed South. Democrats had already captured a majority of the popular vote in 1876, even though Hayes had eked out a win in the Electoral College. In post-Reconstruction America, political momentum seemed to be on the Democratic side. As Grant scholar Ronald White recounts, "Republicans were desperate to find a candidate who could win."[38]

Party regulars proposed nominating him in 1880. Their leaders were senators Roscoe Conkling (R-NY), Donald Cameron, (R-PA), and Joshua Logan (R-IL). These senators, and others in their Stalwart faction, repeatedly clashed with Hayes over matters of patronage, and civil service reform.[39] They anticipated better treatment from a new Grant Administration.[40]

On the opening day of the convention, the *Chicago Tribune* wrote scathingly of these men and the political turmoil they promoted.

> The candidacy forced upon General Grant by a clique of grasping, self-constituted dictators has excited and convulsed the whole Republican Party. . . . Never in the history of political conventions has there been such a condition of affairs as now confronts the Republican Convention which meets today in this city. The New England States, New Jersey, Ohio, Michigan, Iowa, Kansas, Indiana, Wisconsin, Minnesota, and the three Pacific Coast states are practically unanimously here protesting against another term for Grant.[41]

Chernow quotes Buck Grant, the General's son, about Grant's attitude toward these preparations. "While father was abroad, his political friends arranged that he should try again for a third term, and had gone so far in their arrangements that when he returned he felt in justice to them, that he ought to go on." John Sherman says of Grant, "He made no open declaration of his candidacy, but it was understood that he was very willing to again accept the office of President."[42] The presidency, Grant felt, was something he should neither pursue, nor refuse.[43]

Notwithstanding strong sentiment for Grant among the Stalwarts, the party was badly fractured.[44] Opposition coalesced around Senator James G. Blaine of Maine, whose supporters were termed the Half-Breeds.[45] Another major candidate was Sherman, who stoked resistance to Grant by stressing the public's traditional hostility to a third term.[46] Indeed, that issue was the animating principle of the anti-Grant forces. On May 26, 1880, the *New York Tribune* reported,

> Those who believe that General Grant cannot be elected, or ought not to be nominated for a third term, are compactly united by that belief, although they have preferences for several different candidates. It is not "anything to beat Grant" with them, but their action is governed by a strong conviction that his nomination ought not to be made; that it would be fatal to the party and dangerous to the country. With these men, the preference for some other candidate is a secondary and subordinate motive. . . . In this particular position, the opponents of the third term have nothing to prevent their acting together heartily and resolutely until the third term issue is put completely out of the way by decisive defeat.[47]

Grant's backers tried to dismiss these concerns by noting that his would not be a third *consecutive* term.[48] Political scientist Charles R. Lingley wrote about the pragmatism that was the basis for this position. "The country was thoroughly hostile to the election of one man to the presidency for three successive times, but considerable numbers of people, thinking Grant the only possible winner in 1880, found in the idea that three non-consecutive terms would not destroy the tradition, something which allowed them to choose the man whom they desired, and yet not break or appear to break the long-standing custom."[49] However, this theory was pilloried in 1880, and the idea would never gain traction.[50] Both the original House and Senate versions of the Twenty-second Amendment, and the final ratified text, addressed the overall length of service, making irrelevant whether terms were consecutive or not.

Grant allowed supporters to put his name forward.[51] While not manifesting a public thirst for the job, he privately much desired to win.[52] In 1868, when he was a political candidate for the first time, Grant had made no effort to seek the nomination. The most prominent hero of the war, he had merely to wait for the politicians to reach out to him.[53] He approached the 1880 nomination pretty much the same way.[54] By then, circumstances were quite different.

In the 1880 convention, a candidate would need at least 379 votes for nomination. From the first, Grant was the leader, securing more than 300 votes on the initial ballot. While they both opposed Grant and felt affirmatively about each other, Blaine and Sherman never cobbled together an alliance that would allow one or the other to win.[55]

Grant and his managers hoped to impose unit rule voting on the delegates.[56] This would allow a candidate to control the votes of an entire delegation if he commanded a majority within that delegation. Such a rule would work to Grant's advantage, as it would enable him to avoid the effects of large delegations dividing their votes. The *Chicago Tribune* editorialized against it.

> The unit rule is the enslavement of the many for the profit of the few. Three men have taken the contract to nominate General Grant for President, and they propose by placing shackles on a number of the delegates and voting them as slaves to carry out the contract, and this against the indignant protests of the people who these delegates were appointed to represent. To undertake make such a rule the permanent policy of the Republican Party is an attempt to destroy that party by making it odious to the American people as a mere corporation of office-brokers and political spoilsmen.[57]

If the unit rule had been in effect, Grant might have won.[58] However, on June 5, 1880, the Convention rejected it by a vote of 479 to 276.[59]

Unlike the Democrats, which required their nominees to win support of two-thirds of the delegates, Republicans only mandated a simple majority to prevail.[60] Nevertheless, these three factions would deadlock the Convention for thirty-five ballots. It was the most contentious Republican Convention ever, and remains so even to the present day. Grant's support remained firm, but insufficient to put him over the top. On the 36th ballot, Representative James Garfield (R-OH), who had been a leader for Sherman, received a majority when Sherman and Blaine delegates defected to him.[61] The movement to Garfield was sudden and electric. He had won a single vote on the 33rd ballot, seventeen on the 34th, fifty on the 35th, and then surpassed a majority with 399 on the 36th.[62] Even on that ballot, Grant received 306 votes, a testament to the durability of his support from the Stalwarts.[63]

As was the practice at the time, potential nominees stayed away from these proceedings. Thus, while Republicans were meeting in Chicago, Grant was home in Galena, Illinois. Ever ambitious, Julia Dent Grant believed that her husband could achieve a breakthrough by appearing at the Convention. Grant rejected her advice out of hand. "How I entreated him to go on Sunday night and appear on the floor of the Convention, but no! He said he would rather cut off his right hand," recounted Julia in her memoirs. "I said, 'do you not desire success?' 'Well, yes, of course,' he said, 'since my name is up. I would rather be nominated, but I will do nothing to further that end.'"

Julia was dismayed. "Oh Ulys," I said, "how unwise, what mistaken chivalry. For heaven's sake go—and go tonight. I know they are already making their cabals against you. Go, go tonight—I beseech you." But Grant refused. "Julia, I am amazed at you."

In her memoirs, Julia lamented, "The result is known by all."[64]

Grant was chagrined that his friends had misled him about the breadth of opposition to his candidacy. Had he been aware that victory was uncertain, he may never have allowed his name to go forward. Badeau bemoaned, "He was never so fit to be President as when his party rejected him."[65]

Although Grant did not send Garfield a congratulatory telegram, he ultimately swallowed his pride and campaigned to elect the ticket.[66] Thereafter, Grant endorsed a constitutional amendment to limit presidents to a single seven-year term.[67]

Even though he had been stymied in his quest for the nomination, the specter of a third term for Grant continued to haunt the former president. The week prior to Election Day, the St. Paul, *Daily Globe* ran the editorial headline "Something for Republicans—The Third Term Danger Still Imminent." The paper was concerned that, apart from keeping Republicans in power, a vote for Garfield in 1880 meant that Grant would return to the White House in 1884. "Only a few months ago, even, one-half of the Republican Party was alarmed at the portentous shadow of a third term under Grant, which they feared was the entering wedge to destroy our republican form of government and set up an empire on its ruins." Endorsing the Democratic ticket, the editorial insisted that "Garfield is the stepping stone to Grant and the third term. Grant and the third term are the stepping stones to an empire built upon the ruins of the Republic."[68]

On November 2, 1880, Garfield and New York's Chester A. Arthur prevailed over Democrats Winfield Scott Hancock of Pennsylvania and William H. English of Indiana, winning in the Electoral College by 214 to 155. Democrats strongly dominated voting margins in sweeping the South. As a consequence, Garfield won the popular vote by fewer than 2000 votes out of some nine million cast.

Of the 1880 election, Senator Blaine observed, "The salient and most serious fact of the Presidential election was the absolute consolidation of the Electoral vote of the South; not merely the eleven states that composed the Confederacy, but the five others in which slaves were held at the beginning of the civil struggle. The leading Democrats of the South had been steadily aiming at this result from the moment that they found themselves compelled by the fortunes of war to remain citizens of the United States."[69]

He was destined to serve as president for only six months. On the morning of Saturday, July 2, 1881, inside the Baltimore and Potomac Railroad Station in Washington, DC, Charles Guiteau shot Garfield.

Guiteau was a thirty-six-year-old frustrated office seeker, rebuffed in his hopes to become minister of France. Police immediately arrested him. In

Guiteau's pocket was a letter addressed to the White House. It said, in part, "The President's tragic death was a sad necessity, but it will unite the Republican Party and save the Republic. . . . I had no ill-will toward the President. His death was a political necessity. . . . I am a Stalwart of the Stalwarts." When arrested, he declared to police, "I am a Stalwart and Arthur will be President."[70]

Although original bulletins indicated the incident was fatal, later reports corrected this to say that Garfield's wounds were grievous, but that the president might survive. Medical care proved ineffective, even counterproductive. The president lingered for two months, and died at age 49 at 10:35 in the evening of Monday, September 19, 1881. Vice President Chester Arthur, who had been placed on the Republican ticket at the insistence of the Stalwart faction, took the oath at his home in New York City, and finished the final 42 months of Garfield's term.[71]

Arthur hoped for election in his own right, but was unsuccessful in his pursuit of the 1884 Republican nomination, which went to James G. Blaine.[72] In the general election, New York Governor Grover Cleveland narrowly defeated Blaine.

Seeking a second term in 1888, Cleveland lost to former Indiana Senator Benjamin Harrison. The incumbent swept the old Confederate States, with majorities sufficient to prevail in the national popular vote by 0.8 percent. However, Harrison narrowly won Cleveland's home state of New York and defeated the president in the Electoral College 233 to 168.

Four years later, in 1892, Cleveland returned the favor. The only president to regain the White House after losing it, the Democrat beat Harrison by three percent in the popular vote and by a resounding 277 to 145 in the Electoral College.

Cleveland chose to retire at the end of his second term, which enabled former Representative William Jennings Bryan of Nebraska to capture the 1896 Democratic nomination. Only 36 years old, Bryan electrified his party's convention with a speech demanding relaxation of tight money adherence to the Gold Standard. "You shall not press down on labor this crown of thorns," he proclaimed. "You shall not crucify mankind upon a cross of gold."

In the general election, Bryan opposed former Ohio Governor William McKinley. While McKinley ran a traditional "front-porch" campaign from his home in Canton, Ohio, Bryan embarked on a whistle-stop campaign that lasted from August to November and covered 18,000 miles.[73] Bryan endorsed bimetallism currency policy, and other populist economic programs.[74] These enabled him to carry most of the Great Plains and Rocky Mountain states, in addition to the Solid South, but McKinley won the Northeast and Great Lakes regions.[75] He beat Bryan by nearly 5 percent in the popular vote and prevailed in the electoral vote 271 to 176.

McKinley successfully sought reelection in 1900. The Republican ticket also included New York Governor Theodore Roosevelt, who replaced McKinley's first Vice President Garrett Hobart.[76] Bryan was again the Democrat. This time, he carried every Southern state, but was less successful outside that region. McKinley beat Bryan by 6 percent in the national popular vote, and won emphatically in the Electoral College 292 to 155.

NOTES

1. In his memoirs, Senator James G. Blaine also attributed the loss to the receding of the Civil War and Reconstruction in the public imagination. Republicans had borne the standard on those issues. "The popular conviction of the necessity of Republican rule was losing much of its force," Blaine explained. James G. Blaine, *Twenty Years in Congress,* vol. II (Norwich, Connecticut: Henry Hill Company, 1886), p. 567.

2. Stephen W. Stathis, "The Twenty-second Amendment: A Practical Remedy or a Partisan Maneuver," *Constitutional Commentary*, 1990, p. 64.

3. "General Grant's Party," *The New York Herald* (New York, NY), March 4, 1875, p. 6. *Chronicling America: Historic American Newspapers*. Library of Congress, https://chroniclingamerica.loc.gov/lccn/sn83030313/1875-03-04/ed-1/seq-6/ (accessed June 9, 2019).

4. "Grant and the Third Term," *The Andrew County Republican* (Savannah, Missouri), May 7, 1875, p. 4. *Chronicling America: Historic American Newspapers,* Library of Congress. https://chroniclingamerica.loc.gov/lccn/sn85034076/1875-05-07/ed-1/seq-4/ (accessed June 9, 2019).

5. Republican Stalwarts in the Senate, known for being enamored of the spoils system, pressed Grant to run for a third term in 1876. Ron Chernow, *Grant* (New York: Penguin Press, 2017), p. 809. Many of these same Stalwarts also pushed Grant for a third term in 1880, after he had declined to run in 1876. As to Julia, Grant's biographer, Ron Chernow, notes, "She had relished being First Lady as only someone could whose social ambitions had been cruelly mocked during her early years of marriage. In the White House, she had finally attained a grandeur that satisfied her White Haven upbringing and she had radiated pleasure in the spotlight." Chernow, p. 810.

6. "As newspapers stepped up their attacks on Grant and his administration over the scandals, the president chose to follow his usual pattern—he did not respond. But a posture that had been effective in the Army hurt more than it helped him as president. As Grant refused to refute or even reply . . . many came to believe he should bear some responsibility for the misdeeds of his associates. . . . In May 1876, weighed down by scandals and tied to the crimes committed by men in whom he had placed his trust, Grant lost all credibility as a third-term presidential candidate." Ronald C. White, *American Ulysses: A Life of Ulysses S. Grant* (New York: Random House, 2016), pp. 568–569.

7. Congressional Quarterly, in a 1927 report, asserted that "Grant desired renomination to succeed himself when his second term drew to a close." "The Third Term Tradition in American Politics (1927)," *Editorial Research Reports* 1927 (Vol.

1) (Washington, DC: CQ Press). http:/library.cqpress.com/cqresearcher/cqresrre192 7031900 (accessed October 8, 2018).

8. Blaine, p. 657.

9. Chernow, p. 810. But Grant did not entirely close the door. The letter also stated, "I would not accept a nomination if it were tendered, unless it were to come under such circumstances as to make it an imperative duty—circumstances not likely to arise." Grant's letter responded to the resolution from the Convention opposing a third term. CQ Researcher, "The Third Term Tradition in American Politics," *CQ Press*, www.library.cqpress.com (accessed October 8, 2018). Once the Pennsylvanian Republicans passed their resolution, Republicans in nine more states made similar declarations. Lingley, pp. 311–312.

10. Ibid.

11. "Grant and the Third Term," *The Daily Gazette* (Wilmington, Delaware), June 4, 1875, p. 4. *Chronicling America: Historic Newspapers*. Library of Congress. https ://chroniclingamerica.loc.gov/lccn/sn82014805/1875-06-04/ed-1/seq-2/ (accessed June 9, 2019).

12. "Grant's Third-term Letter," Editorial from the *New York Sun,* quoted in *The Jasper Weekly Courier* (Jasper, Indiana), June 18, 1875, p. 3, *Chronicling America: Historic American Newspapers,* Library of Congress. https:chroniclingamerica.loc.gov/lccn/sn84023963/1875-06-18/ed-1/seq-3/ (accessed June 10, 2019).

13. Julia Dent Grant, *The Personal Memoirs of Julia Dent Grant*, reprint (New York: G.P. Putnam's Sons, 1975), p. 186.

14. Quotations from the state resolutions are set out in the *West Jersey Pioneer* (Bridgeton, New Jersey) April 1, 1880. Library of Congress. https://chronicling-america.loc.gov.

15. "Editorials," *Northern Ohio Journal* (Painesville, Ohio), June 12, 1875, p. 2. *Chronicling America: Historic American Newspapers*. Library of Congress. https://chroniclingamerica.loc.gov/lccn/sn84028194/1875-06-12/ed-1/seq-2/ (accessed June 9, 2019).

16. "Grant's Third Term Blunder," *The Louisiana Democrat* (Alexandria, Louisiana), 16 June 1875, p. 3. *Chronicling America: Historic American Newspapers*. Library of Congress. https://chroniclingamerica.loc.gov/lccn/sn82003389/1875-06-16/ed-1/seq-3/ (accessed June 9, 2019).

17. Michael J. Korzi, *Presidential Term Limits in American History: Power, Principles, and Politics* (College Station: Texas A&M University Press, 2011), p. 61.

18. In 1875, the House also considered a constitutional amendment for a single six-year term. The Judiciary Committee reported it, but it could not secure a two-thirds majority. The Democrats tried again in 1876, but with similar results. Ames, p. 128.

19. CQ Researcher, "The Third Term Tradition in American Politics," CQ Press, www.library.cqpress.com. (accessed October 8, 2018).

20. Isabel Wilkerson, *The Warmth of Other Suns: The Epic Story of America's Great Migration* (New York: Random House, 2010), p. 37–38.

21. William H. Rehnquist, *Centennial Crisis: The Disputed Election of 1876* (New York: Alfred A. Knopf, 2004).

22. In that day, candidates did not go to party conventions to accept their nominations. Instead, once the nomination was made, a party committee would visit the candidate to notify him formally that he had been nominated. The candidate would accept via a letter to the party leadership. As to the major parties, this tradition remained intact until 1932, when Franklin Roosevelt flew to Chicago to accept his nomination in person from the Democratic Convention still in session.

23. Ari Hoogenboom, *Rutherford B. Hayes: Warrior and President* (Lawrence, Kansas: University Press of Kansas, 1995), pp. 266–267.

24. *The New York Herald* (New York, NY), July 16, 1876, *Chronicling America: Historic American Newspapers*, Library of Congress, https://chroniclingamerica.loc.gov/lccn/sn83030313/1976-07-16/ed-1/seq-6/ (accessed June 9, 2019).

25. "Rutherford B. Hayes' Inaugural Address," rbhayes.org. (accessed October 8, 2018).

26. John Russell Young, a journalist who accompanied Grant on the world tour, was intrigued by the General's political rehabilitation. Young "clearly saw the logic of a Grant third-term candidacy in 1880. Grant's popularity had soared—a remarkable turnabout from four years earlier, when scandals, reconstruction, hard times, and eight years of familiarity had all conspired to turn the public against its two-term president. 'Grantism' had become an insult, linked to corruption." Kenneth D. Ackerman, *Dark Horse: The Surprise Election and Political Murder of President James A. Garfield* (New York: Carroll & Graf Publishers, 2003), pp. 43–44.

27. *St. Johnsbury Caledonian* (St. Johnsbury, Vermont), September 26, 1879. Library of Congress. https. chronclingamerica.loc.gov.

28. Ibid.

29. John Sherman, *John Sherman's Recollections of Forty Years in the House, Senate, and Cabinet: An Autobiography,* Volume 2 (Chicago: The Werner Company, 1895), p. 766.

30. Adam Badeau, *Grant in Peace: From Appomatox to Mount McGregor, a Personal Memoir* (Hartford: S.S. Scranton & Co., 1887), pp. 317–318.

31. "The Third Term Finesse," *The New York Herald*, quoted in *The Weekly Kansas Chief* (Troy, Kansas), January 8, 1880, p. 1. Chronicling America: Historic American Newspapers. Library of Congress. https://chroniclingamerica.loc.gov/lccn/sn82015484/1880-01-08/ed-1/seq-1/ (accessed June 11, 2019).

32. "Ohio," *Chicago Daily Tribune,* May 29, 1880, p. 7. *Chronicling America: Historic American Newspapers*. Library of Congress. https://chroniclingamerica.loc.gov/lccn/sn84031492/1880-05-29/ed-1/seq-7/.

33. "The Presidency," *The Indianapolis Leader* (Indianapolis, Indiana), May 22, 1880, p. 1. Library of Congress. https://chroniclingamerica.loc.gov.

34. John Adams (Great Britain), Thomas Jefferson (France), John Quincy Adams (Russia), and James Buchanan (Great Britain) served in diplomatic postings before their presidencies.

35. "I had not met him for more than a year, during which period he had gone through his wonderful experience in the Far East, had obtained his knowledge of China and Japan, and conceived an Oriental policy for this country which he believed so important that a desire to achieve it was certainly one reason why he was so anxious to return to power." Badeau, p. 320.

36. Ibid.
37. Chernow, p. 890.
38. White, p. 617.
39. Blaine, p. 657. "A combination which included Senators Conkling, Cameron, and Logan, with their dominant personal influence and political force, and which aimed at the consolidation of the three great states of New York, Pennsylvania, and Illinois, presented a formidable force.
40. Ackerman, p. 19.
41. "Will Grant Withdraw," *Chicago Daily Tribune* (Chicago, Illinois), June 2, 1880, p. 4. *Chronicling America: Historic American Newspapers*. Library of Congress. https:/chroniclingamerican.loc.gov/lccn/sn84031492/1880-06-02/ed-1/seq-4/ (accessed June 11, 2019).
42. Sherman, p. 766.
43. Chernow, p. 892. In a letter to his friend, Elihu Washburne, Grant disclaimed pursuing an active candidacy, although he remained open to being nominated, if that were the will of the Convention. White, p. 618.
44. In 1880, the Pennsylvania Republican Convention, which had opposed a third term in 1876, was dominated by Grant forces. They endorsed the former president for nomination and buried a resolution that would have reprised their 1876 message. Lingley, 313.
45. "Elevated to the U.S. Senate in 1867, Blaine built a strong organization of moderate 'Half-Breeds'—a term that began as an insult against Republicans who had wavered in their loyalty for Grant, but became a compliment as Grant's scandals mounted through the 1870s." Ackerman, p. 19.
46. Hoogenboom, p. 416. Garfield chronicler Candice Millard notes, "The idea of a third term, for anyone, was controversial, and the two terms Grant had already served as president had been notoriously rife with corruption. He was, however, still a national hero." *Candice Millard, Destiny of the Republic: A Tale of Madness, Medicine, and the Murder of a President* (New York: Doubleday, 2011), p. 11. Blaine states, "With all the respect and affection for the illustrious commander of the Union armies, there was a deep and earnest feeling against a third term. This sentiment was not personal to General Grant." Blaine, p. 658.
47. "No Compromise with a Third Term," *New-York Tribune*, May 26, 1880, p. 4. *Chronicling America: Historic American Newspapers*. Library of Congress. https://chroniclingamerica.loc.gov/lccn/sn83030214/1880-05-26/ed-1/seq-4/.
48. In 1912, Theodore Roosevelt advanced the exact same argument.
49. Lingley, p. 314.
50. On February 26, 1880, the *Lancaster Daily Intelligencer* wrote. "The pretext on which the change is made is that as Grant has been out of office one term, the danger of election to a third term does not exist. But it is apparent that this is but a pretext. . . . Establish this precedent, and when Grant asks a fourth and a fifth term, it will be his to command. He will already have been honored above Washington and nothing that he can ask more can be refused him." "A Victory that is a Defeat," *Lancaster Daily Intelligencer* (Lancaster, Pa.), February 26, 1880, p. 2. On the eve of the 1880 convention, Representative J. Warren Keifer (R-OH) stated, "I regret that

General Grant has permitted his name to be used for a third Presidential term. There is no precedent for it. His friends claim that the objection is only to continuous terms and not to the number of terms. But there are many people personally and politically friendly to General Grant who do not wish to set a precedent for a third term, especially in a time when there is no great exigency impending over the country." "Ohio: Special Dispatch to the *Chicago Tribune*," *Chicago Daily Tribune,* May 29, 1880, p. 7. Keifer served in the House from 1877 to 1885 and again from 1905 to 1911. From 1881 to 1883, he was speaker.

51. Badeau, p. 322. "While Grant stayed aloof, his self-appointed 'friends' took over. Grant never directly approached the three Senate bosses, Conkling, (John) Logan, and (Don) Cameron—his triumvirate—for help. Still, during their months of highly public work lining up delegates, he never discouraged them." Ackerman, p. 47.

52. Ibid., p. 41.

53. Ibid., p. 48.

54. "In 1868, and again in 1872, he had been given the Republican nomination for president on the first ballot. No one believed he would win the nomination as easily this time, but few expected him to lose." Millard, p. 31.

55. Sherman, p. 774.

56. Blaine, p. 658.

57. "The Unit Rule," *Chicago Daily Tribune* (Chicago, Illinois), 02 June 1880, p. 7. *Chronicling America: Historic American Newspapers*. Library of Congress. https:/chroniclingamerican.loc.gov/lccn/sn84031492/1880-06-02/ed-1/seq-4/ (accessed June 11, 2019).

58. On May 31, 1880, the *Chicago Tribune* published an analysis of the effect of the projected unit rule on the delegates. A majority in the convention was 379 votes. The *Tribune* claimed that Grant had 284 votes, with an additional ninety six who would be bound to him if unit rule were imposed but who would otherwise defect. With unit rule in place, Grant would have a majority of two votes. If unit rule were not imposed, anti-Grant delegates would outnumber Grant delegates by 190 votes. *Chicago Daily Tribune* (Chicago, Ill.), May 31, 1880. *Chronicling America: Historic American Newspapers*. Library of Congress. https://chroniclingamerica.loc.gov/lccn/sn84031492/1880-05-31/ed-1/seq-4/

59. Sherman, p. 773; Blaine, p. 662.

60. The Democratic two-thirds rule existed to protect Southern influence within the party. This rule could sometimes produce lengthy balloting fights, such as the forty-six ballots it took to nominate Woodrow Wilson in 1912 or the astounding 103 ballots required for John W. Davis' nomination in 1924. Preparing for the Convention, Homer Cummings, then a Roosevelt adviser and later U.S. Attorney General, criticized the two-thirds rule as providing for tyranny by the minority. "The two-thirds rule is a misnomer," wrote Cummings. "It is in fact a one-third rule, because it permits a determined minority to block action and paralyze the normal function of the Convention." Homer Cummings, "The Two-thirds Rule," Memorandum dictated June 17, 1932, Franklin Delano Roosevelt Library, Democratic National Conventions, Box143, www.fdrlibrary.marist.edu/_resources/images/psf/psf000531.pdf (accessed July 20, 2018). Franklin Roosevelt was nominated on the fourth ballot in

1932, after leading on the first three ballots, but it was unclear whether he could have survived further balloting. Once in control of the party machinery, FDR ensured that Democrats dropped the two-thirds rule for the 1936 Convention. Since then, Democrats have nominated by majority vote.

61. At no point an active candidate, Garfield received only a single vote on the first ballot, and had no substantial support until the thirty-fifth ballot. At that time, Garfield received fifty votes, principally from Indiana and Wisconsin, but Ohio continued to hold firm for Sherman. William Ralston Balch, *The Life of James Abram Garfield* (Philadelphia: Hubbard Brothers, 1881), pp. 473–475. Ohio broke for Garfield on the 36th ballot, at which time support for Blaine and Sherman utterly collapsed.

62. James D. McCabe, *Our Martyred President: The Life and Public Services of Gen. James A. Garfield* (Philadelphia: National Publishing Company, 1881), p. 471.

63. Grant's delegates were exceedingly proud of their stance and wore their fealty as a badge of honor. "They remained steadfast at 306. In future years, they called themselves the '306,' proud they had stayed loyal to their hero." White, p. 621.

64. Julia Dent Grant, pp. 321–322.

65. Badeau, p. 321.

66. Chernow, p. 906. According to the New York Sun, a decidedly Democratic paper, Grant came around after he and several of his Stalwart allies secured Garfield's agreement over patronage issues, and as well, to set Grant up for a third-term nomination in 1884. Regardless of what understandings the Stalwarts thought they had, such soon fell apart. Stalwart leader, Senator Roscoe Conkling (R-NY) got into a major, unsuccessful fight with President Garfield over patronage. "Grant's Campaign," *The Sun* (New York [N.Y.]), October 16, 1880, p. 2. *Chronicling America: Historic American Newspapers*. Library of Congress. https://chroniclingamerica.loc.gov/lccn/sn83030272/1880-10-16/ed-1/seq-2/. Ironically, it was Garfield's recalcitrance on patronage that led to his assassination by a demented and disappointed office seeker.

67. Ibid., p. 902.

68. "Something for Republicans: The Third Term Danger Still Imminent," *Daily Globe* (St. Paul, Minnesota,) October 30, 1880, p. 2. *Chronicling America: Historic American Newspapers*. Library of Congress. https://chroniclingamerica.loc.gov/lccn/sn83025287/1880-10-30/ed-1/seq-2/ (accessed June 11, 2019).

69. Blaine, p. 670.

70. "A Great Nation in Grief," *New York Times*, July 3, 1881, p. 1.

71. Ackerman, pp. 151–160. See, also, "The President Dead," *New York Times*, September 20, 1881, p. 1.

72. Ibid., p. 438.

73. Michael Kazin, *A Godly Hero: The Life of William Jennings Bryan* (New York: Alfred A. Knopf, 2006), pp. 66–67.

74. The Democrats "demanded the free and unlimited coinage of silver and gold at the ratio of 16 to 1, denounced the protective tariff, advocated government regulation of trusts and railroads, called for enlarged powers of the Interstate Commerce Commission, and blasted the Supreme Court's ruling that the income tax was unconstitutional." Robert W. Merry, *President McKinley: Architect of the American Century* (New York: Simon & Schuster, 2017), p. 132.

75. Merry, p. 142.

76. Hobart died in 1899. Roosevelt was a peripatetic campaigner. "In eight weeks of campaigning, he traveled 21, 209 miles in delivering 673 speeches to an estimated three million people in twenty-four states encompassing 567 town and cities." Merry, p. 447.

Chapter 4

A Tradition under Severe Pressure

Theodore Roosevelt (1912)

On Friday afternoon, September 6, 1901, Leon Czolgosz, an anarchist, shot President William McKinley at the Pan American Exposition in Buffalo, New York. It was the third presidential assassination in thirty-five years.

McKinley underwent immediate surgery. In its aftermath, White House medical announcements indicated he might survive.[1] However, the president lingered for just over a week, and died on September 14, only six months into his second term.[2] Later that day, his vice president, Theodore Roosevelt, took the oath as president. In 1904, Roosevelt sought election in his own right. There was no contest for the Republican nomination.[3] In November, voters elected him in a landslide, at the time the greatest in modern American history. Roosevelt prevailed in the popular vote by 56.4 percent to 37.6 percent for Democrat Alton B. Parker, and won every state outside the former Confederacy, except for Kentucky. Once again, the South performed well and predictably for Democrats. Roosevelt's best state in the region was Tennessee, where he exceeded 43 percent. He received less than 10 percent in South Carolina, Mississippi, and Louisiana. The electoral vote count was 336 for Roosevelt to 140 for Parker.[4]

Roosevelt had been uncertain about the outcome, determined and desperate to win the mandate of election in his own right.[5] Four days prior to the balloting, he wrote to his friend, Senator Henry Cabot Lodge. "I think everything is going well," observed the president anxiously, "but we are in the last hours of the campaign, everyone is tired and nervous, and the air is thick with rumors."[6]

Then came the vote, which exceeded Roosevelt's most optimistic hopes. The morning after the election, he wired Lodge, "Have swept the country by majorities which astound me."[7]

On election night, Roosevelt proclaimed that he would not again run for the presidency. He composed the announcement himself. Shortly after 10:00 PM, in the White House corridor, standing outside the Red Room, he handed it to a secretary.[8] It was very much his own decision, not the work of advisers. The statement read, "On the fourth of March next, I shall have served three and one-half years, and the three and one-half years constitute my first term. The wise custom which limits the President to two terms regards the substance and not the form. Under no circumstances will I be a candidate for or accept another nomination."[9]

By 1908, Roosevelt would have seven and a half years as chief executive. Because he was only elected once to the presidency, some Republicans sought to dodge the two-term tradition by claiming that it applied to two elective terms. Roosevelt considered this a technicality; the reality was that he would have served nearly two entire terms. To have prolonged his presidency in 1908 would have contradicted the spirit of the custom.

Roosevelt's statement ended this debate before it really began. In the autobiography, Roosevelt explained, "The reason for my choice of the exact phraseology used was twofold. In the first place, many of my supporters were insisting that, as I had served only three and a half years of my first term, coming in from the Vice Presidency when President McKinley was killed, I had really had only one elective term, so that the third term custom did not apply to me; and I wished to repudiate this suggestion. I believed then (and I believe now) the third term custom or tradition to be wholesome and, therefore, I was determined to regard its substance, refusing to quibble over the words usually employed to express it."[10]

Roosevelt's closest political associates, even if they knew he harbored such sentiments, did not expect the announcement when it happened. In a postscript to a lengthy congratulatory letter from Lodge to Roosevelt, dispatched the morning after the election, the Senator stated, "I read your speech with profound interest and admiration. I know, of course, how you felt in regard to another term. It had not occurred to me that you would say it at that precise moment. It was the moment of all others in which to say it, and it will give you, if such a thing were needed, more strength than ever in the confidence of your countrymen."[11]

Roosevelt replied immediately, delighted with Lodge's encouragement. "I am particularly pleased that you approved of my utterance about the third term being made just when it was."[12]

The president surprised not only Lodge, but even the First Lady, Edith Roosevelt.[13] According to Roosevelt's biographer, H.W. Brands, Edith enjoyed the White House, was concerned about her husband turning himself into a lame duck for the entire second term, and worried about how a still youthful Roosevelt would adjust to the post-presidency.[14] Roosevelt's concealing his plans from Edith seems much like Grant in 1876 keeping secrets from Julia. In both cases, the president knew his wife would not be pleased, and preempted her objection with a public announcement.

In his autobiography, Roosevelt laid out two reasons for his announcement. The first was to rebut allegations that he suffered from an overbearing desire for power. "My opponents during the campaign had laid much stress upon my supposed personal ambition and intention to use the office of President to perpetuate myself in power."[15] The second was his respect for the two-term tradition, then more than a century old. These two considerations interrelated. In 1912, when Roosevelt ran again, he distinguished between the entrenchment of power when a president sought to perpetuate himself after two consecutive terms and the absence of such entrenchment if he had sat out a time.

Brands assesses that, "In the very moment of victory, when delusions of grandeur should have held him in their grasp, if they ever would, he renounced power. A nobler or more dramatic gesture was hard to imagine of a politician; in making it, Roosevelt believed he would confirm once and for all his claim to serve not his own self-interest but only the public good."[16]

Thereafter, Roosevelt had reservations about the pledge, as he confronted the reality of leaving office with much on his agenda left to do. "When I felt obliged to insist on retiring and abandoning the leadership, now and then I felt ugly qualms as to whether I was not refusing to do what I ought to do, and abandoning great work on a mere fantastic point of honor."[17]

Those misgivings also had a peculiar political dimension. Roosevelt believed that, if he ran in 1908, he could crack the Democrats' hold on the Solid South.[18] It was a bold claim. Once the South was "redeemed," Democrats shut out Republicans in the old Confederacy election after election. In seven campaigns, from 1880 through Roosevelt's own in 1904, Republicans won zero electoral votes in that region.

Archibald Butt, Roosevelt's military aide and friend, recalled a 1908 conversation with the president. "You know," stated Roosevelt,

> my chief regret in not making the race this year is that I am not able to demonstrate the fact that I can carry Georgia. I am convinced that I would carry Georgia, Virginia, and possibly Louisiana. . . . I would carry those states for the reason that I am not sectional; I have not got a sectional bone in my body. I imbibed the traditions and folklore of the South from my mother; my earliest training and principles were Southern.[19]

Notwithstanding these temptations, Roosevelt kept his word. An important principle was involved. "I believe in a strong executive," he affirmed several years after declaring the pledge. "I believe in power; but I believe that responsibility should go with power, and that it is not well that the strong executive should be a perpetual executive."[20] In time, his misgivings would give way to profound regret.[21] Historian Doris Kearns Goodwin asserts, that "in all likelihood, had Roosevelt not declared against a third term on the eve of his overwhelming victory in 1904, he would have pursued a third term."[22]

As the 1908 election approached, Roosevelt was determined to secure his legacy even if he was not on the ballot to defend it. His first choice of a successor was Secretary of State Elihu Root, who declined.[23] Then, he turned to his Secretary of War William Howard Taft of Ohio.

Taft was a reluctant candidate,[24] who preferred appointment to the Supreme Court.[25] Roosevelt finally prevailed on Taft to run, and made it known that he wanted him nominated.[26]

Roosevelt was in firm command of the party apparatus. It bent to the President's will, although not without dissension. Some grumbling came from potential nominees that Roosevelt pushed aside to get the prize for Taft, or from delegates who feared that Taft could not win the general election.[27] And some came from Roosevelt partisans, sizeable in number, who nurtured the hope that he would rescind his promise and seek reelection. As Doris Kearns Goodwin comments, "So long as the merest possibility remained that Roosevelt might rescind his pledge and run for a third term, many Republicans would not commit to anyone else."[28] To skirt criticism about his running for a third term, Roosevelt's argued that another four years would amount to a "second elective term."[29]

Such maneuvering amounted to nothing.[30] Notwithstanding the apprehensions of Taft's supporters, in particular his wife Nellie, that Roosevelt would change course and run again, the president held firm.[31]

Although intrigued by the continued interest he received from within the party, Roosevelt fretted about what people might think if he reversed on the pledge. Kearns Goodwin writes, "Even as he warmed to the popular clamor for a third term, Roosevelt suspected that many of those who called for his re-election 'would feel very much disappointed' if he actually ran and would include that he had fallen 'short of the ideal they had formed as to the integrity of his character and the credibility of his word."[32]

Thus, Roosevelt would not be a candidate, so long as it was plain that Republicans would be willing to nominate Taft in his place.[33] "If the people knew Taft, there would be no doubt of his election," the president mused. "They know what he has done, but they don't know the man. If they knew him, they would know that he can be relied upon to carry out the policies which I stand for. He is committed to them just the same as I am and has been made the mouthpiece for them as frequently as I."[34]

The 1908 Republican Convention met in Chicago in June. The keynoter was Convention Chairman Henry Cabot Lodge, understood to be the president's spokesman. When he mentioned Roosevelt's name, the galleries erupted for a forty-nine-minute raucous demonstration, but unlike the Convention that nominated Wendell Willkie in 1940, delegates would not be stampeded to make a nomination.[35] Maintaining control of the proceedings, Lodge asked the Convention to honor Roosevelt's disclaimer. "The President has refused what his countrymen would gladly have given him," announced Lodge. "He says what he means and means what he says, and his party and his country will respect his wishes as they honor his high character and public service."[36] Taft won more than 70 percent of the vote on the first ballot, routing supporters of Pennsylvania Senator Philander Knox and New York Governor Charles Evans Hughes.[37]

As Roosevelt stated, Taft had a distinguished record of public service, spanning nearly twenty years. He had been Solicitor General of the United States, a judge on the Sixth Circuit Court of Appeals, the first civilian governor of the Philippines, and later Secretary of War. In the general election, Taft ran against William Jennings Bryan, twice previously the Democratic nominee. Bryan expected to win.[38] Although a Republican victory was not a foregone conclusion when the campaign began, Taft prevailed handily.[39] On March 22, 1909, barely two weeks following the end of his presidency, Roosevelt left the country for an African safari.[40] As he departed, he was but fifty years old, regretful to exit the White House, but content to have honored his pledge, and pleased by an election outcome he had actively abetted.[41] Roosevelt would be gone from the United States for more than a year, returning home in June 1910.

Almost from the start of Taft's administration, and continuing as it unfolded, Republican Progressives were unhappy. There were concerns about Taft's appointments. According to Roosevelt scholar David Pietrusa, Taft had promised to keep all of Roosevelt's cabinet, but wound up retaining just two of them. Certain holdovers from Roosevelt's administration left under acrimonious circumstances. The firing of Gifford Pinchot, originally a Roosevelt appointee to head the National Forest Service, was a prime example of Taft charting his own course, and it deeply irritated Roosevelt.[42]

Compounding the discontent, Progressives considered Taft to be a captive of reactionary party leaders in Congress. Particularly controversial was a fight over tariff policy. In general, Progressives were free traders. Old Guard Republicans, such as Senate Finance Committee Chairman Nelson Aldrich (R-RI) and Speaker Joseph Cannon (R-IL), were steadfast protectionists. Taft initially appeared willing to join Progressives in challenging them, but ultimately signed the highly protectionist Payne-Aldrich Tariff Act of 1909.

For his part, Taft had a considerably less expansive view of presidential power than did his predecessor. "The true view of the Executive functions is, as I conceive it, that the President can exercise no power which cannot be fairly and reasonably traced to some specific grant of power or justly implied and included within such express grant as proper and necessary to its exertion. Such specific grant must be either in the Federal Constitution or in an act of Congress passed in pursuance thereof." Roosevelt's perspective, as Taft described it, was wildly more expansive, even dangerous.

> My judgment is that the view . . . of Mr. Roosevelt, ascribing an undefined residuum of power to the President is an unsafe doctrine and that it might lead under emergencies to results of an arbitrary character. . . . The mainspring of such a view is that the Executive is charged with responsibility for the welfare of all the people in a general way, that he is to play the part of a Universal Providence and set all things right, and that anything that in his judgment will help the people he ought to do, unless he is expressly forbidden not to do it.[43]

It had become obvious that Roosevelt's heir apparent was not his clone. As a consequence, he grew disillusioned with the incumbent president, and fretted that Taft was a weak leader.[44]

Tensions appear to have arisen almost from the beginning of Taft's administration. Letters written by Archie Butt, an aide to both Roosevelt and Taft, and published in 1930 after Taft's death, shed light on the split. As reported in the 1930 New York Times, "From what the letters contained about the rupture between President Taft and his predecessor in the White House, it would appear that Colonel Roosevelt began to be dissatisfied with the Taft way of doing things almost from the moment of Mr. Taft's inauguration." In one of the letters, Butt quotes Roosevelt, "I hope that my policies may be made into law, but I may have to come back in four years and enter the fight."[45]

Moreover, Roosevelt harbored a personal grievance against Taft, deepening the split. In 1911, Taft's Justice Department brought an antitrust suit against United States Steel, involving an acquisition made during the prior administration. Roosevelt had signed off the acquisition. The lawsuit claimed he had been deceived. Roosevelt felt blindsided by the litigation and angrily denied being duped.[46]

Roosevelt returned to America in 1910, having remained publicly mute on his attitudes toward the Taft's administration.[47] At the beginning of July, he endorsed the campaigns of various progressive insurgents. This sparked a third-term boom, promoted by former U.S. Ambassador to Mexico David E. Thompson. But Roosevelt did not immediately engage.[48] However, in late summer, he reentered the political arena with a three-week speaking tour. Apart from campaigning for Republicans in that election year, he wanted to propound a vision for progressive government. These speeches gained wide public attention.[49]

The most famous of them was at Osawatomie, Kansas, on August 31, 1910, in which he advocated for significant government intervention to promote the general public welfare, a graduated income tax, strengthened government intervention in business and labor policy, and enhanced government control over natural resources.[50] "We are face to face with new conceptions of the relations of property to human welfare," exclaimed Roosevelt, "chiefly because certain advocates of the rights of property as against the rights of men have been pushing their claims too far. The man who wrongly holds that every human right is secondary to his profit must now give way to the advocate of human welfare, who rightly maintains that every man holds his property subject to the general right of the community to regulate its use to whatever degree the public welfare may require it." He continued, "but I think we may go still further. The right to regulate the use of wealth in the public interest is universally admitted. Let us admit also the right to regulate the terms and conditions of labor, which is the chief element of wealth, directly in the interest of the common good."[51]

Roosevelt called the policy the New Nationalism. These forward-leaning positions contrasted sharply with Taft's and those of Republican conservatives in Congress.[52] Pietrusa notes how radical Roosevelt's departure was, not only from Republican orthodoxy but from the former president's own record in office.

> The mildly progressive "Square Deal" of Roosevelt's White House days no longer interested him. . . . He decried socialism and communism, but his "New Nationalism" placed the collective above the individual, the federal over the state and local, and scorned the traditional American system of checks and balances.[53]

The *Topeka State Journal* noted the vividness of Roosevelt's positions. "Since his return from Africa, more than two months ago, he has been silent in regard to his views on the specific issues of the day. The former President broke his silence today in a speech which left no doubt as to where he stands."[54]

Progressive newspapers were enthralled. The *Detroit Times* gushed, "Theodore Roosevelt has once more exposed himself to the charge of being the best politician the country has ever known. We doubt if Roosevelt would deny the charge; at any rate we don't think he should, for he isn't that kind of politician. The *Times* only wishes there were more of his kind in politics."[55]

"In Theodore Roosevelt's Osawotomie speech the word national and nationalist occurred over and over again. . . . The seed was sown that men might take into consideration the whole people—the bond in common," said the *Richmond Palladium and Sun-Telegram*.[56]

The *Aberdeen Herald* added, "In this battle, not less than 80 percent of the people are in sympathy with the progressives, and in aligning himself with them, former President Roosevelt acted as was expected by all who have noted his course all through his public life."[57]

Clearly, Roosevelt stirred Progressive spirits. But did this speaking tour foretell a presidential candidacy? The press was unsure what to make of it, in light of the two-term tradition. "We are not disposed to believe Mr. Roosevelt wants a third term as president and prefer to await further developments before attacking him on that score," wrote the *Durham Recorder*. "We believe Roosevelt has a different card up his sleeve but what it is we cannot just make out. He works too far in the future to be taken as an ordinary politician. Watch him."[58]

Meanwhile, doubts about Taft's leadership were not limited to Roosevelt and the Progressives. Voters made that evident. The 1910 mid-term elections wound up being calamitous for Republicans, who lost fifty-eight seats in the House of Representatives, giving way to a Democratic majority. While control of the Senate did not change, Republicans shed nine seats. The defeat exceeded the GOP's worst expectations.[59] There was a strong possibility that opposition to Taft for the 1912 nomination would materialize.[60] Wisconsin Senator Robert LaFollette, already a leader among Progressive elements, prepared a challenge.[61]

As he assessed matters early in 1911, neither did Roosevelt believe LaFollette could wrest the nomination from Taft, nor did he think Taft could be reelected. At the same time, he did not want to acquiesce in conservative control of the party, or to fracture the GOP, either of which would boost prospects for a Democratic victory. Unsure of what to do, Roosevelt initially resisted the temptation to lead an emerging movement of Progressives.[62]

While he was philosophically sympathetic to a LaFollette candidacy, Roosevely did not rule out his own.[63] The senator was skeptical, expecting that the former president would declare himself once he assessed that Taft was vulnerable enough to overtake.[64]

Roosevelt's posturing and positioning not only troubled LaFollette, but also worried the White House.[65] Representatives from both LaFollette and Taft sought assurances from Roosevelt that he would not run. In a December 13, 1911, letter to Senator Lodge, Roosevelt described a delegation, from exactly whom it is not clear, who asked him to put to rest rumors that he would run in 1912. However, the former president declined to do so. He told Lodge, "For your private information, I may mention that ___ and ___ have been to see me to urge me to make an announcement that I would refuse the nomination if offered to me! Of course, I refused point blank. I told them that I emphatically did not want the nomination, and should regard it as a misfortune if it came, and that I did not believe there was any chance of its coming, but that I should certainly not definitely state that if it did come in the form of a duty I would refuse to perform the duty; in other words, that as Abraham

Lincoln used to say, no man can justly ask me to cross such a bridge until I come to it."[66]

As the incumbent, Taft commanded the party organization. Roosevelt's prospects for a third term depended on appealing to Progressive factions, which, if sufficiently mobilized, might overwhelm them. The former president staked out positions likely to gain their support. On February 21, speaking before the Ohio Constitutional Convention in Columbus, he endorsed direct primaries, as well as the "initiative, referendum, and recall" policy, dear to the Progressive program, but beyond that, he supported public referenda to overturn state judicial decisions related to constitutional questions.[67] These positions, especially the one on judicial recall, may have appealed to Progressives, but they deeply alienated other Republicans.

Writing about referenda to countermand judicial decisions, Alice Roosevelt Longworth opined, "I think that proposal, more than any other one thing, lost him the nomination. It gave his opponents the angle from which to attack him as a dangerous radical, and really distressed his most sincere friends and supporters, who felt that anything that undermined respect for the judiciary was a 'menace to our institutions.' The fact that his proposal merely applied to a certain type of decision on constitutional questions was never made generally clear. It was exploited as an attack on judicial power as a whole."[68]

Major newspapers commented negatively on this idea.[69] As well, staunch Roosevelt friends, who were otherwise regular Republicans, already had misgivings about his turn to the left and were appalled by his proposal for referenda on court decisions. One such supporter was his friend, Henry Cabot Lodge. Both in private correspondence and in public speeches, Lodge had distanced himself from Roosevelt on key aspects of the Progressive agenda. For example, in a December 18, 1911, letter to the former president, Lodge stated, "As for the recall of the judges, that is a matter on which I feel very strongly. I think the independent court is more essential to freedom." Lodge described recall as "a summary form of impeachment." He also opposed referenda in lieu of legislation. "My objection is a fundamental one, that the mass of voters (and I include myself) are unable to legislate by a 'yes' or 'no' vote at the polls. I do not believe that you can get good legislation in that way."[70]

Throughout the winter of 1911–1912, Roosevelt maintained he was not running but signaled he might accede to a convention draft.[71] A draft would mitigate criticism over a third term, which Roosevelt was loathe to confront if he could avoid it.[72] If the call came, he would not decline to serve.[73] Meanwhile, he did what he could to ensure its appearance, engineering a letter from seven Progressive Republican governors encouraging him to run.[74] Roosevelt received their letter on February 10, 1912. On February 25, he made public his reply that he would accept the nomination if the Convention tendered it. "I deeply appreciate your letter," he said "and I realize the heavy responsibility it puts on me, expressing as it does, the carefully considered convictions of the men elected by popular vote to stand at the heads of government in their several states. I will accept the nomination for president if it is tendered to me, and I will adhere to this decision until the convention has expressed its preference."[75] Primed to get going, Roosevelt had told a reporter several days earlier, "My hat is in the ring. The fight is on and I am stripped to the buff."[76]

The *Chicago Journal* was unimpressed with the charade. "There is in that statement the inference that Mr. Roosevelt now responds to duty's call; that he might not have sought a third term if the eight governors had not laid the 'heavy responsibility upon me.'" The *Journal* would have none of it. "All other issues in the campaign of 1912 are dwarfed by the Third Term issue. Greater than currency, greater than tariff, greater than trusts, is the issue of the Third Term."[77]

The *St. Louis Republic* concurred. "There is no suggestion of shrinking modesty or the difference of doubt in Theodore Roosevelt's response to the handful of Governors who recently offered him a third term. On the contrary, he throws himself into their arms with an emphasis that must prove somewhat discouraging even to them. . . . Never before was there so poor an excuse for violating the best traditions of the republic. Never before did a weak pretender more gravely accept distinction that can never be his."[78]

In her memoirs, Alice Roosevelt Longworth acknowledged that the exchange of correspondence had been prearranged for appearance's sake. She described the gubernatorial communication as a "somewhat 'cooked' letter that did not take Father by surprise."[79]

Facing this new challenge, Taft quickly countered. By the end of February, the president produced telegraphic communications from nine governors, supporting his reelection.[80]

Meanwhile, a faction of Democrats in Congress tried to derail the incipient Roosevelt momentum. On February 1, 1912, Representative James Luther Slayden (D-TX)[81] introduced a measure that reprised the language of Springer's anti-Grant resolution of 1875. It was referred to committee. He also indicated he would introduce a constitutional amendment restricting presidents to a single six-year term. Slayden was confident his resolution would pass. "I think that until recently there has hardly been any doubt that the overwhelming majority of the citizens of this country are oppose to the election of a President to a third term," said Slayden. House Majority Leader Oscar Underwood (D-AL)[82] chimed in. "I am opposed to a third term in the White House for any man, no matter how wise, able, or patriotic he may be," adding "I am opposed to the third-term idea. Two terms of four years each is long enough for any man to spend in the office of President." Representative

John Nance Garner (D-TX), then Assistant Majority Whip had another, quite practical, reason to support his fellow Texan: Roosevelt would be harder to beat than Taft. "I hope the Slayden resolution will be passed," said Garner, "because I believe it will aid in the elimination of Colonel Roosevelt as a factor in the present political situation. I want to see him put out of the running. I believe the democratic nominee this year will be able to defeat President Taft, I am not certain that we could beat Colonel Roosevelt." Slayden wanted affirmative action, quickly. The *Washington Star* thought he would prevail. "There will be a hearing or two on it, and there seems to be no doubt that it will be favorably reported to the House for action. Its passage by the body seems assured."[83]

On February 6, Slayden tried to accelerate matters. On the House Floor, he moved to suspend the rules, which would have the effect of discharging his resolution from committee and bringing it up for immediate consideration. Although a two-thirds vote was necessary to adopt the motion, Slayden believed no more than twenty Representatives would oppose it. Slayden may have been correct, if members were willing to vote. But most preferred to avoid the question, either because they were Republicans who wanted Roosevelt for president and hoped to duck the third-term issue, or, they were Democrats who did not want to look like they feared Roosevelt's candidacy. The vote came on a related procedural question. With an affirmative vote necessary to allow Slayden to proceed, the count was fifty in favor and ninety opposed. "The attempt of Representative Slayden to force action on his resolution failed in obtaining any crystallization of sentiment on presidential third terms," commented the *New York Times*. "It was almost unanimously admitted that, on its merits, an anti-third-term resolution would be favored by nine-tenths of the House membership, but the wisdom of taking such action as was proposed today is variously viewed, and the desire of factions on both sides to 'play politics' wrecked the plan."[84]

Roosevelt formally declared his candidacy on February 21, 1912. The Honolulu *Hawaiian Star* was dismayed. Its commentary was a vivid example of how, in many instances, the third-term issue served to overshadow the merits of Roosevelt's effort. "Washington served for two terms in the presidential office and there he stopped, going back resolutely to private citizenship and leaving in that act a solemn admonition to the nation to beware of the hero worship which might make the presidency a life tenure of a strong and popular man," noted the *Star*. "There were those who, in years to come, tried to give a third term to the great popular hero who had saved the nation in civil war, but the sound sense of the country rose against it and passed the chief office on to other deserving hands. It was not to be said, as Cassius warned Brutus, 'that these wide walks encompassed but one man.' If Theodore Roosevelt receives a third term, who shall forbid him a fourth? Precedents will have been thrown away, the moorings cut! Who, other than he could make conditions ripe, four years hence, for another adventure?"[85]

From Texas, the *El Paso Herald* agreed. "In view of firmly established precedent, wise custom, and well-grounded popular sentiment, and in view furthermore of Roosevelt's own declarations in respect to it, all talk of a third term for Theodore Roosevelt in the presidency should cease. If persisted in, the result is predestined, inevitable. If the national convention of the Republican Party should make the fatal mistake of nominating him, the people of the United States at the polls would confirm the precedent of a century by overwhelming defeat for him who would seek to break it."[86]

The distinction between accepting a nomination if offered, and actually seeking a third term, was lost on many people. Roosevelt could not escape criticism that he was breaking his no-third-term pledge. He received plenty of it. "That Theodore Roosevelt's utter repudiation of a pledge twice given and which should have been held sacred by him, is disgusting and repulsive to all men of honor and a sense of decency, no matter to what party they belong," wrote the Butler, Missouri *Weekly Times*. The *Kansas City Journal* concurred. "Colonel Roosevelt is very anxious to impress the country that there is a vast difference between 'becoming a candidate' and accepting a nomination if it is tendered. . . . Taking him at his word, it is yet plain and inescapable that he has violated his pledge. . . . His 'hat is in the ring' and he is actively giving encouragement and aid to those who are managing his campaign" The *New York World* commented, "Among citizens of commanding prestige and influence, Theodore Roosevelt alone has endorsed Theodore Roosevelt's third term candidacy. No great lawyer has endorsed it. No great jurist has endorsed it. No great educator has endorsed it. No great publicist or student of government has endorsed it. No United States Senator of the first rank has endorsed it. No representative in Congress of the first rank has endorsed it. No governor whose political influence extends beyond the borders of his own state has endorsed it. Hardly half a dozen newspapers of power and in importance has endorsed it."[87] During March, a great many smaller papers around the country would reprint the *World's* editorial in full.[88]

To win, Roosevelt would have to stir and unify the Progressive Republican faction, the very voters to whom LaFollette hoped to appeal. In this, he succeeded. Many imagined Roosevelt as the more compelling candidate, causing them to abandon the senator.[89] This was so, even though Roosevelt carried the burden of the third-term issue and LaFollette did not.

Of LaFollette's fair weather friends among Progressives, the *Topeka State Journal* complained that they "have persuaded Colonel Roosevelt to really believe . . . that he must lead the country out of the morass and sloughs of despond to a solid national footing. They have persuaded Colonel Roosevelt to believe that unless he gave them his consent to accept a nomination, should it be tendered to him, that he would be shirking a duty. . . . This paper is thus disposed to blame these uneasy deserters of LaFollette, rather than Colonel Roosevelt, much as his yielding to their importunities is to be regretted."[90]

Once Roosevelt made himself available, LaFollette's candidacy was dead.[91]

Roosevelt's open break with Taft caused the incumbent great consternation and split the Republican Party.[92] Some of Roosevelt's closest allies were distressed. Secretary of War Henry Stimson endorsed Taft in a March 5 Chicago speech, announcing "I entered into public life under the inspiration of Theodore Roosevelt. . . . But I believe that those who are forcing him, contrary to his original intention, into the arena against Mr. Taft, are jeopardizing instead of helping the real cause of progress in the nation."[93]

Senator Lodge, long a Roosevelt partisan, shared his anguish. While the senator could not bring himself to oppose Roosevelt, he emphasized his differences with his friend's platform, especially as to referenda on judicial decisions. "I am opposed to the constitutional changes advocated by Colonel Roosevelt in his recent speech in Columbus," wrote Lodge. "I have very strong convictions on those questions which, during the past three or four years, I have expressed in public with such force of argument as I could command. But Colonel Roosevelt and I for thirty years, and wholly apart from politics, have been close and most intimate friends. I must continue to oppose the policies which he urged at Columbus, but I cannot personally oppose him who has been my lifelong friend, and for this reason I take no part whatever in the campaign for the presidential nomination."[94]

On February 28, shortly after issuing his statement of neutrality, Lodge sent a letter to Roosevelt, in which he expressed the torment of not being able to endorse him.

> I could not abandon my convictions, and to come out for you, holding and known to hold the views I have expressed, would have stultified me and made me worse than useless to you. As for going against you in any way, or supporting anyone else against you, that I could not do. . . . I cannot tell you how much I have suffered from these harsh necessities and so I shall say no more.

Roosevelt replied on March 1, assuring Lodge that their friendship was intact. "I don't know whether to be most touched by your letter or most inclined to laugh over it. My dear fellow, you could not do anything that would make me lose my warm personal affection for you."[95]

Roosevelt's strategy to win the nomination was to prevail decisively in the primaries.[96] Thirteen states held them. Winning would help mitigate criticism over third-term ambitions, by making his candidacy look like a response to public demand. As Roosevelt's scholar, Edmund Morris, explained,

"Roosevelt intended to use his huge primary vote to persuade the party as a whole not to ratify the exclusion of his delegates, and to accept that progressivism was natural, desirable evolution of Republican doctrine."[97] Roosevelt was confident that success in the primaries would enable him to reach the Convention with a lead in committed delegates.[98]

Taft made sure that Roosevelt could not easily dodge the third-term issue. On April 25, several days before the Massachusetts primary, the president spoke in Boston. "Mr. Roosevelt ought not to be nominated in Chicago because in such a re-nomination, the Republican Party will violate our most useful and necessary government tradition—that no one shall be permitted to hold a third presidential term." The president went on to say, "There is not the slightest reason why, if he secures a third term, and the limitation of the Washington, Jefferson, and Jackson tradition is broken down, he should not have as many terms as his natural life will permit.[99] If he is necessary now to the government, why not later?"[100]

Throughout the campaign, Taft would continue to use the third-term issue against his rival. Two months later, campaigning in the Ohio primary, the president argued,

> Theodore Roosevelt doesn't understand the nature of our government or know what liberty regulated by law is. He is a man of great ability, but of little constitutional restraint, and is impatient of legal restraint. He is a dangerous man to intoxicate with the compliment of a third term.[101]

Because Roosevelt had cited the two-term tradition in his Election Night declaration, he knew he would have to distinguish the circumstances confronting him from those prevailing in 1904. The day after Taft's speech, Roosevelt did so. It made all the difference, he argued, if one ran as a private citizen, rather than an incumbent, perpetuating himself through patronage and the other powers of his office.[102] The evil was pursuing three *consecutive* terms, Roosevelt insisted, not a third term *per se*.[103]

Editorializing the next day, the *New York Times* was unimpressed by Roosevelt's hair-splitting.

> We are sure that every man of honest and candid mind must deeply regret that an ex-President of the United States has embarked upon an undertaking which he finds it necessary to serve by such a pitiful sophistication. . . . It is a disagreeable necessity which compels us to withhold full faith from the public statements of an ex-President of the United States.[104]

In his autobiography, published in 1913, Roosevelt expanded upon this distinction that engendered so much skepticism. He began with a vigorous defense of the two-term custom. "The Presidency is a great office, and the power of the President can be effectively used to secure a re-nomination, especially if the President has the support of certain great political and financial interests. It is for this reason, and this reason alone, that the wholesome principle of continuing in office, so long as he is willing to serve, an incumbent who has proved capable, is not applicable to the Presidency. Therefore, the American people have wisely established a custom against allowing any man to hold that office for more than two consecutive terms." This rationale vanished, however, when a candidate no longer wielded these powers. "But every shred of power which a President exercises while in office vanishes absolutely when he has once left office. An ex-President stands in precisely the position of any other private citizen, and has not one particle more power to secure a nomination or election than if he had never held the office at all."

"The reasoning on which the anti-third term custom is based has no has no application whatever to an ex-President," Roosevelt insisted, "and no application whatever to anything but consecutive terms." To apply it regardless of this distinction was a "mere formula," he argued, and "a potential source of mischievous confusion."[105]

During the campaign, when challenged on why his 1912 bid did not repudiate his 1904 pledge, he again rationalized that he promised not to seek a third consecutive term, not that he would never again run for president. "What we need to do in the third-term matter is to pay attention to the substance and not the form," Roosevelt wrote. I cared nothing for the fact that I have not had two elective terms, for of course the only possible justification for the third-term theory is that it shall be a third consecutive term."[106] Roosevelt's theory was that an outsized presidency and the potential for corruption correlated with uninterrupted tenure in office. Sitting out a term, he theorized, would mitigate these evils.

However, skeptics in the press were unpersuaded. Opposing the third-term candidacy, the *El Paso Herald* reasoned, "While beyond question, the chief academic objection to a third term is disposed of when another administration intervenes, nevertheless the feeling against a presidential tenure of more than eight years is as firmly fixed in American political tradition as any other policy that may be called national." Thus, the paper construed the two-term tradition to mean the number of years a person had served, rather than if he had served them consecutively.[107]

Roosevelt's primaries strategy bore fruit. He won nine of fourteen races, including Taft's home state of Ohio,[108] as compared to two each for Taft and LaFollette.[109] In the primary states, Roosevelt secured a majority of the overall vote, approximately 1.2 million ballots, as against 860,000 for Taft and 350,000 for LaFollette.[110] Of the delegates selected, Roosevelt won 278, Taft got 48, and LaFollette won 36.[111] Such victories were sizeable, but nevertheless insufficient to wrest the nomination. In nonprimary states, of which there were many, Taft controlled delegate selection through patronage and dominance of party organizations.[112] This was especially true in southern states.[113]

Roosevelt-friendly press denounced what it believed to be undemocratic tactics from Taft organizations. *The Detroit Times* editorialized, "The National Committee of the Republican Party is opening the doors of the White House today to Theodore Roosevelt to serve his third term in the Presidency, just as surely as day follows night, if as a result of its treasonable methods, Taft is the nominee of the Chicago convention, and providing the Democrats fail in Baltimore to nominate a progressive."[114]

As the convention approached, the incumbent exercised tight control over the Credentials Committee, enabling numerous credentials contests to be resolved in Taft's favor.[115] Alarmed and angered by these developments, Roosevelt publicly deplored them. For example, on June 8, he condemned the replacement of two Roosevelt delegates from Alabama with Taft supporters. "Again and again we have sent to the penitentiary election officials for deeds morally not one whit worse than what was done by members of the national committee," Roosevelt proclaimed.[116]

Soon thereafter, he traveled to Chicago, where the Convention was about to begin. He denounced the Republican machinery, who he charged was stealing the nomination from him. Addressing thousands of supporters[117] in a June 17 speech titled "The Case Against the Reactionaries," Roosevelt concluded, "If we are true to ourselves by putting far above our own interests the triumph of the high cause for which we battle, we shall not lose. It would be far better to fail honorably for the cause we champion than it would be to win by foul methods the foul victory for which our opponents hope. But the victory shall be ours, and it shall be won as we have already won so many victories, by clean and honest fighting for the loftiest of causes. We fight in honorable fashion for the good of mankind; fearless of the future; unheeding of our individual fates; with unflinching hearts and undimmed eyes; we stand at Armageddon, and we battle for the Lord."[118]

It was to no avail. The party machinery worked as Taft needed it to do.[119] On June 22, with sufficient numbers of his delegates seated, Taft won the nomination.[120]

The *Chicago Tribune* labeled Taft's victory a triumph of bossism. "The suicidal success won in a fraud packed convention by the discredited remnants of standpat leadership in the Republican Party has served only to throw into higher relief the progressive leadership of Theodore Roosevelt," said the *Tribune*. "The bosses were compelled to do their worst to beat him. They were compelled to expose the ruthless extremes of machine rule, trickery, bullying, and fraud."[121]

Taft was satisfied, not just with his victory, but also with what he had stopped.[122] Doris Kearns Goodwin observes, "He believed he had already achieved the victory he wanted by preventing Roosevelt from taking over the Republican Party and moving it in an incomprehensibly radical direction that threatened to upset the constitutional separation of powers and destroy 'the absolute independence of the judiciary.'"[123]

In the immediate aftermath, Progressives gathered at Orchestra Hall, across town. Their meeting presaged the national launching of the Progressive Party—colloquially known as the Bull Moose Party—which would run Theodore Roosevelt for a third term.[124]

"Following the adjournment of the Taft convention," reported the *Boston Globe*, "the Colonel plans to have his followers issue a call for a Roosevelt Progressive convention, which will meet in five or six weeks, probably in Chicago, if they want him to be their candidate for President, he will accept and make the fight, he says."[125]

Indeed, the formal nomination would come six weeks later. Meanwhile, the party began to gather adherents. "In all of his recent public utterances," reported the *Cincinnati Enquirer*, "Colonel Roosevelt has urged the welcoming into the party of former Republicans and Democrats on an exactly equal footing."[126]

On August 4, Roosevelt left his home at Oyster Bay, Long Island, drove to Manhattan, and boarded an overnight train to Chicago. As he did, he insisted that he would not accept the nomination unless he approved of the platform committee's final report. That proved not to be an obstacle.[127]

Roosevelt formally accepted the Bull Moose nomination in a two-hour address on August 5, 1912.[128] In doing so, he fractured the Republican vote and dramatically enhanced the likelihood that the Democrats' nominee, Woodrow Wilson, would win the general election.[129]

William Jennings Bryan did not agree. Campaigning in Denver for Democrats, Bryan warned of dangers inherent in breaching the two-term tradition. "It would open a door which no man might be able to close."[130]

The third-term issue was an albatross weighing down Roosevelt's candidacy that fall. Among voters to whom he might have appealed, it could be a complication. Some who might have overlooked the problem if he was the party nominee, would not do so for an independent. And others found the third term so alienating that they found it reason enough to support Taft or defect to Wilson. In 1912, scientific opinion polls did not exist, so it is difficult to pinpoint the impact of the third-term issue.[131] However, it is inescapable that both political opponents and big-city and small-town press inveighed against it constantly. One can infer that they considered its effect on the public potent, as a way to undermine Roosevelt.

The Olathe, Kansas *Mirror* wrote on September 26 of a campaign infected with "unscrupulous ambition, with contempt for law, precedent, and patriotic emotion." It rebuked the notion of perpetuating "presidential terms indefinitely," what it called Roosevelt's "Napoleonic ambition," and "the present grave menace to American institutions." It beseeched voters to "place the seal of condemnation upon Roosevelt, his menacing ambition," and "his defiance of law and precedent of more than a hundred years standing."[132]

That same month, the Muncie, Indiana, *Evening Press* editorialized, "Third termism implies not merely life tenure. It means the centralization of power and its consolidation in the fewest hands. Aiming at autocracy, absolutism, and self-perpetuation, it sets itself against the principles and underpinning of all our institutions. If there were no tradition to oppose and resist its pretensions, however plausible, its very nature, quality, and argument should be sufficient to expose and defeat it."[133]

Just before the election, the *Brooklyn Daily Eagle* stated, "For the first time in the history of the country, the people have a chance to deal with what Jefferson described as a demonstration of ambitious views, plus the repudiation of solemn pledges. For the first time they have a chance to grant or withhold what Washington, Jefferson, Madison, and Monroe renounced as patriots. Coming generations will be vitally affected by the outcome. It should not be in doubt."[134]

Even when the third term was not itself the main topic at hand, hostile press could find a way to work it into stories focusing on other issues. For example, an article in the Wagoner, Oklahoma, *Record-Democrat* critical of Roosevelt and tariff policy carried the headline "Roosevelt and Reciprocity Issue: Insincerity and Demagogism of Third Term Candidate Shown."[135]

Most press outlets gave the third term such treatment, but not all. At length, the *Perry County Times*, of New Bloomfield, Pennsylvania, rebutted a key myth surrounding the two-term tradition: that George Washington considered a third term dangerous to national institutions. "A man sixty-six years of age," the paper noted, "who had for eight years led the often forlorn hope of an armed revolution, who for eight years had guided the uncertain steps of an infant nation, desired rest." In a modern context, the issue was vastly overblown, it concluded. "To say today that a third term for one man in the office of President of the United States would endanger its existence as a republic is to declare the failure of that form of government."[136]

In November 1912, Americans elected Woodrow Wilson with 41.8 percent of the popular vote, as against 27.4 percent for Roosevelt, and 23.2 percent for Taft. Eugene Debs, the candidate of the Socialist Party, received approximately 6 percent. This breakdown translated into a resounding victory for Wilson in the Electoral College, where the Democrat won 435 electoral votes, as against eighty-eight for Roosevelt and eight for Taft. Both as to the popular vote and the electoral vote, Roosevelt's performance was the best in American history for a third-party candidate, even to this day. However, his chance for a third term was quashed once he no longer was able to run as a major party nominee.

World War I commenced in August 1914, midway through Wilson's first term. Roosevelt was an outspoken critic of Wilson's policy to avoid entanglement in the fighting. Assessing how most effectively to challenge these policies, and how best to assure himself a political future, Roosevelt pondered returning to the Republican Party and running again under its banner. While Progressives had rallied to his New Nationalism platform, many did not share his bellicosity on the war.

Early in 1915, the political reunion was yet incomplete. Among Republicans, there remained resentment and wariness for Roosevelt the renegade. And, for his part, Roosevelt was suspicious of the Old Guard that had blocked him in 1912. On February 6, Roosevelt wrote to Lodge, outraged by reports that conservatives were positioning Taft to be nominated again. "There are a great many Progressives, including myself, who under no circumstances would support Taft." Roosevelt wrote. He was confident that if Taft were the candidate, "the Progressives as a whole will either come out for Wilson or run a third ticket." Implicit was reprise of 1912: Republicans split, perhaps with Roosevelt as a third-party candidate, and Wilson elected.[137]

Lodge responded on February 8 to assure Roosevelt that Taft rumors were unfounded. "I cannot believe there is the slightest possibility of Taft receiving the Republican nomination," replied the senator.

On March 31, 1916, Roosevelt and Lodge met for lunch in New York with Elihu Root, who had served twice in Roosevelt's cabinet, but who, as chairman of the 1912 Republican Convention, had helped steer proceedings in Taft's direction.[138] Two other leading Republicans, Robert Bacon and General Leonard Wood, also attended.[139] In 1912, this group was emblematic of the party split, with Roosevelt and Bacon embracing the Progressives and Root remaining loyal to Taft.[140] The principal issue that bonded them in 1916 was criticism of Wilson's alleged failures on preparedness.[141] The press prominently publicized the meeting, which appeared to signify party reunification.[142]

Roosevelt die-hards among Republicans hoped to nominate him against Wilson in 1916. If TR could secure such a third-term nomination, they surmised, the Republican split of 1912 might close.[143] Progressives entered into discussions with Republican leaders to explore this possibility, but the negotiations fizzled.[144] The memories of 1912 were too fresh.[145] Charles Evans Hughes, former associate justice of the Supreme Court and New York governor, was in a commanding position to secure the nomination. He won on the third ballot, in major part because he proved to be an acceptable common denominator.[146]

Progressives dreamed of again having Roosevelt lead them as a third-party candidate, as a way to breathe new life into their party. They had done poorly in the 1914 mid-term elections. Without a galvanizing figure, the party might utterly disintegrate.[147] Unable to engineer Roosevelt's nomination to lead the Republican ticket, they were determined to nominate him themselves.

Convening in Chicago at the same time as the Republicans, the Progressives tendered Roosevelt their nomination. This time, he rebuffed them.[148] Instead, the former president rallied support for Hughes.[149]

Progressives were not easily deterred. At a meeting they held in Chicago to coincide with the Republican National Convention in the same city, they nominated Roosevelt anyway, However, Roosevelt was satisfied with Hughes' positions on key issues and demurred. Longworth reports that, after several weeks, "Father wrote the Progressive National Committee, saying that he would support Hughes and recommending that his fellow Progressives should do the same."[150]

On behalf of the Republican ticket, Roosevelt participated actively in the 1916 general election campaign.[151] Meanwhile, without Roosevelt to carry their standard, the Progressives were leaderless, disintegrating as a political force. Again unified, the Republicans nearly unseated Wilson, but failed.[152]

As the 1920 election loomed, it was widely anticipated that the former president would again seek the White House.[153] Roosevelt allowed this talk to fester, suggesting at that relatively early stage his openness to a draft.[154] Others had ambitions for the party nomination, but Roosevelt was the nation's most prominent Republican, and the one most and longest identified with criticism of the incumbent Democratic administration.

Roosevelt himself imagined a 1920 campaign.[155] He was already framing a platform for it.[156] Had he made the run, it is unlikely that any other figure would have the stature to prevent his nomination or, for that matter, keep him from winning the general election.

However, a third term was not to be. Unwell and hospitalized during the weeks following the 1918 mid-term election,[157] Roosevelt died at home of a coronary embolism early in the morning of January 6, 1919.[158] He was 60 years old.

The 1920 Republican Convention met in Chicago. Delegates split their votes among eleven candidates. Republicans nominated Senator Warren Harding of Ohio, an old-line Taft loyalist, on the tenth ballot, after party bosses meeting in the legendary "smoke-filled room" at the Blackstone Hotel helped to designate him as a compromise candidate. Harding and his running mate, Massachusetts Governor Calvin Coolidge, opposed Ohio Governor James Cox and Assistant Secretary of the Navy Franklin Roosevelt. The Republicans captured 60.3 percent of the popular vote and swept thirty-seven of forty-eight states on the way to a 404 to 127 triumph in the Electoral College.

NOTES

1. "The patient stood the operation well, pulse of good quality, rate of 130, and his condition at the conclusion of operation was gratifying. The result cannot be foretold. His condition at present justifies hope of recovery." "President Shot at Buffalo Fair," *New York Times*, September 7, 1901, p. 1.

2. Ibid., pp. 479–482.

3. H.W. Brands, *T.R.: The Last Romantic* (New York: Basic Books, 1997), p. 504.

4. www.presidency.ucsb.edu (accessed September 8, 2018). Roosevelt's was the largest percentage of the popular vote since the 1820s. Ibid., p. 517.

5. Doris Kearns Goodwin, *The Bully Pulpit: Theodore Roosevelt, William Howard Taft, and the Golden Age of Journalism* (New York: Simon & Schuster, 2013), p. 420.

6. *Selections from the Correspondence between Theodore Roosevelt and Henry Cabot Lodge, 1884–1919, Volume II* (New York: Charles Scribner's Sons, 1925), p. 107.

7. Ibid.

8. Alice Roosevelt Longworth, *Crowded Hours* (New York: Charles Scribner's Sons, 1933), p. 64. See also, Goodwin, p. 421.

9. Brands, *T.R.*, p. 514. Roosevelt ended his campaign on a strong note, issuing a stinging rebuttal of Democratic charges that corporations had controlled the president's campaign through political contributions. Election day came immediately thereafter and afforded him a resounding victory. "Purged by his last minute blast at Parker, astounded at the extent of his sweep, and reverential to the memory of George Washington, he dictated a quick statement to reporters at 10:30 PM in the White House vestibule." It was his renunciation of a run for a third term. Edmund Morris, *Theodore Rex* (New York: Random House, 2001), p. 364.

10. Ibid., p. 213.

11. *Selections*, p. 109.

12. Ibid., p. 110.

13. "Roosevelt may have raised with her the general subject of serving only two terms, but he seems to have kept her in the dark that he was going to abjure a third term before his second term began. Doubtless he did so for the same reason he declined to tell Lodge: that he feared she would try to change his mind—as indeed she would have tried, as she later admitted to Owen Wister." Brands, *T.R.*, pp. 514–515.

14. Ibid., p. 515.

15. Theodore Roosevelt, *The Autobiography of Theodore Roosevelt* (New York: Charles Scribner's Sons, 1913), pp. 213–214. Roosevelt wrote that he did not specify that he would not be a candidate in 1908, because to do so would allow others to infer that he might run again in later elections. "I had no such intention, and had no idea that I would ever be a candidate again." Roosevelt, p. 214.

16. Ibid., pp. 516–517.

17. Brands, *T.R.*, p. 628.

18. He had been far from successful in doing that in the 1904 election, but he continued to harbor the idea that he, and he alone among Republicans, was capable of a breakthrough.

19. Lawrence F. Abbott, ed., *The Letters of Archie Butt* (Garden City, New York: Doubleday, Page, and Company, 1924), pp. 66–67. Roosevelt's mother, Martha Bulloch Roosevelt, was a Georgian. Major Archibald Butt died during the sinking of the Titanic on April 15, 1912.

20. Brands, *T.R.*, pp. 628–629.

21. Pointing to his wrist, he later told H.H. Kohlsaat, a presidential historian, "I would cut my hand off right there, if I could recall that written statement," Ibid., pp. 515–516. See also, Kearns Goodwin, *Bully Pulpit*, p. 423.

22. Ibid., p. 523. Presidential scholars Leonard W. Levy and Louis Fischer assess the pledge as "one of the noblest gestures Roosevelt ever made." However, they add, "in view of the pain it caused him to keep the promise and the frustrations that dogged him as an ex-President, it was the biggest mistake of his political career." Levy and Louis Fischer, eds., *Encyclopedia of the American Presidency, Vol. 3* (New York: Simon & Schuster, 1994), p. 1332.

23. Levy and Fischer, p. 1334.

24. Brands, *T.R.*, pp. 518–519.

25. Patricia O'Toole, *When Trumpets Call: Theodore Roosevelt After the White House* (New York: Simon & Schuster, 2005), p. 78. Taft never really got comfortable with the job, and pined for the chance to serve on the Supreme Court. "After sixteen months in office, Taft still had trouble conceiving of himself as the chief executive of the United States." Ibid., p. 95. In 1921, Taft finally got the opportunity to sit on the Court, when President Warren Harding appointed him as chief justice. Taft served until a month before his death in 1930.

26. O'Toole, *Trumpets*, p. 79. "Roosevelt launched a private campaign of persuasion, engineering a boom of support for Taft's candidacy. In personal letters and meetings, he repeatedly insisted he would 'do all in his power' for Taft, though he could say nothing in public." Kearns Goodwin, *Bully Pulpit,* p. 518.

27. There were qualms about Roosevelt hand-picking Taft as a successor. In a July 24, 1908, letter to his mother, recounting a discussion with the President, Butt wrote, "I said that to me the great danger to Mr. Taft came from the residuary legatee idea, but that I thought this would be counteracted by the fact that Mr. Taft would also be the legatee of the President's popularity." Roosevelt concurred. "There will be no backward step under Taft." Abbott, p. 67.

28. Kearns Goodwin, *Bully Pulpit*, p. 523.

29. "As the winter went on, Taft's nomination became more and more certain, despite the furious advocacy of other candidacies—by the candidates themselves and by those who resented Father's dictation. Also despite the determination of some of Father's ardent supporters that Father himself should run again. I think it was Jonathan Bourne who gave birth to the phrase 'second elective term.' But Father was a hundred times more resourceful and determined than any one of his followers or opponents." Longworth, p. 148.

30. "Roosevelt registered thorough satisfaction with the outcome. Breaking his official silence, he congratulated the country and the party on a stellar nominee, a

man, he suggested, who would make as good a President as almost any who had ever served." Brands, *T.R.*, p. 628.

31. Kearns Goodwin, *Bully Pulpit*, p. 523.

32. Ibid., pp. 523–524.

33. Roosevelt held open the possibility of running, if necessary to forestall nomination of a conservative to succeed him. In 1908, he did not consider Taft a conservative, so he was content to stick with his pledge as long as Taft prevailed at the Convention. O'Toole, *Trumpets,* p. 79. "In case Taft's canvass failed to take off, however, he would not foreclose the possibility of his candidacy." Kearns Goodwin, *Bully Pulpit*, p. 524.

34. Abbott, p. 66.

35. "The delegates kept their places, and when it was all over there was no danger of a third term or 'second elective term' in that convention." Longworth, p. 150. See also, Kearns Goodwin, *Bully Pulpit*, pp. 543–544.

36. Kearns Goodwin, *Bully Pulpit*, p. 544.

37. Taft went on to appoint Knox as his Secretary of State and put Hughes on the Supreme Court as an Associate Justice.

38. "Not since Grover Cleveland's last campaign had Democrats been so united, and they were running on a tough, anti-corporate platform that seemed in sync with the reformist mood of the nation." Michael Kazin, *A Godly Hero: The Life of William Jennings Bryan* (New York: Alfred A. Knopf, 2006), p. 162.

39. Taft received 51.6 percent of the popular vote, besting Bryan by eight points. The Democrat prevailed in all the old Confederate States, and also won in Maryland, Kentucky, Nevada, Colorado, and his home state of Nebraska. In the Electoral College, Taft got 321 votes to Bryan's 162. www.presidency.ucsb.edu (accessed September 8, 2018).

40. Writing to his sister-in-law on the morning after Taft's election, Butt said, "The President is simply radiant over Taft's victory. Certainly, he looks at the result as an endorsement of his own policy." Abbott, p. 153.

41. "Roosevelt made no secret of his reluctance to leave office. 'If I had conscientiously felt at liberty to run again, and try once more to hold this great office,' he acknowledged, 'I should greatly have liked to do so and to continue to keep my hands on the levers of this mighty machine.'" Kearns Goodwin, *Bully Pulpit,* p. 564.

42. David Pietrusa, *TR's Last War* (Guilford, Connecticut: Lyons Press, 2018), p. 20.

43. Taft, pp.139–145.

44. See Kearns Goodwin, *Bully Pulpit*, pp. 583–599. See, also, O'Toole, *Trumpets*, pp. 96–97.

45. "New Butt Letters Tell Taft History," *New York Times*, September 4, 1930, p. 23.

46. James C. German, Jr. "Taft, Roosevelt, and United States Steel," *The Historian,* vol. 34, no. 2 (August 1972), pp. 598–613, 611. https://www.jstor.org/stable/24442959 (accessed December 26, 2018).

47. "Greetings have come from the jungle and the plain, but it is said by those who have made it their work to inquire in the right places that nothing Mr. Roosevelt has written can in any way be considered as passing judgment upon anything that has

been done in a political or administrative way since he has left this country." *American Falls Press.* (American Falls, Idaho), February 05, 1910. *Chronicling America: Historic American Newspapers.* Library of Congress. https://chroniclingamerica.loc.gov/lccn/sn86063041/1910-02-05/ed-1/seq-9/.

48. "The ex-president was pitching hay when he was asked as to his attitude toward the proposal. His reply was a point blank refusal to talk about the matter, the refusal being emphasized by a fierce scowl. . . . He knows that if he desires it, a string sentiment can be worked up within the Republican Party, or at least in the insurgent element of it. Roosevelt, as far as known, has not given the slightest encouragement as yet to these importunities." "Refuses to Talk of a Third Term," *The Richmond Palladium and Sun-Telegram* (Richmond, Ind.), July 16, 1910, p. 2. *Chronicling America: Historic American Newspapers.* Library of Congress. https://chroniclingamerica.loc.gov/lccn/sn86058226/1910-07-16/ed-1/seq-2/.

49. "By one estimate, more than a million people came out to see Roosevelt on his speaking tour, and if they were not ready to demand his candidacy, they were thrilled to see him." O'Toole, *Trumpets*, p. 103.

50. The site was a battlefield on which, in 1856, anti-slavery and pro-slavery forces fought in the lead up to Kansas statehood and the Civil War. "Roosevelt Speaks at Osawotomie," *The Topeka State Journal*, August 31, 1910, p. 1.

51. Theodore Roosevelt, "New Nationalism Speech," *Osawotomie, Kansas*, August 31, 1910. www.teachingamerican history.org (accessed October 6, 2018). "Climbing on to a kitchen table that doubled as a speaking platform, Roosevelt delivered the most radical speech he had ever made, placing him *ipso facto* in 'the front rank' of the insurgent forces." Kearns Goodwin, *Bully Pulpit*, p. 643.

52. James Chace, *1912: Wilson, Roosevelt, Taft & Debs – the Election that Changed the Country* (New York: Simon & Schuster, 2004), p. 57.

53. Pietrusa, p. 22.

54. "Roosevelt Speaks at Osawatomie," *The Topeka State Journal* (Topeka, Kan.), August 31, 1910, p. 1. *Chronicling America: Historic American Newspapers.* Library of Congress. https://chroniclingamerica.loc.gov/lccn/sn82016014/1910-08-31/ed-1/seq-1/.

55. Editorial Page of *The Detroit Times* (Detroit, Mich.), September 02, 1910, p. 16. *Chronicling America: Historic American Newspapers.* Library of Congress. https://chroniclingamerica.loc.gov/lccn/sn83016689/1910-09-02/ed-1/seq-16/e.

56. "The Common Cause," *The Richmond Palladium and Sun-telegram* (Richmond, Ind.), September 05, 1910. *Chronicling America: Historic American Newspapers.* Library of Congress. https://chroniclingamerica.loc.gov/lccn/sn86058226/1910-09-05/ed-1/seq-4/.

57. "Roosevelt with Progressives," *Aberdeen Herald* (Aberdeen, Chehalis County, W.T.), September 1, 1910, p. 4. *Chronicling America: Historic American Newspapers.* Library of Congress. https://chroniclingamerica.loc.gov/lccn/sn87093220/1910-09-01/ed-1/seq-4/.

58. "Short Chats with the Editors," *The Durham Recorder* (Durham, N.C.), September 15, 1910, p. 4. *Chronicling America: Historic American Newspapers.* Library of Congress. https://chroniclingamerica.loc.gov/lccn/sn84020731/1910-09-15/ed-1/seq-4/.

59. Kearns Goodwin, *Bully Pulpit,* p. 451.

60. Anticipating the electoral outcome, Senator Elihu Root (R-NY) believed the Republicans would have to abandon Taft for Roosevelt or some other progressive. Root did not believe that, under such conditions, the party could safely renominate Taft. "Root Wants Teddy Again." *The Hawaiian Star* (Honolulu [Oahu]), October 29, 1910, p. 13. *Chronicling America: Historic American Newspapers.* Library of Congress. https://chroniclingamerica.loc.gov/lccn/sn82015415/1910-10-29/ed-1/seq-13/.

61. Ibid., pp. 100–103.

62. In January 1911, Progresive leaders formed the National Progressive Republican League. Fearing that membership would be construed as a third term bid, he declined to join. O'Toole, *Trumpets*, p. 120.

63. Ibid., pp. 103–104. To oppose Taft openly, "would have called attention to Roosevelt's blunder in selecting Taft to succeed him and would raise (from its shallow grave) the suspicion that Roosevelt coveted another term." O'Toole, *Trumpets*, p. 99.

64. "Roosevelt consistently said that he did not wish to run and consistently refused to promise he would not, a bit of straddling that convinced LaFollette that TR was holding himself aloof only because he believed that Taft was certain to win the nomination." Ibid., p. 122.

65. Nellie Taft anticipated Roosevelt would get into the race, with disastrous consequences for her husband's presidency. To her husband she observed, "I suppose you will have to fight Mr. Roosevelt for the nomination, and if you get it he will defeat you. But it can't be helped. If possible, you must not allow him to defeat you for the re-nomination." Kearns Goodwin, *Bully Pulpit,* p. 646.

66. Theodore Roosevelt and Henry Cabot Lodge, *Selections from the Correspondence between Theodore Roosevelt and Henry Cabot Lodge, 1884–1919,* Volume II (New York: Charles Scribner's Sons, 1925), p. 417. In the published version of the letter, omits the identities of those who called on Roosevelt.

67. Theodore Roosevelt, "A Charter of Democracy," Address Before the Ohio Constitutional Convention, February 21, 1910, www.theodore-roosevelt.com (accessed October 6, 2018).

68. Longworth, pp. 186–187.

69. Kearns Goodwin, *Bully Pulpit,* pp. 679–680.

70. Roosevelt and Lodge, pp. 417–418. However, these differences were surpassed by Roosevelt's Columbus proposal to overturn court decisions by vote. On February 28, 1912, Lodge wrote, "I found myself opposed to your policies declared at Columbus with great force in regard to changes in our Constitution and principles of government as I understand them. . . . I knew of course that you and I differed on some of these points but I had not realized that the difference was so wide." Ibid., pp. 423–424.

71. As Roosevelt put it, "while wildly improbable, it was yet possible that there might be a public demand which would present the matter to me in light of a duty which I could not shirk." Brands, *T.R.*, p. 699. Roosevelt's posture toward a draft was quite similar to that of his cousin, Franklin, in 1940. While active pursuit of a third term could appear unseemly, responding affirmatively to a draft could seem noble. Both Roosevelts worked to engineer to have themselves drafted.

72. Presidential scholar Harold J. Laski, writing in 1940, when no third-term bid had yet been successful, observed, "Certainly the pressure of public opinion against a third term is very strong. There is not only the power of tradition, in a country where tradition exercises very great authority. There is an important truth in the argument of Professor Cushman that the American people would grow very restive under a long executive term of office." Laski, pp. 65–66.

73. Brands, *T.R.,* p. 700.

74. H. W. Brands writes, "He still wished to maintain the appearance that he was acting only in response to public demand. In mid-January, he contacted a handful of progressive-minded Republican governors and suggested that they write him a letter asking point-blank what his intentions were." Ibid., p. 701. The seven governors were from West Virginia, Nebraska, New Hampshire, Michigan, Kansas, Missouri, California, and Wyoming.

75. In a press statement, Roosevelt republished the Governors' letter and responded to it, Chace, p. 106.

76. Kearns Goodwin, *Bully Pulpit*, p. 681.

77. "The Greatest Issue of All: Roosevelt and the Third Term." *The Leon Reporter* (Leon, Iowa), 07 March 1912, p, 4. *Chronicling America: Historic American Newspapers*. Library of Congress. https://chroniclingamerica.loc.gov/lccn/sn87057096/1912-03-07/ed-1/seq-4/.

78. Ibid.

79. Longworth, p. 185.

80. These governors represented Minnesota, Iowa, Washington, Maryland, Pennsylvania, Tennessee, Utah, Delaware, and Rhode Island.

81. Slayden served in the House from 1897 to 1917.

82. Underwood was in the House from 1897 to 1915 and in the Senate from 1915 to 1927.

83. "Oppose Third Term," *Washington Evening Star*, February 2, 1915, p. 4.

84. "Third-Term Fight Shelved by House," *New York Times*, February 6, 1912, p. 2.

85. "The Great Lesson of the Day," *The Hawaiian Star* (Honolulu [Oahu]), February 22, 1912, p. 4. *Chronicling America: Historic American Newspapers*. Library of Congress. https://chroniclingamerica.loc.gov/lccn/sn82015415/1912-02-22/ed-1/seq-4/. It should be observed that at the time of the 1916 election, World War I had been underway for more than two years. Under President Wilson's leadership, the United States had stayed out of the war. From the sidelines, Roosevelt strongly criticized the President. Had Roosevelt himself been elected in 1912, it is wholly conceivable that America would have entered the war much sooner, and that the conflict may have been unresolved in 1916. If that were so, Theodore Roosevelt may have claimed a duty to continue as commander in chief, much as Franklin Roosevelt did in 1944. Thus, the speculation of the *Hawaiian Stars* editorial is not really farfetched.

86. "No Third Term," *El Paso Herald* (El Paso, Tex.), February 13, 1912, p. 4. *Chronicling America: Historic American Newspapers*. Library of Congress. https://chroniclingamerica.loc.gov/lccn/sn88084272/1912-02-13/ed-1/seq-6/.

87. "Lonely Mr. Roosevelt," *Butler Weekly Tines* (Butler, Missouri) March 7, 1912, p. 4. Library of Congress, *Chronicling America: Historic American Newspapers*. http://chroniclingamerica. gov loc. (accessed June 20, 2019).

88. For example, on March 14, the Guntersville, Alabama *Democrat* did so under the headline "Lonely Mr. Roosevelt." The March 12 Racine, Wisconsin *Journal* did so under "Roosevelt's Awkward Squad." The March 8 Hutchinson, Kansas *Gazette* did so under "After the First Five Days."

89. The Roosevelt-LaFollette situation is quite similar to the race of the 1968 Democratic nomination. Drawing on opposition to the Vietnam War, Senator Eugene McCarthy campaigned in the March 12, 1968, New Hampshire primary against President Lyndon Johnson. Johnson won the primary by six points. With weakness in Johnson's candidacy exposed, Senator Robert F. Kennedy (D-NY) announced his candidacy. Anti-Johnson Democrats who had been supporting McCarthy quickly abandoned him and joined the Kennedy bandwagon.

90. *The Topeka State Journal* (Topeka, Kan.), March 6, 1912, p. 4. *Chronicling America: Historic American Newspapers*. Library of Congress. https://chroniclinga merica.loc.gov/lccn/sn82016014/1912-03-06/ed-1/seq-4/

91. A half-century later, something similar happened in the Democratic Party. Senator Eugene McCarthy (D-MN) challenged the renomination of President Lyndon Johnson. McCarthy's candidacy evoked enthusiasm, to the point that he made an excellent showing in the New Hampshire primary. The effect was to bring Senator Robert Kennedy (D-NY) into the campaign. For the most part, Kennedy eclipsed McCarthy as Johnson's main challenger. The Kennedy campaign ended with the Senator's assassination on June 6, 1968.

92. Brands, *T.R.*, pp. 706–707.

93. Ibid.

94. Roosevelt and Lodge, p. 423.

95. Ibid., p. 424.

96. "It had long been Roosevelt's plan to obtain the nomination as much as possible through direct primaries. This would allow him to say that the people had called on him to lead them, and give him the right to accuse Taft of being a creature of political bossism." Chace, p. 109. "Taft, as expected, ran strongest in states closely controlled by the party organization, while Roosevelt gained ground where primaries afforded voters more direct access to the delegate selection process." This included a big win for Roosevelt in the Ohio primary, held in Taft's home state. Brands, *T.R.*, pp. 712–713.

97. Edmund Morris, *Colonel Roosevelt* (New York: Random House, 2010), p. 194.

98. As the Convention opened, Roosevelt had 411 committed delegates, Taft had 201, LaFollette had 36, 136 delegates were uninstructed, and the credentials of 254 were contested. Stacy A. Cordery, *Alice: Alice Roosevelt Longworth, from White House Princess to Washington Power Broker* (New York: Viking, 2007), p. 226.

99. In 1912, Roosevelt was 54 years old, precisely the midpoint age for starting a presidency. Eleven presidents had been aged less than fifty-four years. Two had been 54. Thirteen had been aged above fifty-four years. Roosevelt seemed hale and

hearty, making possible the extended tenure in White House. "The Presidents by Age at Inauguration," www.robinsonlibrary.com (accessed September 20, 2018).

100. Edmund Morris, *Colonel Roosevelt*, p. 185. In a 1927 article on the two-term tradition, Congressional Quarterly stated, "The third term issue was raised against him, and contributed to his defeat in the three-cornered contest, although it was contended that all objection to a third term had been removed by his surrender of the presidency for four years." "The Third Term Tradition in American Politics (1927)," *Editorial Research Reports* 1927 (Vol. 1), Washington, DC: CQ Press. http:/library.cqpress.com/cqresearcher/cqresrre1927031900 (retrieved October 8, 2018).

101. "Taft in Youngstown, Roosevelt in Canton, End Strenuous Day." *Evening Star* (Washington, D.C.), May 15, 1912, p. 10. *Chronicling America: Historic American Newspapers*. Library of Congress. https://chroniclingamerica.loc.gov/lccn/sn83045462/1912-05-15/ed-1/seq-11/.

102. Morris, *Colonel Roosevelt*, p. 185. Although Taft was seeking a second term, he expressed a personal preference for a single term of six or seven years. Such an arrangement would promote executive independence, wrote Taft, and avoid the distractions associated with a reelection campaign. Moreover, "the absorbing and diverting interest in the reelection of the incumbent, taken by those federal civil servants who regard their own tenure as dependent upon his, would disappear." William Howard Taft, *Our Chief Magistrate and His Powers* (New York: Columbia University Press, 1916), p. 4.

103. Campaigning in Ohio on May 16, Roosevelt encountered a heckler who asked him about the third term. The Colonel responded by citing the 1880 involvement of Taft's father, Charles P. Taft, in a Grant third-term movement. "I will appeal from the son to the father and ask you to accept the sound common sense as to the ridiculous folly of raising any talk about a third term when the terms are not consecutive and the man out of power has no earthly means of influencing a single officeholder, a single privileged representative of the privileged class." "Discloses Tafts as Third Termers," *Chicago Tribune*, May 17, 1912, p. 2.

104. "Of Course," *New York Times*, February 28, 1912, p. 10.

105. Roosevelt, *Autobiography*, pp. 214–215.

106. Cordery, p. 697.

107. "No Third Term," *El Paso Herald* (El Paso, Tex.), February 13, 1912, p. 6. *Chronicling America: Historic American Newspapers*. Library of Congress. https://chroniclingamerica.loc.gov/lccn/sn88084272/1912-02-13/ed-1/seq-6/.

108. Roosevelt won forty-five of fifty counties and thirty-two of forty-two delegates. It must be noted that when Roosevelt won Taft's home state, he was returning the favor from the March 26, New York primary. In that contest, held in Roosevelt's home state, Taft secured two-thirds of the vote.

109. After Roosevelt trounced Taft in in May 21 Ohio primary, Roosevelt claimed that the nomination had been decided. His campaign chairman, Senator Joseph M. Dixon (R-MT), issued a statement calling for Taft's withdrawal. "The Republican Party is bigger than the ambition of any one man. The one wise and patriotic thing to be done is for Mr. Taft and his managers now to accept the unanimous verdict of the Republican primary states and withdraw from the contest." "Asks Taft to Withdraw," *The Topeka State Journal,* May 22, 1912, p. 1. *Chronicling America: Historic*

American Newspapers. Library of Congress. https://chroniclingamerica.loc.gov/lccn/sn82016014/1912-05-22/ed-1/seq-1/. (accessed June 22, 2019). Dixon served in the House from 1903 to 1907 and in the Senate from 1907 to 1913.

110. Chace, p. 113.

111. O'Toole, *Trumpets*, p. 171.

112. Roosevelt-friendly press denounced what it believed to be undemocratic tactics from Taft organizations. *The Detroit Times* editorialized, "The National Committee of the Republican Party is opening the doors of the White House today to Theodore Roosevelt to serve his third term in the Presidency, just as surely as day follows night, if as a result of its treasonable methods, Taft is the nominee of the Chicago convention, and providing the Democrats fail in Baltimore to nominate a progressive."

113. "T.R., who had perfected presidential control of the Republican Party, had given it to Taft, who was now using it to thwart him." Ibid. p. 109. "The ex-President won most of the primaries, but his own invention, the patronage -and organization-based steamroller, worked as effectively against him as it had once worked in his behalf." Levy and Fisher, p. 1334. "A President of the United States" Roosevelt said, "can, if he knows how to use the machinery at his disposal, re-nominate himself even though a majority of his party is against him." "The Third Term Tradition in American Politics," *Editorial Research Reports* 1927 (Vol. 1) (Washington, DC: CQ Press). http:/library.cqpress.com/cqresearcher/cqresrre1927031900 (accessed October 8, 2018). See also, Kearns Goodwin, *Bully Pulpit*, pp. 684–685. Five hundred thirty-nine votes were necessary for nomination. The Southern states, which did not have primaries, supplied 366 delegates to the Convention. CQ Press, Ibid. See, also, Pietrusa, pp. 24–25.

114. "Opening the White House Doors for Teddy in Chicago," *The Detroit Times* (Detroit, Mich.), June 13, 1912, p. 12. *Chronicling America: Historic American Newspapers*. Library of Congress. https://chroniclingamerica.loc.gov/lccn/sn83016689/1912-06-13/ed-1/seq-12/. (accessed June 22, 2019).

115. The Convention Rules Committee resolved 235 of these disputes for Taft and only nineteen for Roosevelt. If Roosevelt had won at least 50 of these contests, he would likely have prevailed in the balloting. Ibid., p. 116. "The Taft majority on the National Committee had indeed deprived Roosevelt of delegates legitimately his and in its wrath had awarded every debatable seat to Taft." O'Toole, *Trumpets*, p. 176.

116. "Roosevelt Calls Committee's Act Morally a Crime," *Chicago Tribune*, June 9, 1912, p. 1.

117. The pro-Roosevelt *Chicago Tribune* estimated that 5000 were in the auditorium, filling it to capacity, with an additional 10,000 unable to enter. "Roosevelt Warns of Peril to Nation: Throng Acclaims His Fight for Right," *Chicago Tribune*, June 18, 1912, p. 1.

118. "Case Against the Reactionaries," June 17, 1912, Chicago, www.theodore-roosevelt.com (accessed September 15, 2018).

119. Lewis Gould writes, "To understand how the Chicago convention turned out as it did, it is necessary to recognize the superior skill of President Taft in winning re-nomination. The portly chief executive is often portrayed as a genial boob, but in this case he grabbed the initiative from Roosevelt in mid-1911 and never lost it.

His personal secretary, Charles D. Hilles, began rounding up delegate commitments within the GOP during the summer of 1911 and continued through a nationwide tour that Taft made in the autumn of that year. The two men also recognized the key role of the Republican National Committee and solidified Taft's dominance of its membership in December. Their strategy emerges in the Hilles Papers at Yale University which, when opened in the 1960s, provided detailed evidence of Taft's strategy." Lewis Gould, "Why TR Lost the Republican Nomination in 1912: What New Research Shows," www.historynewsnetwork.org (accessed June 22, 2019).

120. Taft won 561 votes, Roosevelt got 107, LaFollette had 41, and 344 delegates abstained from voting. Chace, p. 122.

121. "The Fight Up to Date," *Chicago Tribune*, June 24, 1912, p. 6.

122. Post-election news accounts, published in the Barboursville, Kentucky *Mountain Advocate*, reported that Taft "regarded Colonel Roosevelt's third term aspirations as a menace to popular government. Even before he was re-nominated at Chicago last June, Mr. Taft said to some of his intimate friends that he regarded his nomination more important than his election, because his nomination, he believed, would end Roosevelt's campaign for the Presidency." *Mountain Advocate* (Barbourville, Ky.), November 15, 1912. *Chronicling America: Historic American Newspapers*. Library of Congress. https://chroniclingamerica.loc.gov/lccn/sn87060032/1912-11-15/ed-1/seq-1/.

123. Kearns Goodwin, *Bully Pulpit*, p. 711.

124. Senator William Borah's biographer, Claudius O. Johnson, recounted how the senator tried to talk Roosevelt out of a third-party campaign. Borah had been a Roosevelt supporter, who felt that the former president had been unjustly denied the nomination. Nevertheless, the senator was disturbed about the possibility of a rump party, which he knew would divide the Republican vote. Borah went to Roosevelt's suite at the Blackstone Hotel to plead with him not to run. The conversation went nowhere. Roosevelt tried to talk Borah into joining Progressives, which Borah refused. "I have always been opposed to a third-party movement," argued the senator. "I think it is a great mistake. I not only cannot go, but I would not like to see your friends go over there and commit you, practically nominate you, on a third ticket." Irritated, Roosevelt insisted that the movement could not be stopped. "If they do not nominate me, they will nominate LaFollette." Roosevelt proceeded with his plans. Claudius O. Johnson, *Borah of Idaho* (New York: Longmans, Green, and Co., 1936), p. 140. See, also, Cordery, p. 227.

125. M.E. Hennessey, "Roosevelt Plans Later Convention," *Boston Globe*, June 22, 1912, p.8.

126. "Curtain is Ready to Rise," *Cincinnati Enquirer*, August 5, 1912, pp. 1–2.

127. Ibid.

128. Morris, *Colonel Roosevelt*, pp. 223–225.

129. Turmoil from the party split also cost Representative Nicholas Longworth (R-OH), husband of Alice Roosevelt Longworth, his seat in Congress in 1912. He returned to the House after winning the 1914 election, became speaker in 1925 and served until his death in 1931.

130. "Bryan Begins Tour," *Boston Globe*, September 15, 1912, p. 8.

131. Bizarrely, the third-term issue even arose in connection with an assassination attempt on Roosevelt. On October 14, in Milwaukee, Wisconsin, one John Schrank

shot and wounded Roosevelt. A month later, Schrank entered a guilty plea. In those proceedings, the district attorney asked about the assassin's motive. "I intended to kill Theodore Roosevelt the third termer," the defendant responded. "I did not want to kill the Progressive Party. I shot Roosevelt as a warning to other third termers." "Alienists to Quiz Man Who Shot T.R.," *Journal Gazette* (Mattoon, Illinois), November 13, 1912, p. 8. Roosevelt was in the hospital for five days, during which all 1912 presidential candidates suspended their campaigns.

132. "To Kansas Republicans," *The Olathe Mirror*, September 26, 1912, pp. 1–2.

133. *Muncie Evening Press*, September 16, 1912, p. 4.

134. "The Issue of Issues," *Brooklyn Daily Eagle,* November 3, 1912, p. 18.

135. "Roosevelt and Reciprocity Issue, *The Record-Democrat* (Wagoner, Oklahoma), October 17, 1912, p. 4.

136. "The Third Term," *Perry County Times*, October 10, 1912, p. 4.

137. This threat was not confined to the possibility of a Taft candidacy. If the Republicans chose someone else the Progressives deemed too conservative or Old Guard, such as New York Senator Elihu Root, then the fracturing of the Republican vote would persist, along the lines of 1912. Pietrusa, p. 90.

138. Root had been Secretary of War from 1899 to 1904 and Secretary of State from 1905 to 1909. He served in the Senate from 1909 to 1915.

139. Bacon was Taft's appointee as Ambassador to France. Wood served with Roosevelt in the Rough Riders during the Spanish-American War, and under Taft as Army Chief of Staff.

140. In 1912, Wood was on active military duty as Army Chief of Staff. Pietrusa, p. 61.

141. Pietrusa, p. 102.

142. Morris, *Colonel Roosevelt*, pp. 452–453, Pietrusa, p. 103.

143. Morris, p. 457, Pietrusa, p. 140.

144. Pietrusa, pp. 139–140.

145. Nonetheless, Roosevelt was disappointed. "Against all instincts, he had allowed himself to believe that the miracle might happen, that the Republican nomination he had always wanted (in preference to that of 1912) was coming to him just as Americans realized that he, of all the men in the world, was probably the best equipped to arrest the general breakdown of civilization." Ibid., p. 459.

146. For an account of the 1916 convention proceedings that led to Hughes' nomination, see Pietrusa, pp. 127–142.

147. In 1914, the Progressives lost three of their nine House seats and won no Senate seats. They also did poorly in gubernatorial and state legislature races. Their main influence on the election was to serve as a spoiler. Continuing to divide the Republican electorate, they helped elect Democrats in 39 House seats and four Senate seats. Pietrusa, p. 49.

148. "Those who had followed Father in 1912, and with him organized the Progressive Party, were urging him to be their candidate again. He and Mother had gone on a trip to the West Indies, on the way home from which he put out a statement defining his position. In it he indicated that he did not wish the nomination, that he would not fight for it, and would not permit any fight to be made for him." Longworth, pp. 239–240. "No one appreciated the Progressives' weaknesses better than he did, and

after their collapse in the 1914 state and congressional elections, he actively conspired to scuttle the party." Levy and Fisher, p. 1335. See, also, Pietrusa, p. 156, for Roosevelt's letter provisionally declining the Progressive nomination.

149. Although not close allies, Roosevelt and Hughes had a history of political cooperation in the New York Republican Party. In 1906, Roosevelt helped to engineer Hughes' nomination for Governor by the State Republican Convention. Hughes was elected that November, for the first of two terms, then two years long. Betty Glad; *Charles Evans Hughes and the Illusions of Innocence* (Urbana, Illinois: University of Illinois Press, 1966), p. 65. Roosevelt also agreed to patch up differences with Taft. The two former presidents held a unity meeting in September at New York's Union League Club. Ibid., p. 81. The rapprochement was complete in 1918, following a meeting between the two at Chicago's Blackstone Hotel. Ibid., p. 263.

150. Longworth, p. 241.

151. "He supported Hughes vigorously, made many speeches—speeches rather less for Hughes than against Wilson." Ibid., p. 241.

152. In the Electoral College, Wilson won 277 to 254. The president won 49 percent of the popular vote, to 46 percent for Hughes.

153. "It was pretty generally believed that had Father lived he would have been the nominee of the Republican Party. His death made the fight an open one." Ibid., p. 304.

154. "Republican leaders visited him to see if he would accept the Republican nomination. He responded that he would not actively seek it, but if party leaders came to him and said they were convinced he was the only man who could be elected and that they were all for him, he would not refuse." Chace, p., 264. See also Brands, *T.R.*, p. 808.

155. He declined the possibility of running in 1918 for New York Governor. As he told his sister, "I have only one fight left in me, and I think I should reserve my strength in case I am needed in 1920." Morris, *Colonel Roosevelt*, p. 531.

156. Ibid., p. 548. O'Toole, *Trumpets*, p. 401.

157. Roosevelt's health deteriorated sharply in the winter of 1918–1919, and he was in substantial discomfort. "At various times, he was told he was suffering from multiple rheumatism, lumbago, sciatica, or gout." Morris, *Colonel Roosevelt*, p. 544. As well, he had endured a serious pulmonary embolism several weeks in late 1918. He was also depressed over the death of his son, Quentin, who was shot down in aerial combat over France in July 1918. Ibid., pp. 548, 553. See also, Pietrusa, pp. 247–279 for an account of Roosevelt's physical deterioration.

158. Immediately after the former president's death, his physicians issued a statement. It read, "Colonel Roosevelt had been suffering from an attack of inflammatory rheumatism for almost two months. His progress had been entirely satisfactory and his condition had not given cause for special concern. On Sunday, he was in good spirits, and spent the evening with his family, dictating letters. He retired at 11 o'clock, and at four o'clock in the morning, his manservant who occupied an adjoining room, noticed that, while sleeping quietly. Colonel Roosevelt's breathing was hollow. He died almost immediately, without awakening. The cause of death was an embolism." "Theodore Roosevelt Dies Suddenly at Oyster Bay Home," *New York Times*, January 7, 1919, p. 1.

Chapter 5

A Tradition in Unexpected Jeopardy

Woodrow Wilson (1920)

Held in Baltimore at the end of June, the 1912 Democratic Convention was contentious. Principal candidates were Governor Woodrow Wilson of New Jersey and Speaker of the House James Beauchamp ("Champ") Clark of Missouri. Clark was the early leader, but on the 46th ballot, Wilson secured the two-thirds majority necessary for nomination.

Two weeks before the Democrats convened, Republicans met in Chicago to renominate President William Howard Taft. Theirs was a bitter gathering, in which forces of the incumbent were able to overcome an insurgency aimed at nominating former President Theodore Roosevelt.

At its essence, the Taft-Roosevelt contest had been fundamentally an ideological struggle between conservatives and progressives. Alienated by the triumph of the conservatives, and feeling that Roosevelt had been unfairly denied the Republican nomination, progressives moved to form a new party. Roosevelt would lead it. Because he did, the Progressive Party immediately gained national stature. No political movement in American history ever rose so far so fast. Roosevelt was on a quest for a third term, the first time in American history there was such a candidacy on a general election ballot. To try taking the edge off this precedent-shattering step, some of his supporters framed it merely as a quest for a second elected term.

Seeing the Republican divide, and anticipating Roosevelt's Progressive Party nomination, Democrats inserted in their platform a plank endorsing a one-term limit for president. It reprised their 1896 platform. Doing so might appeal to voters worried about the prospect of Roosevelt's election breaching the two-term tradition. The 1912 platform read, "We favor a single presidential term, and to that end urge the adoption of an amendment to the Constitution making the President of the United States ineligible to re-election, and we pledge the candidates of this Convention to that principle."[1]

The Republican platform was silent on the subject, but Taft announced his personal support for one six-year term.

Although Governor Wilson ran on the single-term plank, he did not like it. Once elected, he worked to ensure it would not be implemented. In the interim between Wilson's November 1912 election and his March 4, 1913, inauguration, pertinent legislation appeared.

The third session of the 62nd Congress convened on December 2, 1912, and adjourned on March 3, 1913. Several weeks prior to adjournment, the Senate approved S. J. Res. 78, a constitutional amendment proposed by Senator John D. Works (R-CA)[2] to limit the presidential tenure to a single six-year term, just as the Democrats had proposed in their 1912 platform.[3]

Senate debate took five session days.[4] It previewed many of the arguments that characterized the 1947 proceedings on the Twenty-second Amendment. The Senate ultimately passed a proposal that not only limited the president to only one six-year term, but touched upon the service of anyone who had acceded to the office and had a partial term.[5] Service as president for any duration whatsoever meant a lifetime exclusion from ever coming back to run again.

During these proceedings, various floor amendments were unsuccessfully proposed.

- Senator Augustus Bacon (D-GA)[6] proposed to limit an elected president to one term of four years duration. It lost 25 to 42.[7]
- Senator Joseph Bristow (R-KS)[8] offered an amendment that would have empowered Congress to provide for the recall of a president by popular vote. The amendment went down 10 to 58.[9]
- An amendment by Senator Elihu Root (R-NY)[10] would have applied the single six-year term to anyone serving as president after March 4, 1917. This would have exempted the 1913–1917 term to which Woodrow Wilson had just been elected. The Senate rejected Root's amendment by a voice vote.
- Senator Gilbert Hitchcock (D-NE)[11] would affix the six-year limitation to any president elected after the constitutional change was ratified. The cap would not apply to the partial term of a vice president who had succeeded to office. Hitchcock's amendment was defeated 27 to 37.[12]
- Senator Thomas H. Paynter (D-KY)[13] offered an amendment to extend to six years the term of the president who was serving at the time of ratification. Senator Works endorsed this proposal, because it would make explicit what was already implicit in the joint resolution. Notwithstanding Works' endorsement, the lost by 30 to 36.[14]
- Senator George T. Oliver (R-PA)[15] specified that the six-year term would begin with the presidential inauguration following ratification. The amendment failed 13 to 52.[16]

- Senator George Sutherland (R-UT)[17] offered an amendment specifying that adoption of the constitutional change would not extend the term of whoever was president at the time of ratification. The amendment was defeated 29 to 38.[18]
- An amendment from Senator Robert L. Owen (D-OK)[19] would have abolished the Electoral College. A state's governor would certify the outcome of its popular vote to the President of the Senate. The weight of the state's vote would be the same strength as it had been under the Electoral College system. The amendment was rejected 32 to 36.[20]
- Senator John Sharp Williams (D-MS)[21] offered an amendment to restrict prospectively a president to two four-year terms, and counting as one of those terms any fraction of a full term that an individual may have served.[22] The amendment lost on a voice vote.
- Senator Porter J. McCumber (R-ND)[23] proposed to limit a president to two four-year terms, and further provided that an individual who had succeeded to office and served a majority of that term would be eligible to run only once thereafter. The McCumber's amendment lost 3 to 51.[24]

The remarkable thing about the McCumber's amendment is that it is precisely the formula that the Twenty-second Amendment put into the constitution years later. Why was it so badly defeated? Fundamentally, senators considered that it unnecessarily codified existing practices. "This would change the Constitution, it is true," observed Senator William Borah,[25] "but it would not change that which has become the unwritten law of this country, and it gives rise to the question: what brings on this discussion and this proposed constitutional amendment at this time? What tendency has there been on the part of the people to break away from the precedent heretofore established and from the rule so long prevailing?" Borah continued, "We have now experimented for a hundred and odd years; there has been no infraction of the rule, and every time the question has been presented to the American people, they have rejected the proposition."[26] Senator Works responded, "This amendment proposed by the Senator from North Dakota is simply a provision against a third term. I think it would be a useless amendment of the Constitution." Works added, emphatically, "The people of this country in all its history have never elected any man to a third term as President of the United States and, in my judgment, they never will."[27]

Thereafter, S. J. Res. 78 passed, putting the Senate on record for a single six-year term.

Nearly three weeks remained before adjournment, potentially sufficient time for the House of Representatives to concur. Woodrow Wilson might have a lot of influence on whether that would happen. So, where did the president-elect stand? During the Senate debate, Republicans tried to draw answer out of Senator James E. Martine (D-NJ).[28] Part of the New Jersey

Democratic machine, the senator had come to office in the same year that voters elected Wilson the state's Governor. Perhaps Martine could elaborate on the president-elect's views.

Martine refused to state categorically that Wilson, if eligible for reelection, would decline a second term. Nevertheless, he implied that the president-elect would look favorably on the amendment. "I said that he has declared on a number of occasions in favor of one term," noted Martine. "I further stated that it was the policy of our party, as declared in the Baltimore convention, to favor one term, and President-elect Wilson had declared, and redeclared his adherence to the platform of the Baltimore convention."[29]

In fact, Wilson was determined to sink the legislation. Quietly, the president-elect contacted Representative A. Mitchell Palmer (D-PA), a Wilson loyalist, who served on the House Judiciary Committee. Although only in his second term in Congress, Palmer was already influential among House Democrats.[30] Wilson told Palmer to bury the amendment. Palmer passed the word, and the House sat on it, taking no action before adjourning *sine die* on March 3, 1913.

The Democratic platform never again mentioned limits on presidential tenure. Free to seek a second term, Wilson secured reelection in 1916, notwithstanding the reuniting of the Republican Party under Charles Evans Hughes. Before his presidency ended, Wilson would actually consider seeking a third term.

Wilson's initial years were notable for singular accomplishments in domestic policy.[31] Although the war in Europe commenced in August 1914, during his second year, the president had been able to steer the United States clear from involvement in the conflict. This remained true notwithstanding attacks on shipping, as well as the 1915 sinking of the Lusitania, which cost the lives of 1198 persons, including 128 Americans.[32] Primarily a passenger vessel, and flying British flag, the Lusitania was also transporting munitions to Britain. The Wilson's administration vigorously protested the incident to Germany, which promised to refrain from attacking passenger liners without warning. Having lodged this complaint, Wilson did not seek a declaration of war. Thus, he was able to run his 1916 campaign on the slogan "He kept us out of war." Republicans, most notably Theodore Roosevelt, vehemently disagreed with Wilson's policies, but a sufficient number of voters seemed content.

In an effort to bring an apparently endless war to a conclusion, Germany announced a policy of unrestricted submarine warfare against all vessels entering European war zones.[33] Publicized on January 31, 1917, this strategy would interdict supplies destined for British and starve them into defeat.[34] The new policy took effect the following day.

Germany anticipated that its new policy might bring the United States into the war as a belligerent, but hoped the expanded submarine warfare would finish off the British before the full effects of American intervention were brought to bear. To mitigate the possible effects of American engagement, Germany had in mind a distraction. From Berlin, the German Foreign Minister, Arthur Zimmermann, sent a note on January 19, 1917, to the German Ambassador in Mexico. The Zimmermann note proposed a military alliance between Germany and Mexico, if America joined the allies.

The text of the Zimmermann Note read: "We intend to begin on the first of February unrestricted submarine warfare. We shall endeavor in spite of this to keep the United States of America neutral. In the event of this not succeeding, we make Mexico a proposal of alliance on the following basis: make war together, make peace together, generous financial support and an understanding on our part that Mexico is to reconquer the lost territory in Texas, New Mexico, and Arizona. The settlement in detail is left to you. You will inform the President of the above most secretly as soon as the outbreak of war with the United States of America is certain and add the suggestion that he should, on his own initiative, invite Japan to immediate adherence and at the same time mediate between Japan and ourselves. Please call the President's attention to the fact that the ruthless employment of our submarines now offers the prospect of compelling England in a few months to make peace."

Seen from the vantage point of the 21st century, Zimmermann's note appears bizarre. But it came within the context of periodic tensions that had existed for years between the United States and its neighbor. Thus, his approach was not wholly outlandish, even if difficult to implement.[35] In addition, Zimmermann recommended that Mexico attempt to coax Japan into joining their anti-American alliance.

Zimmermann's efforts to neutralize the U.S. war capacity did not work. However, when publicized in early March, they helped galvanize the American public to support entering the fighting.[36] An additional, and important, consideration was the sinking during March of three American merchant vessels and other naval attacks, per Germany's new submarine warfare policy. These incidents also provoked American opinion, and deepened Wilson's distrust for the Kaiser's government.[37] On the evening of Monday, April 2, 1917, the president addressed a Joint Session of Congress to seek a declaration of war. On the floor of each chamber, there was vigorous debate and some dissent. By a vote of 82-6, the Senate approved the Declaration on April 4. The House followed suit on April 6, 373-50.

On December 4, 1918, less than a month after the Armistice ending fighting on the Western Front, Wilson journeyed to France to take part in peace negotiations. The United States, France, and Great Britain were the leading powers in shaping the Treaty of Versailles. At Wilson's insistence, the peacemakers included the League of Nations Covenant in the Treaty. This contradicted the advice of numerous Republican senators, openly expressed in a resolution they introduced on March 3, 1919, who believed that the treaties to conclude the war should be separate from structuring an international organization to keep the peace.[38] Not binding, and indeed never voted-upon, the resolution was a harbinger of major problems Wilson would confront in the Senate. The president chose to ignore it.

On June 28, 1919, signatories gathered at the Hall of Mirrors in the Palace of Versailles, west of Paris. After the ceremonies, Wilson headed home, pleased about the praise heaped on the treaty by governors, legislatures, and publications.[39] On Thursday, July 10, 1919, two days after he arrived back in the United States, Wilson spoke in the Senate chamber to present the treaty in person.[40] "Dare we reject it," he queried, "and break the heart of the world?"[41]

Many senators seemed skeptical. Wilson had a sobering three-hour meeting on August 19, 1919, with members of the Senate Foreign Relations Committee. This discussion revealed much discontent with the treaty, and helped to shape the president's view that he must mobilize public opinion to move the Senate. Wilson's secretary, Joseph Tumulty, offered insight on the meeting. "Although, at this conference of August 19, 1919, the President had frankly opened his mind and heart to the enemies of the Treaty, the opposition instead of moderating seemed to grow more intense and passionate. The President had done everything humanely possible to soften the opposition of the Republicans, but, alas, the information brought to him from the Hill by his Democratic friends only confirmed the opinion that opposition to the Treaty was growing and could not be overcome by personal contact of any kind between the President and the members of the Foreign Relations Committee."[42]

Wilson therefore planned a national tour, on which he could take his case to the people.[43] Reading the mood of their colleagues, and concerned that support for the Treaty, as submitted, was lacking, Democratic senators urged the president on.[44]

On September 3, 1919, Wilson embarked on a cross-country rail trip to summon up public support.[45] His staff worried whether he would have the strength and stamina to complete it, and told him so. Said Tumulty, "As I looked at the President, while he was talking, I made a comparison between the man, Woodrow Wilson, who now stood before me and the man I had met many years before in New Jersey. In those days he was a vigorous, agile, slender man, active and alert, his hair but slightly streaked with gray. Now stood before me discussing the necessity for the Western trip, he was an old man, grown grayer and grayer, but grimmer and grimmer in his determination, like an old warrior, to fight to the end."[46]

Wilson felt exhausted, but insisted on going. "In the presence of the great tragedy which now faces the world," he told Tumulty, "no decent man can count his own personal fortunes in the reckoning. Even though, in my condition, it might mean the giving up of my life, I will gladly make the sacrifice to save the Treaty."[47]

The president paid substantial personal attention to the itinerary, demanding addition of more stops, and rejecting suggestions from the staff that opportunities be built-in to rest.[48]

Beginning in Columbus, Ohio, on September 3, he traveled 8,000 miles in 22 days and made over 30 major addresses.[49] Along the way, he often suffered from severe headaches.[50]

In the main, the public gave Wilson a friendly reception.[51] Encouraged, he planned a second trip, this one to New England, where he would have an opportunity to challenge Lodge on the senator's home turf. However, on September 25, in Pueblo, Colorado, the president collapsed.[52] Wilson's physician, Dr. Cary Grayson, was adamant that remaining stops be foregone and the president return to the White House.[53]

Reluctantly cancelling the remainder of his trip, the president returned to Washington.[54] Back at the White House on October 2, 1919, he suffered a major stroke, which incapacitated him for weeks. While Wilson was out of action, debate on the president's most fervent priority, the League of Nations, consumed the Senate. Wilson had staked the nation's reputation on securing a favorable outcome there. Victory would cement his standing as a great president. Defeat would cause him to contemplate vindicating his position by running for a third term.

In the Senate, there were three voting blocs. One was composed entirely of Democrats. Led by Senator Gilbert Hitchcock (D-NE),[55] it supported Wilson's insistence that the Senate approve the treaty without any modifications. Hitchcock was the senior Democrat on the Foreign Relations Committee. A second group included Republican senators who were willing to consent, but subject to reservations that would either express distinctive views about provisions in the treaty or qualify American obligations to the League of Nations.[56] Senator Henry Cabot Lodge (R-MA), chairman of the Foreign Relations Committee, led the reservationists.[57] There was a third group, composed of thirteen Republicans, who wanted to reject the treaty outright. No collection of reservations could mollify them. Led by Senator William Borah (R-ID), they were known as the irreconcilables.

Floor proceedings began on September 10, 1919. The Foreign Relations Committee had recommended four reservations to the covenant and forty-five amendments. Not wanting to create a circumstance where renegotiation of the treaty would be plainly necessary, the Senate rejected all the amendments. Nevertheless, many senators were open to adding reservation as a basis on which to consent.[58]

On November 19, 1919, Lodge proposed a resolution of ratification with fourteen reservations. The Senate had agreed to each of them individually during Floor proceedings.[59] The day before, Hitchcock visited the White House to ascertain whether Wilson was open to Democrats supporting this proposal, or at least some of it. However, the president was adamant that the Senate reject all reservations.

In particular, the president took exception to one that concerned Article 10 of the League Covenant.[60] Article 10 provided that the Council of the League of Nations[61] could recommend military action to defend a member state against aggression.[62] In his August White House meeting, Wilson represented to the senators that such a recommendation would not bind the United States to participate, but would create a moral obligation. Wilson was open to exchange diplomatic notes to the effect that American forces could only be committed with Congress' consent. However, he opposed the Senate's writing this into the resolution of ratification. To do so would require a renegotiation of the treaty, Wilson insisted.[63]

Hitchcock hoped in vain that Wilson would demonstrate some flexibility. There was none.[64] Instead, Wilson returned a note to Hitchcock that exclaimed, "The resolution in that form does not provide for ratification, but rather for the nullification of the treaty."[65]

Wilson chronicler Arthur Link states,

> His mind remained relatively clear; but he was physically enfeebled, and the disease had wrecked his emotional constitution and aggravated all his more unfortunate personal traits. . . . When Wilson made his decision, on November 17, to reject the Lodge reservations, he was still a very sick man. His mind could function well in certain circumstances, but his whole emotional balance had been shattered.[66]

As the letter was being prepared, Edith Wilson, who had assumed significant responsibilities during her husband's illness, asked the president whether a compromise with Lodge was possible. "She recounted that, turning his head on the pillow and stretching out his hand to take hers, he had answered in a voice she would never forget, 'Little girl, don't you desert me; that I cannot stand. Can't you see that I have no moral right to accept any change in a paper I have signed without giving to every other signatory, even the Germans, the right to do the same thing? It is not that I will not accept; it is the Nation's honor that is at stake."[67]

Wilson's note to Hitchcock circulated widely in the Senate and became public. Thus instructed, most Democrats stuck with him. For ratification to occur, sixty-four affirmative votes were needed if all ninety-six senators voted. However, the Lodge resolution went down 39 to 55. The thirteen irreconcilables combined with the Democrats. Then, Senator Oscar Underwood (D-AL) proposed an alternative resolution of ratification that would have consented to the treaty with no reservations at all. The Senate defeated Underwood's proposal by a nearly identical vote of 38 to 53. Voting in the negative were the irreconcilables plus the reservationists.

According to Lodge, "The vote on the resolution of Senator Underwood had a peculiar importance and is generally forgotten. It demonstrated that the Covenant of the League of Nations as proposed by President Wilson could under no circumstances have been accepted by the Senate."[68]

The outcome suggested the need for compromise and that some form of reservations would be necessary to secure the Senate's consent. Informal bipartisan negotiations ensued, in January 1920, lasting for two weeks. Nine senators were involved, five Republicans and four Democrats. The discussions caused great consternation among the irreconcilables, who were not included in them. Alerted to the talks by Alice Roosevelt Longworth, Senator Borah pressured Lodge not to give in, including a threat to seek Lodge's removal as party leader.[69]

Negotiations produced several agreements, although none covering the contentious reservation to Article 10. Failure to strike a compromise on that point was an important reason that discussions broke off, although they might have failed anyway because of pressure from the irreconcilables to scuttle them.[70]

Lodge brought the treaty back up in the Senate on February 16, 1920. The resolution of ratification contained the fourteen reservations that were included the prior November, but modified as recommended by the bipartisan group. As debate progressed, some of the revisions were adopted; in other cases, the Senate reverted to the original reservation language.

On March 19, 1920, the Senate made one last attempt to approve the treaty, with reservations. Wilson still refused to compromise.[71] This time, the resolution commanded a 55 to 39 majority, but was still seven votes short of two-thirds.[72] Lodge was confident that he had sufficient Democratic votes to put across a resolution of ratification with reservations, and indicated so to Corinne Roosevelt Robinson, Theodore Roosevelt's sister. But Wilson remained firm, and held enough Democrats to prove the Senator wrong. After the vote, Lodge told her, "just as I thought I had everything settled and that my number of Democratic votes was ample in every way, a sinister, unseen hand came out from the White House and drew away many votes, and I could do nothing." The same day, the Senate passed a resolution returning the Treaty of Versailles to the president.

Badly wounded and bitterly disappointed, Wilson considered running in the 1920 election for a third term. He foresaw his campaign being a referendum on U.S. entry into the League of Nations.[73] To set the stage, he sent a letter to be read at the January 8, 1920, Jackson Day Dinner, an annual conclave of leading Democrats. In the letter, Wilson laid out his hypothesis that 1920 was a chance to convert the forthcoming election into a referendum on the League. "If there is any doubt as to what the people think on this vital matter, the clear and single way out is to submit it for determination at the next election to the voters of the nation, to give the next election the form of a great and solemn referendum, a referendum as to the part the United States is to play in completing the settlements of the war and in the prevention in the future of such outrages as Germany attempted to perpetuate."[74]

An accomplished orator, Wilson imagined summoning his strength to reprise his 1919 campaign for the League. However, there was insufficient strength to summon. The president was far too debilitated by the stroke to carry on a national campaign.

While Wilson never announced his willingness to run, he also never disclaimed it.[75] Encouraged by First Lady Edith Wilson, Tumulty tried to convince the president to stand down and openly declare he would not seek a third term, arguing that such a step would de-politicize the Treaty. However, said Tumulty, "Wilson saw nothing to be gained from such a gesture. It would only hand the leadership of the party to William Jennings Bryan; and he felt it presumptuous to decline something that he had not been offered." As historian Patricia O'Toole notes, Wilson's unwillingness to step aside generated substantial problems for his party. "By refusing to sideline himself, Wilson signaled that he was available, and Democrats found themselves in a fix. They could not openly disown the president, but they could not indulge him either—because of his health and because they did not feel Democrats could win if they flouted the two-term tradition."[76]

Meanwhile, Wilson was concocting a third-term bid. He conceived a circumstance in which the Democratic Convention deadlocked and turned to him as the savior of the party and of the League.[77] Other candidates were available, but Wilson was not impressed.[78] Among them were Ohio Governor James Cox; William Gibbs McAdoo, who was Wilson's son-in-law and former Treasury Secretary; Attorney General A. Mitchell Palmer; and former Secretary of State and party nominee, William Jennings Bryan.

Capable as these men might be for smaller tasks, Wilson thought, they either lacked capacity or vision to grapple with the biggest job of all: saving the structure of world peace.[79] It was a precursor to the kind of indispensability assessment that Franklin Roosevelt would make as his second term wound down in 1940.

The more Wilson considered this idea, the more it appealed to him and the more he fancied he could make it happen. Wilson's biographer, Scott Berg, writes of the run-up to the 1920 Democratic Convention, "President Wilson, however, continued to fool himself into believing he would run for a third term, and some surrounding him nursed the delusion. So began the most surreal few weeks in the Wilson Presidency, a moment when nobody could bring himself to tell the emperor that he was not wearing any clothes."[80]

To enhance his prospects, the president sat for a June 17, 1920, interview with Louis Seibold of the *New York World.* It occurred in the interregnum between the two party conventions. When asked about who the Democrats should nominate, the incumbent was cagey. "Wilson had declined to Seibold's question about the kind of man the Democratic Party should choose as its candidate. He has not come forward in the promotion of any Democratic presidential nomination. He was, however, clear on the chief issue. The League of Nations was too great a concept for mere political skullduggery."[81]

Public reaction to the interview was that it was tantamount to a declaration of candidacy, stirring ample speculation about a third term.[82] Leading Democrats, including some members of Wilson's cabinet, tried to dissuade him, but he was determined to preserve the chance he might run.[83] Dr. Grayson was appalled. He spoke with Senator Carter Glass (D-VA), formerly in the cabinet as secretary of the treasury, and chair of the Democratic Platform Committee. Telling Glass that a campaign would kill Wilson, he urged the senator to take all possible steps to stifle the chance for it.[84]

The 1920 Democratic Convention opened in San Francisco on July 5. Prominently displayed was a large portrait of Wilson, which along with a speech by Convention Chairman Homer Cummings, evoked immense enthusiasm from the delegates. Cummings wired Wilson, "There can be no doubt that the Convention is with you and for the League of Nations overwhelmingly. . . . It is a Wilson convention in spirit and purpose."[85]

As Wilson foresaw, and indeed hoped, the Convention nominating process soon became a messy affair. The White House had adopted a position of neutrality, from which it refused to budge.[86] Delegates mainly divided their votes between Cox, McAdoo, and Palmer. The deadlock persisted, ballot after ballot. "In Washington, the President appeared indifferent," writes Berg, "but as one ballot followed another with no candidate emerging, Wilson took increasing interest in reports that came over the in-house telegraph wire."[87]

Secretary of State Bainbridge Colby was in San Francisco by agreement with Wilson to assess the circumstances and attend to the president's political interests. They agreed to communicate in code.[88] Observing the deadlock, and the delegates' apparent affection for the president, Colby sent Wilson a wire on July 2. He believed that the central issue of the campaign would be entry into the League, and that public support for Democrats would be galvanized if Wilson were the candidate.[89] Moreover, he assessed that circumstances were ripe to position Wilson for the nomination.

Telling Wilson that the deadlocked Convention could suspend the rules to allow the President to be nominated by acclamation[90] Colby said he would put Wilson's name forward unless the president instructed him not to do so.[91] On the president's behalf, Edith Wilson responded positively.[92]

Wilson's friends at the convention now got word of this scheming and were outraged. Among them was Secretary of the Navy Josephus Daniels. On July 4, the group met with Colby and reproached him. "I never saw more indignation and resentment in any small gathering," wrote Daniels. All present insisted that he ought not to have sent such a message without first conferring with them, and some of his colleagues told him it was a cruel thing to have done in view of the state of the President's health."[93] In light of his condition, they concluded, a campaign was wholly impractical. And they raised a further important objection. The country would resent an effort to secure a third term.[94] Confronting their strenuous objections, Colby stalled, telling the president in a further coded message that the time was not ripe to execute the plan. Meanwhile, on the 44th ballot, the voting deadlock broke, and the Convention nominated Cox. Wilson was chagrined, feeling betrayed.[95]

At no time did Convention leaders show interest in the idea of renominating Wilson. Quite the opposite. Apart from their concern over the president's health,[96] many Democrats simply opposed challenging the two-term tradition.[97]

One can speculate that the result would have been different if Wilson had been in good shape. Daniels certainly thought so. "I think we were all agreed that, if Wilson had been in robust health, the people would have drafted him to run as the incarnation and embodiment of 'the solemn referendum' on the League of Nations."[98] Daniels added that, "if Wilson had been a well man, he would, in my opinion, have been willing to break the old three-term jinx in devotion to the League."[99] One can imagine Wilson, recalling the crowd response to his September 1919 tour, believing he could galvanize public opinion to endorse him and his League, and vanquish his enemies.

Democrats adopted a platform endorsing the League. After nominating Cox on the forty-fourth ballot, they chose Assistant Secretary of the Navy Franklin Roosevelt (D-NY) as his running mate. In the general election, this team would oppose the Republican ticket of Senator Warren Harding (R-OH) and Governor Calvin Coolidge (R-MA). Denied the chance to vindicate the League by winning a third term, the president was decidedly unhappy.[100]

Although Wilson was not a candidate, and took little part in the campaign, the League was the predominant issue facing the electorate.[101] Harding and Coolidge won election with 60.32 percent of the vote. They carried every state outside the old Confederacy, except for Kentucky, and narrowly prevailed in Tennessee.[102] They took the oath of office on March 4, 1921. Leaving the White House, Woodrow and Edith Wilson moved into 2340 S Street NW, in Washington, DC.

It was predictable that Harding, along with a Republican majority in Congress, would foreclose entry into the League and attempt to undo aspects of Wilson's domestic legacy. In retirement, the former president labored over ideas to serve as a platform for the 1924 Democratic nominee. Remarkably, Wilson left open the possibility that he might again be a candidate.[103] However, Wilson's health continued to deteriorate. He died on February 3, 1924, his ambition to return to the White House unfulfilled.

NOTES

1. "Democratic Party Platforms: 1912 Democratic Party Platform: June 25, 1912," www.presidency.ucsb.edu (accessed September 2, 2018).
2. John D. Works was a senator from 1911 to 1917.
3. The vote was 47–23, on February 1, 1913. Tom Wicker, "Six Years for the President," *New York Times*, June 26, 1983, www.nytimes.com (accessed October 7, 2018).
4. The Senate initially debated it on December 9–10, 1912. Further proceedings were deferred so the Senate could conduct impeachment proceedings against Judge Robert W. Archbald. The Senate returned to it during sessions on January 30–February 1, 1913.
5. If the amendment had been in effect in 1904, Theodore Roosevelt would have been ineligible to run, because he would have already served as a president for forty-two months of McKinley's second term.
6. Augustus Bacon was a Senator from 1895 until his death in 1914.
7. *Congressional Record,* January 30, 1913, p. 2266.
8. Joseph Bristow served in the Senate from 1909 to 1915.
9. *Congressional Record*, January 30, 1913, p. 2274.
10. After having served as Secretary of War under President William McKinley and Secretary of State under President Theodore Roosevelt, Elihu Root was a senator from 1909 to 1915.
11. Gilbert Hitchcock served in the House from 1903 to 1905 and again from 1907 to 1911. He was a senator between 1911 and 1923.
12. *Congressional Record*, January 31, 1913, p. 2354.
13. Thomas H. Paynter was in the House from 1889 to 1895 and in the Senate from 1907 to 1913.
14. *Congressional Record*, January 31, 1913, p. 2360.
15. George T. Oliver was a senator from 1909 to 1917.
16. *Congressional Record*, January 31, 1913, p. 2263.
17. George Sutherland was in the House from 1901 to 1903, in the Senate from 1905 to 1917, and was later an Associate Justice of the Supreme Court from 1922 to 1938.
18. *Congressional Record,* February 1, 1913, p. 2419.
19. Robert L. Owen served in the Senate from 1907 to 1925.
20. *Congressional Record*, January 31, 1913, p. 2362.

21. John Sharp Williams was in the House from 1893 to 1909 and in the Senate from 1911 to 1923.

22. This would have put into law the arrangement Theodore Roosevelt informally observed, counting his partial term as one term, his elected term as a second, and then ending his presidency in 1908.

23. Porter J. McCumber served four terms in the Senate, from 1899 to 1923.

24. *Congressional Record*, January 31, 1913, p. 2360.

25. William Borah was a senator from 1907 to his death in 1940.

26. *Congressional Record*, January 31, 1913, p. 2356.

27. Ibid.

28. James E. Martine served one term in the Senate, from 1911 to 1917.

29. *Congressional Record*, January 30, 1913, p. 2275.

30. Palmer served in Congress from 1909 to 1915. Later, as Wilson's last Attorney General, he was associated with the Palmer Raids, targeted against immigrants with leftist and allegedly anarchist views. This period is also known as the Red Scare.

31. Leading examples would be the Federal Reserve Act, the Clayton Antitrust Act, legislation establishing the Federal Trade Commission, and the Revenue Act of 1913.

32. As part of Germany's policy of unrestricted submarine warfare within a declared exclusion zone, one of its submarines sank the Lusitania off the Irish coast on May 7, 1915. "Wilson had to respond, so dramatic was the incident, so atrocious was the deed in the eyes of the American people, so flagrant was the violation of elementary national rights." Arthur S. Link, *Woodrow Wilson: Revolution, War, and Peace* (Wheeling, Illinois: Harlan Davidson, Inc., 1979), p. 41. Notwithstanding these terms, a German submarine sank a cross-channel ferry on March 24, 1916, prompting additional American protests and a threat to sever diplomatic relations if Germany repeated such attacks. Ibid., p. 44. In the aftermath, Germany mollified the United States by issuing the Sussex Pledge, which constrained the rules of engagement for its submarines. On January 31, 1917, Germany effectively rescinded this pledge by announcing a policy of unrestricted submarine warfare in the North Atlantic. On April 6, 1917, at the president's request, Congress declared war on Germany.

33. This announcement effectively ended the Sussex Pledge. "The staggering announcement of unrestricted U-boat warfare was equivalent to a declaration of war on the United States." Thomas A. Bailey, *Wilson and the Peacemakers* (New York: The MacMillan Company, 1947), pp. 5–6. The war zones included waters around the United Kingdom, France, Italy, and the eastern Mediterranean. Link, p. 64.

34. "Naval spokesmen, armed with elaborate memoranda, guaranteed absolutely that an unrestricted submarine campaign against all maritime commerce, belligerent and neutral, could reduce Great Britain to starvation and surrender within five months." Link, p. 58.

35. Mexico had long-standing grievances against the United States, stemming from the Mexican War of the 1840s. These were gravely exacerbated during Wilson's tenure. American troops landed in Veracruz in April 1914 after a naval incident, engaged in combat, suffered casualties, and remained there for much of the year. O'Toole, pp. 101–105. During the period March 1916 to February 1917, under Wilson's orders, and commanded by General John J. Pershing, some 5000 American

troops crossed the border and plunged 800 miles into Mexico in pursuit of Pancho Villa, who had led several cross-border incursions into the United States. Mexico protested this lengthy violation of its sovereignty. O'Toole, pp. 199–200.

36. "This fantastic cablegram was intercepted and decoded by the British, and, when published, caused a tremendous revulsion of feeling in America, more so than the vastly more significant announcement of unrestricted submarine warfare. The East had generally been favorable to war following the announcement of the U-boat campaign, but the South and West had been rather apathetic. The Zimmermann note did more than anything else to fuse the disunited United States." Bailey, p. 7. Scholar David Stevenson takes a somewhat different view, arguing that while Wilson published the note to provoke public opinion, its impact was sensational, but temporary at best. "It swayed the Senate less than the House of Representatives, and the filibusterers received hundreds of supporting letters from their constituents, even if Wilson and most newspapers condemned them. . . . By mid-March coverage had almost disappeared, and in April few newspapers highlighted it as a reason for intervention." David Stevenson, *1917: War, Peace & Revolution* (Oxford: Oxford University Press, 2017), p. 61.

37. Link, pp. 70–71.

38. Senator Philander Knox (R-PA) served in the Senate from 1904 to 1909 and from 1917 until his death in 1921. During the Taft's administration, he was Secretary of State. In early March, Knox and Senator Henry Cabot Lodge organized a resolution, which thirty-nine Republican senators signed. Lodge read it aloud in the Senate on March 3, 1919. The resolution said, in part, "it is the Sense of the Senate that the negotiations on the part of the United States should immediately be directed to the utmost expedition of negotiating peace terms with Germany satisfactory to the United States and to the nations with whom the United States is associated in the war against the German Government, and that the proposal for a league of nations to insure the permanent peace of the world should then be taken up for careful and serious consideration." (emphasis added). Henry Cabot Lodge, *The Senate and the League of Nations* (New York: Charles Scribner's Sons, 1925), pp. 120–121.

39. Lodge, pp. 106–107.

40. "It was the first time a President had presented a treaty in person to an open session of the Senate." John Milton Cooper, Jr., *Breaking the Heart of the World: Woodrow Wilson and the Fight for the League of Nations* (New York: Cambridge University Press, 2001), p. 118. "The presence of Lodge and Borah among the Senators delegated to meet him and escort him to the chamber raised a laugh. There was scattered applause on his appearance, the Republican side in stern silence, Medill McCormick and (Philander) Knox remained seated." Longworth, p. 286.

41. Cooper, Jr., p. 118.

42. Joseph Tumulty, *Woodrow Wilson as I Know Him* (Garden City, New York: Doubleday, Page & Company, 1921), pp. 424–425.

43. Link, pp. 112–113. Relative to this meeting with the committee, its chairman, Senator Henry Cabot Lodge, wrote, "Having failed in securing any Republican votes on the terms and conditions which he desired, President Wilson then made up his mind to appeal to the country." Lodge, *The Senate and the League of Nations*, p. 150. Tumulty, pp. 424–425.

44. Ibid., p. 434.

45. Three Senators, William Borah (R-ID), Hiram Johnson (R-CA), and Medill McCormick (R-IL), trailed Wilson and made speeches of their own to contradict him. Cooper, p. 167.

46. Tumulty, p. 435.

47. Ibid.

48. Ibid., p. 438.

49. Link, p. 113.

50. "He suffered from violent headaches each day, but his speeches never betrayed his illness." Tumulty, p. 439.

51. As noted by John Milton Cooper, Wilson's generally favorable public reception did not necessarily translate into support from senators for the treaty. In any case, after Pueblo, the effort was cut short and not renewed. Cooper, pp. 190–191. "While the first meeting in Columbus was a disappointment as to attendance, as we approached the West the crowds grew in numbers and the enthusiasm became boundless." Tumulty, p. 446.

52. Reporting on his affliction, the New York Times ran the headline, "The President Suffers a Nervous Breakdown." Phyllis Lee Levin, *Edith and Woodrow* (New York: Scribner, 2001), p. 332. White House bulletins after his October 2, 1919, stroke, reinforced this misleading impression. Ibid., p. 354.

53. Grayson awakened Tumulty at 4:00 AM on September 26, to report that Wilson was gravely ill. "As we walked toward the President's car, the Doctor told me in a few words of the President's trouble and said that he greatly feared it might end fatally if we should attempt to continue the trip, and that it was his duty to inform the President that by all means the trip must be cancelled." Tumulty, pp. 446–447.

54. Grayson, along with his secretary, Joseph Tumulty, and Edith combined to persuade the president to terminate the trip, beginning with scrapping a scheduled stop in Wichita. Convincing him was not easy. "Don't you see," Wilson told Tumulty, "if we cancel this trip Senator Lodge and his friends will say that I am a quitter, that the trip was a failure. And the treaty will be lost." Gene Smith, *When the Cheering Stopped: The Last Years of Woodrow Wilson* (New York: William Morrow and Company, 1964), pp. 84–85.

55. Gilbert Hitchcock served in the House from 1907 to 1911 and in the Senate from 1911 to 1923.

56. This position received notable outside backing from former pro-Treaty leaders such as President William Howard Taft and 1916 Republican nominee Charles Evans Hughes. Their engagement helped to legitimize the idea that supporting reservations was not inconsistent with support for the Treaty. Link, pp. 131–132.

57. Lodge considered the League as "an alliance charged to intervene anywhere in the world in order to maintain the existing distribution of power in the world." He forcefully objected to its implications for American sovereignty, and insisted on strong reservations to protect the sanctity of American constitutional processes. Ibid., pp. 134–135.

58. Marian McKenna, *Borah* (Ann Arbor: University of Michigan Press, 1961), p. 163.

59. Under the Constitution, two-thirds of senators voting is the required threshold for consent. Disposition of any amendments, reservations, conditions, declarations, and provisos happens by majority vote. Any of these is included in the resolution of ratification, which is the mechanism for the Senate to consent. The two-thirds threshold applies only at the end, on passage of the resolution of ratification.

60. Article 10 provided, "The Members of the League undertake to respect and preserve as against external aggression the territorial integrity and existing political independence of all Members of the League. In case of any such aggression or in case of any threat or danger of such aggression the Council shall advise upon the means by which this obligation shall be fulfilled."

61. The League Council much resembled today's United Nations Security Council. The United States was to have been a permanent member of the Council.

62. Lodge recounted that, during Wilson's August 19 meeting with the Foreign Relations Committee, senators asked the president about the authorship of Article 10. The president claimed it as his own. As adopted by the Senate during November 13, 1919, deliberations in the Committee of the Whole, the reservation (Reservation Number 3) read: "The United States assumes no obligation to preserve the territorial integrity or political independence of any other country or to interfere in controversies between nations—whether members of the League or not—under the provisions of Article 10, or to employ the military or naval forces of the United States under any article of the treaty for any purpose, unless in any particular case the Congress, which, under the Constitution, has the sole power to declare war or authorize the employment of the military or naval forces of the United States, shall by act or joint resolution so provide." Lodge, p. 184.

63. See the written record of Wilson's August 19 meeting with the Committee on Foreign Relations, as set out in Appendix IV of Lodge, pp. 313–317. "To his mind, the reservations offered by Senator Lodge constituted a virtual nullification on the part of the United States of a treaty which was a contract and which should be amended through free discussion of all the contracting parties. . . . He was unalterably opposed to having the United States put in the position of seeking exemptions and special privileges under an agreement which he believed was in the interest of the entire world, including our own country." Tumulty, pp. 452-453.

64. "He believed, very deeply, that the one issue now at stake was whether the United States would join the League of Nations and give leadership to it wholeheartedly and without reservations, or whether it would join the League grudgingly, with no promises to maintain the peace of the world. To Wilson, the difference between what he stood for and what the Republicans would agree to was the difference between the success or failure and the life or death of mankind's best hope for peace." Link, pp. 123–124.

65. Levin, p. 378.

66. Link, pp. 121–122.

67. Levin, p. 379. His statement to Edith is in full accord with his comments about renegotiation during his August 19, 1919, meeting with the Senate Foreign Relations Committee.

68. Lodge, p. 192.

69. Cordery, p. 285. Apart from being Chairman of the Committee on Foreign Relations, Lodge was then the Senate Republican Leader. Outraged that Lodge might reach a compromise that would yield a two-thirds majority for the treaty, Borah located and interrupted the meeting. He confronted Lodge, threatening to denounce him openly on the Senate Floor and demand election of a new Leader. "Lodge informed his conferees, who had been awaiting his return with some impatience, that he could not go on—that the agreement was off." Johnson, p. 247. As a consequence of Borah's pressure, the resolution of ratification was resubmitted in March was much the same as the Lodge proposal the Senate rejected the previous November. McKenna, p. 168.

70. Senator Hitchcock was quoted in the January 31, 1920, *Washington Post*, "There was no dramatic climax to the conferences. It was agreed by all that unless some compromise could be worked out on Article 10 it would be useless to continue the meetings." See the account of this in Lodge, p. 204.

71. As to Wilson's staunch defense of Article 10, Lodge wrote, "He would not consult, he would not advise, he would not consider any change of meaning or consequence. He was determined to have the treaty in every essential point exactly as he had approved it in Paris, and nothing else." Lodge, pp. 215–216.

72. Levin, p. 438. Alice Roosevelt Longworth was working with the irreconcilables against the treaty. She reported that they feared Wilson would accept the modified reservations as "merely interpretive" and would free Democrats to vote for the treaty with the reservations appended. "Our apprehensions that Mr. Wilson might accept the reservations were laid to rest on the eighth of March. The president wrote to Senator Hitchcock at length, especially in regard to any reservation on Article X." In Wilson's letter, he said "I hear of reservationists and mild reservationists, but I cannot understand the difference between a nullifier and a mild nullifier." Longworth was relieved. "So to our great satisfaction, Mr. Wilson insisted on our moral obligation to unreserved ratification and refused to recede one iota from that position. That settled the defeat of the treaty." Longworth, p. 301.

73. The president spoke of this to his physician and confidant, Dr. Cary Grayson. "With the approach of the national conventions, he daydreamed of taking a referendum for his treaty to the people. In idle moments, he drafted a series of questions for the electorate—did they wish to make use of his services as President, did they approve of the way in which the Administration had conducted the war, did they wish the Treaty of Versailles ratified?" A. Scott Berg, *Wilson* (New York: G.P. Putnam's Sons, 2013), p. 684. "As the spring wore on, Wilson convinced himself that the election had to be a referendum on the League and he was the one to lead the fight." Patricia O'Toole, *The Moralist: Woodrow Wilson and the World He Made* (New York: Simon & Schuster, 2018), p. 459. At the end of the document, he listed potential Cabinet nominees for his next administration. Levin, p. 447.

74. Link, p. 125.

75. Ibid.

76. O'Toole, *The Moralist*, p. 461.

77. "Wilson had conjured a plot in which the Democratic Convention would find itself in a 'hopeless tie-up,' and with the world in so much turmoil, the Peace Treaty

with its League of Nations would become the dominant issue. Then, Wilson added, 'there may be practically a universal demand for the selection of someone to lead them out of the wilderness.'" Ibid.

78. Levin, pp. 446–447.

79. Ibid., p. 459.

80. Berg, p. 688.

81. Levin, p. 449.

82. "Wall Street sources let it be known the President was the betting favorite to secure the Democratic nomination." Smith, p. 160.

83. Ibid.

84. Ibid., p. 161. To a Democratic operative, Grayson confided, "No matter what others may tell you, no matter what you may read about the President being on the road to recovery, I tell you that he is permanently ill physically, is gradually weakening mentally, and can't recover. He couldn't possibly survive the campaign." Ibid.

85. Levin, p. 451.

86. Tumulty, p. 496.

87. O'Toole, p. 690.

88. "Wilson asked Colby to stay in touch with him and wait for the deadlock. They would conceal their dealings from Tumulty by wiring each other in code." O'Toole, *The Moralist*, p. 462.

89. Josephus Daniels, *The Wilson Era: Years of War and After: 1917–1923* (Chapel Hill: University of North Carolina Press, 1946), p. 555.

90. In 1940, Colby would appear before a Senate Judiciary Committee subcommittee headed by Senator Edward Burke (D-NE) to denounce the possibility of a third term for Franklin Roosevelt. None of the senators asked Colby about his role in encouraging a third Wilson term two decades earlier. However, it is likely they did not know about it. In 1946, Josephus Daniels, who had been Wilson's Secretary of the Navy, wrote an account of the Wilson era. In it, he disclosed Colby's maneuverings, saying that he was revealing a twenty-five-year-old secret. Ibid.

91. Ibid., p. 556.

92. Levin, p. 451. The way Scott Berg puts it, when faced with Colby's maneuver, the president did not object. Berg, p. 690. Gene Smith recounts, "Tumulty saw the wire and frantically begged the First Lady to wire Colby that this thing not be done. She refused." Smith, p. 163.

93. Daniels, p. 556. Others present included Cummings, Postmaster General Albert Burleson, Treasury Secretary (later, senator) Carter Glass, and journalist Ray Stannard Baker. Levin, pp. 451–452.

94. Ibid., p. 452. "They forced a chagrined Colby to send another telegram to the President, this time rescinding his plan—explaining that the Democratic leaders did not command votes sufficient either to set aside convention rules or to nominate him and that such a public display would only injure the party's chances in the upcoming election—as well as any hope left for the League." Smith, pp. 163–164.

95. "Wilson, humiliated, was pitiful in his complaints that all his circle, including Grayson, and even his wife, had lost interest in him because he was now judged hopeless." Ibid. After learning of Cox's nomination, Wilson, "who could literally go

for years without using a stronger term than 'damn' or 'hell' burst into a stream of profanities and obscenities." Smith, p. 164.

96. In a conversation with the doctor, Virginia Senator Carter Glass "told Grayson bluntly that he did not think the Convention could be induced to nominate a man in the President's disabled condition, and that even if he were in robust health, the Democrats, to say nothing of the nation, did not seem prepared to overcome their antipathy to a third term." Ibid.

97. "The Democrats opposed to a third term for Wilson were numerous enough to defeat a motion to suspend the rules, and when they did, Tumulty said, Wilson would suffer a public humiliation at the hands of his own party." O'Toole, *The Moralist*, p. 462.

98. Ibid.

99. Ibid., pp. 557–558.

100. As Berg notes, Wilson's stenographer, Charles Swem, observed that the president was embittered by the Convention outcome. Ibid., p. 691.

101. O'Toole, *The Moralist*, pp. 464–465. Lodge reported, "It was pushed to the front and kept there throughout the whole campaign. It was the predominant issue and completely overshadowed all others. . . . The League of Nations was the one question above all others which the people wished to hear discussed. Mr. Wilson desired and had demanded an appeal to the people. That appeal was duly made and fully met and the result is history." Lodge, *The Senate,* p. 210.

102. In most Southern states, Harding received around 30 percent of the vote. He got 49.3 percent in Kentucky. However, his total in Mississippi was 14 percent and in South Carolina, he got 4 percent.

103. "Support for his own candidacy presented itself almost every day, as the house on S Street became a mecca for liberals." Berg, p. 722.

Chapter 6

A Tradition Interpreted

Calvin Coolidge (1928)

Calvin Coolidge became the 30th President of the United States on August 2, 1923, after the death in office of his predecessor, Warren Harding. The following year, he won a full term with a resounding general election victory. Coolidge prevailed with 54 percent of the popular vote, against nearly 29 percent for Democrat John W. Davis. Senator Robert LaFollette, running on a Progressive Party ticket captured almost 17 percent. In the Electoral College, Coolidge won 382 votes, against 136 for Davis and thirteen for LaFollette. The president was victorious in every state outside the old South, with the exception of LaFollette's home state of Wisconsin.

Coolidge had served 19 months of Harding's unexpired term, far shorter than the 42 months that Roosevelt had been president after the McKinley assassination. Should that partial term, in addition to his full four years, be construed as constituting two terms, prejudicing his renomination in 1928? Coolidge thought not. In his autobiography, he wrote, "While I am in favor of continuing the long-established custom of the country in relation to a third term for a President, yet I do not think that the practice applies to one who has succeeded to part of a term as Vice President. Others might argue that it does, but I doubt if the country would so consider it."[1]

Another eminent Republican figure also took this view. Charles Evans Hughes, the party's 1916 nominee, and former Supreme Court Justice and Secretary of State, asserted that the incomplete term Coolidge served should not constitute a barrier to the president's further election. In the May 21, 1927, *Washington Evening Star*, which carried the banner "Lindbergh in Paris," there appeared a story by the paper's political reporter, Gould Lincoln. Its headline read "Hughes Supports Coolidge for 1928: Leaders Consider His Stand as Political Utterance of Utmost Significance." Wrote Lincoln,

"His assertion that Mr. Coolidge will be re-nominated and re-elected indicates that he does not consider that the third-term issue will be a real obstacle either in the nominating convention or in the general election. Coming from an authority on American government of the eminence of Mr. Hughes, this opinion doubtless will have no little effect upon public opinion."[2]

Members of the Republican National Committee seemed to agree. In the spring of 1927, the *Star*, then the capital's leading newspaper, surveyed how RNC committee men and committee women saw the third-term issue. It asked three questions: "1. In your opinion, would another term of office for President Coolidge constitute a 'third term' as the phrase is generally understood? 2. In your opinion, would the so-called 'third term' issue be a serious obstacle either to the nomination or re-election of President Coolidge in 1928? 3. In your opinion, is President Coolidge the logical candidate of the Republican Party in 1928?" Overwhelmingly, the committee members refused to construe a Coolidge run in 1928 as a third-term candidacy. They also opined that the two-term tradition would present no meaningful barrier to his reelection.[3]

None of the respondents was more outspoken than Charles Hilles of New York, who replied, "If Mr. Coolidge had served for the practical equivalent of two terms, our devotion to tradition might make a candidacy for further service of doubtful propriety; but it would be proof of idolatrous devotion to tradition to attack him after less than six years of service, during only four of which he served in his own right. It would be a foolish taboo."[4]

The national committee members had on their mind winning the next election, and no candidate was more likely to produce a good result than Coolidge. However, there were also some prominent dissenters. Chief among them was Columbia University President Nicholas Murray Butler, who believed that what mattered was the number of times a president took the oath. Coolidge had taken it twice. Thus, Butler argued that if Coolidge ran in 1928, he would be seeking a third term and, on that basis, would be defeated. Butler predicted the president would not run.[5]

Progressive elements within the Republican Party, remnants of the movement that nominated Theodore Roosevelt in 1912, formed the Anti-Third Term League. Launched on May 29, 1928, and based in New York, it began operations by sending 10,000 letters to Republicans seeking recruits to the cause. In part, the letter read,

> The Republican Party faces a grave danger. Should it nominate a candidate for President for a third consecutive term, it would violate a sacred tradition of the country and place itself in the attitude of repudiating one of its fundamental principles. . . . If the Republican Party should nominate a candidate for a third consecutive term, all other issues would be lost sight of in the campaign.

The letter predicted that, "the party would be accused of trying to set up a dictatorship." The League did not organize around any alternative nominee, but simply oppose a Coolidge nomination on principle.[6]

On August 2, 1927, on the fourth anniversary of his accession to the presidency, Coolidge was in Rapid City, South Dakota. At a press conference, he handed reporters a set of notes, each of which carried an identical message: "I do not choose to run for President in 1928." In response to questions, the president would not comment further.[7]

Many political observers had expected Coolidge to seek reelection. Thus, his announcement came as a shock. Friend and foe struggled to interpret it. As the *Washington Evening Star* reported, "Instead of clarifying the situation as the time approaches for active campaigning to get underway for the 1928 national conventions, the action of Mr. Coolidge brought a vast outpouring of opinions which graphically illustrated the uncertainty in the minds of both friends and opponents of the administration."[8]

Many observers imagined that Coolidge was actually open to and angling for a draft.[9] Such a strategy would showcase popular demand, and mitigate criticism that the candidate was breaching the two-term tradition.[10] Thus, they did not necessarily accept Coolidge's terse statement as his final word on the subject.

As political commentator David Lawrence noted, on the day after the statement, "President Coolidge literally means what he said when he announced that he did not 'choose to run for the presidency in 1928' and thus means also that he has placed squarely before the Republican Party the decision of whether he shall be drafted at the next Republican national convention to be the nominee for the presidency." Mr. Lawrence continued, "He knew that if the Republican Party did choose him by acclamation, the responsibility for the 'third term' would be on the Republican Party itself, and if the Republican Party was victorious at the polls. . . . the decision would then be the public opinion of the United States as expressed by the majority in a referendum."[11]

Confusion lingered. A month after Coolidge's announcement, the *Washington Evening Star* carried the front page headline, "Republicans Hold President Still 1928 Possibility." Under the byline of its political reporter Gould Lincoln, the article stated,

> The Republican preconvention campaign is in a state of suspended animation. The reason for this is simple. Leader after leader of the Republican Party has publicly announced that he does not consider that President Coolidge has eliminated himself from the presidential race by his 'I do not choose to run' statement. . . . It has become increasingly apparent that unless the President makes it crystal clear that he will not have the nomination and make the race under any circumstances, the chances are he will be re-nominated.

On the other hand, it was possible that the laconic president meant what he said. With a potential vacuum at hand, aspirants, such as Secretary of Commerce Herbert Hoover, began contemplating their own candidacies. Hoover, who hoped to run in 1928 if Coolidge retired, but who refused to challenge the president, was among many Republican leaders confused by the announcement. In August 1927, Hoover was meeting at Bohemian Grove in northern California with his key advisers. "Like so many weaving spiders, they gathered in camp to spin out theories as to what Coolidge meant by his statement. Was he through with politics? Was he putting the onus on his party to enlist him for another term? Was there some connotation to the phrase 'I do not choose' that only New Englanders understood?"[12]

Third-term issues aside, there were other factors that might persuade Coolidge to retire. In his memoirs, the president expressed concern that another term would damage his health and his wife's. "Although my own health has been practically perfect, yet the duties are very great and ten years would be a very heavy strain. It would be especially long for the mistress of the White House. Mrs. Coolidge has long been in more than usual good health, but I doubt if she could have stayed there for ten years without some danger of impairment of her strength."[13]

Moreover, Professor Robert E. Gilbert of Northeastern University argues that the president suffered from acute depression following the 1924 death of his son, Calvin. The second of two children, the sixteen-year old died from infection after getting a blister from playing tennis on the White House lawn. According to Gilbert, "The President was overwhelmed with a deep and enduring grief. Both the American Psychiatric Association and the National Institutes of Health have specified symptoms of a major depressive episode. These include hypersomnia or insomnia, changes in appetite, decreased energy, feelings of guilt, recurrent thoughts of death, indecisiveness, loss of interest in nearly all activities, complaints of bodily indispositions, increased irritability, spitefulness and suspiciousness, deterioration in work performance. After his son's death, Calvin Coolidge showed signs of all of these symptoms. He began to sleep as many as fifteen hours out of every twenty-four and ate incessantly, sometimes to the point of abdominal distress. He complained of exhaustion and of feeling much older than his years."[14]

Coolidge's own words strongly hint at his depression.

> We do not know what might have happened to him under other circumstances, but if I had not been President, he would not have raised a blister on his toe, which resulted in blood poisoning, playing lawn tennis in the South Grounds. In his suffering, he was asking me to make him well. I could not. When he went, the power and the glory of the Presidency went with him. . . . I do not know why such a price was exacted for occupying the White House.[15]

Coolidge's father died two years later, in 1926. The President was unable to be with him as he passed away. Coolidge's comment was similarly grim. "It costs a great deal to be President," he lamented.[16]

Coolidge's biographer, Amity Shlaes, observes that the president was experiencing exhaustion and burnout from more than four years on the job.[17] In his autobiography, Coolidge states, "The Presidential office takes a heavy toll of those who occupy it and those who are dear to them. While we should not refuse to spend and be spent in the service of our country, it is hazardous to attempt what we feel is beyond our strength to accomplish."[18]

Coolidge was also committed to limited government and restrained political power. As he expresses it, "A President should not only not be selfish, but he ought to avoid the appearance of selfishness. The people would not have confidence in a man that appeared to be grasping for office." Extended tenure, he wrote, would diminish a president's capacity to act in the public interest. "It is difficult for men in high office to avoid the malady of self-delusion. They are constantly surrounded by worshipers. . . . They live in an artificial atmosphere of adulation and exaltation which sooner or later impairs their judgment."[19]

Coolidge believed that the natural rhythm of politics diminishes the effectiveness of presidents as their second terms wore along.

> It is necessary for the head of the nation to differ with many people who are honest in their opinions. As his term progresses, the number who are disappointed accumulates. Finally, there is so large a body who have lost confidence in him that he meets a rising opposition which make his efforts less effective.[20]

Term limits were in the public interest, Coolidge felt. "The chances of having wise and faithful public service are increased by a change in the presidential office after a moderate length of time."[21] By retiring when he did, before he lost touch with the people and his presidency became stale, Coolidge would vindicate these values.

Notwithstanding all this, the president seemed to have left matters open. "I do not choose to run," was not exactly an unequivocal, "Shermanesque" renunciation.[22] What if a draft materialized? The president kept both his party and would-be aspirants guessing. As Herbert Hoover's biographer, Kenneth Whyte, notes, "To ascertain the President's plans, Hoover visited Coolidge twice in 1927, after the announcement, and again on the eve of the Convention in 1928. During these visits, Coolidge encouraged Hoover's candidacy, but never ruled out his own.

Coolidge would remain silent all the way through the Convention, behaving like a man who hoped for a deadlock so he could be drafted for another term."[23]

"Silent Cal" remained reticent. "I never stated or formulated in my own mind what I should do under the circumstances," he writes, adding, "but I was determined not to have that contingency arise."[24]

Coolidge dispatched his secretary, Everett Sanders, to the Republican Convention, then meeting in Kansas City. Sanders carried instructions the President wanted communicated to state delegations that they should not vote for Coolidge. It speaks to the ambiguity of his 1927 statement, and the various interpretations given it, that Coolidge could write of his instructions to delegates, "Had I not done so, I am told, I should have been nominated."[25]

Thus, Coolidge appears to have wanted to leave the door to nomination ajar. He announced he would not seek another term, claimed he did not want to be nominated, and maneuvered to avoid being confronted with a proffered nomination. But he did not instruct Everett to say that he would decline the nomination if the delegates insisted on offering it to him. Indeed, in his autobiography, Coolidge wrote, "The report that he had talked with me on the telephone after his arrival, and I had told him I would not accept if nominated, was a pure fabrication."[26] Coolidge foreclosed nothing, and gave himself room to pivot if the Convention insisted on running him. As Kenneth Whyte comments, "Chief Justice Taft, one of the few White House intimates, had no doubt that Coolidge wanted to be re-nominated in 1928."[27]

The possibility that Coolidge wished to keep alive was one his opponents acted preemptively to kill. One of them was Senator Robert LaFollette, Jr. Elected to the Senate on September 29, 1925, to fill a vacancy created by the death of his father, "Young Bob" shared his dad's progressive politics, and proved to be an ongoing irritant to the incumbent Republican president.

Although Coolidge had served only a portion of Harding's term, if elected again in 1928, he would be the longest serving president ever. LaFollette was troubled about the implications he claimed this presented for constitutional government.[28] On January 31, 1928, the Wisconsin senator introduced S. Res. 128, to express the Sense of the Senate that the two-term tradition must be observed.

The first clause of the resolution was identical to the 1875 Springer Resolution the House had passed to deter Grant from seeking a third term in 1876.[29] It read:

> Resolved, That it is the sense of the Senate that the precedent established by Washington and other Presidents of the United States in retiring from the presidential office after their second term has become, by universal concurrence, a part of our republican system of government, and that any departure from this time-honored custom would be unwise, unpatriotic, and fraught with peril to our free institutions.[30]

LaFollette also added a second clause, aimed at boxing in Coolidge.[31] It read:

> Resolved, that the Senate commends observance of this precedent by the President.[32]

The 1875 Springer Resolution, which served as LaFollette's model, passed the House rapidly, without debate. LaFollette's proposal would not move so easily. The Senate considered it during three session days. The resolution was debated briefly on Tuesday, February 7, 1928, dominated the session of Thursday, February 9, and was subject to a last round of debate, amendments, and final disposition on Friday, February 10.[33]

LaFollette scholar, Patrick Maney, describes the GOP dilemma. "The resolution created a problem for Senate Republicans. If they voted against it, they would pass up the opportunity to commend their president. Worse yet, they would leave themselves open to charges that they did not believe Coolidge when he said he would not seek another term. If they supported it, they would go on record as opposed to his re-nomination, and some still hoped he would run again."[34]

LaFollette denied that his resolution cast aspersions on the president. Given the August 2 disclaimer, and Coolidge's reinforcement of that statement in December 6, 1927, remarks before the Republican National Committee, LaFollette argued the paragraph should be understood as commending the president for fealty to the two-term tradition.[35] Walsh read the language differently, as an attempt to box Coolidge in. "It suggests a fear that in an emergency, the President may change his mind and the Senate begs him not to do so."[36]

Senator Simeon Fess (R-OH), another Coolidge ally, took the Floor to oppose LaFollette and to contest the wisdom of term limits. Newspapers had identified Fess as conspiring to draft Coolidge and positioning the president to acquiesce. During the Floor debate, against repeated taunts from Democrats, Fess insisted that Coolidge's disclaimer was sincere, and that the president was not concocting a campaign, but that it would nonetheless be proper for him to be nominated if the party demanded it.[37] Fess explained, "All I can say is that, in light of that statement, to my mind meaning that he does not want to run in 1928, in case the convention should tender him the nomination when he does not want it, when he does not seek it, when he has made it known to everybody that he does not want it, there would be no honor in his not accepting it."

In the Constitutional Convention, Fess noted, the Framers did not term limit any federal officeholder, Fess noted. As a result, many Members of Congress accumulated substantial seniority. Fess thought this had proven to be in the public interest. "As we believe that unlimited tenure in this body captures experience and capitalizes ability, so it seems to me it is equally true in the case of the President." Fess went on, "It would be better for us to continue the practice of not limiting tenure, except by a vote of the people."[38]

Fess believed that because Coolidge had served only nineteen months of Harding's term, it was too short a period to apply the two-term limit. Senator Borah disagreed, asserting that Coolidge had been able to run for election in 1924 on the basis of his performance after Harding died.

Thus, Borah asserted, "My opinion is that the construction which would be placed on the tradition . . . would be that if the party had held office twice or held the term, whether long or short, and exercised the powers of the presidency, he would be regarded as having two terms." Fess was non-plussed. "Even if he had served but one day?" Finding no way to draw a line, Borah replied, "Even had he served but one day."[39] If a president had taken the oath twice, Borah concluded, he had served two terms.

Although he believed in the desirability of the two-term tradition, Borah said he would not support constitutional amendment. If the custom were to remain in force, it should be because the voters demanded it, and for no other reason. "I am perfectly willing to leave it to the judgment of the people of the electorate," articulated the senator. "I would not write it into the Constitution of the United States."[40]

Borah acknowledged that emergencies could arise "in which the people would judge it better to have the president for the third time than to change under the circumstances." He imagined a situation in which the Civil War had begun near the end of Lincoln's second term rather than at the outset of the first. "The American people would have insisted on his being President again, and he would have been President."[41]

The senator did not think such emergency conditions existed in 1928, so he did not support a third term for Coolidge. However, he wanted to preserve for voters, then and for all time, the right to decide that question for themselves.

As he summed it up, "I am perfectly willing to leave it to the people. . . . In other words, I would not write it into the Constitution of the United States. I would leave it a tradition."[42] Almost two decades later, Democrats opposed to the Twenty-second Amendment would fully embrace this argument.

Borah was by no means alone in this thinking. Senator David Reed (R-PA) was unwilling to put term limits in the Constitution.[43] In particular, he worried about how to construe partial terms, and uniformly applying a rigid formula to them. Rather than have Congress draw an arbitrary line, Reed deferred to voter judgment.

Like Borah, Reed believed that emergencies might justify exemptions. One such example, Reed cited, was Reconstruction, which occurred after Lincoln's death, and which suffered from problems Lincoln might have solved. "I think we can all agree that it would have been of infinite benefit to all our people, in all probability, if President Lincoln served three full successive terms instead of one term and a few weeks. Had he been in office for eight years longer, most of the agony of Reconstruction and the unwisdom of the Reconstruction policies would, in all probability, been avoided. There may be exceptions, as I think there was an exception in that case. The people can be trusted to say whether the circumstances of any particular case justify a departure from this tradition." Thus, Reed asserted, "I do not believe that, as a general rule, it would be wise to put this provision into the Constitution."[44]

Meanwhile, what would the Senate do about the LaFollette resolution? Senator Fess remained deeply troubled over the words "unpatriotic and fraught with peril to our free institutions." Harrison asked whether Fess would support the resolution if the Senate struck those words from it. For Fess, that was not enough. He felt the Senate should not affirm a political custom, even if it did so with less pejorative language. "There may arise cases where the peril would come in not departing from the tradition," answered the senator.

Fess dismissed the LaFollette resolution as simply a political document aimed at the 1928 election, rather than a statement of constitutional theory. "The Senator from Wisconsin . . . made perfectly clear that one of the reasons for the introduction of the resolution is a fear that the President might be a candidate under certain circumstances, and he thinks the resolution, if adopted, would at least assist in preventing that happening. I would not vote for any suggestion of that kind at all," said Fess.[45]

As the session on February 9 wound down, LaFollette took the Floor. He had intended to commend Coolidge for observing the two-term limit, until he listened to that day's debate. Fess' remark that Coolidge had not foreclosed accepting nomination, and could honorably take it, had caused LaFollette to rethink his position. "I wish to say that if the construction placed upon the President's language by the Senator from Ohio is correct, then I agree that the second paragraph should be stricken from the resolution."

LaFollette persisted, "I felt that if I offered this resolution without the provision commending the President for his action in observance of the anti-third-term tradition, I would be subject to the charge that I did not take his statement as having been made in good faith, but for the purpose of subterfuge and deceit."[46] Thus, if the language was not removed, the Senate would be commending the President for a step he had not taken. When it came time for amendments, LaFollette proposed deleting that paragraph. The Senate agreed.

Fess told the Senate that Coolidge had decided not to be an active candidate for personal reasons that were fundamentally similar to Washington's, rather than as a declaration of constitutional principle. "So far as I can learn from what the President says to me, he wants to leave the office on the 4th of March, 1929; he is tired of the office and does not care to be a candidate."

This comment prompted Senator Walsh to respond, "The Senator has made a statement which I have heard no one else in the country make. He tells us that when the President made the statement, as he did on two occasions, it was his opinion that the President did not have under consideration at all the anti-third-term tradition. I understand that statement to have been made by the Senator from Ohio. Am I correct?" Fess' reply was stark. "I am morally certain that the third-term idea had nothing whatever to do with the President's statement."[47]

Walsh was incredulous. "It is my opinion that the President did have in mind the anti-third-term tradition and that he declined to be a candidate because of that tradition. I think the Senator's statement is not fair to the President."

But Fess was sure he knew better. "I think if the Senator will make a little investigation, he may have that opinion modified."[48]

Senator Pat Harrison (D-MS)[49] claimed that Republican opposition to the resolution was hypocritical. Almost all senators who had spoken against it supported Taft over Roosevelt in 1912. When they had done so, most referenced the custom against third terms. "In their speeches, I dare say—and I call upon them now to disclaim it if it is not true—they went from one end of their States to the other saying that Roosevelt should not be elected because it would be in contravention of the traditions of the Government and the precedent established by Washington, Madison, and Jefferson."[50]

Senator Thomas Heflin of Alabama reinforced Harrison, and raised the stakes.[51] "The two-term tradition is as much a part if this Government as if it were written into the Constitution or the law so far as the sanction of the American people is concerned," the Senator insisted. "They believe in it and they want it respected."[52]

The Senate was obligated to pass the resolution, argued Heflin. Failure to do so would imply that the Senate had been indifferent to a central feature of the unwritten Constitution. "The Senate will have shown the country that it has no conviction on the subject and no desire to prevent a step toward monarchy in America."

Previewing the very arguments Franklin Roosevelt's opponents would make a decade later, Heflin added, "A President with the power to fill the offices of this country, to direct legislation, to veto it, to bestow favors upon powerful interests can build a machine that would be almost impregnable. He could, by using his power, nominate himself for a second term and also for a third term."[53]

After debate wound down, the voting began. It was a debacle for Coolidge's allies. Connecticut Senator Hiram Bingham[54] moved to refer the resolution to committee. He cited three reasons. The first was that the committee could determine whether such a hortatory resolution was appropriate for the Senate to consider. Second, he wanted the committee's expertise on whether, if proper, the language should be modified to allow for cases of national emergency. Third, the committee could consider whether the proper course would be to amend the Constitution.[55] Bingham's motion failed 52 to 27.

Senator Matthew Neely (D-WV)[56] proposed adding a proviso after LaFollette's second clause. It read, "That if the President should change his mind and choose to become a candidate for re-election, the last paragraph of this resolution shall be held void and of no effect." The Senate rejected the amendment by voice vote.[57]

Fess proposed an amendment to strike the second clause altogether. LaFollette responded, "To my astonishment, and I think to the astonishment of the country, the President's closest political friends in the Senate, led by the Senator from Ohio, object to the clause of commendation on the ground that the President did not, by the express language which he employed, foreclose his acceptance of a nomination if it were tendered him by the convention. In view of the sources from which this objection emanates, and in view of the authentic character which must be given their interpretation of the President's intent, I accept the amendment to the resolution striking out the concluding paragraph."[58] Thus, the Senate removed the language.

Fess sought to amend the resolution so that it applied to two elective terms, which would amount to exempting Coolidge from its application in 1928. Heflin countered that the amendment would have the effect of allowing a president to serve eleven years and eleven months. "Yes," responded Fess, "and he might serve eight years and one day, too." The amendment was defeated 73 to 6.[59]

Bingham proposed an amendment to make an exception to the two-term tradition in the case of emergencies. The Senate rejected the amendment by voice vote.[60]

Fess moved to delete "unpatriotic and fraught with peril to our national institutions." By voice vote, the Senate refused the amendment.[61]

Fess proposed to strike the words "unpatriotic and fraught with peril to our free institutions." The amendment also failed on a voice vote.[62]

As placed before the Senate for a vote, the LaFollette resolution read:

> Resolved, That it is the sense of the Senate that the precedent established by Washington and other Presidents of the United States in retiring from the presidential office after their second term has become, by universal concurrence, a part of our republican system of government, and that any departure from this time-honored custom would be unwise, unpatriotic, and fraught with peril to our free institutions.

By 56 to 26, the Senate agreed to the resolution. The fifty-six supporters included eighteen Republicans, principally from the progressive wing, thirty-seven Democrats, and one Senator from the Farmer-Labor Party. The twenty-six opponents included twenty-two Republicans and four Democrats.[63]

Resolutions like LaFollette's in the Senate in 1928 or Springer's in the House in 1875 have no legal effect, but they are a way that the Senate and House can express themselves on matters of public consequence. Without question, S. Res. 128 drew support for many different reasons, including support for a custom that by then was deeply engrained in America's political culture. While Congress had never seen fit to amend the constitution, both Houses were now on record as reinforcing the two-term tradition against presidents who might think to challenge it. It was the last time either chamber would speak to the issue until Franklin Roosevelt ran in 1940 for a third term. By then, the roles of the parties reversed. The Republicans, especially the Old Guard element, treated the two-term tradition as sacrosanct, while many Democrats breezed right by it. The old axiom once more proved true: where one stands depends on where one sits.[64]

On February 21, 1927, the day before LaFollette proposed the first version of his resolution, Representative Benjamin Fairchild (R-NY)[65] introduced a constitutional amendment that would have resolved the two-term tradition in Coolidge's favor. The Fairchild proposal read, "In addition to the prohibitions mentioned in subdivision 7 of section 1 of Article II of the Constitution, no person shall be eligible to the office of President who has previously served two terms whether by election, or by succession due to the removal, death, resignation, or inability of the President where the term by succession shall have continued for a period of two years or more."

Intending to give Coolidge breathing space to accept nomination, Fairchild would have permitted a person to seek the presidency who had succeeded to the office, served one day less than half of his predecessor's term, and then been elected once in his own right. Although the verbiage differs from the text of the Twenty-second Amendment, the concept is essentially identical.[66] With little time left in the session, the House took no action on Fairchild's legislation, and on March 3, 1927, the 69th Congress adjourned.

NOTES

1. Calvin Coolidge, *The Autobiography of Calvin Coolidge* (Plymouth, Vermont: The Calvin Coolidge Memorial Foundation, 1989), p. 240 (original edition published 1929).

2. Gould Lincoln, "Hughes Supports Coolidge for 1924," *Washington Evening Star*, May 21, 1927, p. 1.

3. Gould Lincoln, "President is Held Strongest GOP Possibility of 1928," *Washington Evening Star*, April 20, 1927, p. 1.

4. Lincoln, p. 1.

5. "The Third Term Tradition in American Politics (1927)," *Editorial Research Reports* 1927 (Vol. 1), Washington, DC: CQ Press. http:/library.cqpress.com/cqresearcher/cqresrre1927031900 (accessed October 8, 2018).

6. "The Anti-third Term League," *Washington Evening Star*, May 30, 1927, p. 8.

7. Amity Shlaes, *Coolidge* (New York: HarperCollins Publishers, 2011), pp. 381–382.

8. "President Confuses Politicians by Employing Word 'Choose'; Out of Race, Associates Declare," *Washington Evening Star*, August 3, 1927, p. 1.

9. "After all, Coolidge had often played coy before. It might be his way of timing his campaign. Coolidge was simply saying that if he ran, it would be on the people's vote, not his own." Shlaes, p. 382.

10. Ulysses Grant had a similar idea in 1880. Theodore Roosevelt floated such thinking in 1912 and in the run-up to his anticipated 1920 campaign. On the same basis, Woodrow Wilson hoped for a draft at the 1920 Democratic Convention. In 1940, Franklin Roosevelt tried to manipulate the Democratic Convention to draft him, believing that it would neutralize criticism about the third term.

11. David Lawrence, "President Places Decision on Party," *Washington Evening Star*, August 3, 1927, p. 1.

12. Kenneth Whyte, *Hoover: An Extraordinary Life in Extraordinary Times* (New York: Alfred A. Knopf, 2017), p. 323.

13. Coolidge, pp. 240–241.

14. Robert E. Gilbert, "Calvin Coolidge: The Disabled Chief Executive," www.historynewsnetwork.org (accessed September 20, 2018). See also, Robert E. Gilbert, *The Tormented President: Calvin Coolidge, Death, and Clinical Depressions* (Westport, Connecticut: Praeger, 2003). President Herbert Hoover's biographer, Kenneth Whyte observes, "Coolidge grew distracted and listless, sleeping more than twelve hours a day. He was given to bouts of rage and irascibility, aimed at his wife, his Cabinet secretaries, and even his barber. Grace Coolidge observed that after Calvin Jr.'s death, her husband never regained his 'zest for living.'" Whyte, p. 302.

15. Coolidge, p. 190. In a 1992 interview, the president's first son, John, stated, "Calvin was my father's favorite. It hurt him terribly." Douglas Martin, "John Coolidge, Guardian of President's Legacy. Dies at 93," *New York Times*, June 4, 2000. www.nytimes.com (accessed September 23, 2018).

16. Coolidge, p. 192. The President's mental state was not helped by losing command of his own political destiny. Instead of being able to maneuver a draft, Coolidge saw Herbert Hoover amass growing support. "The President was in a miserable state of mind as the convention approached. His bouts of rage were more frequent. His doctor saw signs of 'mental disturbance' and diagnosed a temporary derangement. While his unhappiness undoubtedly owed more to the loss of his son than any other factor, it did not help that Hoover was elbowing him toward the wing." Whyte, p. 340.

17. Shlaes, p. 385.

18. Coolidge, p. 239.

19. Ibid., p. 241.
20. Ibid.
21. Ibid.
22. The term "Shermanesque" relates to an oft-cited quotation from General William Tecumsah Sherman, who disclaimed interest in running for president over a series of late Nineteenth Century elections. "If nominated, I will not run. If elected, I will not serve," Sherman is reputed to have said. Charles Bracelen Flood, *Grant and Sherman: The Friendship that Won the Civil War* (New York: Farrer, Strauss, and Giroux, 2005), pp. 293–294.
23. Whyte, pp. 339–341.
24. Coolidge, p. 244.
25. Ibid.
26. Coolidge, p. 244.
27. Whyte, p. 323.
28. "Believing the chief executive to be the 'most powerful individual in the world,' he warned that 'establishment of the precedent that one man may continue to wield this power for longer than eight years would make a definite step toward the abrogation of popular government." Patrick J. Maney, *Young Bob: A Biography of Robert M. LaFollette, Jr.* (Madison: Wisconsin Historical Society Press, 2003), p. 56.
29. LaFollette was not the first Member of Congress to attempt a reprise of the Springer Resolution. In a 1912 effort to forestall a comeback for Theodore Roosevelt, Representative James Luther Slayden (D-TX) introduced a similar resolution, but it received no action. Lingley, p. 316.
30. *Congressional Record*, January 31, 1928, p. 2253.
31. The Senator believed that "financial and industrial interests" would demand Coolidge's nomination, that Coolidge had not actually closed the door, and that the president would accept the nomination after an orchestrated draft. Maney, p. 57.
32. Ibid.
33. "Senate Declares Against Third Term By 56 to 26 Vote," *New York Times*, February 11, 1928, p. A1.
34. Maney, p. 57.
35. *Congressional Quarterly,* p. 2781.
36. Ibid.
37. Ibid., February 9, 1928, p. 2788. For example, Senator Joseph Robinson pushed Fess hard on colluding with Coolidge to evade the disclaimer. "Why did the Senator seek to coerce, or to persuade, if he prefers that term, the President into violating his construction of his proper relationship to the campaign of 1928? Why did the Senator from Ohio try to induce him to run when he said he did not want to?" Ibid., p. 2786. In a similar vein, Senator Heflin asked Fess, "Does the Senator believe that when the President said, 'I do not choose to run,' he meant 'I will not accept the nomination if tendered me?'" Ibid., p. 2788.
38. Ibid.
39. *Congressional Record*, February 9, 1928, p. 2784.
40. Ibid.
41. Ibid.

42. Ibid.
43. David Reed served in the Senate from 1922 to 1935.
44. *Congressional Record*, February 10, 1928, p. 2832.
45. *Congressional Record*, February 9, 1928, p. 2789.
46. Ibid., p. 2790.
47. Ibid.
48. Ibid.
49. Pat Harrison served from 1911 to 1919 in the House and in the Senate from 1919 to his death in 1941.
50. *Congressional Record*, February 10, 1928, p. 2837.
51. Thomas Heflin was in the House from 1904 to 1920 and in the Senate from 1920 to 1931.
52. *Congressional Record,* February 10, 1928, p. 2838.
53. Ibid.
54. Hiram Bingham III was a senator from 1927 to 1933.
55. *Congressional Record*, February 10, 1928, p. 2839. Coolidge ally, Samuel Shortridge (R-CA), argued in support of Bingham's motion, "I think it would be wise to refer this resolution to the Committee on the Judiciary; and that committee, perhaps sympathizing with the purpose of this resolution, might suggest and report an amendment to the Constitution." Ibid., p. 2831. Shortridge was a senator from 1921 to 1933.
56. Matthew Neely had an extensive and complicated history in Congress. He served in the House from 1913 to 1921 and again from 1945 to 1947. He was a senator from 1923 to 1929, again from 1931 to 1941, and finally from 1949 until his death in 1958.
57. *Congressional Record,* February 10, 1928, p. 2840.
58. Ibid.
59. *Congressional Record*, February 10, 1928, p. 2841.
60. Ibid.
61. Ibid., p. 2842.
62. Ibid., p. 2841.
63. Ibid., p. 2842.
64. In a 1916 article appearing in the *Texas Review,* Charles R. Lingley chronicled this venerable phenomenon. He noted that progressive Republicans who opposed the possibility of a Grover Cleveland candidacy in 1896, because it would contradict the two-term tradition, supported Theodore Roosevelt in 1912. In both cases, there would not be a third consecutive term, so the facts were similar. The differences were political. Lingley, pp. 307–308.
65. Benjamin L. Fairchild served in the House from 1917 to 1919, 1921 to 1923, and 1925 to 1927.
66. The Fairchild proposal read, "In addition to the prohibitions mentioned in subdivision 7 of section 1 of Article II of the Constitution, no person shall be eligible to the office of President who has previously served two terms whether by election, or by succession due to the removal, death, resignation, or inability of the President where the term by succession shall have continued for a period of two years or more."

Chapter 7

A Tradition Breached

The Third Term of Franklin Delano Roosevelt (1940)

Calvin Coolidge did not run in 1928. In that year's presidential election, Republican Herbert Hoover, Coolidge's Secretary of Commerce, kept his party's winning streak intact, prevailing over Democrat Al Smith, the governor of New York. Smith was the first Roman Catholic nominated for president by a major party. It seems certain that his religion cost him a number of Southern states.[1] Virginia, North Carolina, Tennessee, Texas, and Florida all voted Republican, as almost none had done since Reconstruction.[2] Hoover won nearly 60 percent of the popular vote and forty states, trouncing Smith in the Electoral College 444 to 87.

Thereafter, the Great Depression, which began in 1929, generated an economic and political upheaval in the country. Republicans lost 52 House seats in the 1930 election, leaving them with a two-seat majority. However, Congress did not convene until March 4, 1931. Between November and March, there were several special elections in which Democrats were successful. Thus, by the time the new Congress met, Democrats had a one-seat margin in the House. Republicans lost six Senate seats in 1930, leaving them with a 50–46 majority. It seems safe to speculate that their losses that year would have been greater, but for the fact that only one-third of senators stand for election every two years.

Starting in 1932, Franklin Delano Roosevelt prevailed in four successive presidential elections, putting together a diverse political coalition that enabled Democrats to supplant Republicans as America's dominant party. Saddled with the blame for miserable economic conditions, Republicans had little prospect of reelecting Herbert Hoover as president in 1932. For seven decades since its formation, the Grand Old Party had dominated politics in most of the country. The Depression provoked a massive realignment. Roosevelt won forty-two of forty-eighty states in 1932 and prevailed in the

Electoral College 472 to 59. In the House of Representatives, Republicans dropped 101 seats; in the Senate, they lost a dozen.

Even though the party out of power usually becomes stronger after mid-term elections, Republican erosion accelerated in 1934. The GOP lost fourteen more seats in the House and another nine senators. Their political distress continued in 1936. The Republican presidential nominee, Kansas Governor Alf Landon, won only Maine and Vermont. There suffered further deterioration in Congress, with the loss for twelve more representatives and seven additional senators.

Following these three successive landslides, GOP membership was reduced to a mere eighty-eight in the House and sixteen in the Senate, the direst position for a minority party since the Civil War.[3] The Republican Party seemed on the brink of extinction.[4]

Thereafter, momentum shifted. A recession in 1937, a bruising struggle that same year over Roosevelt's effort to pack the Supreme Court, and a sense that the New Deal was running out of steam, opened the door to a strong off-year Republican comeback in 1938. The GOP gained seventy-two seats in the House of Representatives and seven in the Senate. The outlook for a Republican victory in the 1940 presidential appeared reasonably good, especially if FDR followed precedent and retired. In thirty-seven quadrennial elections until that time, no incumbent president had been a candidate for a third term, consecutive or otherwise.

However, even if he tried to break new ground, FDR might face the same third-term backlash that had damaged Grant in 1880 and Theodore Roosevelt in 1912. As 1940 approached, it was difficult to gauge how vexatious a problem it would be.

Then, the president stepped forward. Never renouncing interest in a third term, FDR maneuvered to block any other Democrat from emerging as a possible replacement. As international conditions worsened in the first half of 1940, a rationale to keep him on the job materialized.

As the presidential election year approached, a third term was far from a sure thing, even if Roosevelt wanted it. The demise of his plan to pack the Supreme Court, foreign policy conflicts with Congress over neutrality legislation,[5] the failure of his attempted 1938 purge of conservative Democrats,[6] broadly felt economic reversals,[7] and widespread Republican gains in the 1938 general elections,[8] all suggested a president on dwindling political reserves.

Republicans felt momentum moving in their direction. It was not blind optimism. Writing about opinion polls taken in December 1938 and again several months later, Roosevelt scholar John Jeffries reports, "A majority of those polled thought FDR would lose if he ran again for President, and in early 1939, only about one-third favored a third term for Roosevelt."[9]

One prospective Republican nominee was Manhattan District Attorney Thomas E. Dewey, only 38 years old in 1940. Dewey's rise had been meteoric. Already known as a crusading prosecutor, Dewey had come close to defeating Democratic New York Governor Herbert Lehman in the 1938 election, losing by just 100,000 votes out of nearly 4.7 million. Dewey actually outdistanced Lehman by more than 300,000 votes on ballots cast on the Republican and Democratic lines. Winning more than 400,000 votes on the American Labor Party line saved the incumbent.

Dewey's near-success propelled him onto the national stage. He oozed confidence, even arrogance, telling a journalist, "Don't you realize that Franklin Roosevelt is the easiest man in the world for me to beat?"[10]

Another leading candidate was Michigan Senator Arthur Vandenberg. A former newspaper editor, Vandenberg came to the Senate in 1928. During the 1930s, he had developed a reputation as a staunch opponent of the New Deal and a committed isolationist in foreign policy. Few senators were such ardent defenders of the neutrality laws.

The third prominent Republican was Ohio Senator Robert Taft. Elected to the Senate in 1938, Robert Alfonso Taft was the son of William Howard Taft, the 27th president and, later, Chief Justice. He provoked intense loyalty among party conservatives, was highly respected by his colleagues, and would later become the leader among Senate Republicans. A distant, generally aloof personality, Taft was less attractive to the broader electorate.[11]

Former President Herbert Hoover, crushed in the 1932 election, hoped for a comeback.[12] Of all the prospective candidates, none had more experience. Hoover imagined a deadlocked convention that might turn to him.[13]

Taft was the first of these Republicans formally to declare his candidacy, announcing in August 1939.[14] The eventual nominee, Indiana's Wendell Willkie, only emerged as a viable possibility late in the nominating process, virtually on the eve of the June 1940 Republican Convention itself.[15]

Among Democrats, the picture was murky. Would Roosevelt retire? No one knew. Would he anoint a successor? One could only speculate.

Vice President John Nance Garner, an outright opponent of a third term for Roosevelt, hoped to run for president.[16] FDR's principal rival for the 1932 nomination, Garner agreed to join the ticket after a deal brokered by William Randolph Hearst caused the California and Texas delegations to support Roosevelt in exchange for taking Garner for vice president. The deal cleared the way for Democrats to nominate Roosevelt on the fourth ballot.

A former speaker of the House and a thirty-year veteran of service in that chamber, Vice President Garner was helpful to FDR in moving early New Deal legislation through Congress. However, although Roosevelt and Garner served together for eight years, friendship and true partnership never materialized. Policy differences between them widened, especially after the president's failed attempt to pack the Supreme Court.[17] Writes FDR biographer Ted Morgan, "Cabinet meetings had become unpleasant, with FDR and Garner baiting each other."[18] Over time, their differences became open and obvious, with Garner emerging as a *de facto* leader of the conservative coalition in Congress.

Some Democrats seemed open to a Garner candidacy, certainly if Roosevelt were out of the picture. Some may have assumed, probably incorrectly, that Garner would foster continuation of Roosevelt's policies. The president, himself, was not deceived on this point.[19] Conservative elements, Garner among them, were still influential within the Democratic Party. If Roosevelt were gone, this faction could recapture control of a party they felt the New Deal had hijacked.[20]

An additional potential candidate was Postmaster General James Farley, chairman of the Democratic National Committee and instrumental in Roosevelt's two previous elections.[21] Farley was a Roman Catholic. Leading Catholic clergy, such as Cardinal George Mundelein of Chicago, worried about a repeat of that rejection and, in a July 1939 meeting, urged Farley not to run. It seems likely that the Cardinal, who had just dined with Roosevelt, was passing along a message from the president. Farley was not convinced, believing that anti-Catholic bias would not prove to be the barrier in 1940 that it had been to Al Smith in 1928.[22]

Garner and Farley were old political allies, and periodically discussed the 1940 nomination between themselves, each sizing up the other, while commiserating about Roosevelt. In early July 1939, Vice President Garner and Postmaster General Farley dined on Capitol Hill. He told Farley, "I want to let you know just where I stand and exactly how I feel. I mean on this third-term business. Jim, I can't support a third term and will fight any third term for the good of the party." Garner inquired as to Farley's position on the issue. Farley responded that he, too, looked negatively on a third term.[23]

On July 23, 1939, Farley told Roosevelt, "I'm sure Jack is not interested in being a candidate. He is willing to let his name be used if necessary, and only if necessary, as a candidate by those opposed to a third term."[24] Frustrated with Roosevelt's unwillingness to step aside, Garner formally declared his candidacy in December 1939.

Another prominent possibility was Secretary of State Cordell Hull, who could have been formidable. However, while Hull might have run if FDR had stepped aside, at no time did the Secretary signal a willingness to unseat him.

Yet further possibilities periodically mentioned in news reports included former Indiana Governor Paul McNutt,[25] House Speaker William Bankhead of Alabama, South Carolina Senator James F. Byrnes,[26] Administrator of the Reconstruction Finance Corporation Jesse Jones,[27] and Montana Senator Burton K. Wheeler.[28]

State Democratic leaders could only speculate on the president's intentions. Among them, support for a third-term candidacy began slowly to coalesce.[29] It did so because key Democrats believed prospects for the party in 1940 would improve with him on the ballot.[30] It was similar to the calculation that some Republican powers made about Grant in the run-up to the 1876 election.

The problem for would-be nominees was that Roosevelt had for several years "frozen the field" by failing to disclaim the possibility of running for a third term. To preserve his own options for the maximum time, he offered an array of confusing signals and misdirection about who he might otherwise support.[31] In such a climate, no other potential candidate could gain momentum.

For example, in 1938, Roosevelt encouraged Farley to seek the governorship of New York in that year's elections, claiming it would be a useful foundation on which to base a 1940 presidential candidacy. Notwithstanding the president's encouragement, bordering on insistence, Farley refused.[32] Then, on July 23, 1939, Roosevelt met with Farley and expressly disclaimed the possibility of a third term. In his memoirs, Farley recounts the conversation. "'Jim, I am going to tell you something I have never told another living soul.' Roosevelt dropped his voice to an impressive whisper. 'Of course, I will not run for a third term. Now I don't want you to pass this on to anyone, because it would make my role difficult if the decision were known prematurely.'" Farley pledged to keep the secret, only to be dismayed as Roosevelt quickly told the same story to others.[33]

Hull had a similar experience. He writes about a 1940 conversation with Roosevelt prior to the surrender of France. Then, as at other times, FDR seemed to promote Hull's candidacy. "As late as about June 20, 1940, when I saw the President at the White House, he again referred to the statement he had made at repeated intervals since October 1938, that he wanted me to be his successor. On this occasion, he still gave me no indication that he intended to run again, in fact, just the opposite."[34] Within ten days, Roosevelt would reverse course and actively discourage Hull.[35]

Such prevarications kept competitors off balance, while leaving the door open for FDR. As the president's son, Elliott, writes, "Father made a practice of dropping a few words of good cheer to most of them as part of his strategy of keeping everyone guessing."[36]

H. W. Brands recounts a conversation between Farley and Garner in the early months of 1940. "What's the Boss going to do?" Garner asked. "Your guess is as good as mine," Farley replied. Garner volunteered, "I guess he's going to run," and added, "Hell, he's fixed it so nobody else can run."[37]

As Burns remarks, "He had not only encouraged existing candidates to contend with one another, but had also adroitly enlarged the field so that potential opposition would be fragmented and thus more manageable."[38]

Eleanor Roosevelt hoped her husband would not be a candidate, and urged him to groom a capable successor. It was fruitless. "Franklin always smiled," she wrote, "and said he thought people had to prepare themselves, that all he could do was to give them opportunities and see how they worked out. I felt that he, without intending to do so, dominated the people around him and that so long as he was in the picture, it was very hard for anyone to rise to a position of prominence."[39] Dunn reflects, "No one else stood out, though several—Jack Garner, Burton Wheeler, Jim Farley, Paul McNutt, and Cordell Hull—hoped against all odds, for the nomination. And hope was about all they had, since they could not openly campaign or build a popular following so long as Roosevelt had not declared his intentions."[40]

Jim Farley grew fed up with all of FDR's dissembling. In a July 7, 1940, conversation with Roosevelt, he told the president he would seek the Democratic nomination. With candor and vehemence, he described the state of confusion Roosevelt had engineered. "Notwithstanding the fact that you have put all the other candidates out of the picture by maneuvering delegates into a state of mind where many feel they must nominate you whether or not you want the nomination, I am going to allow my name to go before the Convention."[41] Farley also informed the president of his resignation as party chairman and his refusal to manage the general election campaign in the event the Convention should nominate Roosevelt.[42]

Historian Charles Peters attributes Farley's decision to anger at Roosevelt backing away from a promise generally tendered five months earlier not to seek a third term, which Peters thinks would have opened the door to a Hull-Farley ticket, and mitigated the anti-Catholic sentiment that damaged Smith in 1928.[43] Putting to rest the belief that a Catholic could not win national office was one of Jim Farley's greatest priorities.

Burns asserts that FDR's refusal to commit was characteristic of a desire to postpone decisions until absolutely necessary to make them. "His method through most of his career was to keep open alternative lines of action," wrote Burns, "to shift from one line to another as conditions demanded, to protect his route to the rear in case he wanted to make a sudden retreat, and, foxlike, to cross and snarl his trail in order to hide his real intentions."[44]

The press was as mystified as the politicians about what Roosevelt would do. At the Gridiron Club dinner on December 9, 1939, he was in attendance as White House correspondents displayed an eight-foot papier-mâché statue of him shaped like a Sphinx, related to his refusal to disclose his 1940 plans.[45]

In his memoirs, Roosevelt's speechwriter and confidant, Sam Rosenman, describes three plausible reasons why the president could have decided to forego another term. Foremost among them was the weight of the two-term tradition. It could only be a negative, but how much of one? It had been nearly thirty years since Theodore Roosevelt had attempted it. No one had done so as the nominee of a major party. During the relative infancy of polling, the public's response was hard to gauge. And attitude could change amid fluid circumstances. "True, he had broken many traditions and precedents before," Rosenman noted, "but the third-term tradition was such deep-rooted one! He knew the political dangers of breaking it, and the political handicaps of a third-term candidacy."[46]

Indeed, there was the real possibility that longer service in the White House could complicate the president's legacy. The country was growing more conservative. During Roosevelt's second term, Congress had reasserted itself at his expense. Born in the Court-packing fight of 1937, a powerful coalition of Southern Democrats and Republicans had formed on Capitol Hill. Not without reason, Roosevelt worried about ideological backsliding. In February 1940, he said to his progressive ally, Senator George Norris, "Did you ever stop to think that if I should run and be elected I would have much more trouble with Congress in my third term and much more bitterness to contend with as a result of running for a third term than I ever had before."[47] Under such conditions, retirement seemed attractive.

FDR contemplated a change of pace.[48] Observed Rosenman, "He had felt the crushing physical and mental burdens that eight years in the White House could impose upon a President."[49]

At his home in Hyde Park, FDR could manage his Presidential Library, work on his memoirs, and comment periodically on current affairs. Indeed, he had signed a lucrative contract with *Collier's* magazine in January 1940 for a series of twenty-six articles over a three-year period, for which he would earn $75,000 annually.[50] The articles were to run after he left office. The wage was equivalent to what a president earned at the time.

Frances Perkins, FDR's longtime Secretary of Labor, was present at a 1940 conversation Roosevelt had with Dan Tobin of the Teamsters' Union. Tobin urged the president to stay on the job. Citing health, fatigue, and competing interests, Roosevelt demurred.

> No, Dan, I just can't do it. I've been here a long time. I am tired. I really am. And besides, I have to take care of myself. This sinus trouble I've got, the Washington climate makes it dreadful. . . . No, I can't be President again. I have to get over this sinus. I have to have a rest. I want to go home to Hyde Park. I want to take care of my trees. I have a big planting there, Dan. I want to make the farm pay. I want to finish my little house on the hill. I want to write history.[51]

In 1938, Roosevelt built Top Cottage, a private retreat adjacent to Springwood, his Hyde Park, New York, family home. In 1939, he laid the cornerstone of his Presidential Library, also at Springwood. Roosevelt's neighbor, Daisy Suckley, describes some of the preparations. "Every time he came to Hyde Park in the winter and spring of 1940, he brought large gobs of stuff—papers, documents, statues, presents—to be taken to the attic and sorted out for the library."[52]

While making these preparations, Roosevelt avoided making any early retirement announcement. Instead, he held open the possibility he might actually seek a third term, so what capacity he had to dominate politics and policy would not dissipate.[53]

Notwithstanding all this, there were weighty reasons why he should run, after all. A big one was that it would serve to perpetuate the socioeconomic transformation the President started. Far from the ideologically tight parties of the present era, 1930s Democrats ranged from highly conservative elements, to left-leaning activists, powerful unions, and big-city machines.[54] Electing another Democratic Administration to follow Roosevelt's would not necessarily mean continuity of New Deal policies, and even if a successor attempted them, he might not successfully work with contrarian coalitions in Congress. As we have seen, Roosevelt himself already worried about Congress veering right. How would a new president fare who had less prodigious political skills? As Ted Morgan observes, "He was afraid the reactionary South would control the convention and nominate a so-called middle-of-the-roader."[55]

FDR was determined that his successor be a liberal Democrat, philosophically in tune with the New Deal.[56] He must keep intact and energize the disparate coalition that had propelled him into office. As Roosevelt biographer Nathan Miller notes, "In January 1939, he announced that he could not support any Democrat who was not a New Dealer."[57] Thus, Roosevelt had been grooming Harry Hopkins, former head of the Works Progress Administration, and, increasingly, the president's confidant.

Hopkins' scholar, David Roll, drawing upon the adviser's notes, describes a spring 1938 conversation between Hopkins and Roosevelt about a possible Hopkins candidacy.

> Speaking of his own 'personal disinclination' and the opposition of Mrs. Roosevelt to his running for a third term in 1940, FDR ticked off the liabilities of the possible Democratic candidates for president. . . . Roosevelt said that if Hopkins could recover his health by 1940, he could head off Farley, secure the nomination, and get elected.[58]

In 1938, the president elevated Hopkins to the cabinet, appointing him as Secretary of Commerce, and made sure he was well-covered in the press. In his Pulitzer Prize winning book about the Roosevelt-Hopkins relationship, Robert Sherwood writes,

> There is no question that in 1938 Roosevelt did all he could—and that was a very great deal—to aid the Hopkins build-up. When the President was photographed

> at a baseball park or on the back platform of a train, or on a fishing cruise, he had Hopkins at his elbow. . . . It was plain to see that while Hopkins was receiving this preferred treatment, other potential candidates were not.[59]

However, Hopkins' physical condition proved too fragile to run for president.[60] With the Hopkins option unworkable, Roosevelt did not embrace anyone else.[61]

Rosenman writes, "He knew that a reactionary or conservative Democratic candidate would never receive the votes of labor, and that without the support of labor, a Democratic victory would be highly improbable."[62] None of the other active potential nominees seemed to fit the bill, Roosevelt thought, and he doubted that anyone who did could command sufficient support to secure the nomination.[63]

A second major reason to consider running was the dire world situation. The president had little faith that other Democrats could manage world affairs as well as he could.[64] By not disclaiming a third-term candidacy, he avoided becoming a lame-duck and preserved his effectiveness in addressing these conditions.[65]

International disorder figured prominently in the president's thinking. Confronted with aggression, the democracies had responded impotently. In Asia, the Roosevelt years had coincided with aggressive Japanese militarism, which actually began in 1931, when Japan invaded Manchuria during President Hoover's term, The United States refused to recognize Japanese claims on the mainland of Asia.[66] After investigation, the League of Nations condemned but could not reverse the aggression.[67]

Through the early to middle 1930s, tensions between Japan and China were severe. Then, in 1937, six months into Roosevelt's second term, Japan launched a war against China proper.[68] From a gruesome fight for Shanghai in the autumn of 1937 to the Rape of Nanking that soon followed, Japan conducted its war on China with extreme brutality.[69] Moreover, Japanese ambitions to dominate Asia challenged America's Pacific interests and those of its allies.[70]

In Europe, political instability was unraveling steadily. In 1935, Fascist Italy further damaged the League of Nations by attacking Abyssinia (Ethiopia), provoking protests from League members but no collective response.[71] In 1936, Germany and Italy combined to support Fascist General Francisco Franco in the Spanish Civil War. Franco was victorious, toppling Spain's Republican Government and installing a military dictatorship. That same year, Hitler contravened the Treaty of Versailles by occupying the Rhineland. In March 1938, National Socialists effected the Anschluss, which joined Germany and Austria together in a Greater Reich. Later in 1938, the Munich Conference acknowledged and appeased German territorial claims to the Czech Sudetenland.[72] The consequence was to render Czechoslovakia militarily indefensible. In March 1939, Germany seized the remainder of country, which surrendered without a fight. Germany and the Soviet Union concluded a non-aggression pact in August 1939, which contained a secret protocol dividing Polish territory. Within weeks, Germany attacked Poland and the Soviets claimed their portion. In 1939, the Soviets absorbed the Baltic States of Lithuania, Latvia, and Estonia, and launched a four-month attack on Finland.[73]

After a hiatus in the winter of 1939-1940, the shooting war began again in Europe with German conquests of Denmark, Norway, and the Low Countries. On May 10, 1940, Germany attacked France. Seeing German success, on June 10, 1940, Mussolini's Italy piled on, and itself declared war on France.[74]

By June 14, Marshal Philippe Petain, France's military commander, announced that further resistance would be futile and declared Paris an open city. Opposing him, and desperate, French President Paul Reynaud wired an appeal to Roosevelt on the same day. "Wounded France has a right to turn to the other democracies and say to them, I have claims on you. No one who has feelings of justice could deny this; but it is one thing to approve and another thing to act. We know how great a place ideals have in the life of the great American people. Would it still hesitate to declare itself against Nazi Germany?" Reynaud continued, "It is necessary that swarms of war planes come from the other side of the Atlantic to crush the evil force which is dominating Europe." Reynaud noted that although the United States had done everything possible for France within the restrictions of the neutrality laws, such relief was insufficient. He described his cable as a "final appeal."[75]

Reynaud believed he might rally support for further resistance if his people knew that America would become a belligerent.[76] Roosevelt offered emotional solidarity but nothing more. "The American people will not forget the brilliant, courageous, and effective resistance which you carried on as the head of your Government in the name of France. The American people and their Government share the conviction that the ideals which France has exemplified for so many generations—the ideals of human liberty, of democracy, and of the highest form of human civilization—will still triumph, and that France herself will ultimately regain her full independence and freedom."[77]

The situation was already too desperate. On June 22, France surrendered. Completing the downward spiral, on September 27, 1940, Germany and Italy combined with the Japanese militarists in signing the Tripartite Pact, which committed each signatory to the defense of the others in the event of attack.

No good news interrupted these cascading negative developments. Believing that circumstances justified, if not impelled, a third-term candidacy, Roosevelt positioned himself to run.

Skeptical as he was about other Democrats handling these conditions, Roosevelt had even less confidence in the Republicans, whose leading candidates were active isolationists.

"He was thoroughly frightened at the prospect of a Republican President who would be backed or controlled by the old leaders of the Republican Party," stated Rosenman. "He knew that a reversal of his foreign policy of all out assistance to Britain short of war would deprive her of the arms she needed so desperately, and would cause a disastrous break in British morale."[78] This situation posed a potential existential danger to the United States. "With Britain out of the way, he was sure we were high on the list of nations, if not first on the list, that Hitler intended to attack," Rosenman added.[79]

Top Democrats expected that the Republicans would nominate Michigan Senator Arthur Vandenberg.[80] He had been a senator since 1928, and a spokesman for the party during its leanest years. The public knew him better than they knew either Dewey or Taft. Opinion polls taken at the start of 1940 confirmed his early front-runner status.[81] After the war, the Senator would emerge as one of the great architects of American engagement in foreign affairs.[82] But that was not the Vandenberg of the 1930s, who Roosevelt knew to be a staunch isolationist and an advocate of neutrality legislation.[83] FDR vehemently disagreed with those attitudes and hoped to prevent them from roosting in the White House. The internationalist candidacy of Wendell Willkie, Roosevelt's actual opponent, did not materialize until too late to have any bearing on this calculation.[84]

So when, exactly, did the president decide to run? No one has been able to establish the time for certain. As Herbert Parmet and Marie Hecht write, "Any attempt to pinpoint accurately the precise date when Roosevelt made up his mind to be the Democratic candidate in 1940 is presumptuous."[85]

Richard Moe, Chief of Staff to Vice President Walter Mondale, and author of a book on the 1940 campaign, explains that Roosevelt was notoriously non-transparent about his judgments and took no one into his confidence.

> His practice of solitary decision making had begun early for him, an only child raised on an isolated estate. . . . The practice continued through his youth and early adulthood until it became deeply ingrained. . . . For whatever reason, he always withheld something of himself, even from Eleanor.[86]

Joseph P. Lash, Mrs. Roosevelt's close friend, bears out the truth of this irony. "Franklin had kept her in the dark up to the very last moment about his decision to accept the nomination." It was, in fact, a nomination she did not want him to seek.[87] In principle, Eleanor believed in the two-term custom. "My own personal option—and not as the wife of a President—is that except in extraordinary circumstances, we should stick to our traditions."[88] As FDR made his choice, the decision was not collaborative, but the president's alone.[89]

Others in the president's immediate family were similarly unaware, and actually had decided that FDR would retire. His son Elliott wrote in 1975, "None of us in the family had a clue to what he intended. He spoke so often of the books he was going to write, the good times at Hyde Park he was looking forward to, the travels he would undertake with Mother, that we concluded he had made his choice."[90]

While no one could establish precisely when Roosevelt made decision, the deciding factor was the catastrophe in Europe.

Thomas Jackson, an adviser who Roosevelt would later nominate to the Supreme Court, noted, "The approach of the war in Europe and the complications there were decisive things that were changing his mind. . . . With the war coming, he was not willing to see a war economy turned over to somebody else."[91]

Presidential Counselor Thomas Corcoran agreed with that assessment, keying it to Germany's invasion of Denmark in April 1939, resuming active hostilities after a winter lull. "The Democratic Convention was held in Copenhagen," Corcoran concluded.[92]

After the German attack on France, there remained a last possibility Roosevelt might still exit. During World War I, the Western Front stabilized after an initial German onslaught. If this repeated, the emergency would be menacing but nonetheless contained, allowing Roosevelt to step aside. In May, with the military situation unresolved, FDR affirmed to Undersecretary of State Sumner Welles that he had no interest in a third term.[93]

However, history did not repeat. During the first war, the Western front held for four years.[94] But in 1940, it fell apart in six weeks. Rosenman asserts this outcome sealed the president's decision to run. "If France had withstood the Hitler attack in May 1940, and if the war had then developed into a drawn-out stalemate as World War I did between 1915 and 1917, I am sure Roosevelt would not have consented to be nominated in July 1940."[95] Instead, there were stark conditions and, apart from the president himself, a leadership vacuum. Added Rosenman, "If he had felt that a liberal, internationalist Democrat could have been nominated who had a fair chance of election, I am again sure he would not have consented to be nominated." Rosenman clarifies, "By 'consenting,' I mean that he was not an active participant or seeker of the nomination in 1940 in the sense that he was in 1932. He was not going to go out and actively seek delegates. He was not going to ask any delegate to vote for him."[96]

In his memoirs, former Secretary of State Cordell Hull writes, "The third term was an immediate consequence of Hitler's conquest of France and the specter of Britain standing alone between the conqueror and ourselves. Our dangerous position induced President Roosevelt to run for a third time."[97]

Hull was among many people who were opposed to a third term in principle, but gravitated to Roosevelt under conditions of extreme peril. While the Secretary worried about excessive concentration of power in a long-tenured executive, there were overriding considerations. "I myself was strongly opposed to the third-term idea," Hull stated in his memoirs. "I feared lest it set a precedent for some future President to abuse the power entrusted to him. I felt it had only one justification. This was that we were then in the midst of a terrible international crisis, when Western civilization seemed in the greatest danger in its history; if Roosevelt did not run, another Democratic nominee might have lost; and it would have been disastrous in that event for the Government to be left without a real head during the two and a half months between the election and the Inauguration."[98]

These conditions also had a major effect on public opinion. "As the crisis deepened, Roosevelt's popular backing mounted sharply," writes James MacGregor Burns. "Millions of Americans forgot their concern for the third-term tradition as they instinctively rallied behind their leader against the threat outside."[99]

Thus, one arrives at the indispensable man.[100] In Roosevelt's own thinking, he was the only candidate whose record, outlook, and experience, could unite the party and put it in a position to win.[101] Among Democrats, there were dissenters, as Senate hearings would soon bring out, but most of his party followed him.[102]

On Monday, June 24, 1940, two days after the French surrender, the Republican Convention opened in Philadelphia. On its eve, the president made a powerful, preemptive political strike by appointing two prominent Republicans to his cabinet. One, to be Secretary of War, was Henry Stimson. He had served as Secretary of War under President Taft and as Secretary of State under President Hoover. The other, to be Secretary of the Navy, was Frank Knox, Landon's vice presidential running mate in 1936.[103] Both were committed internationalists.[104] Indeed, Roosevelt had considered naming Landon himself as Secretary of War, but did not when the governor conditioned his taking the job on Roosevelt's renouncing a third term.[105] Republican National Committee Chairman John Hamilton denounced Stimson and Knox, purporting, in effect, to expel them from the party.[106]

The emerging catastrophe in international affairs tended to discredit GOP isolationists.[107] The 1940 Republican platform disdained engagement in foreign wars, embraced strict observance of the neutrality laws, and stated that U.S. national defense requirements would have to be satisfied before sending aid to any other nation. Perniciously influencing the platform was Representative Hamilton Fish (R-NY). He arranged for a group of isolationist Republican Congressmen to testify before the platform committee, meeting in Philadelphia. It later came to light that the German embassy in Washington subsidized the cost of this travel.[108]

The platform section on national defense began, "The Republican Party is firmly opposed to involving this Nation in foreign war. We are still suffering from the ill effects of the last World War: a war which cost us a twenty-four billion dollar increase in our national debt, billions of uncollectible foreign debts, and the complete upset of our economic system, in addition to the loss of human life and irreparable damage to the health of thousands of our boys." On aid to the allies and Roosevelt's willingness to stretch the neutrality laws, the platform declared, "we deplore explosive utterances by the President directed at other governments which serve to imperil our peace; and we condemn all executive acts and proceedings which might lead to war without the authorization of the Congress of the United States. Our sympathies have been profoundly stirred by invasion of unoffending countries and by disaster to nations whose ideals most closely resemble our own. We favor the extension to all peoples fighting for liberty, or whose liberty is threatened, of such aid as shall not be in violation of international law or inconsistent with the requirements of our own national defense."[109]

Dewey was in tune with these sentiments. Taft opposed compulsory military training and openly condemned Stimson and Knox for joining the cabinet.[110] American intervention in World War I deeply disillusioned Vandenberg. He concluded that profit-hungry munitions manufacturers fomented sentiment for war. He would become a leading opponent of the September 1940 Bases-for-Destroyers and December 1940 Lend-Lease deals, both of which assisted the British before American entry into the war.[111]

However, among Republicans there was a potential nominee with a very distinctive outlook, consistent with emerging conditions, and one who arrived in Philadelphia with no delegates pre-pledged to him at all.[112]

Until late in 1939, Wendell Willkie had been a Democrat, and not just nominally so.[113] He was a delegate from Indiana to the 1924 Democratic Convention. An ardent Wilsonian, he had been attracted to liberal causes, supporting inclusion in the 1924 Democratic platform of U.S. entry into the League of Nations[114] and condemnation of the Ku Klux Klan.[115] Willkie was a delegate to the 1932 Convention that nominated FDR to a first term in the White House,[116] and he remained active in that party well into the 1930s.[117]

Willkie had practiced law in Akron, Ohio. Among his clients was a public utility company. His work for them introduced him to the world of public power regulation, and ultimately to a lead counsel position in New York with the Commonwealth and Southern Corporation, a public utilities holding company. At the beginning of 1933, Willkie assumed its presidency. As an industry leader, he became a leading and highly visible antagonist to Roosevelt's policies on power generation, via numerous articles and interviews, as well as through testimony before Congressional committees.[118] Among the Administration's major domestic initiatives was creation of the Tennessee Valley Authority, which would negatively affect Commonwealth and Southern's position in many States.[119] Cast as a New Deal opponent, Willkie began to draw press attention, including from publications like *Fortune, Look, Barron's, Life*, and *Time*.[120]

Energetic and charismatic, Willkie came to the attention of Russell Davenport, Managing Editor of *Fortune*.[121] Through Davenport, and Irita Van Doren of the *New York Herald Tribune*, the transplanted Hoosier gained a following among prominent journalists, business interests, and the still potent Eastern Establishment Republicans.[122] He initially spoke and wrote on domestic topics.[123] However, Willkie, the committed supporter of the League of Nations, remained a strong internationalist. Thus, he also addressed the need to confront the rising Fascist menace.[124] Spurred on by his supporters in journalism and business, Willkie began to introduce himself to delegates for the 1940 Convention.[125] Meanwhile, under the leadership of New York attorney Oren Root, Willkie Clubs began to spring up around the United States.[126]

Dewey's strategy was to dominate the primaries, hoping that doing so would give him irresistible momentum at the Convention.[127] Indeed, Dewey won nearly half of them. However, in 1940, primaries were neither as numerous nor as influential as they are today.[128] While Dewey was the early Convention front-runner, his lead was surmountable.[129] Willkie's immensely favorable press coverage, alongside deteriorating international conditions, enabled him to mount a powerful challenge. Pro-Willkie operatives gained control over the Convention machinery.[130] By manipulating distribution of tickets, they were able to pack the Convention Hall galleries with Willkie supporters. "We Want Willkie" was their incessant and vocal demand.[131] In addition, delegates received many thousands of grassroots communications urging Willkie's nomination. Gradually, a political stampede developed.[132]

As balloting commenced, Dewey was the leader, commanding 360 votes of 501 needed for nomination. Taft was the second with 189. On the first ballot, Willkie had 105.[133] Vandenberg scholar Hendrik Meijir observes, "Dewey might have gone over the top had he picked up Vandenberg's seventy-six delegates. He offered Vandenberg the vice presidency." Vandenberg offered to take the first spot, serve one term, and support Dewey in 1944. In the alternative, he offered to flip a coin to see who would end up as the nominee for president and who for vice president. Dewey declined, and the coalition never materialized.[134]

Over the course of five ballots, Dewey faded, leaving Willkie and Taft to contest at the end. Willkie secured a plurality on the fourth ballot and a majority on the sixth. By motion of Ohio Governor John Bricker, a Taft leader, Willkie's nomination was made unanimous.[135] It was a breathtaking outcome.[136] Oregon Senator Charles McNary, the Senate's Minority Leader, became Willkie's running mate.[137]

In good measure, Willkie prevailed because he fit the moment and faced divided opposition that did not coalesce around one of the more established candidates. The Republican establishment never really warmed to Willkie, who had little history within their party and whose views contradicted their 1940 platform. Their disdain for him became vivid after the campaign was over.

Willkie appeared before the Convention in person, the first Republican nominee ever to do so.[138] The party formally notified him of the nomination on August 16, 1940, in Rushford, Indiana. The next day, on a sweltering summer afternoon, before a crowd estimated at 250,000, Willkie accepted in a speech in nearby Ellwood, his boyhood home. However, Willkie's speech failed to ignite his campaign.

Robert Jackson was a close Roosevelt associate who FDR later appointed to the Supreme Court. He was also American Chief Prosecutor at the Nuremberg Trials. Of Willkie's Ellwood speech, Jackson wrote, "Willkie had an enormous buildup at the time of the Convention. He looked like a very formidable candidate. The buildup kept going on and on and on until his acceptance speech, which was to be the great speech that would inflame the country and scourge Roosevelt out of office. It was oversold, tremendously oversold."[139]

After the Convention, Willkie had spent 37 days in Colorado, ostensibly organizing his campaign. Party leaders believed the sojourn was too long, and that Willkie had lost valuable momentum that his nomination generated.[140]

Roosevelt held Willkie in high regard, and worried that the Republican could prevail in the general election. He understood his opponent was a magnetic figure, unburdened by a lengthy political record or by retrograde isolationism. "Roosevelt considered Willkie the most formidable opponent for himself that the Republicans could have named," noted Sherwood.[141]

Other prominent Democrats, such as Harold Ickes and William O. Douglas, assessed the situation in similar terms.[142] In July 1940, the president told Farley, "You know if the war should be over before the election, and I am running against Wendell Willkie, he would be elected."[143] However, the war did not end before the election, nor did it stalemate. As the world situation fell apart, support for Roosevelt solidified.[144]

Three weeks after Willkie's victory in Philadelphia, the Democrats convened in Chicago. Their choice of a convention site reflected the tightly competitive nature of Illinois politics in that day as well as the presumed centrality of the state to a Democratic victory in November.[145]

Chicago was also home to the political machine of a reliable Roosevelt support, Mayor Edward Kelly. African-American voters were key to his power. Since Lincoln's time, they mostly had been Republicans, but the New Deal fostered their migration to the Democrats.[146] Hoover won a majority of

African-American voters in 1932. But Roosevelt carried approximately 70 percent of their vote in 1936.[147] A major Depression-era movement of African-Americans from the South to northern cities amplified these changes.[148]

Chicago was one of those cities long governed by Republicans. After the New Deal, the Democrats would perpetually rule there. Kelly's Chicago machine would be instrumental in manipulating Convention proceedings to Roosevelt's advantage.[149]

FDR was loathe to challenge the two-term tradition head on. Rosenman describes a conversation with the president two days before the Convention opened. "He said he did not want to give the appearance of making any effort for the nomination."[150] Instead, FDR sought to organize a "draft." It involved a political three-step: first, a disclaimer of interest in the nomination; second, ensuring that delegations went to the Convention uncommitted to any other candidate;[151] and, third, acquiescing in an orchestrated demand for his candidacy.[152]

Roosevelt decided that abandoning the two-term tradition required a deft sidestep and not a frontal assault.[153] He would try arranging for his party to call him to duty.[154] FDR chronicler James MacGregor Burns comments, "Unhappily for the President, he could not openly lift a finger to bring about such a draft. To do so would be to sharpen the very fears that lay behind the no-third-term feeling, the fears that had dogged Roosevelt all through his second term—the fears of a dictatorial leader grasping for more and more power."[155] Feigning detachment and nonchalance, the president cruised the Potomac as the Convention got underway.[156]

Meanwhile, the delegates in Chicago were confused and agitated. Historian David Roll observes, "The Democratic National Convention opened on Monday, July 15, 1940, and for the next thirty-six hours confusion reigned. Some delegates resented Hopkins for trying to control the process and were appalled at his abrasive and imperious attitude."[157]

Cloistered in a suite at Chicago's Blackstone Hotel, Hopkins busied himself promoting FDR's interests. At the president's insistence, Hopkins got word to Senate Majority Leader Alben Barkley to make a public declaration that FDR would not be an avowed candidate. Some of Roosevelt's closest advisers were against having any such statement made, likely out of concern that the president could lose control of the Convention. When they urged this position on the president, he was unyielding.[158]

In his capacity as permanent chairman, Barkley spoke to the delegates on the Convention's second night, July 16, 1940. The senator added the following remarks at the conclusion of his prepared speech:

> I and other close friends of the President have long known that he has no wish to be a candidate again. We know, too, that in no way whatsoever has he exerted any influence in the selection of delegates or upon the opinion of delegates.

> Tonight, at the specific request of the President, I am making this simple fact clear to the Convention.
>
> The President has never had, and has not today, any desire or purpose to continue in the office of the President, to be a candidate for that office, or to be nominated by the Convention for that office.
>
> He wishes in all earnestness and sincerity to make clear that all the delegates to this Convention are free to vote for any candidate.
>
> That is the message I bear to you from the President of the United States.[159]

With Garner and Farley openly seeking the nomination, Mayor Kelly arranged for a pro-Roosevelt demonstration to galvanize the Convention Hall.[160] T. D. McGarry, Chicago's Superintendent of Sewers, controlled the Chicago Stadium's loudspeaker system, and staged the whole affair. Situated in the arena's basement, McGarry repeatedly broadcast, "We want Roosevelt!" Delegates responded with a 53-minute floor demonstration. Hopkins and others passed the word that the president was willing to respond by accepting a "draft."[161] With that, opposition mostly withered.

To reinforce the fiction of a draft, Roosevelt's team, led by Hopkins and James F. Byrnes, tried to induce Garner and Farley to allow Roosevelt to be nominated by acclamation, without need for a ballot.[162] During a July 15, 1940, telephone call, Roosevelt himself tried unsuccessfully to coax Farley into acquiescence. "By the way, Jim, there are a lot of stories in the papers. . . . They are writing stories about there being no need for a ballot," Roosevelt told him. Farley was unpersuaded. "There just has to be a ballot. You and I both know there must be a ballot and that any effort to prevent a ballot or roll call will be the one thing that's needed to wreck the Democratic Party in November." Roosevelt replied, "Of course, of course. I agree with you on the situation, but the papers are talking."[163] As Farley states in his memoir, "Every effort was being directed at winning the nomination by acclamation, in an effort to convince the country there was a real draft."[164]

Farley was convinced that a majority of the delegates were against the third term and preferred not to renominate Roosevelt.[165] However, if they were unhappy with being steamrolled, they had nowhere else to turn. As Farley writes, "Murmurings of mutiny grew until the delegates grew downright ugly, but the president's maneuvering over the years saved the day. Delegates lacked a rallying point for revolt and were forced to surrender, grumblingly and glumly, on the never genuine threat that Roosevelt might not run and thus leave the party without its greatest vote getter."[166]

Garner and Farley never went along with the ruse of the draft. They never withdrew their names, but FDR crushed them in the Convention roll call. Alabama Senator Lister Hill put Roosevelt in nomination.[167] The call of states began after midnight on July 17, 1940. Farley and Garner allowed their names to be put up, but it was no contest. The tally was Roosevelt 946 ½, Farley 72

½, Garner 61, Maryland Senator Millard Tydings 9 ½, and Hull 5.[168] Roosevelt was in. Because unit rule was in effect for some state delegations, the balloting did not capture the true measure of anti-Roosevelt sentiment.[169]

Doris Kearns Goodwin states, "Though the nomination had not come in the exact form Roosevelt wanted—the 'draft' would never be able to shake off the quotation marks surrounding it, since votes had been cast for other candidates—it had been achieved nonetheless, and without the kind of party split that might have hurt the chances for victory in November."[170]

Nevertheless, Roosevelt's manipulation was not over. He insisted that the Convention nominate longtime Secretary of Agriculture Henry Wallace of Iowa for vice president, replacing Garner. Open revolt among the delegates was incipient.[171]

Roosevelt's original preference for a successor was Secretary of State Cordell Hull, a former senator and representative from Tennessee.[172] Hull was also Eleanor's choice.[173] In early July, having signaled to Hull that he intended to seek a third term, FDR attempted to convince the Secretary to join him on the Democratic ticket. "Almost immediately, the President began urging me to run with him as Vice President," recalled Hull. "He called me to the White House and pleaded with me for some two hours and forty minutes. I declined and stood firm in my declination." When Hull declined, the president pivoted toward Wallace. "A night or so later, the President telephoned me at my apartment. He again pressed his offer with much emphasis. Again, I refused. . . . He then said, 'If you don't take it, I'll have to get Henry Wallace to run.'"[174]

A former Republican,[175] and a staunch New Dealer,[176] Henry Wallace was well regarded in the farm states, but deeply unpopular with many Democrats, especially Southerners. However, qualms about him reached beyond conservative elements of the party. Even his fellow progressives doubted Wallace could stir electoral and financial enthusiasm.[177] Farley thought him a mystic.[178] But the president was not to be denied, brushing aside alternatives suggested by the First Lady and other confidants.[179]

The president was determined to command the direction of his party, regardless of such misgivings. Roosevelt outlined for Frances Perkins[180] his reasons for choosing Wallace. The Secretary had been an innovative and formidable leader at the Department of Agriculture, as well as being a firm internationalist. Wallace would strengthen the ticket with Midwestern farmers, who tended to support Republicans, and mitigate their isolationist tendencies. Moreover, Roosevelt liked working with Wallace, considered him trustworthy, and saw him as a committed liberal.[181]

Roosevelt scholar Susan Dunn observes, FDR "believed in healthy—even polarizing—partisanship."[182] Wallace would serve that purpose, bringing an unmistakable ideological cast to the ticket,[183] as opposed to the marriage of convenience with Garner that was instrumental for Roosevelt to secure the

1932 nomination.[184] Informed by Harry Hopkins that Wallace faced substantial opposition, Roosevelt told his secretary, Grace Tully, he would condition his running on the delegates' acceptance of his choice. "Well, damn it to hell, they will go for Wallace or I won't run, and you can jolly well tell them so."[185] He indicated much the same thing to Rosenman. "Well, I suppose all the conservatives in America are going to bring pressure on the Convention to beat Henry. The fellow they want is either Jesse [Jones] or [Speaker] Bankhead. I'm going to tell them that I won't run with either of those men or with any other reactionary—I've told them that before and I'll tell them again."[186]

Roosevelt went so far as to handwrite a note refusing the nomination in the event the delegates did not accept Wallace.[187] Dated July 18, 1940, the Convention's closing day, the original draft of the note stated, in part:

> Until the Democratic Party makes clear its overwhelming stand in favor of liberalism, and shakes off *all* the shackles of control by conservativism and reaction, it will not continue its march of victory.
>
> It has been without question that certain influences of conservatism and reaction have been busily engaged in the promotion of discord since this Convention convened.
>
> That being the fact and the case, I in all honor cannot and will not condone or go along with the fact of that party dissension.
>
> It would be best not to straddle ideals.
>
> It would be best for America to have the fight out.
>
> Therefore, I give the Democratic Party the opportunity to make that historic decision by declining the honor of the nomination for the Presidency. I so do.[188]

Rosenman polished the letter into final form, but the president never dispatched it.

For the president, the delegates' unhappiness could prove ominous, the forerunner of a party split. Doris Kearns Goodwin states, "By Thursday afternoon, July 18 . . . the Convention had spun out of control. The galleries were packed with placards for a dozen different candidates. . . . Everywhere one went, the name of Henry Wallace was met by jeers and catcalls."[189]

Witness to the festering discontent, Frances Perkins called Roosevelt to urge that he reconsider his decision not to attend the Convention. He responded, "I thought it all through both ways. I know I am right, Frances. It will be worse if I go. People will get promises out of me that I ought not to make. If I don't make promises, I will make new enemies. If I do make promises, they'll be mistakes." Perkins replied, "Can't you suggest something." "How would it be if Eleanor came?" asked the president. Thus, to quell the opposition, the White House dispatched Eleanor Roosevelt to Chicago.[190]

The strategy worked. "You cannot treat it as you would treat an ordinary nomination in an ordinary time," Eleanor implored the delegates. "We people in the United States have got to realize today that we face a grave and serious situation." She continued, "We cannot tell from day to day what may come. This is no ordinary time. No time for weighing anything except what we can do best for the country as a whole, and that responsibility rests on each and every one of us as individuals." The responsibility for the campaign would rest not just on Roosevelt, but on a united party. "No man who is a candidate or who is president can carry this situation alone."[191]

Her speech infused sufficient calm into the proceedings, and the Convention nominated Wallace after considerable pressure by the president's operatives.[192] The nominee skirted through with 627 votes out of 1100 possible.[193] In the aftermath, many at the Convention remained upset. To avoid stirring the pot and reigniting the controversy, Byrnes and Hopkins urged Wallace not to address the Convention.[194] He complied.

With Wallace on the ticket, FDR could signify his acceptance. How would he do so?

Throughout his political career, the president had shown a talent for the dramatic. This was never truer than in 1932, when he was first the nominee, and electrified his party by appearing in person to accept the nomination.[195] On July 2, 1932, Roosevelt flew from Albany to Chicago, and addressed the delegates at Chicago Stadium.

The president's son, Elliott Roosevelt, sheds light on the reason for this tradition-shattering event. "Weeks earlier, he decided to fly so that he could deliver his acceptance speech in person, not dawdle across the country by train. . . . He wanted to demonstrate by this gesture that he was a man of vigorous action, not the semi-invalid depicted without fail by his enemies in both parties. Above all, he knew that by smashing precedent by accepting on the spot, he could thrill the voters with a sense of decisive leadership and get his campaign off to an instant start."[196]

To the delegates, Roosevelt exclaimed,

> The appearance before a National Convention of its nominee for President, to be formally notified of his selection, is unprecedented and unusual, but these are unprecedented and unusual times. I have started out on the tasks that lie ahead by breaking the absurd traditions that the candidate should remain in professed ignorance of what has happened for weeks until he is formally notified of that event many weeks later.
>
> My friends, may this be the symbol of my intention to be honest and to avoid all hypocrisy or sham, to avoid all silly shutting of the eyes to the truth in this campaign. You have nominated me and I know it, and I am here to thank you for the honor.

> Let it also be symbolic that in so doing I broke traditions. Let it be from now on the task of our Party to break foolish traditions. We will break foolish traditions and leave it to the Republican leadership, far more skilled in that art, to break promises.

Roosevelt concluded his remarks with a stirring guarantee. "I pledge you, I pledge myself, to a new deal for the American people."[197]

When nominated in 1936, Roosevelt addressed the Democrats in person once more. But in 1940, wanting to leave the impression of the executive preoccupied with the emergency, he declined to attend the Convention, and accepted by radio hookup from the White House.[198]

In his remarks, the president indicated that, notwithstanding the outbreak of hostilities in Europe, it had been his intention to step down:

> When the conflict first broke out last September, it was still my intention to announce clearly and simply, at an early date, that under no conditions would I accept re-election.

As the political and military situation deteriorated, declared Roosevelt, it was necessary to defer personal preferences and give way to the national good:

> Every day that passed called for the postponement of personal plans and partisan debate until the latest possible moment. The normal conditions under which I would have made public declarations of my personal desires were wholly gone.

Instead, he declared his willingness to continue in public service:

> Lying awake, as I have on many nights, I have asked myself whether I have the right, as Commander in Chief of the Army and Navy, to call on men and women to serve their country, or to train themselves to serve and, at the same time, decline to serve my country in my own personal capacity, if I am called upon to do so by the people of my country.[199]

Having been "drafted" by the 1940 Convention, Roosevelt announced he would subject himself to a second draft, meaning the will of the voters in the general election:

"Only the people themselves can draft a President. If such a draft should be made upon me, I say to you in the utmost simplicity, I will, with God's help, continue to serve with the best of my ability and with the fullness of my strength."[200]

The third term was an important issue during the general election campaign. Even so, it was less prominent than it might have been because, for a while, Willkie did not emphasize it.[201] To the contrary, as the party conventions drew near, Willkie professed he wanted Roosevelt to run.

On March 15, 1940, Wendell Willkie appeared before the Commonwealth Club in San Francisco. A press account states, "Before the speech Willkie expressed hope that President Roosevelt would seek a third term and predicted that if he did, the President would be 'licked.'" In the same interview, Willkie said, "President Roosevelt is the ablest spokesman, and in a Democratic country it is essential we vote for or against the ablest advocate. If he runs, we can debate the New Deal to everybody's satisfaction."

In an April 26, 1940, article he prepared for publication in *Look* magazine, Willkie went back to this theme. He taunted, "In spite of what I consider sound reasons for maintenance of the anti-third term tradition, I think Franklin D. Roosevelt should be the Democratic nominee for President in 1940."[202]

Willkie's comment set him aside from more conventional Republicans who were appalled by and fearful of a third-term candidacy, claiming it carried the seeds of dictatorship. "Mr. Roosevelt is the champion New Dealer," Willkie wrote for *Look,* "the outstanding advocate of the philosophy which holds that that the government's control over the individual shall be extended and intensified."

Whether that should be the governing philosophy of the United States should be the central issue of the 1940 campaign, Willkie insisted. However, he surmised, no New Dealer besides Roosevelt could win nomination. If the Democrats passed over Roosevelt, a sharply defined, partisan debate on New Deal policies would not occur. Having the debate was more important than adhering to tradition, Willkie argued. "Since the New Deal is an issue which transcends even a sound political tradition, let its champion be its representative in 1940."[203]

In the *Look* article, Willkie went even further to minimize the importance of the two-term custom. He expressly endorsed the Framers' decision not to limit presidential terms. "The four-year term has proved to be about right," he observed, "and in setting no limit to the number of times a man may be re-elected, the Fathers were apparently very wise. . . . The people, the Fathers thought, were perfectly capable of deciding for themselves how many terms a President should serve," a judgment he argued history had vindicated.[204] As the campaign wore along, and Willkie saw the need to consolidate support from anti-third-term Democrats, he diametrically reversed his position.

By April, two months before Roosevelt appears to have finally decided to run, Willkie expected FDR to be the nominee. He told the *Look* readers, "There is absolutely no telling at the present writing whether Mr. Roosevelt will run for office a third time, or not. But so far, every political move that he has made in the current campaign has been a move in that direction, a move to keep the way open should he decide to try it."[205]

In his article, Willkie dismissed as "glib" and inauthentic arguments from Roosevelt supporters in favor of another term. As Willkie summarized them, there were three points. The first was that Roosevelt was needed to address emergency conditions in Europe.[206] The second was that only Roosevelt could beat the Republicans.[207] The third was that Roosevelt alone could provide the leadership America required.[208]

Willkie argued that Roosevelt's true reason was different. It was to reinforce a government-dominated political philosophy. "The real reason why the New Dealers want Mr. Roosevelt for a third term is because they think that he—along with them—is dedicated to the principle of State power, and to the perpetuation of that power."[209]

Insisting that the key issue in the election was political philosophy rather than adherence to a custom, Willkie stated, "We should all rather beat the champ."[210]

He appeared to have a chance to do so. August polling from Gallup showed the Republican winning in twenty-four states, compromising a majority in the Electoral College.[211] However, this proved to be Willkie's apogee; as the campaign unfolded, his support began to disintegrate, then swing positively but insufficiently back in his direction as the end neared.[212]

In his August 17, 1940, acceptance speech Willkie proclaimed, "I propose that during the next two and a half months, the President and I appear together on public platforms in various parts of the country, to debate the fundamental issues of this campaign. These are the problems of our great domestic economy, as well as of our national defense: The problems of agriculture, of labor, of industry, of finance, of the government's relationship to the people, and of our preparations to guard against assault."[213]

The speech was lengthy, and almost entirely focused on a stinging critique of the New Deal. But near the end, Willkie turned to the third term. "And also, I should like to debate the question of the assumption by this President, in seeking a third term, of a greater public confidence than was accorded to our presidential giants, Washington, Jefferson, Jackson, Lincoln, Cleveland, Theodore Roosevelt, and Woodrow Wilson."[214]

This was an issue his advisers and prominent Republicans urged him to emphasize, because they believed it would appeal to disaffected Democrats, who abhorred the prospect of a third term. For example, John Cowles, publisher of the *Minneapolis Star* and other papers, as well as a leading Willkie adviser, wired the candidate on May 20, 1940. Cowles was concerned that the Democrats were trying to exaggerate the sense of national emergency in order to justify a third term for FDR. "Say something along the following line," Cowles proposed, "the real national emergency confronting America, if any emergency is confronting us, is the survival of democracy. We do not serve the cause of democracy elsewhere in the world by allowing it to perish by default in the United States. Democracy that depends on one man or one party ceases to be democracy. . . . America loses every free ideal it cherishes if it unwittingly establishes dictatorship in this nation in the name of combatting it across the seas."[215]

The third-term issue became more prominent in Willkie's campaign as the fall campaign intensified. In print material and speeches, Willkie repeatedly referred to Roosevelt at the "third-term candidate." Seeing the issue as a way to dislodge Democrats from their party loyalty, Willkie campaigned on it even in territory with deep Democratic roots. In Amarillo, Texas, Willkie exclaimed, "the people of the South are faced with a conflict of traditions. In order to keep that 80-year-old Democratic tradition, they must abandon another tradition. That tradition is 150 years old." Willkie went on,

> The only difference between this great democracy of ours and totalitarianism is the continuation in office of one man. . . . The people who have lost their democracy and their liberty are the people in countries where one man said, "I am indispensable."[216]

The third-term emerged elsewhere in the country as the wedge issue of 1940. Columnist L. R. Conner noted in a mid-September dispatch from Columbus, "It continues to become more and more apparent in Ohio that the basic issue in this presidential campaign is the third term." Although Ohio papers split over foreign and domestic policy issues, they coalesced for Willkie over the third term. Conner described, "the almost universal decision of Ohio newspapers is to unite in opposition to a third term for President Roosevelt."[217]

Willkie went into high gear on the third-term issue in a speech he made on October 14, 1940. His remarks got front-page coverage in the next day's *New York Times.*

"Perhaps it may seem to some in this troubled world we face the preservation of the third term tradition is a small thing. We see a world aflame. We see abroad ruthless military aggression trampling upon the rights of free peoples. . . . Oppressed by the difficulties of these problems, it is understandable that some of our people should feel that the preservation of a mere tradition is relatively unimportant."

"If it were merely a tradition that was being challenged, I would agree. Traditions are not sacred; principles are" Citing Washington and Jefferson, he declared, "The men who established the third term tradition knew that power long contained in the hands of one man will inevitably and insensibly corrupt him. They knew that no man is to be trusted with prolonged and increasing power."[218]

Willkie continued, "The principle of rotation in office should never be dispensed with because there will never be a time when real difficulties will not exist and furnish a plausible pretext for dispensing with that principle." Subsequent presidents—Madison, Monroe, and Jackson—by word and deed, had reinforced this idea, Willkie proclaimed. He added, "And since those days, the principle against a third term has been reinforced by every thoughtful political leader in American public life." Twice, it was the Republicans who rebuffed attempts to violate it, Willkie noted, meaning the attempts by Grant and Theodore Roosevelt to return to office. However, he stressed "justice compels us to say that it is the Democratic Party that has been preeminent in upholding this unwritten law." Apart from anti-third-term declarations by Democratic presidents, and from Democrats in Congress, the party had twice included express platform planks strenuously opposing the third term.

But Progressives had transformed the party, Willkie alleged.

> The Democratic Party would not be seeking to violate that principle had not the Democratic Party been kidnapped by the New Deal. . . . It is the New Deal of Hopkins, Ickes, Corcoran, Cohen, and Wallace which has captured the Democratic Party.

Willkie called these Roosevelt acolytes "the little clique of power-hungry men who hide behind his smiling mask." It was to them, and not to the country, that Roosevelt was indispensable. Willkie insisted. "We know that many real leaders of that party are not behind this movement."

Over the span of eight years, Roosevelt had accumulated enormous powers, Willkie exclaimed. Some of that was the work of a compliant Congress; in addition, the president had declared sixty-seven emergencies as a basis to act unilaterally. And then there was his Court-packing plan. "Congress rebuked his attempt to pack the Supreme Court," noted Willkie, but Roosevelt had over time been able to fill vacancies with "five of his closest followers." If FDR were given a third term, Willkie charged, he would dominate the entire federal judiciary.

Willkie concluded, "This is the pattern of dictatorship—the usurpation of power by manufactured emergencies; the circumvention of the Legislature, the capture of the courts. The pattern calls for the creation of one dominant party in which all power is vested. It calls for the indefinite rule of one indispensable man." In these circumstances, fundamental American institutions were at risk. "This is the way democracy has been destroyed."[219]

Six months earlier, Willkie had urged Roosevelt to step into the arena, so that the philosophy of the New Deal could be debated and vanquished. By October, the fight had been reframed into a battle over the conditions for constitutional government.

The day before the November election, Willkie made a nationwide radio address from New York. He again hit the third-term issue hard, rejecting the contention that deteriorating conditions in Europe justified ignoring the unwritten constitution.

> The argument that you should thrust aside the tradition against a third term on the grounds that we are faced with an international crisis—that argument is false and it is a dangerous one. To thrust aside that tradition is to assume that only one man has the ability to take us through these emergencies. That means that democracy must surrender in the face of any trouble. It means that whenever our government says it sees an emergency, we must forego our democratic institutions until the government is pleased to return them to us.[220]

Perpetuating a president in office would undermine the relationship between the executive and the other branches, Willkie charged, destroying constitutional checks and balances. "If to the terrible concentration of power in the hands of the third-term candidate, and the subversion of the other departments of government, there is to be added continual tenure of office, then the last step in the destruction of our democracy has been taken."

Those who opposed Roosevelt on the third-term issue often voiced concern that breaching tradition would lead to constitutional ruin. They worried that a third term would lead to a fourth and beyond. For one election, the excuse could be preparing for war; in another it could be winning the war; in yet another, it could be arranging and preserving the peace.[221] Without voluntary term limits rooted in tradition, or ones imposed by the constitution itself, there was no limiting principle. At the end of that political rainbow, could be tattered constitutional protections and the prospect of dictatorship. In his address, Willkie hit on these concerns. "Let us remember that dictatorship always begins by asking the people to give up some law or tradition for some special reason. The reason given may even seem logical. The motives behind it may be honorable and sincere. But if you give in to such reasons, little by little the structure of democracy is taken away from you without your realizing it."[222]

The same day, Willkie issued a statement supporting a constitutional amendment to limit presidential tenure to eight years or fewer. To justify it, Willkie contended that a tradition once broken was subject to repeated violation, unless specifically barred by law.[223]

"If once our common law against a third term be repealed," Willkie declared,

> there is no further law to restrain him or any of his successors . . . from an indefinite number of terms. And that repeal of that law will be final. It can never be revoked. Never again can there be a tradition against as many terms as a President can take for himself. The third term candidate's own future administrations and those of all subsequent Presidents would be directed to a further series of their re-elections and the people would not get the disinterested service to which they are entitled.

Willkie concluded with a promise. "When elected, in order to prevent any subsequent demonstration of such ambitious views, in my first message to Congress I shall recommend that they submit a Constitutional Amendment limiting the time any one President may serve to eight years or less."[224]

Although there was not any fundamental difference between the candidates on the direction of foreign policy, Willkie criticized what he alleged was Roosevelt's failure to prepare the country and its armed forces. Mindful of public opinion, which was sympathetic to Britain but opposed to armed intervention, both candidates proclaimed intention to keep America out of the war.[225]

In general, Willkie's internationalist sentiments simplified matters for Roosevelt, because it divorced certain sensitive issues from the partisan campaign. Willkie scholar Charles Peters observes, "Understanding the wrenching choices that he (Roosevelt) faced that summer of 1940 is the key to understanding the significance of Willkie's nomination. Only if we realize how close a call those days were for Roosevelt, the United States, and Britain, can we comprehend how essential was Willkie's role in the steps the President took to prevent Britain's collapse and to prepare this country for its entry into World War II."[226]

At a time preceding Pearl Harbor, when isolationism ran strongly within the Republican Party, any of the other nomination prospects would likely have framed their response differently.[227]

As the election drew near, respected political analysts were predicting a close outcome. Syndicated columnist David Lawrence reported from Chicago on October 22, 1940, "Surveys of this Midwestern section indicate clearly that there is a uniform tide rolling in Illinois, Indiana, Michigan, Wisconsin, and that it is strongly in the direction of Wendell Willkie." Lawrence attributed this voter trend principally to, "the idea that tradition must not be lightly brushed aside."[228] The same day, *The Washington Star*'s Gould Lincoln told readers, "Lukewarmness for a third presidential term—even for Franklin D. Roosevelt—on the part of Democratic leaders in Congress and in many of the states is not helping the Roosevelt candidacy." He added, "these leaders are 'going along' with the President outwardly, but doing little—and quietly many of them would shed no tears if Mr. Roosevelt is defeated." Lincoln continued, "A third presidential term is entirely against the democratic principles upon which these Democrats have stood for many years, and they do not believe it is a good thing for the country." He observed that the president was suffering an erosion of support among Catholic voters. "There is an indication," Lincoln claimed, "among many Catholics to oppose a third term on principle."[229]

Franklin Roosevelt was in Cleveland on Saturday, November 2, 1940. He proclaimed that worsening world conditions was the reason for his third-term candidacy, and that he fully expected a new term would be his last. "There is a great storm raging now," said the president. "It makes things harder for the world. And that storm, which did not start in this land of ours, is the true reason that I would like to stick by these people of ours until we reach the clear, sure footing ahead. We will make it—make it before the next term is over." And he proclaimed, "When that term is over, there will be another President."[230]

On November 3, 1940, the Sunday before Election Day, Representative Joseph W. Martin, Jr., chairman of the Republican National Committee, predicted victory for the Willkie-McNary ticket, adding that they would secure a Republican majority in the House of Representatives. Martin was specific about these claims. "Willkie and McNary will receive a minimum of 324 electoral votes in the Tuesday election and Republicans will capture at least 50 additional seats in the House, bringing the Republican total in that body to 228, or 10 more than a majority."[231] Edward J. Flynn, chairman of the Democratic National Committee, predicted a different outcome. The president would amass at least 427 electoral votes.

In the RNC's election eve statement, Martin put the third term front and center. "Millions of Democrats in every State in the Union will vote for Willkie and McNary in a desire to prevent the breaking of our sacred tradition against a third term and to keep this country out of war. Millions of independent voters will go to the polls on Tuesday to give their support to Wendell Willkie and Charles McNary as the best safeguard for the preservation of our American form of government."[232]

In the end, the third-term controversy did not amount to much. "It was in vain that Mr. Willkie raised the third term issue against the President," wrote the *Washington Evening Star's* Gould Lincoln. "Nor was Mr. Willkie's charge that a third term would lead to a dictatorship effective in overturning the results."[233]As Robert Jackson comments, "Republicans kept talking about the third term issue, but nobody was taking that seriously."[234] Presidential scholar Stephen Stathis concurs, "The third term issue had little discernible effect on voters in the 1940 election, but it did generate widespread public interest during the campaign."[235]

The president won the 1940 election by a popular vote margin of 27 million to 22 million, in percentage terms, 54.7 percent to 44.8 percent. Willkie won ten states, the largest of which was Michigan. Margins in other industrial states, such as New York, Ohio, and Illinois, were tight, but the South remained solid for Democrats,[236] so even if Willkie had carried them, Roosevelt would have prevailed in the electoral vote.[237] Eighty percent majorities in the South also ensured a healthy popular vote margin nationally for FDR.[238] The overwhelming public support Roosevelt enjoyed in the region kept almost all Southern politicians on board with the president, notwithstanding their rift with him during the unsuccessful purge of 1938.[239] From public works, to rural electrification, to agriculture, the New Deal had transformed the South, bringing tangible benefits of government intervention. At the same time, keeping his broad coalition together, Roosevelt did not challenge the racial politics that animated the region.[240]

Martin's prediction for the electoral vote was drastically off. In the Electoral College, the president won 449 to 82. Martin was similarly wrong about the House of Representatives. He had predicted a gain of fifty seats; in fact, the Republicans lost seven seats. Ed Flynn's projection was almost exactly correct.

FDR's victory was decisive, even though narrower than his 1936 landslide against Kansas Governor Alf Landon. In 1936, Roosevelt received 60.8 percent of the popular vote and won every state except Maine and Vermont, giving him a total of 523 out of 531 electoral votes.[241]

In the immediate aftermath of the election, *Life* magazine editorialized about Roosevelt's chance to unify Americans, as he distinctly had not done following his victory in 1936. "He had had a great opportunity before, at the beginning of his second administration in 1937, to become the leader not of a party or class but of a united people. But as storm clouds gathered abroad, the nation remained racked and torn by internal dissension. Now, his opportunity unfulfilled, his work unfinished, he had asked and won another chance."[242]

Joe Martin assessed the main reason Willkie lost. "There are times, and 1940 was one, when the party that best seems able to prosecute a war seems invincible. In the last analysis, the people trusted Roosevelt's experience in coping with the situation that confronted the country."[243] Willkie biographer David Levering Lewis concurs, believing that the Republican was "trapped into the necessity of representing himself as an improved version of Roosevelt in order to defeat Roosevelt. A great many Americans, however, found the genuine specimen more satisfying in comparison."[244]

NOTES

1. Hoover personally decried religious intolerance, and said so in his August 11, 1928, nomination acceptance address. His campaign focused on touting the economic prosperity that he believed would earn Republicans another term in the White House. However, as Kenneth Whyte observes, "Inevitably, given the virulence of anti-Catholic sentiment, not all in his party followed his example. . . . The flow of anti-Catholic literature increased markedly throughout the country as the race intensified." Whyte, p. 351.

2. Tennessee voted for Harding in 1920.

3. During the Civil War, Democratic strength in Congress was badly diminished due to the secession of the Southern states. At the opening of the 39th Congress,

elected in 1864, Republicans held 45 of 53 seats in the Senate and 140 of 188 seats in the House.

4. In the presidential election of 1936, the Republican defeat was so total that Landon exceeded 45 percent of the vote in only four states. Susan Dunn, *Roosevelt's Purge: How FDR Fought to Change the Democratic Party* (Cambridge, Massachusetts: The Belknap Press of Harvard University Press, 2010), p. 3.

5. Francis O. Wilcox, "American Government and Politics: The Neutrality Fight in Congress: 1939," *The American Political Science Review,* Vol. 33, No. 5 (October 1939), pp. 811–825. The first Neutrality Act passed in 1935. Mindful of the pronounced isolationist strain in U.S. public opinion, Roosevelt unenthusiastically signed it and successor legislation. "FDR reluctantly acquiesced to the bill because of his understanding of the strong American opposition to becoming involved in conflicts abroad, as it had in World War I, and his desire not to endanger his domestic program." John W. Jeffries, *A Third Term for FDR: The Election of 1940* (Lawrence, Kansas: University of Kansas Press, 2017), p. 36.

6. British scholar Piers Brendon had an interesting take on the effect of the purge. Most writers interpret the purge as a failure for Roosevelt, but Brendon actually saw it as a benefit to him. "The more divided the Democrats became," Brendon wrote, "the more it appeared only Roosevelt could unite them." Piers Brendon, *The Dark Valley: A Panorama of the 1930s* (London: Jonathan Cape, 2000), p. 437.

7. By 1938, recessionary conditions had returned. Unemployment increased by 2.5 million persons, which was a gain of nearly 5 points, farm prices and manufacturing fell, and the stock market lost value precipitously, giving back half the gains it had made after bottoming out in 1933. See Brendon, p. 436, also Joshua M. Brown, "Stock Market Crash: Think 1938, not 2008," *Christian Science Monitor*, August 4, 2011, www. csmonitor.com. "Early on, Republicans had been bullish about the prospect of retaking the White House. Despite all of Roosevelt's initiatives, there were still more than ten million unemployed, and the national debt had soared to an unprecedented $36 billion." Richard Moe, *Roosevelt's Second Act: The Election of 1940 and the Politics of War* (Oxford: Oxford University Press, 2013), p. 147.

8. Republicans gained 81 House seats, 8 Senate seats, and 13 governorships. Many attractive new Republican faces emerged. *Time* magazine wrote that Republicans looked strong for 1940, unless somehow there were a "Rooseveltian miracle." Steve Neal, *Dark Horse: A Biography of Wendell Willkie* (Lawrence, Kansas: University of Kansas Press, 1984), p. 57.

9. Jeffries, p. 34.

10. Neal, p. 60. Dewey was not simply boasting. He had private polls that showed him defeating Roosevelt. Moe, p. 149.

11. "Although Taft had remarkable credentials and keen ambition, his talents as a politician were less impressive. . . . Taft, who came across as stiff, pedantic, and standoffish, had a metallic voice and rushed delivery. . . . A man of obvious integrity, Taft was better liked by his associates than Dewey, but his attractive personality in small groups did not translate to his appearance on the hustings. The serious, studious, formal Taft resembled, critics said, 'a chemistry professor, bank president, possibly a Sunday school superintendent.'" Jeffries, p. 49.

12. Whyte, pp. 565–566.

13. "Hoover, still bitter about the turn of events since 1929, continued to persist in his hopes for vindication; but despite his status as a respected, and for some revered figure in the party, his time as the GOP's presidential nominee had come and gone." Jeffries, p. 45. Hoover hoped that the primaries would be dominated by unpledged delegates and "favorite son" candidacies. The latter was a mechanism by which a political figure could win a primary within his own state and thus, for horse-trading purposes, control his state delegation at the convention. The combination of such outcomes would result in the kind of open convention that Hoover hoped would eventually select him. Neal, p. 64. "But there was little enthusiasm among GOP leaders for the man whom the nation had so overwhelmingly rejected in 1932." Ibid. "He was damaged beyond political repair by the failure of his presidency and the anti-Hoover mythology artfully perpetuated by Roosevelt." Whyte, p. 566.

14. Jeffries, p. 51.

15. "Indeed, a late winter poll of Republican delegates to the party's 1936 convention showed no support for Willkie, and he did not even appear on the Gallup survey of presidential preferences until late April, when he polled a bare three percent." Jeffries, p. 55.

16. "Throughout the first term, Garner was an invaluable member of the new administration as it pursued revolutionary solutions to address the Great Depression. Garner used his political contacts in both the House and Senate to assist passage of Roosevelt's agenda. As presiding officer of the Senate, he sometimes descended to the Senate floor to personally lobby for bills." University of Virginia Miller Center, U.S. Presidents: Franklin D. Roosevelt, "John Nance Garner (1933–1941)." www.millercenter.org.

17. Herbert S. Parmet and Marie B. Hecht, *Never Again: A President Runs for a Third Term* (New York: The MacMillan Company, 1968), pp. 10–11.

18. Ted Morgan, *FDR: A Biography* (New York: Simon & Schuster, 1985), p. 518.

19. Roosevelt did not support Garner as a successor, or wish him to continue in the Vice presidency past 1940. To his Cabinet, Roosevelt quipped, "I see that the Vice President has thrown his bottle—I mean his hat—into the ring." Kathryn Smith, *The Gatekeeper: Missy LeHand, FDR, and the Untold Story of the Partnership that Defined a Presidency* (New York: Touchstone, 2016), p. 218.

20. "Democratic voters favored Garner as Roosevelt's successor, and the Vice President's support among them shot up from 20 percent in December 1938 to 42 percent in March 1939. . . . Whatever his actual desire for the presidency may have been, he was clearly ready to head the opposition to Roosevelt, the New Dealers, and a third term." Jeffries, p. 89. However, a clear majority of Democrats remained with Roosevelt over Garner in a head-to-head choice between the two. "Democrats polled in May 1939 as to whom they wanted to see elected President preferred FDR to Garner by 56–22 percent." Ibid. As to hijacking, Dunn quotes North Carolina Senator Josiah Bailey to the effect that Roosevelt liberals "have come into the house which was built by others and intend to take possession and drive the builders out. We'll not let anybody take the Democratic Party away from us." Dunn, *Purge*, p. 86.

21. See James A. Farley, *Jim Farley's Story: The Roosevelt Years* (New York: McGraw-Hill Book Company, Inc., 1948), pp. 175–177. Richard Moe writes that

Roosevelt would never have allowed Farley to be nominated for president. "He didn't think Farley was qualified or that he could be elected." Moe, p. 185.

22. "Farley and Garner, both of them unhappy about the direction of the New Deal, their own declining influence in the administration, and the possibility of FDR seeking a third term, had discussions as early as November 1937 about the 1940 nomination." Jeffries, p. 86.

23. Farley, pp. 171–172. For his part, Garner had substantial misgivings about the possibility of a third Roosevelt term. Ibid., pp. 213–214.

24. Ibid., p. 184.

25. Roosevelt initially worked to sideline McNutt by appointing him United States High Commissioner to the Philippines. Farley, p. 71. After government reorganization legislation passed in 1939, he appointed McNutt as Administrator for the Federal Security Administration, an amalgam of agencies that served as the precursor to the Department of Health Education and Welfare. "A few days later, McNutt was named Federal Security Administrator, which occasioned no little surprise in official circles, but was no surprise to me, because I saw in the move an adroit maneuver to silence Paul's campaign for the nomination." Farley, p. 170.

26. By 1940, Byrnes had served nine years in the Senate, following 14 in the House. He would later hold major positions in Roosevelt's wartime administration, be Truman's Secretary of State, and become governor of South Carolina. Byrnes was mistrusted by liberal elements of Roosevelt's coalition, especially labor. When Roosevelt replaced Wallace on the ticket in 1944, Byrnes expected to be FDR's choice for vice president. He had gotten Senator Truman to agree to make a nominating speech, only to be chagrined when Roosevelt selected Truman in his place.

27. Jones was well liked by business Democrats, however he faced opposition from labor and other New Deal elements. "He was neither a liberal nor a New Dealer. He was alleged to have opposed the nomination of Hugo Black to the Supreme Court because Black was too liberal." Parmet and Hecht, p. 12.

28. A prairie populist, Wheeler had run for vice president with Wisconsin Senator Robert LaFollette on the Progressive Party ticket in 1924. He was the first senator to endorse FDR for president in 1932, but later became the president's staunch opponent, not only in the 1937 Court-packing fight, which Wheeler led, but also on war preparation measures. The senator was an outspoken isolationist. Wheeler could have been a compromise candidate. "His fight against the Court plan and subsequent break with FDR might endear him to the conservatives, whereas his overall record might make him acceptable to the liberals." Parmet and Hecht, p. 12. More likely, no faction would fully trust Wheeler and he was certain to face Roosevelt's enmity.

29. In 1938, a poll of Democratic Governors showed only six of thirty-eight supporting the idea. Three were opposed. All others were non-committal. Eugene W. Hickok, Jr., "Pique Over Principle: Partisan Politics and the Twenty-second Amendment" in *Restoring the Presidency: Reconsidering the Twenty-second Amendment* (Washington, DC: The National Legal Center for the Public Interest, 1990), p. 39.

30. For example, on March 27, 1940, the Maine Democratic Convention adopted a resolution encouraging Roosevelt to seek a third term. It began by citing the fact that the Framers had not foreclosed it when writing the Constitution, and cited the "world crisis" as the rationale for breaking the two-term tradition. "Whereas it is important

and of vital concern to the peace and security of our nation, in this great world crisis, that the United States of America should have in the next four years a President who is able to cope and deal with trying and grave problems, and a leader whose efforts are dedicated to world peace and to keep the youth of America out of war," said the resolution, Maine delegates to the Convention would pledge their vote to Roosevelt. If the president declined to run, they would vote for Farley. Franklin Delano Roosevelt Library, Democratic National Conventions, Box 143, www.fdrlibrary.marist.edu/_resources/images/psf/psf000531.pdf (accessed July 20, 2018).

31. Farley, p. 186.

32. Ibid., pp. 142–143.

33. Ibid., p. 186.

34. Cordell Hull, *The Memoirs of Cordell Hull, vol. 1* (New York: The MacMillan Company, 1948), p. 858.

35. Hull, p. 859.

36. Elliott Roosevelt and James Brough, *A Rendezvous with Destiny: The Roosevelts in the White House* (New York: G.P. Putnam's Sons, 1975), p. 256.

37. H.W. Brands, *Traitor to His Class: The Privileged Life and Radical Presidency of Franklin Delano Roosevelt* (New York: Doubleday, 2008), p. 553.

38. James MacGregor Burns, *Roosevelt: The Soldier of Freedom* (New York: Harcourt, Brace, Jovanovich, 1970), p. 503.

39. Doris Kearns Goodwin, *No Ordinary Time: Franklin and Eleanor Roosevelt: The Home Front in World War II* (New York: Simon and Schuster, 1994), p. 106.

40. Dunn, *Purge*, p. 135.

41. Farley, p. 252.

42. Jeffries, p. 107.

43. Charles Peters, *Five Days in Philadelphia: The Amazing "We Want Willkie" Convention of 1940 and How it Freed FDR to Save the Western World* (New York: PublicAffairs, 2005), p. 129.

44. Burns, p. 409.

45. "The purpose of portraying Roosevelt as a Sphinx was to let it be known to the President that the press was flummoxed by his persistent reluctance to make clear whether he would run for re-election in the contest of November 1940." Nicholas Wapshott, *The Sphinx: Franklin Roosevelt, The Isolationists, and the Road to World War II* (New York: W.W. Norton, 2015), p. ix.

46. Samuel I. Rosenman, *Working with Roosevelt* (New York: Harper & Brothers, 1952), p. 200.

47. Morgan, p. 519.

48. "Roosevelt wanted to be a country squire just as his mother always pictured him, raising trees and improving his working farm. He wanted to be an elder statesman, issuing brilliant solutions for complex problems from his Hudson River retreat. He wanted to be a scholar going over his papers and writing the definitive history of the New Deal from his lovely Memorial Library." Parmet and Hecht, p. 175.

49. Rosenman, p. 200.

50. Morgan, p. 527.

51. Frances Perkins, *The Roosevelt I Knew* (New York: The Viking Press, 1946), p. 126.

52. Kearns Goodwin, *No Ordinary Time*, p. 108.

53. "The Congressional rebellion against the President's power and possibly against the continuance of the New Deal could best be controlled by a man whose days in office were not numbered. As long as he was a possible candidate, he could make policy. On the other hand, if he announced his candidacy, he would become more a political figure and less a President, and thus his prestige would suffer." Parmet and Hecht, p. 10.

54. "In 1938, even though Democrats held staggering majorities of nearly four-fifths of the seats in both chambers of Congress, that huge Democratic majority was deceptive, for a real division in the vast Democratic ranks had existed for several years." Dunn, *Purge*, p. 5. For instance, Dunn mentions by name 13 Democratic senators who often found ways to limit or otherwise undercut the New Deal. Ibid. Such conservative defections were not limited to Congress. Former Party leaders such as John W. Davis and Al Smith, the 1924 and 1928 Democratic nominees respectively, had been frequent critics of Roosevelt. Davis would testify in person in 1940 Senate hearings, and submit written testimony for a 1945 Senate hearing, declaring his outspoken opposition to a third term. For his part, Smith would endorse Governor Landon, FDR's 1936 Republican opponent, as well as Wendell Willkie's 1940 candidacy.

55. Morgan, p. 516.

56. "In June (1939), Harry Hopkins told the United Press that, in time, he would urge FDR to seek the 1940 nomination. Nevertheless, he was unwilling to give up his own presidential ambitions. . . . Shortly afterward, he became seriously ill again. . . . A visit to the Mayo Clinic helped him to recover enough to go home to Georgetown, but he was confined to the house for eight months. His presidential hopes were cancelled." Parmet and Hecht, p. 18. "With respect to Hopkins' prospects, FDR identified his liabilities as his divorce (though he had a happy marriage with his second wife before her death in 1937) and his health. Assuming a return to health, Roosevelt told Hopkins that he could be elected and would be a better president than other possibilities." Jeffries, p. 87. Hopkins went on to be FDR's point-man at the 1940 Convention and then served as a principal adviser and confidant during the war.

57. Nathan Miller, *FDR: An Intimate History* (Garden City, New York: Doubleday & Company, 1983), p. 445.

58. David L. Roll, *The Hopkins Touch: Harry Hopkins and the Forging of the Alliance to Defeat Hitler* (Oxford: Oxford University Press, 2013), p. 45.

59. Robert E. Sherwood, *Roosevelt and Hopkins: An Intimate History* (New York: Harper & Brothers, 1948), p. 99.

60. In December 1937, Hopkins had major surgery at the Mayo Clinic to treat stomach cancer. "The surgeons said the operation was successful, but Hopkins would suffer the aftereffects of this operation for the rest of his life." Moe, pp. 43–44. "It was evident by 1939 that Hopkins' candidacy was stillborn . . . during the crucial pre-convention months, he was either sick in bed or convalescing. There was no other New Dealer in sight to pick up the banner." Lash, p. 615.

61. Roosevelt and Brough, *A Rendezvous*, p. 254.

62. Rosenman, p. 201.

63. Ibid.

64. "Throughout 1938, the world situation deteriorated. And as the situation worsened, the President became increasingly aware that many New Dealers backed away from any international involvement because they feared it might mean less interest in domestic reform." Parmet and Hecht, p. 13.

65. Roosevelt and Brough, *A Rendezvous*, p. 256.

66. Henry L. Stimson and MacGeorge Bundy, *On Active Services in Peace and War* (New York: Harper Brothers, 1947), pp. 234–236.

67. Via the mechanism of the Lytton Commission, the Council of the League of Nations investigated the situation in Manchuria. After approximately a year, the Commission issued a report that was highly negative toward Japan. "It was a masterful summary of events in Manchuria and a decisive judgment against Japan on all major issues. . . . Its arraignment of Japan was unanswerable. . . . At last, after months of debate and delay, the League of Nations on February 24 (1933), with Japan alone dissenting, adopted a report accepting in full the findings of the Lytton Commission and refusing to recognize the puppet regime in Manchuria." In response, Japan withdrew from the League of Nations. Ibid., pp. 260–261.

68. The war began on July 7, 1937, with an incident at the Marco Polo Bridge near Beijing.

69. Peter Harmsen, *Shanghai 1937: Stalingrad on the Yangtze* (Havertown, Pennsylvania: Casemate Publishers, 2013).

70. "A careful reading of the diplomatic negotiations that preceded Pearl Harbor can lead to no conclusion but that it was American support for China—American refusal to repudiate the principles of Hay, Hughes, Stimson, and Hull—which proved the final cause of the breakdown of negotiations and the beginning of war. If at any time the United States had been willing to concede to Japan a free hand in China, there would have been no war in the Pacific. The lines of division laid down so clearly in February 1932, led straight to Pearl Harbor." Stimson and Bundy, p. 256.

71. Tim Bouverie, *Appeasement: Chamberlain, Hitler, Churchill, and the Road to War* (New York: Random House, 2019), pp. 72–81.

72. Adolf Hitler of Germany, Neville Chamberlain of Great Britain, Benito Mussolini of Italy, and Edouard Daladier of France attended the conference in September 1938. Czechoslovakia was not represented.

73. "The Russian attack on Finland intensified Roosevelt's concerns about the defense of the United States, and he expressed his anxiety in his State of the Union message on January 4, 1940. . . . 'We must see the effect on our own future if all the small nations of the world have their independence snatched from them.'" Miller, p. 443.

74. At a commencement address at the University of Virginia, FDR departed from his prepared remarks to condemn Italy for this action. "On this 10th day of June 1940, the hand that held the dagger has struck it into the back of its neighbor," exclaimed the president. www.presidency.uscb.edu. "XXXII President of the United States Franklin D. Roosevelt, "Address at the University of Virginia, May 10, 1940." According to Nathan Miller, Undersecretary of State Sumner Welles urged the president to drop this vivid reference from the speech to avoid complicating relations with Italy. However, Roosevelt was livid with Mussolini and insisted on keeping the language in his remarks. Miller, p. 447.

75. Franklin Delano Roosevelt Library, Box 29, "France 1940," www.fdrlibrary.marist.edu/_resources/images/psf/psfa089.pdf (accessed July 21, 2018).

76. Churchill endorsed Reynaud's plea, emphasizing the effect that a French collapse would have on Britain. To Roosevelt, the Prime Minister cabled, "This moment is supremely critical for France. A decision that the United States will, if necessary, enter the war might save France. Failing that, in a few days French resistance may have crumbled and we will be left alone." Brands, *Traitor*, p. 551.

77. Ibid. America's refusal to engage in hostilities in, or on behalf of France, was consistent with long-standing U.S. policy. For example, on April 4, 1940, before the German attack, French War Minister Edouard Daladier wrote to Roosevelt about discussions with U.S. Ambassador to France William Bullitt. "I feel I should tell you that during the past two years when I was Prime Minister, Ambassador Bullitt always said to me that in case of a European conflict, France should make her own decisions, knowing that, according to the opinion of Ambassador Bullitt, the United States would not enter the war." Franklin Delano Roosevelt Library, Box 31, "France 1940, Bullitt, William C." www.fdrlibrary.marist.edu/_resources/images/psf/psfa0306.pdf (accessed July 21, 2018).

78. Ibid., p. 203.

79. Ibid.

80. "Asked whether Vandenberg would be the Republican nominee, Democratic Party Chairman James A, Farley replied 'undoubtedly.'" Hendrik Meijer, *Arthur Vandenberg: The Man in the Middle of the American Century* (Chicago: University of Chicago Press, 2017), p. 139. For his part, Roosevelt expected the Republicans to nominate Taft. Jeffries, p. 61.

81. Neal, p. 57.

82. "My convictions regarding international cooperation and collective security for peace took firm form on the afternoon of the Pearl Harbor attack. That day ended isolationism for any realist," wrote Vandenberg. Lawrence J. Haas, *Harry and Arthur: Truman, Vandenberg and the Partnership that Created the Free World* (Lincoln, Nebraska: Potomac Books, 2016), p. 17.

83. For example, Vandenberg opposed repealing arms embargo restrictions. Anything other than strict adherence to the embargo would take the country down a very slippery slope. "Repealing the arms embargo probably won't get us into a war," the senator reasoned, "but it's like taking the first drink of whiskey. After a while, you're drunk." Neal, p. 58.

84. Roosevelt was grateful, however, that Willkie's nomination eased political divisions that could have existed if one of the other Republicans had been the candidate. "He considered this nomination a 'Godsend to the country,' for it tended to remove the isolationist-interventionist issue from the campaign (at least, until the final days) and thereby prevented the splitting of the people into two embittered factions," stated Robert Sherwood. "The importance of this consideration could hardly be overestimated." Sherwood, p. 174. Elliott Roosevelt concurs, "If Britain collapsed before Election Day, which seemed more than likely, and my parent's aid-for-the-allies program thereby fell into disrepute, Willkie might well be the next President, but there was little chance that he would strike any bargains with the Nazis." Roosevelt and Brough, *A Rendezvous*, p. 265.

85. Parmet and Hecht, p. 176.

86. Moe, pp. 177–178.

87. Joseph P. Lash, *Eleanor and Franklin* (New York: W.W. Norton and Company, 1971), p. 612.

88. Lash, p. 616.

89. Ibid., pp. 614–615.

90. Roosevelt and Brough, *A Rendezvous*, p. 254.

91. Robert H. Jackson, *That Man: An Insider's Portrait of Franklin D. Roosevelt,* edited and introduced by John Q. Barrett (New York: Oxford University Press, 2003), p. 39.

92. Parmet and Hecht, p. 176. Along the same line, Tully opines, "If the world had remained at peace, I am sure that Mr. Roosevelt would have retired in January 1941." Grace Tully, *FDR: My Boss* (New York: Charles Scribner's Sons, 1949), p. 236.

93. He proclaimed to Welles that "a third term movement would make him vulnerable to attacks that everything he had done was to serve his ambition." Morgan, p. 516.

94. The large infusion of American troops to buttress exhausted French and British forces was instrumental in holding this line. Major German offensives in 1918 nearly succeeded, but for the involvement of the U.S. armed forces. See Stephen Rabalais, *General Fox Conner* (Philadelphia and Oxford: Casemate Publishers, 2017), pp. 35–148.

95. Rosenman, p. 203.

96. Rosenman, p. 203. David Fromkin adds, "The collapse of France changed Roosevelt's calculations. It was the decisive foreign policy event in his presidency, for before it occurred, he had seen no need to bring the United States into the war. After it happened, however, he saw no way to keep America out of it. . . . Taking a dim view of his party, his Congress, and all of the candidates who proposed to take his place, FDR, who has already decided to carry on himself, decided to do so with a new team." David Fromkin, *In the Time of the Americans* (New York: Random House, 1995), p. 516.

97. Hull, p. 855. The Secretary writes of a July 3, 1940, conversation with Roosevelt, less than two weeks before the Democratic Convention opened. "The President began to speculate on how he himself might win under certain circumstances. His tone was that of deprecating the idea of running. He thought he could win in November unless the war should stop." Roosevelt, who had spoken to Hull about being his successor, began pointing out the Secretary's political weaknesses. "The President's whole tone and language during our conversation was a complete reversal of what it had been ten days before, when he was advocating my candidacy." Hull, p. 859.

98. Hull, p. 861. In 1916, President Woodrow Wilson had similar concerns, exacerbated by the fact that prior to the Twentieth Amendment (1933), there was a four-month transition period between the presidential election and the March 4 Inauguration. Believing he might lose to Republican Charles Evans Hughes, Wilson pondered appointing Hughes Secretary of State, after which Wilson and Vice President Thomas Marshall would resign. Under the presidential succession laws then in effect, Hughes would have become President. O'Toole, *The Moralist,* p. 228.

99. Burns, p. 422.

100. "Roosevelt had great ambivalence about his decision to accept or to reject a third term. He wanted the New Deal to continue, and he thought it imperative for the safety of the world that his foreign policy prevail. His superb political sense told him that he alone, of all the Democrats, could be reasonably certain of success." Parmet and Hecht, pp. 174–175. "Roosevelt believed that the war was coming to the United States, and the question was who could lead the country through it and keep it united and focused, as Lincoln had during the Civil War? It was the President's inability to answer this question to his satisfaction that caused him to believe there was no one except himself who had a chance of accomplishing that. . . . In FDR's case, it can safely be said that he believed he was better prepared to govern in a time of national crisis than anyone else, since he had already done so." Moe, pp. 176–177.

101. "The President's policies had received an impressive endorsement from the American people in 1936. . . . He was most of all anxious that these proven policies, domestic and foreign, should be carried on." Tully, p. 237.

102. Senator Elmer Thomas (D-OK) reflected this attitude transformation. "If times were normal, I would not favor a third term for President Roosevelt, [but] I consider 1940 an abnormal year." Kearns Goodwin, *No Ordinary Time*, p. 108. Thomas served in the House from 1923 to 1927 and was a senator from 1927 to 1951.

103. The appointments threw the Republicans off stride. "Master Stroke by Roosevelt Stuns GOP," read a headline in the *Atlanta Constitution*; its reporter called FDR's appointments a 'demolition bomb tossed into the Republican camp.'" Dunn, p. 99. Missy LeHand's biographer, Kathryn Smith argues that the Stimson and Knox nominations were "hard evidence that FDR was now committed to a third term." Kathryn Smith, p. 224. "The appointment of Stimson and Knox was announced on June 20, and Stimson speedily learned that he was a highly controversial figure. The chairman of the Republican National Committee read him out of the party, and Republican pique was general. The Republicans were about to begin their convention, and their minds were so firmly fixed on politics that they insisted on describing the President's maneuver as a political dodge." Stimson and Bundy, p. 324.

104. "FDR had pulled off an enormous coup. Not only had he greatly strengthened his Cabinet in two critical positions, but he had broadened the appeal of his internationalist foreign policy by enlisting two prominent Republicans who were in support of it." Moe, p. 162. George Reedy, President Lyndon Johnson's Press Secretary, said of the appointments, "It was a very shrewd move by any standard. It nailed down the concept that the conduct of the war was an enterprise in which the President deserved the support of all of the people regardless of their attitude toward his politics. It disarmed the opposition and gave Roosevelt elbow room which he would not otherwise have had." George E. Reedy, *The Twilight of the Presidency* (New York: The World Publishing Company, 1970), p. 129.

105. Burns, p. 424.

106. David Levering Lewis, *The Improbable Wendell Willkie* (New York: Liveright Publishing Corporation, 2018), pp.141–142. Not all Republican leaders approved of his denouncing Stimson and Knox, preferring to frame the appointments as having improved the Cabinet. "Republican Fight Looms on War Issue at the Convention," *New York Times*, June 23, 1940, pp. 1–2.

107. "The one thing that made Willkie acceptable to a nominating majority of the convention . . .was his internationalist pedigree. To many Republicans, the isolationists, including such Senate stalwarts as Arthur Vandenberg of Michigan and Robert Taft of Ohio had become an embarrassment." Brands, *Traitor,* p. 552. See also, Lewis, p. 112.

108. Neal, p. 84. See, also, Lewis, p. 139.

109. Republican Party Platforms, "Republican Party Platform of 1940," June 24, 1940. Online by Gerhard Peters and John T. Woolley, *The American Presidency Project.* http://www.presidency.ucsb.edu/ws/?pid=29640.

110. Dunn, *Blueprint,* p. 108. "If Taft had been nominated, he would have vigorously opposed the efforts FDR made to aid Britain and to enact a military draft in this country. This isn't a matter of speculation; it's on the record in innumerable speeches that Taft made and, more significantly, in actual votes in the Senate against measures as Lend-Lease and the Selective Service bill." Peters, p. 4.

111. Haas, p. 11. Bases for destroyers allowed the transfer of fifty U.S. destroyers in exchange for basing rights on British possessions.

112. Willkie was at zero percent in opinion polls taken three months before the Convention. Peters, p. 4. He won no primaries and received six-tenths of one percent of the overall votes cast in those primaries. "1940 Republican Presidential Primaries," www.wikipedia.org.

113. He switched parties and became a Republican in November 1939. Neal, p. 54.

114. Lewis, pp. 56–57. Moe, p. 152. In their platform, the Democrats supported conducting a national referendum on League membership.

115. The proposal to condemn the Klan failed by a single vote. Lewis, p. 59. See also www.presidency.ucsb.edu/ws/index.php?pid=29593. However, he did successfully battle the Klan at the local level in Akron, Ohio.

116. Even then, Willkie was an internationalist, and supported an unsuccessful platform plank reaffirming support for the League of Nations. Peters, p. 30.

117. Richard Norton Smith, *Thomas E. Dewey and His Times* (New York: Simon and Schuster, 1983), p. 295.

118. "From the beginning of the Roosevelt presidency, Willkie was among the New Deal's outspoken critics. He first shouted his opposition in April of 1933 following FDR's proposal to build the Tennessee Valley Authority." On April 14, 1933, he made his initial appearance before Congress, testifying in front of the House Military Affairs Committee, which oversaw the Army Corps of Engineers. Steve Neal, *Dark Horse: A Biography of Wendell Willkie* (Lawrence, Kansas: University of Kansas Press, 1984), pp. 28–29.

119. To acquire Commonwealth and Southern properties by eminent domain, the Tennessee Valley Authority offered $48 million. Willkie refused the offer, publicly denounced it, and wound up settling with the government for $78 million. In July 1939, after Willkie successfully concluded these negotiations, he appeared on the cover of Henry Luce's *Time* magazine. Lewis, p. 119.

120. Neal, pp. 32–38. Henry Luce, who published *Time* and *Life,* appreciated Willkie's staunch anti-Nazi views. "The puffery from Luce's publications was shameless and endless. On May 13, 1940, *Life* devoted an unprecedented eleven-page

spread to Willkie that concluded, 'In the opinion of most of the nation's political cognoscenti, Wendell Lewis Willkie is by far the ablest man the Republicans could nominate for President in Philadelphia next month.'" Peters, p. 39.

121. A majority of the Convention would be 501 votes. On the first ballot, Dewey secured 360, Taft, 189, and Vandenberg 76. Willkie received 105. On the fourth ballot, Willkie took the lead. Taft was the last man standing as Willkie secured his sixth ballot victory. Dunn, *Blueprint,* pp. 114–115.

122. "A handful of likeminded northeastern national committeemen believed that the party of Lincoln, absent new leadership and a retooled platform, was destined for yet another rejection that might leave it on life support after 1940." Lewis, p. 105.

123. Willkie published a major essay in the April 1940 issue of *Fortune.* Titled, "We the People: A Foundation for Political Recovery," it was a searing critique of the New Deal. Lewis, p. 125.

124. Willkie was still a Democrat in September 1939 when the war began in Europe. "In the months ahead, Willkie would speak out with increased frequency on the European war and American vulnerability. The war transformed Willkie from a big-business critic of the New Deal into a champion of freedom. And it gave his candidacy a new purpose." Neal, p. 52.

125. "Wendell Willkie came out of nowhere. . . . He combined his sallies against Roosevelt with a willingness to align the United States with Great Britain in the fight against Germany. This set him apart from Vandenberg, Taft, and Dewey—and endeared him to East Coast publishers and financiers who could abide neither the New Deal nor isolationism." Meijer, p. 167.

126. Moe, 156–157.

127. "Dewey recognized that his one chance for the nomination lay with his party's primary voters. While Taft confined his efforts to Republican professionals and Southern rotten boroughs, and Vandenberg waltzed around a formal declaration of candidacy, Dewey set out to demonstrate overwhelming popular support, enough to deflect Old Guard opposition with the sweet smell of success." Richard Norton Smith, p. 297.

128. That year, twelve states had primaries. Dewey won five of them and secured just under half of the overall vote in all primaries. "Republican Presidential Primaries, 1940," www.wikipedia.org.

129. Moe, p. 151.

130. Ralph Williams was the head of the Convention's Committee on Arrangements. He died on May 16, 1940, of a heart attack. Williams had been a Taft supporter. His replacement was his vice chair, Sam Pryor of Connecticut. The Willkie boom had its origins among Connecticut Republicans. Pryor combined his roles as Arrangements chair and Willkie partisan to create conditions at the Convention very much in Willkie's favor. Among them was the ability to pack the galleries with Willkie supporters. Lewis, pp. 137–138.

131. Neal, pp. 105–106.

132. Ibid., p. 107.

133. Lewis, pp. 146–147.

134. Meijer, pp. 167–168.

135. Turner Catledge, "Republicans Nominate Wendell Willkie for the Presidency on the Sixth Ballot," *New York Times,* June 28, 1940, www.archivenytimes.com (accessed July 12, 2019).

136. Until Donald Trump's nomination and general election victory in 2016, Willkie's come-from-nowhere nomination stood as perhaps the most extraordinary upset in U.S. political history. "Gallup described Willkie's rise as the most astonishing phenomenon in the brief history of polling." Neal, p. 85. Assessing the outcome, Senator Taft's wife, Martha, expressed, "They say this is the first unbossed convention in the Party's history; I hope it's the last." "The Age of Taft," *Time*, January 20, 1947, p. 23.

137. McNary, in fact, hoped to be the beneficiary of a deadlocked convention and secure the presidential nomination. He was not, in the first place, a Willkie enthusiast. Neal, p. 93. When the vice presidential nomination was offered to him, McNary initially refused. Party leaders, worried about Willkie's weakness in the West states, implored McNary to join the ticket. Eventually, the Oregon senator agreed. Neal, pp. 117–119. It was a classic example of regional ticket balancing.

138. Ibid., p. 121. To columnist Walter Winchell, Roosevelt said of Willkie, "He's grass-roots stuff. The people like him very much. His sincerity comes through with terrific impact. The people believe every word he says. We are going to have a heck of a fight on our hands with him." Neal, p. 122.

139. Jackson, p. 41.

140. Ibid., p. 132. "His stock had dropped sharply in the polls since Philadelphia and the momentum had clearly shifted to the President. And for the rest of the fall, he would be playing catch up against the consummate professional." Ibid., p. 141.

141. Sherwood, p. 174.

142. Neal, p. 119.

143. Farley, pp. 252–253. To the contrary, Grace Tully writes, "The Boss was never worried about the outcome of the 1940 campaign. He had considerable respect for Wendell Willkie as an individual and expected him to be a good campaigner. The Indianan's qualities of showmanship appealed to the President, but he never doubted the political strength of his own ticket and the public support of his own policies." Tully, p. 239.

144. An opinion survey taken in mid-September showed that Willkie would prevail by 5.5 percent if the war ended by Election Day, but would lose by 18 points if there was a chance that America might enter the war. Neal, p. 150.

145. Wilkerson, p. 304.

146. The Democratic Party of the 1930s was replete with divisions and opportunism on the race question. As the scholar Isabel Wilkerson observes of the African-American vote, "Suddenly the very party and the very apparatus that was ready to kill them if they tried to vote in the South was searching them out and all but carrying them to the polls. To the Democrats in the North, each new arrival from the South was a potential new vote in their column. It was in the Democrats best interest to mobilize these people, who, now given the chance to vote, might go Republican." Ibid.

147. Against Herbert Hoover in 1932, Roosevelt secured only a narrow majority among African-Americans in New York and averaged 25–30 percent support in six other major American cities, those being Chicago, Cincinnati, Cleveland, Detroit,

Knoxville, New York, Philadelphia, and Pittsburgh. In 1936, among the same voting sample, he won nearly 50 percent in Chicago, over 81 percent in New York, and about two-thirds in the other cities. Within the eight cities, the increase in the Democratic vote between 1932 and 1936 ranged between 60 percent and 250 percent. Nancy J. Weiss, *Farewell to the Party of Lincoln: Black Politics in the Age of FDR* (Princeton, New Jersey: Princeton University Press, 1983), p. 206. This trend continued in 1940. By that time, the conversion of African-Americans from Republican to Democrat was well advanced, so the rate of increase between the 1936 and 1940 elections was not as dramatic, but Roosevelt's candidacy for the third term served to entrench this voting behavior. Weiss, pp. 292–293.

148. "Black voters nationwide realigned their party affiliation because of the growing perception that the interests of the black community were intertwined with local Democratic organizations. Local patronage positions and nationally-administered emergency relief programs in Depression-era Chicago and other cities proved alluring." "Party Alignment and the New Deal," History, Art, and Archives, U.S. House of Representatives, www.history.house.gov (accessed July 29, 2018).

149. "The New Deal had been good to Illinois Democrats and especially to the boss of Chicago's Democratic machine, Edward Kelly, whose men were expected to stampede the Convention for Roosevelt. . . . 'They did not support Roosevelt out of any motive of affection or because of any political issues involved,' recalled Edward Flynn, who would succeed Jim Farley as chairman of the Democratic National Committee. 'Rather they knew that opposing him would be harmful to their local organizations. The Roosevelt name would help more than it could hurt, and for that reason the city leaders went along on the third-term candidacy.'" Brands, p. 554. In 1932, Roosevelt had carried 57.3 percent of the Chicago city vote. This increased to 65 percent in 1936, a boost heavily related to Roosevelt's expanded support in the African-American community. Only 21 percent of African-American voters went for Roosevelt in 1932, but he gained 48.8 percent of their vote in 1936. Weiss, p. 207. "The continued urbanization of blacks, and with it the large concentration of black voters in Northern cities, made the black vote a more significant factor in the Democratic Party's calculations." Weiss, p. 299. In 1940, Roosevelt narrowly carried Illinois, although Kelly machine corruption was a decisive issue in the election of a Republican governor, Dwight H. Green. *Life*, November 18, 1940, pp. 30–31.

150. Ibid., p. 208.

151. "Roosevelt and his allies sought uncommitted delegations or delegations favorable to the President, while Roosevelt, without declaring his candidacy, followed what Arthur Krock called a policy of 'passive acquiescence' to the efforts on his behalf. Those working for a third term wanted to demonstrate such strength for FDR that a 'draft' would be inevitable." Jeffries, p. 102.

152. "Roosevelt's basic problem, if he chose to run, was not how to be nominated . . . but how to secure the nomination in so striking a manner that it would amount to an emphatic and irresistible call to duty. This party call would be a prelude to a call from the whole country at election time." Burns, p. 412.

153. "The two-term limitation had become a cherished tradition, and Roosevelt knew, as 1940 opened, that he would be asking for trouble if he tried to buck it. In political circles in the winter and early spring, the dominant opinion was that

Roosevelt should not run for a third term." Kearns Goodwin, *No Ordinary Time*, p. 107. "All the polls showed a vast majority opposed to a third term as an abstract matter, and a clear majority opposed to a third term for Roosevelt. Yet many people, when further questioned, believed that certain circumstances—especially a crisis—would justify the President's running again." Burns, p. 413.

154. "In view of the no-third-term tradition, and of previous and predictable Republican charges of dictatorship, he believed there must be (or at least appear to be) a genuine draft, if possible by acclamation." Jeffries, p. 108.

155. Burns, p. 413.

156. "Secluded on his boat, Roosevelt appeared neither interested nor involved in the Convention. He had given no clear directions to anyone. He seemed happy to leave convention delegates with the impression that he wanted them to make their own decision. But from backstage—unobtrusively and indirectly—he was pulling the strings." Dunn, *Blueprint,* p. 132.

157. Roll, p. 65. "The delegates, so lively and expansive only four years before, had become irritable at the President's refusal to declare himself. They were worried about the popularity of the Republican presidential nominee, liberal businessman Wendell Willkie. They were worried about breaking the tradition of the third term. But there was no one else they could trust to steer the Democrats to victory. Still, they muttered, if the President wanted a third term, why couldn't he simply come out and say so?" Kearns Goodwin, *No Ordinary Time,* p. 125. Of Hopkins, Richard Moe says, "He would later be roundly accused of arrogance, heartlessness, and of course inattention to the views of the party leaders, most of whom had plenty of views to offer." Moe, p. 207.

158. "He put it on two grounds: first, a personal feeling that he wanted it to be a free and open nomination by delegates released from any pledge or commitment; second, for purposes of history, he wanted it made clear that he was not actively seeking a third term. He wanted this stated as part of the permanent written record of the Convention." Ibid., p. 210. See also, Moe, p.188, and Lash, pp. 619–620.

159. Rosenman, p. 212.

160. When McGarry died in 1976, the *New York Times* wrote, "At a key point in the convention, using a separate sound system in the catacombs under the stadium, Mr. Garry began booming, 'We want Roosevelt' into a microphone. He had arranged for faithful party followers to fill the galleries and they took up the chant. 'New Jersey wants Roosevelt. The people want Roosevelt,' Mr. Garry roared, and the galleries roared back. Millions listening over the radio were stirred by the booming voice that kept the frenzy in the stadium going for about 20 minutes. Few of the bewildered delegates were aware that the voice belonged to the Superintendent of Sewers." T.D. Garry, "'Voice of the Sewers' Who Backed FDR in '40 Dies," *New York Times*, July 3, 1976, p. 24, mobile.nytimes.com (accessed June 3, 2018).

161. "Although he felt that there was no such thing as a bona fide draft by a convention, he was confident that the American people wanted him to be President, and believed that they should be given a chance to vote for him." Rosenman, p. 203.

162. Farley, pp. 260–261. "To prevent the third-term controversy from blemishing the nomination, Roosevelt's supporters planned to have him drafted without the formality of a roll-call vote." Miller, p. 448.

163. Ibid., pp. 271–272. Peters recounts Roosevelt's motive for initiating this difficult and fruitless conversation. "Roosevelt was more worried than he wanted to admit. What if Farley did get enough votes to embarrass him? There was one sure way to prevent that: persuade Farley to forgo balloting and let the President be nominated by acclamation." Peters, p. 134.

164. Farley, p. 260.

165. Ibid., p. 261.

166. Ibid.

167. Dunn, p. 140. Senator Hill would staunchly oppose the Twenty-second Amendment when it came before the Senate in 1947, more vociferously than any other senator.

168. "One hundred and forty-eight votes had been cast against Roosevelt. Earlier that evening, Harry Hopkins had let it be known that Roosevelt would refuse the party's nomination if more than 150 delegates votes against him. The Convention had come perilously close to that limit." Dunn, pp. 141–142. The reason for this threshold related to the legitimacy of the draft. The more overwhelming the number, the more legitimate the draft would seem. Moe, p. 196.

169. Gould Lincoln, "Democrats Face Serious Battles," *Washington Evening Star,* July 16, 1940, p. 1.

170. Kearns Goodwin, *No Ordinary Time,* p. 128.

171. Beyond the Wallace controversy, Frances Perkins details additional reasons for the delegates' discontent. These included resentment at being manipulated by the Kelly-induced Voice from the Sewers. "The delegates did not know what was going on. Those on the platform had no idea that the enthusiasm did not come from the delegates. On the second day, the delegates realized there was something remarkable about it, and by the third day the secret was out. People were angry." Perkins, p. 129. Other problems arose from patronage disputes and the Roosevelt-directed 1938 efforts to purge party dissidents." Ibid.

172. Farley, p. 153.

173. Roosevelt and Brough, *A Rendezvous*, p. 255.

174. Hull, pp. 860–861.

175. Wallace switched parties in 1936. Party leaders, who had toiled for years to elect Democrats, were unhappy with handing the nomination to someone who had not been one of their own. "To the party leaders in Chicago, Wallace was a babe in the political woods. He had started life as a Republican and only recently switched to the Democratic Party." Kearns Goodwin, *No Ordinary Time*, pp. 128–129. One of the ironies of 1940, is that the Republican presidential nominee had recently been a Democrat and the Democratic nominee for vice president had almost as recently been a Republican.

176. In October 1939, on a trip to the West Coast, Secretary Wallace advocated that Democrats nominate Roosevelt for a third term. Believing this was premature, the White House quickly distanced itself from Wallace's comments. Tully, p. 237. But Wallace was by no means the first Cabinet member to advocate it. Ickes had come out publicly for a third term after the Munich Conference of September 1938. Hopkins followed in the summer of 1939. Sherwood, p. 170.

177. Farley, pp. 297–299.

178. Peters, p. 145. Farley was far from alone in this assessment. For example, Party Treasurer Edwin Pauley observed about Wallace, "He was so much the prophet, an unworldly man of mystical leanings and ideas, that it was obvious to all who knew him that he would only make the country a mighty strange president." Quoted in Ferrell, *Choosing Truman,* p. 16.

179. Ibid., pp. 299–300. Knowing of Roosevelt's desire to run with a progressive, but personally skeptical of Wallace, Hopkins recommended William O. Douglas, a committed liberal, who began service on the Supreme Court in April 1939. Roll, p. 66.

180. Secretary of Labor Frances Perkins served in that post from 1933 to 1945, for the entirety of Roosevelt's Presidency, and resigning two months after his death. She was the first woman ever appointed to a Cabinet position.

181. Dunn, *1940,* p. 143. See also, Peters, p. 131.

182. Dunn, *Purge*, p. 230.

183. "I think he chose Wallace because he felt the Secretary of Agriculture was at that time a genuine and sincere liberal and that he had been a loyal member of the Administration." Tully, p. 238.

184. In 1932, a nominee would need to win two-thirds of the delegates. This rule enhanced conservative power within the Democratic Party because it gave the South an effective veto over the nomination. Although he was the strongest contender, Roosevelt could not reach two-thirds until the fourth ballot, when he made a deal demanded by the Texas delegation to bring Garner on to the ticket. See Roosevelt and Brough, p. 290. Once in control of the party machinery, FDR caused the supermajority requirement to be abolished, and the requirement was dropped in time for the 1936 Democratic Convention.

185. Jeffries, p. 114. According to journalist Jack L. Bell, from his oral history at the Truman Library, Roosevelt wanted Wallace because of the strength that the Secretary of Agriculture would bring in from the farm belt. Bell oral history, p. 23.

186. Farley, p. 213. Jesse Jones was head of the Reconstruction Finance Corporation, a federal agency instrumental in combatting the Depression. William Bankhead was Speaker of the House from 1936 to 1940. He died two months after the 1940 Convention.

187. Rosenman took Roosevelt's note and slightly redrafted it, but maintained its fundamental structure and message. The material quoted here is from Roosevelt's original draft.

188. Ibid., p. 216.

189. Kearns Goodwin, *No Ordinary Time,* p. 129.

190. Perkins, p. 132. By telegram, Harold Ickes had also told Roosevelt of the sour mood among the delegates. "The convention is bleeding to death. Your reputation may bleed to death with it." Peters, p. 139. Ironically, Perkins had called Eleanor to encourage her to lobby FDR to appear in Chicago. Mrs. Roosevelt demurred, saying that FDR had already decided to remain in Washington. Then, she reconsidered and became his surrogate. Lash, p. 619.

191. Eleanor Roosevelt, "Address to the 1940 Democratic Convention," The Eleanor Roosevelt Papers Project, www.gwu.edu (accessed July 29, 2018).

192. "Eleanor's statement was just the touch necessary to bring the anti-Wallace factions into line. Perhaps their revolt was chiefly symbolic; perhaps they would have found their way back into the fold. But with Eleanor lecturing them on the obligation to party and country, they had no choice." Brands, p. 559. "There is no doubt in my mind that Mrs. Roosevelt's appearance and her speech about the burdens of the Presidency in critical times saved the day for the President." Farley, p. 302. South Carolina Senator James F. Byrnes and Hopkins led the arm-twisting. Peters, p. 149. "Were it not for Eleanor Roosevelt, Wallace might not have prevailed and the president might have declined to accept the nomination." Roll, p. 66. The irony is that Eleanor was not, herself, a Wallace enthusiast. Lash, p. 612.

193. Farley, p. 302. Elliott Roosevelt reports that FDR, rejection letter at the ready, followed the Convention on the radio, until Wallace was in the clear. "In Washington, Father listened grim-faced to the radio commentators' description of the turbulence in Chicago. . . . Without so much as a fan whirring to cool the room, Father was wet with sweat, his shirt stained dark under the armpits. . . . On the final tally of the first ballot, a handful of states that had asked to pass on the roll call cast their votes for Wallace. . . . One more fight was narrowly won. Father changed his shirt." Roosevelt and Brough, *A Rendezvous*, p. 267.

194. "When Wallace began to move toward the rostrum to accept, Byrnes stopped him from exposing himself and the party via national radio to an embarrassing reception of boos and catcalls." Jeffries, p. 117. See also, Sherwood, p. 179.

195. "May I suggest if the Convention concurs that I come to Chicago at once for the purpose of meeting and greeting the delegates and alternates before they return to their homes, also suggest receiving formal notification of my selection," Roosevelt wrote to his secretary, Marguerite 'Missy' LeHand. Note from Franklin D. Roosevelt to Marguerite LeHand, Series 1: Franklin D. Roosevelt Significant Documents, PPF 3757: LeHand, Marguerite A. (LeHand Scrapbook), Franklin D. Roosevelt Library and Museum.

196. Elliott Roosevelt and James Brough, *An Untold Story: The Roosevelts of Hyde Park* (New York: G.P. Putnam's Sons, 1973), pp. 286–287. "According to at least two important sources, Franklin Roosevelt's dramatic flight and speech to the Democratic National Convention achieved the desired effect. On July 4th, the *New York Times* editorialized, 'Governor Roosevelt put into his appearance and address before the Chicago convention something of the breeziness that naturally went with his flight through the air'. . . . The following day, Claude G. Bowers opined in the *New York Journal*, 'The speech of Roosevelt was a triumph. The delegates found before them a virile figure, physically strong . . . a militant figure with an eagerness to fight.'" David W. Houck and Amos Kiewe, *FDR's Body Politics: The Rhetoric of Disability* (College Station: Texas A&M University Press, 2003), p. 92.

197. Franklin D. Roosevelt, "Address Accepting the Presidential Nomination at the Democratic National Convention in Chicago," July 2, 1932. Online by Gerhard Peters and John T. Woolley, *The American Presidency Project*. http://www.presidency.ucsb.edu/ws/?pid=75174.

198. "Before those of the cabinet who were going to the convention left Washington, we had a talk with Roosevelt about the desirability of his appearance at Chicago.

He said he had definitely made up his mind he would not go. The situation, domestic and foreign, required his complete attention in Washington. He thought it wouldn't look well and would appear that he was putting on pressure." Perkins, p. 128. "The key element in his strategy was to play the Washingtonian role of a statesman far too preoccupied with world crises to involve himself in the crude and vulgar fray of party politics." Dunn, p. 136. "Reasoning that his presence would be seen as an attempt to force the hands of the delegates and ruin the charade of a draft, he remained in the White House working with Rosenman on the acceptance speech." Miller, p. 449.

199. On September 16, 1940, less than two months after Roosevelt's declaration, the president signed into law the Burke-Wadsworth Selective Service and Training Act of 1940. Named for its prime sponsors, Senator Edward Burke (D-NE), an implacable foe of the third term, and Representative James Wadsworth (R-NY), the Act provided for compulsory draft registration for men aged twenty-one to thirty-five.

200. Rosenman, p. 220.

201. "At a chance meeting in the barber shop of the Waldorf-Astoria in New York, James A. Farley pressed him to emphasize the third term as his major issue. Beyond quoting the founding fathers a few times, Willkie chose not to argue the question of the third term." Neal, p. 153.

202. Wendell L. Willkie, "Roosevelt Should Run in 1940," *Look,* April 26, 1940.

203. Ibid.

204. "The confidence that the Fathers had in the people has been amply vindicated. In nearly 150 years only one man, Theodore Roosevelt—has been nominated for a third term, and none has been elected. The issue has arisen on several occasions, but it has always been dismissed." Ibid.

205. Ibid.

206. "If the President seriously intends to keep us out of war, it is difficult to see how the European situation could create an emergency of such a character as to justify shattering this venerable, democratic tradition." Ibid.

207. "There are millions of Democrats in this land who would like to see somebody else try." Ibid.

208. "Among 130,000,000 able-bodied, energetic, level-headed, and imaginative citizens, it is mathematically impossible that no other leader exists." Ibid.

209. Ibid.

210. Ibid. Robert Sherwood disdained Willkie's hubristic strategy. "Even before his nomination, he had challenged Roosevelt to run for a third time, saying that he wanted the privilege of meeting and beating the toughest opponent the Democrats could name. His cry was 'Bring on the Champ!' A shrewder politician would not have said that. The people interpreted Willkie literally as saying, 'The hell with the third term tradition. Let's make this a real fight!' That dramatized the contest—made it an exciting sporting event—and the more popular excitement there was in a campaign, the better it always was for Roosevelt. When Roosevelt agreed to run, people took it not so much as a violation of a tradition as acceptance of a challenge to an old fashioned, bare-knuckled slugfest." Sherwood, p. 176.

211. Lewis, p. 164.

212. Ibid., pp. 171–172.

213. Wendell Willkie, "Address Accepting the Presidential Nomination in Elwood, Indiana," August 17, 1940. Online by Gerhard Peters and John T. Woolley, The American Presidency Project. http://www.presidency.ucsb.edu/ws/?pid=75629.

214. Ibid.

215. Telegram from John Cowles to Wendell Willkie, May 20, 1940. Wendell Willkie Papers, Lilly Library, Indiana University.

216. "Willkie Urges South to Drop Vote Tradition," *Washington Evening Star*, Sept. 17, 1940, p. 1.

217. L.R. Conner, "Third Term Becomes Basic Issue in Ohio; Splits Develop on War," *Washington Evening Star,* September 22, 1940, p. B4.

218. James A. Hagerty, "Willkie Declares New Deal 'Kidnaps' Democratic Party," *New York Times*, October 15, 1940, pp. 1, 12.

219. "Text of Willkie's Address at Rally in Syracuse," *New York Times*, October 15, 1940, p. 12.

220. Text of a radio address by Wendell Willkie on the Columbia Broadcasting System, November 4, 1940, Wendell Willkie Papers, Lilly Library, Indiana University.

221. When Roosevelt died in 1945 of a cerebral hemorrhage, he was sixty-three years old. For some time, he had suffered from congestive heart failure. He thus served three full terms and three months of a fourth. (It was a total twelve years and one month, because ratification of the Twentieth Amendment shortened Roosevelt's second term by six weeks, since it moved Inauguration day from March 4 to January 20.) However, his pronounced illness, which was becoming obvious when he ran for the fourth term was not apparent when he ran for the third. In November 1940, Franklin Roosevelt was fifty-eight years old. Seemingly, he could have remained in office for at least another decade if a rationale could have been developed to keep him there.

222. Ibid.

223. Stathis, p. 65.

224. Statement by Wendell L. Willkie, Republican Presidential Candidate, November 4, 1940, Wendell Willkie Papers, Lilly Library, Indiana University.

225. Susan Dunn, *A Blueprint for War: FDR and the Hundred Days that Mobilized America* (New Haven: Yale University Press, 2018), pp. 1–11.

226. Peters, p. 121. Peters adds, "It is arguable that his impact on this country and the world was greater than most men who actually held the office. At a crucial moment in history, he stood for the right things at the right time. His nomination as the Republican presidential candidate meant that Roosevelt could get away in an election year with doing what had to be done to keep Britain from falling to Hitler and to prepare this country for the great war it would soon have to fight." Ibid., p. 195.

227. Ibid., pp. 195–196.

228. David Lawrence, "Middle West Gains Seen for Willkie," *Washington Evening Star,* Oct. 22, 1940, p. A-11.

229. Ibid. Lincoln cited the examples of Senators Vic Donahey (D-OH), Fred Van Nuys (D-IN), Harry Byrd (D-VA), Carter Glass (D-VA), and Jim Farley.

230. John C. Henry, "Roosevelt Pledges New President After Third Term Ends, as Willkie Charges U.S. Way of Life Is In Peril," *Washington Evening Star*, Nov. 3, 1940, p.1.

231. Statement of Joseph W. Martin, Jr. for the Republican National Committee, November 3, 1940.

232. Ibid.

233. Gould Lincoln, "Late Returns Boost Roosevelt's Lead," *Washington Evening Star,* Nov. 6, 1940, p. 1.

234. Jackson, p. 42.

235. Stathis, p. 65.

236. With the exception of the 1928 anti-Catholic uprising against Al Smith, loyalty to the Democratic Party was unshakable in the South until a split occurred within the Party in 1948, when Senator Strom Thurmond ran for president as a third-party candidate against President Truman. Before the Civil War, Democrats had to vie with Whigs for Southern electoral votes, but once Republicans formed their party in 1854 on an anti-slavery foundation, the South turned solid for Democrats. In 1860, Lincoln was not even on the ballot in Alabama, Arkansas, Florida, Georgia, Louisiana, Mississippi, North Carolina, South Carolina, Tennessee, and Texas, and he received one percent of the vote in Virginia. After Reconstruction, Southern antipathy to Republicans cemented Democratic control there, for offices at all levels of government. As Dunn notes, "The problem was that seventy years after the Civil War, 'Republican' was still a fighting word in the South, and conservative Southern Democrats had a far greater aversion to the party of Abraham Lincoln than to New Deal Democrats. . . . The Democratic Party might have been divided and at odds with itself, but it still mattered deeply to Southerners. It represented far more than a political label and far more than a political machine. It embodied their traditional home, one with deep historical, regional, emotional, and racial resonances." Dunn, *Purge*, pp. 84–86.

237. Roosevelt carried New York by 51.6–48 percent, Ohio by 52–48 percent, and Illinois by 51–49 percent. On the other hand, Willkie received 15 percent of the vote in Georgia, 14 percent in Louisiana, and just over 4 percent in South Carolina and Mississippi. With the notable exception of the 1928 election, in which anti-Catholic sentiment had split the South against Al Smith, Democrats had thus dominated the region since Reconstruction. Wilkerson asserts that African-American voters, assiduously cultivated by Chicago Democrats, were key to Roosevelt's narrow margin in Illinois and, similarly, in the other major industrial states. Wilkerson, p. 305.

238. "The popular vote—27,303,945 for FDR; 22,347,744 for Willkie—decisive though it was, could give Willkie solace. He had attracted five million more votes than Landon, in fact more than any GOP candidate in American history. After the GOP's crushing defeat in 1936, it was back in the game and, fortunately, so was the two-party system." Dunn, p. 264. Outside the Solid South, Willkie had won nearly 48 percent of the popular vote.

239. Neal, p. 129.

240. See, generally, Dunn, *Purge*, pp. 87–88, and pp. 110–111. "If Roosevelt had really wanted to purge conservatives from the Democratic Party, though, all he would have had to do was to take an unambiguous position on the question of race and support equal rights for blacks. That would have done the job, effectively sparking a major exodus of southern conservatives, It would, however, have pushed out many of the region's progressives and populists, a price FDR was not willing to pay." Ibid., p. 236.

241. The northeastern United States was then a Republican stronghold.

242. "Franklin Roosevelt Wins Another Chance to be a Great Leader of a United People," *Life*, November 18, 1940, Vol, 9, No. 21, p. 25.

243. Dunn, p. 265.

244. Lewis, p. 179.

Illinois Representative William M. Springer, who successfully moved a resolution through the House of Representatives in 1875 to forestall a third term bid by President Ulysses S. Grant. Office of Art and Archives, U.S. House of Representatives.

President Ulysses S. Grant declined to seek a third term in 1876, but unsuccessfully sought nomination to a non-consecutive third term in 1880. Brady-Handy Collection, Library of Congress Prints and Photographs Collection.

President Theodore Roosevelt, whose disclaimer of a candidacy in 1908 strongly reinforced the two-term tradition and whose challenge in 1912 threatened to upend it. Baker Art Gallery, Library of Congress Prints and Photographs Division.

The LaFollettes of Wisconsin. Robert, Sr., standing, hoped to lead Progressives in the 1912 campaign, but involuntarily gave way to the Bull Moose candidacy of Theodore Roosevelt. Robert, Jr., sitting, passed a 1928 resolution through the Senate to oppose a third term for Calvin Coolidge. U.S. Senate Historical Office.

Stung by defeat in the Senate of the Treaty of Versailles, President Woodrow Wilson dreamed of a third term candidacy to vindicate the League of Nations. Pach Brothers, NY, Library of Congress Prints and Photographs Division.

Senator William Borah of Idaho, a central figure in Senate foreign policy debates from the Treaty of Versailles to 1930s neutrality laws, pictured with Henry L. Stimson, a member of three presidential cabinets including service as FDR's Secretary of War. U.S. Senate Historical Office.

Franklin Delano Roosevelt and John Nance Garner. Running mates in 1932 and again in 1936, they had become bitter rivals by 1940 when Garner opposed Roosevelt's third term. Franklin D. Roosevelt Presidential Library & Museum.

The Senate Judiciary Committee, circa 1939. Fifth from the left, standing, is Nebraska Senator Edward Burke, who chaired 16 days of hearings in September 1940, opposing a third term for President Franklin Roosevelt. U.S. Senate Historical Office.

Wendell L. Willkie of Indiana, Republican nominee in 1940, opposed Franklin Roosevelt's bid for a third term. Getty Images.

Wendell L. Willkie in Ellwood, Indiana, August 17, 1940, on his way to accept the Republican nomination for President. Getty Images.

Three Vice Presidents, left to right, Alben Barkley, Henry Wallace, and Harry S. Truman. U.S. Senate Historical Office.

President Harry S. Truman and Secretary of State James F. Byrnes, the White House, 1946. Byrnes vainly hoped to be Franklin Roosevelt's running mate in 1944. U.S. Senate Historical Office.

Representative Earl Michener of Michigan, Chairman of the House Judiciary Committee and lead House floor manager for the Twenty-second Amendment. Harris & Ewing Collection, Library of Congress Prints & Photographs Division.

Representative John W. McCormack of Massachusetts, later Speaker. In the 1940s, he led House Democrats in opposing a constitutional amendment to limit presidential terms. Office of Art & Archives, U.S. House of Representatives.

Wisconsin Senator Alexander Wiley, Chairman of the Senate Judiciary Committee, floor manager for the 1947 proceedings on the Twenty-second Amendment. U.S. Senate Historical Office.

Alabama Senator Lister Hill, Franklin Roosevelt's nominator in 1940, and a fierce opponent of the Twenty-second Amendment. U.S. Senate Historical Office.

Senator Robert A. Taft of Ohio, who hoped in 1940, 1948, and 1952 to be the Republican nominee for President. He authored compromise language that became the Twenty-second Amendment. U.S. Senate Historical Office.

New York Governor Thomas E. Dewey, a contender for the 1940 Republican nomination, and the party's choice to oppose Franklin Delano Roosevelt in 1944 and Harry S. Truman in 1948. Greystone Studio, NY, Library of Congress Prints & Photographs Division.

Harry S. Truman, November 3, 1948, holding a copy of the Chicago Tribune, which prematurely headlined his political demise. Getty Images.

Senator Estes Kefauver of Tennessee defeated President Harry Truman in the 1952 New Hampshire primary, generating the President's withdrawal from the race. U.S. Senate Historical Office.

Chapter 8

A Tradition Breached Again

The Fourth Term of Franklin Delano Roosevelt (1944)

Eleven months into Roosevelt's third term, Japan attacked Pearl Harbor, and the United States entered the war. As 1944 dawned, victory remained elusive. Under these conditions, it was possible Roosevelt would seek another term in that year's election. If he did, he had a major advantage. The public was reluctant to change commanders in chief midway through the conflict.[1]

Roosevelt could have had his party's nomination if he wanted it. But did he? Party leaders pressed him for an answer. Early in 1944, a fourth term candidacy was likely, but not certain. It depended on the status of the war and whether his health would hold up. Daisy Suckley's diary for February 24 reflects the conundrum. "The P. is tired, as I have said before. He acknowledges it, & wants to get out of his grueling job, but there is too much demand for him to stay in, not only from this country, but also from all the United Nations—If one could look into the future!"[2]

The President's ambivalence continued into spring.[3] On May 15, 1944, Roosevelt confided in his Chief of Staff, Admiral William Leahy, his preference not to run for a fourth term. "I just hate to run again for election," FDR said. "Perhaps the war will by that time have progressed to a point that will make it unnecessary for me to be a candidate."[4] A week later, he told Suckley, "I haven't even decided if I will run myself." She responded, "What is going to decide you? For you are practically nominated already." The President replied, "What will decide me will be the way I feel in a couple of months. If I know I am not going to be able to carry on for another four years, it wouldn't be fair to the American people to run for another term."[5]

Democratic publicist Charles Michelson, quoted in a March 3 Associated Press article, asserted that Roosevelt would prefer not to run in 1944, but that the burden might be impossible to avoid. "My guess is that Franklin D. Roosevelt would take a case of the hives rather than four years more of the headache that being President means. It will not be so easy a choice as that. Circumstances might arise that would make it impossible for him to lay down the burden." Michelson posited that Roosevelt would see a duty to run, similar to 1940. "Re-election was wise if his motive, and if the people's motive, was based on the thought that, with the impending war, Roosevelt's experience made him the best qualified man to steer the nation through a stormy period." Michelson concluded, "Had it not been for the imminence of war, Roosevelt would never have received the third term nomination; would never, in fact, have gone after it."[6]

Until Roosevelt declared his plans, no other Democrat could make headway toward the nomination.[7] So the party awaited word. As in 1940, if the President were not a candidate, prospects for a Democratic victory would diminish dramatically. David Jordan has written in his study of on the 1944 election, "The leaders of the party simply assumed that Roosevelt would run again; any other possibility looked like disaster for the Democrats."[8]

Even more conservative Democrats, who had longstanding misgivings about the President, really had no alternative to him.[9] In January 1944, the Democratic National Committee unanimously urged the President to seek a fourth term.[10] However, early overtures to Roosevelt produced no commitment, as he was able to use the excuse of ongoing war responsibilities to deflect them.[11]

There was no serious question that Roosevelt would stand for reelection as long as he was physically able to continue. James MacGregor Burns, writes, "By early 1944, there was no doubt in the White House and little outside that he would run again, certainly if the war was not won."

The emergency that was the basis for his third-term candidacy remained unfinished. Even though the end of the war was foreseeable, no one could be sure when the conflict would conclude. Moreover, immensely consequential decisions loomed on how to structure and secure the peace. Who besides Roosevelt was equipped to deal with all that?

Moreover, there was the matter of domestic policy. Within his 1944 State of the Union address, which focused mainly on completing the war and the need for national service legislation, the President sketched out what he termed an "economic bill of rights."

Roosevelt submitted this speech in writing, and not in person. However, he broadcast portions of it to the public. It included ambitious goals for employment, housing, health care, income security, education, farming, and business competition.

"All of these rights spell security," proclaimed the President, "and after this war is won we must be prepared to move forward, in the implementation of these rights, to new goals of human happiness and well-being." He concluded, "I ask the Congress to explore the means for implementing this economic bill of rights—for it is definitely the responsibility of the Congress so to do. Many of these problems are already before committees of the Congress in the form of proposed legislation. I shall from time to time communicate with the Congress with respect to these and further proposals. In the event that no adequate program of progress is evolved, I am certain that the Nation will be conscious of the fact."

These issues had taken a backseat during the war. After the fighting concluded, they would rise in priority. In the State of the Union speech, Roosevelt gave the country a sense of what he thought should command attention. As with foreign policy, who better to lead the fight?

In 1940, FDR worried about a right-leaning retrogression. In 1944, that was still his active concern. Thus, he included a warning in his speech. "One of the great American industrialists of our day—a man who has rendered yeoman service to his country in this crisis—recently emphasized the grave dangers of 'rightist reaction' in this Nation. All clear-thinking businessmen share his concern. Indeed, if such reaction should develop—if history were to repeat itself and we were to return to the so-called 'normalcy' of the 1920's—then it is certain that even though we shall have conquered our enemies on the battlefields abroad, we shall have yielded to the spirit of Fascism here at home."[12]

War chronicler Nigel Hamilton comments, "Delivered in the midst of a continuing world war, the broadcast would, in terms of domestic public policy, be one of the most significant addresses of the twentieth century in America."[13]

With the two-term tradition already broken, retaining Roosevelt during an ongoing war seemed natural. Certainly the argument against extended tenure rang hollower in actual wartime than it did when conflict was merely looming. However, the issue was not quite dead. Speaking in Idaho on February 8, 1944, Wendell Willkie, who hoped to be the 1944 Republican nominee, decried the "dangers involved in giving the President a fourth term." To people who believed that the advantage of keeping Roosevelt in office outweighed the dangers, Willkie asked, "Does this mean then that administrations should never change because change should never be attempted at any but a placid hour?" He warned, "Such a decision would mean the end of democracy. For you and I will never in our lifetime see a placid hour."[14] Notwithstanding this plea, Willkie and other Republicans got little traction on the fourth term issue.

The obstacle to a fourth term was Roosevelt's health, which had eroded drastically during the war.[15] In March 1944, FDR underwent comprehensive medical tests at Bethesda Naval Hospital, under the supervision of Surgeon General Ross McIntire and Navy cardiologist Howard Bruenn. The tests revealed hypertension, hypertensive heart disease, cardiac failure in the left ventricle, and acute bronchitis. Especially alarming were the President's steeply elevated blood pressure and signs of congestive heart failure. Historian David Jordan comments, "Although such a diagnosis made it doubtful that such a patient could lead the country for four more years of a world war and the peace that would follow, Surgeon General McIntire was not about to spread it on the public record, and he ordered Bruenn to keep his conclusions quiet as well."[16]

Bruenn prescribed digitalis, weight loss, and as much rest as humanly possible, but Roosevelt remained terribly ill. According to the journalist Victor Sebestyen, "Roosevelt was warned in 1944 that, with his severe heart problems and weak legs, he would be very lucky to survive a fourth term. But he ignored medical advice and ran for election anyway, believing that his famous luck would hold."[17]

In 1940, the vice-presidential nomination had been important, because Roosevelt insisted on heading an unmistakably progressive national ticket, and was prepared to refuse the nomination if he was not satisfied. In 1944, the vice presidency would again be crucial, but for a very different reason. Ideology mattered much less than choosing someone who could successfully assume the presidency if Roosevelt died in office.[18]

Some Democrats who had opposed the third term in 1940 remained disgruntled, even if powerless to prevent FDR's renomination. One was former Vixe President Garner, who spent the war years in retirement in Uvalde, Texas. He worried that Roosevelt was declining and that Wallace was unfit to be president. In a conversation on February 3, 1943, Garner told Farley, "I think it would be a terrible thing to have Roosevelt elected again. It would not be fair to the country or to him. He cannot last forever, and from what I hear, he is losing ground. The possibility of having Wallace as President is repulsive to me."

Farley concurred. "As long as you brought it up, Jack, I must tell you that I am told the strain is telling on him. . . . Not only is it important that the maker of decisions on the conduct of the war be fresh and vigorous, but the next term will bring the peace making, and it is vital that the negotiations be in strong hands."[19]

By the summer of 1944, Farley had determined to oppose both Roosevelt and Wallace for renomination. But he was doing so from the sidelines, estranged from the White House, no longer a candidate himself, no longer the party chairman, and no longer a member of the President's cabinet.[20] He and Garner were venerable Democrats, but devoid of clout. The possibility that they could generate meaningful opposition to a fourth term was nil.

The 1944 Democratic Convention opened on July 19. Eight days earlier, at the conclusion of a White House press conference, Roosevelt stopped deflecting questions about his candidacy and made public his willingness to run again.[21] As historian Jay Winik observes, "He committed himself to the election as late as humanly possible, husbanding his failing energy and shrewdly limiting the time during which Republicans could make him a target."[22]

On July 11, Roosevelt released an unsolicited letter to party chairman Robert Hannegan. In it, the President stated that he would accept a nomination and would serve if elected, notwithstanding his preference to retire. "For myself, I do not want to run. . . . After many years of public service, therefore, my personal thoughts have turned to the day when I could return to civil life. All that is in me cries out to go back to my home on the Hudson River," wrote the President.[23] However, he added, the war came first. "If the people command me to continue in this office and in this war, I have as little right to withdraw as the soldier has to leave his post in the line."[24]

Columnist David Lawrence wrote,

> Mr. Roosevelt's statement of his willingness to run a fourth time is designed, of course, to answer the chief objection that will be raised against a fourth term, namely, that it is unprecedented and that it is the expression of a personal ambition. He argues that he would prefer not to run, but that the American people must decide in time of war whether he as Commander in Chief shall or shall not remain in office.[25]

At the Convention, which was back in Chicago again, Roosevelt faced only nominal opposition. On the first ballot, he received 1086 votes. Dissident Southern conservatives and Jim Farley personally cast a total of eighty-nine protest votes for Senator Harry F. Byrd of Virginia.[26] Although displeased with the outcome, Farley would not bolt the party. Ever the loyal Democrat, he issued a statement. "I have been opposed on principle to a third or fourth term. For that reason, I voted for the nomination of Senator Byrd of Virginia. Having participated in the proceedings of the Convention, I accept its decision and will support the party nominees."[27]

Nevertheless, there was an ample dose of Convention drama. It occurred on the fight over whether to replace Vice President Henry Wallace. David McCullough notes, "As so many of the Democrats who converged on Chicago understood, the task of choosing a Vice President had unique importance this time. The common, realistic, and not unspoken view was that they were there to pick not one, but two Presidents, and if the identity of the first was clear, that of the second was not."[28]

Wallace had never entirely consolidated his position within the party. Elements who liked him in 1940, such as the strong progressive wing, continued to support him.[29] Others, such as the very substantial array of party conservatives, mostly Southerners, remained opposed, and leaders of the big-city Democratic machines were lukewarm.

The only reason Wallace had gotten as far as he did in 1940 was because Roosevelt insisted on running with him. Four years later, the President did not repeat his demand, so discontent festered.

Fissures in the immensely diverse Democratic coalition were beginning to widen. Roosevelt's candidacy masked them to some degree, but fracturing was particularly evident on the question of retaining Wallace.[30]

Like the 1940 struggle to add Wallace to the ticket, the effort to remove him sparked substantial controversy and open dissent. Disliking the Vice President, and concerned about Roosevelt's health, senior Democrats looked for an alternative. Party Treasurer Edwin W. Pauley, Party Chairman Hannegan, and Roosevelt's appointments secretary, Pa Watson, collaborated to bring dissension over Wallace to the President's attention and to create a sense of urgency to find a replacement.[31] One of those was New York's Ed Flynn, who met with Roosevelt in June 1940, and warned the President that Wallace on the ticket could damage Democrats with independent voters in swing states. "From the moment Flynn informed Roosevelt that the only votes the Vice President could bring were the ones already in FDR's pocket," writes historian James Lacey, "Wallace was doomed."[32]

On July 10, 1944, Vice President Wallace returned to Washington from a trip to Russia and China. He had been gone for nearly two months, during which time his foes within the party leadership worked diligently to undermine his political standing. Plotting against Wallace, which Hannegan had initiated in May, continued among those high in the party machinery.[33] It culminated in a White House meeting on Tuesday evening, July 11, which Roosevelt convened for Democratic leaders. Earlier that day, the President announced he would run again. The leaders he gathered that night were Hannegan, Pauley, Postmaster General Frank Walker, Party Secretary George Allen, and Chicago Mayor Ed Kelly.[34] The convention was little more than a week away.

The leaders reinforced Flynn's message, that Wallace would meaningfully weaken the party ticket in November. The cumulative effect of this discussion, coming after weeks of anti-Wallace lobbying, reinforced Roosevelt's conclusion that a change must occur.

According to FDR's secretary, Grace Tully, there was no falling out between Roosevelt and Wallace. She had often heard the President express satisfaction with Wallace and affirmed his willingness to continue serving with him. However, as opposed to 1940, Roosevelt was open to hearing the views of anti-Wallace factions. According to Tully, "The difference between 1940 and 1944 was that the President was more or less engrossed in the war than in a political issue, and he had less energy to dissipate on multiple problems." Tully asserted that if Roosevelt had stood with Wallace, the Convention would have gone along.[35] But he didn't.

Open to an alternative, Roosevelt discussed several other possibilities, one of whom was a key Roosevelt ally, James F. Byrnes. A former South Carolina Senator, Supreme Court Justice, and, at the time, Director of the Office of War Mobilization, Byrnes, was personally ambitious for the job.[36]

Apart from their effort to derail Wallace, it was also these leaders' mission to sidetrack Byrnes.[37] The South Carolinian was a segregationist, whose civil rights' positions were well within the mainstream of Southern politics at the time, but generated much dissension among African-Americans. Byrnes also drew opposition from urban bosses, unions, and other progressive elements. As well, the leaders highlighted a religious issue. Born a Catholic in 1882, he left the church at the age of 26 to marry an Episcopalian. Catholics were an important voting bloc within the Democratic Party and were skeptical of Byrnes.[38] Taken together, all these liabilities were too much baggage to consider Byrnes.

After extended conversation, it was apparent that neither Wallace nor Byrnes should go forward. If not, then who? The discussion turned to other possibilities, including Missouri Senator Harry Truman. Roosevelt himself raised a dark horse, Supreme Court Justice William O. Douglas, who FDR had put on the bench in 1939.[39] However, none of the leaders shared the President's enthusiasm for the Justice, a political neophyte.[40]

Ending a long evening, Roosevelt concluded, "Bob, I think you and everyone else here want Truman."[41] Not wanting to bear negative tidings personally, Roosevelt dispatched Hannegan to break the bad news to Wallace and Postmaster General Frank Walker to tell Byrnes.[42]

Believing it would be wise to memorialize this conclusion, Hannegan that evening procured from the President a handwritten note, in which FDR said that he would gladly run with Douglas or Truman.[43] Several days later, Hannegan would have this sentiment converted into a letter. Once made public, it helped to secure Truman a spot on the ticket.

Jack L. Bell was a veteran of the Senate press gallery, who knew Truman well from years of covering the Senate. In an oral history for the Truman Library, he observes that Roosevelt had no relationship to speak of with Truman and that the President's actual preference was Douglas. It was Hannegan, disclosed Bell, who actually chose Truman. "He (Roosevelt) really, I think, preferred Douglas, because he thought Douglas would appeal to the liberals and bring out the Democrats. Thank God, it wasn't Douglas. Thank God for Hannegan, you might say in that respect. But FDR wasn't enamored with Truman at all. If he had definitely decided on Truman, he would never have included Douglas. And, of course, I think Harry was thunderstruck, really, that FDR would pick him. FDR didn't, Hannegan did."[44]

Meanwhile, Roosevelt and Wallace met at the White House on July 12, the day following the President's meeting with party leaders. Wallace made a detailed briefing on his overseas trip, and then the conversation turned to politics. FDR told Wallace that the leaders had advised that retaining him would be damaging. Wallace expressed willingness to step aside. Although he had already decided that change was essential,[45] Roosevelt did not accept.

This came as happy news to Wallace, who badly wanted to stand for reelection.[46] While the President was not insisting, in the face of opposition, that the ticket remain intact, he also had not dictated a replacement. "In all his years as a Cabinet officer and then Vice President, Wallace apparently never learned anything about the President's ways," observes James Lacey. "Unable to fire people who were loyal to him, Roosevelt expected them to divine his desires and act appropriately."[47]

Wallace requested Roosevelt to send a letter of endorsement to the Convention Chairman, Indiana Senator Samuel D. Jackson. Wallace hoped that such an expression would give him a boost for the nomination fight he would make at the convention. The President agreed. In Chicago, Wallace would actively seek the nomination, believing he had a chance to win. The Vice President reasoned that no one else could have such an endorsement, and that such an expression from FDR ought to be enough to carry the day.[48]

Wallace was not alone in this assessment. "The Wallace forces, including Sidney Hillman and Phil Murray of the CIO, took the announcement as a sign of hope, since theirs was the only candidate who now had something in writing from the President."[49]

On July 13, Wallace sat down with Hannegan, who urged him to withdraw. Reinforced, albeit deluded, by his discussion the previous day with the President, Wallace demurred.

FDR again met with the Vice President on July 14, telling him that he hoped Wallace would prevail in Chicago, while assuring him of a place in the Administration in case the delegates chose someone else.[50] As the meeting concluded, Roosevelt said, "While I cannot put it just that way in public, I hope it will be the same old team."[51]

As Ted Morgan writes, Roosevelt's assurance "should have been a tip-off for Wallace, who had ten years of close observation of the President's Machiavellian nature behind him, that his goose was cooked."[52]

Roosevelt came through with the promised letter for Wallace, but it was tepid. In correspondence from Hyde Park on July 14, he stated, "The easiest way of putting it is this: I have been associated with Henry Wallace during his past four years as Vice President, for eight years earlier while he was Secretary of Agriculture, and well before that. I like him and I respect him, and he is my personal friend. For these reasons, I would personally vote for his re-nomination if I were a delegate to the Convention."

Then came the disclaimer. "At the same time, I do not wish to appear in any way dictating to the Convention. Obviously, the Convention must do the deciding."[53]

Wallace's backers and his opponents could each find something to tout in the letter. An Associated Press account stated, "Wallace's supporters at once hailed the declaration of presidential views as insuring renomination for him. But in opposition camps, the emphasis was on Mr. Roosevelt's assertion that 'obviously the convention must do the deciding.'"[54]

Roosevelt's 1940 doggedness on Wallace's nomination contrasted vividly with his bland "endorsement" four years later. Notwithstanding the carping about Wallace, it is likely the President could have saved him. Instead, Roosevelt doomed his Vice President by not definitively declaring for him and quieting the dissenters.

As the Wallace situation unfolded, a parallel circumstance developed for Byrnes. At the leaders' meeting, Postmaster General Walker was charged with telling Byrnes a negative report. On Wednesday, July 12, Walker did his duty. Much like Wallace, who rebuffed Hannegan, Byrnes refused to accept his fate, and insisted on having a direct conversation with Roosevelt. Meanwhile, Byrnes learned that the main reason FDR did not select him was because of the presumed effect he would have on the African-American vote.[55]

The following day, Thursday, July 13, Byrnes saw FDR at the White House. Byrnes said that he was inclined to seek the vice presidential nomination, and sought to rebut the theory that his being on the ticket would cost the President votes.[56] During this meeting, Roosevelt told Byrnes about the Wallace letter. "I had to do at least this for Wallace," the President said; however, knowing that the letter was bland and non-definitive, he also expressed confidence that the delegates would nominate Byrnes.[57] Byrnes was therefore neither deterred nor discouraged from pursuing an active candidacy.

Once more, Roosevelt worked by stealth and indirection. Leo T. Crowley, head of the Foreign Economic Administration, was Byrnes' compatriot and strong supporter. Shortly after his meeting with Byrnes, Roosevelt called Crowley, who he knew would soon be seeing Byrnes. Roosevelt did not tell Crowley about the note he gave Hannegan after the July 11 leaders' meeting. But he did say that Hannegan was going to write him a letter asking whether he would object to running with Truman or Douglas, and that he planned to reply that he objected to neither.[58]

On Friday, July 14, Byrnes lunched with Hannegan, Walker, and Crowley. The party leaders importuned Byrnes to shut off his candidacy, claiming it was Roosevelt's desire. They mentioned the Hannegan letter. But their effort to dissuade Byrnes was unsuccessful.[59]

Instead, Byrnes left the meeting and called Roosevelt in Hyde Park, asking him directly whether he wanted to run with Truman or Douglas. The President hedged. He denied expressing a preference for either, stating that his role at the July 11 meeting was to learn who the leaders felt would either assist or diminish the Democratic ticket. "I did not say that I preferred anybody,"

Roosevelt claimed.[60] "They asked if I would object to Truman and Douglas and I said no," the President continued. "That is different from using the word 'prefer.' That is not expressing a preference because you know I told you I would have no preference."[61] To this, Roosevelt added, "After all, Jimmy, you are close to me personally. . . . I hardly know Truman."[62] Armed with this misleading denial, and unaware of the note Hannegan had procured, Byrnes felt he had a green light to run.[63]

Hannegan was confused. Believing Roosevelt had decided on the 11th against Byrnes, the chairman was now unsure. On July 15, he boarded the President's train while it stopped in Chicago. FDR was on his way to California, where he would embark on a naval vessel bound for planning meetings in Hawaii.[64] Hannegan was in Chicago because the Democratic Convention would open there on July 19. His principal objective insofar as the vice presidency was concerned, was to replace Wallace. With whom, mattered less. Again, Roosevelt mentioned that he would be fine to run with either Douglas or Truman. Hannegan emerged from the meeting with another note to that effect, which he gave to Roosevelt's secretary, Grace Tully, to type up.

The document mentioned Douglas and Truman, in that order. However, Hannegan instructed Tully to re-type it to list Truman first.[65] As finally prepared, the letter stated, "You have written me about Harry Truman and Bill Douglas. I should, of course, be very glad to run with either of them and believe that either one of them would bring real strength to the ticket."[66]

Tully wrote in her memoirs, "The reason for the switch was obvious. By naming Truman first it was plainly implied by the letter that he was the preferred choice of the President."[67] The document was postdated to July 19, the day the Democratic Convention would open.

During the meeting on the train, Roosevelt made clear that, notwithstanding the July 11 leaders' discussion, Byrnes also remained personally acceptable to him. However, he anticipated problems with labor. Thus, FDR had an admonition for Hannegan. "Clear it with Sidney," he instructed, referring to Sidney Hillman of the Congress of Industrial Organizations Political Action Committee. This proved to be an insuperable, although not unexpected, stumbling block.[68] As David Jordan reports, Philip Murray, the CIO's president, and Hillman, "made it clear that the CIO-PAC was solidly against Byrnes, that the South Carolinian was regarded as impossible for labor to support."[69] When Roosevelt got word from the party leaders about labor's rejection of Byrnes, the President committed to Truman.

Meanwhile, Truman was unaware of all these Byzantine manipulations. Just before the Senator departed from his Missouri home on the morning of July 14 to drive to Chicago, he got a call from Byrnes. In Truman's words, "As I was about to leave Independence on Friday before the Convention was to meet, James F. Byrnes called and asked me if I would nominate him for Vice President, as the President wanted him to have that position on the ticket."[70] Byrnes did not disclose the efforts Hannegan and others had made to dissuade him on the President's behalf, or that FDR had said he would gladly run with Truman or Douglas. So when Byrnes presented this rather incomplete picture, Truman agreed. The same day, Senator Alben Barkley approached him with a similar request, but Truman demurred, citing his earlier commitment.

In an undated, handwritten note on deposit at his presidential library, Truman recounted what happened when he canvassed the convention for Byrnes.[71] "When I arrived in Chicago, I had breakfast with Sidney Hillman who was a power in the labor section of the Convention. I asked him if he would support Byrnes. He said he would not—that there were only two men he would support. They were Wm. O. Douglas, Justice of the Supreme Court, and Harry S. Truman, U.S. Senator from Missouri. I told him that I was not a candidate and that I had agreed to nominate Byrnes because he told me the President wanted him. Then I had a meeting with Phil Murray head of the C.I.O. and one with Whitney head of the Railroad Trainmen. Both told me exactly what Sidney Hillman had told me. The next morning William Green, head of the A.F. of L., asked me to breakfast at the Parker House. He told me that the A.F. of L. did not like Wallace and that they had decided to support me. I told him my position with Byrnes and that I was not a candidate."[72]

Truman related these conversations to Byrnes, who overtly did not seem concerned. "I reported all these interviews to Mr. Byrnes. He would tell me every time that Roosevelt would say he was for him for Vice President." However, Byrnes was about to be contradicted. Roosevelt had come around to the idea that Truman was the running mate he wanted.[73]

According to Truman, "Roosevelt had decided upon me for the vice presidency, although he did not tell me in advance, but he did not want publicly to turn down Wallace. He had the kindliest heart in the world and never liked to hurt anyone. He would do all sorts of maneuvering to get rid of people he did not want without his being the one to fire them."[74]

In the Truman Library, there exists a second note in Truman's hand, in which he recounts key moments in his political career.[75] One of these was his selection as Vice President at the 1944 Convention.

It began with a visit from Hannegan. "The Chairman of the Democratic National Committee came to see me at the Stevens Hotel and told me that the President wanted me to be the nominee for Vice President on the ticket with him. I was flabbergasted. I told Hannegan that I wanted to stay in the Senate and that I would not take the nomination."

Neither Roosevelt, nor Hannegan, wanted this response. Unwilling to let it stand, they turned the screws on the Senator. The key moment occurred on July 20. Truman reflected, "On Thursday afternoon before the V.P.

nomination was to take place, I was asked to come over to the Blackstone Hotel for a conference. Of course, I went. There I found all the Democratic leaders of the nation and they began to put pressure on me, the country boy, to stand for the nomination for Vice President. Finally, Mr. Hannegan, the Chairman of the Democratic National Committee, called the President in San Diego, Calif. He asked Mr. Hannegan if he had received a commitment from the junior Senator from Missouri. Mr. Hannegan told the President that he had never been in contact with as mulish and contrary a man. Then, the President said, and I could hear him, 'well if he wants to let the Democratic Party and the country down in the middle of a war, that is his responsibility.'"

Truman was perplexed. "I was, to put it mildly, stunned. I stood around for at least five minutes and then I said, 'I'll do what the President wants.'"[76]

Delegates nominated Roosevelt that evening. Although nominations for vice president were supposed to occur the following day, Wallace supporters sensed a possibility to stampede the Convention in his favor if the balloting could begin immediately. The Hannegan-influenced machinery would not comply. After a spontaneous ten-minute demonstration for Wallace, some of it taking place on the convention floor and some in the galleries, Chairman Samuel Jackson recognized a motion to adjourn the evening's session, allowing the potential Wallace momentum to subside.[77] There was a related reason for the break, an opportunity for Hannegan to bring Roosevelt's letter to bear. As reported in the *Washington Evening Star,* "The recess was taken, it was learned, so that the delegates might be able to read—and let it sink in—a letter written by President Roosevelt on July 19 to Democratic National Chairman Robert E. Hannegan, made public at 8 o'clock last night by Mr. Hannegan, saying that the President would be glad to run with Truman or Associate Justice Douglas of the Supreme Court, Undoubtedly, the Truman supporters will use the letter in the contest today."[78]

The nominating process for vice president would thus begin on July 21, as scheduled.[79] When it did, the tussle lasted two ballots. With organized labor's vigorous backing, and that of strongly committed New Dealers, Wallace won a plurality on the first round, but sufficient states voted for other individuals to deny him an absolute majority.[80] On the second ballot, "favorite son" candidates switched to Truman. After eight hours of balloting, the Senator prevailed.[81] He was the candidate with the fewest enemies in a party wracked with internal divisions, thus the one least likely to provoke disgruntlement or rebellion.[82]

As presidential scholar Michael Korzi observes, "Roosevelt and his advisors were predominantly preoccupied with the politics of the vice presidential nomination—that is who would bring the most votes in the general election—rather than leadership qualities of a potential president." Korzi cites the nearly complete absence of preparation Truman had been given during the months between the Democratic convention and Roosevelt's death.[83]

The *Washington Evening Star* reported on the intra-party political turmoil. "Although Senator Truman has been a strong adherent of the New Deal administration, the contest for the vice presidential nomination became a desperate struggle between the New Deal and anti-New Deal factions in the party. . . . Southern anti-fourth-term Democrats, unable to dislodge President Roosevelt in this convention, found Vice President Wallace a vulnerable target. It was in the end the delegations of the southern states which led the stampede to Senator Truman on the second ballot. . . . Not only did many of the delegates fear that Mr. Wallace would lose votes for the Democratic ticket if renominated, but they also knew that if Mr. Wallace won, the report would spread across the country that the CIO had taken over the Democratic Party."[84]

Wallace sent a congratulatory telegram to the man who had ousted him. "Congratulations upon your enlarged opportunity to help the President and the people. Both of us will do our maximum for Roosevelt and what Roosevelt stands for."[85]

In reality, Wallace felt Roosevelt had betrayed him. So did Byrnes.[86]

On July 21, Roosevelt sent Wallace a condolence wire, "You made a grand fight and I am very proud of you." He again dangled the prospect of a Cabinet position for the soon-to-be former vice president. "Tell Ilo not to plan to leave Washington next January."[87]

As in 1940, Roosevelt did not attend the Convention. While it met, he was on a military inspection tour in California. FDR delivered his acceptance speech from his private train parked on a military base, promising that due to wartime conditions, he would not run a traditional campaign. "I shall not campaign, in the usual sense, for the office," declared the President. "In these days of tragic sorrow, I do not consider it fitting. And besides, in these days of global warfare, I shall not be able to find the time. I shall, however, feel free to report to the people the facts about matters of concern to them and especially to correct any misrepresentations."[88] Wrapping himself in the garb of commander in chief, he then proceeded from California to Hawaii for military conferences.

In the 1944 general election, Roosevelt and Truman would face New York Governor Thomas E. Dewey and Ohio Governor John Bricker. Meeting in Chicago at the end of June, the GOP nominated Dewey on the first ballot. In other than wartime conditions, Dewey and Bricker might have won.

The Republican resurgence that began in 1938, and paused in 1940, resumed with a vengeance in the 1942 mid-term elections. Although the public had endorsed Roosevelt for a third term, support for him did not translate into mid-term votes for his party.

Turnout was low in 1942, with just over a third of eligible voters participating. Republicans won eight Senate seats, bringing their total to 38, a long climb up from their nadir of 16 after the 1936 Roosevelt landslide. In the

House, Republicans picked up 47 seats, raising their membership to 209. After the 1936 election, only 88 members of the House had been Republican. In 1943, the comeback continued. After the off-year voting that year, they had governors in 26 of the 48 states, as against the mere six Republican governors still in office after 1936. One of those Republican triumphs had been in New York, which sent Thomas E. Dewey to Albany in November 1942 for the first of three consecutive terms.[89] Thus, it was not far-fetched that the GOP would capture the White House in 1944.[90]

Dewey had become governor of the most populous State in the nation, and the first Republican to hold that office in twenty years. His victory in New York had made him the evident front-runner to lead the party. However, he faced two potentially formidable opponents, Willkie and Ohio Governor John Bricker.[91] Political chatter about a nomination for General Douglas MacArthur never materialized into an actual candidacy

In the years since his 1940 defeat, Wendell Willkie had remained much in the news. On February 12, 1941, he testified before the Senate Foreign Relations Committee in support of Roosevelt's Lend-Lease program, notwithstanding substantial and bitter Republican opposition, both on Capitol Hill and off.[92] Related to this, he also traveled to Britain as Roosevelt's personal representative.

Republican reaction to Willkie support for these initiatives was hostile, undercutting Willkie's position as the party's spokesman.[93] Residual isolationist sentiment in the Republican Party remained powerful and the party's Old Guard were dependably anti-Roosevelt.[94] Willkie's comments in support for Lend-Lease, and his willingness to represent Roosevelt in Britain, were badly out of step with these sentiments.[95] Steve Neal, Willkie's biographer, quotes a letter that John D. Hamilton, Chairman of the Republican National Committee, wrote to a Republican Congressman about Willkie's apostasy. The same chairman that read Stimson and Knox out of the party, Hamilton was never truly at home with the maverick 1940 nominee. Although Willkie was in theory the titular leader of Republicans, Hamilton showed him no deference. "Willkie's statement and subsequent trip to England resulted in a breach between him and Republican members of Congress which, in my opinion is irreparable," stated the Chairman.[96]

Willkie's contrariness on foreign policy continued. In 1942, he made a forty-nine-day world tour, on his own initiative, but with the President's agreement and assistance. A key objective was to emphasize the bipartisan nature of American foreign policy.[97]

These activities received substantial public attention.[98] Willkie followed his 1942 trip with publication the next year of *One World*, which called for American entry into a world organization.[99] More than two million copies were sold within twelve months.[100] While the book was widely acclaimed, it generated more Republican grumbling. Of *One World*, historian Lynne Olson writes,

> It became a runaway bestseller, helping to nudge public opinion toward the idea of a postwar United Nations but also making him even more of a controversial figure within the Republican Party. Dubbing Willkie a "stooge for Roosevelt," the . . . conservative Old Guard never forgave him for his liberalism.[101]

One may conclude that Willkie had well positioned himself as a general election candidate in 1944, but destroyed his already tenuous grip on the Republican Party. "Since his defeat in 1940," writes Neal, "Willkie had frequently blasted congressional Republicans for their isolationism in foreign affairs and conservatism at home. Senator McNary and Representative Martin had warned him that he was hurting his political stock in the party by becoming so closely identified with the Administration's foreign policy."[102]

Indisputable proof would come in the April 4, 1944, Wisconsin primary. Willkie campaigned vigorously there over a thirteen-day period. When the votes were in, Dewey won 17 of 24 delegates, Willkie won none.[103]

After this trouncing, Willkie withdrew from the race. By summer, his health began to decline seriously. On October 8, 1944, Willkie died in New York of heart failure. He was in the hospital for nearly a month, with a range of ailments, not originally life-threatening, but ultimately putting his heart under great stress. Beginning on October 7, Willkie suffered three heart attacks, the last one fatal.[104] An estimable figure, with boundless energy and an outstanding potential for leadership, he was but fifty-two years old.

In a press statement commenting on Willkie's passing, Roosevelt referred to his former rival's outspoken policy positions that left him isolated within the Republican Party. "The nation will long remember Wendell Willkie as a forthright American. Earnest, honest, whole-souled, he also had tremendous courage. This courage, which was his dominating trait, prompted him more than once to stand alone and to challenge the wisdom of counsels taken by powerful interests within his own party."[105]

Ohio Senator Robert Taft, a leading contender in 1940, did not seek the nomination in 1944, preferring to run for reelection to the Senate. In lieu of Taft, Governor John Bricker, emerged as Dewey's principal Convention rival. Bricker won the Ohio primary as a favorite son candidate, but did not contest in other States. His strategy could only succeed if the delegates deadlocked, which they did not. After prevailing on the first ballot, Dewey tapped Bricker for his running mate.[106]

Presidential tenure in office took a relative backseat as an issue in 1944, compared with the stir caused by Roosevelt's third term bid in 1940.[107] The Republican platform made only two references to it. The first was a histrionic statement that extending Roosevelt in office meant the end of the American system of government.[108] The second endorsed a Constitutional Amendment to limit presidential tenure to two four-year terms. The platform started, "We favor an amendment to the Constitution providing that no person shall be President of the United States for more than two terms of four years each."[109] Nevertheless, the subject was merely a sidebar in a campaign fought on Roosevelt's capacity to continue providing the country with vigorous stewardship.[110]

As in 1940, the public had confidence in Roosevelt's capacity to lead the country in war. Opinion surveys, matching Roosevelt against Dewey, showed FDR winning decisively if the war were ongoing without end in sight. If the end seemed near, but the country was still fighting, Roosevelt's lead was slight. If the war had concluded, Dewey would win by a wide margin.[111] Americans seemed to have little interest in turning out a wartime President or in giving him a fourth term if the national emergency abated.[112]

Chronologically, Dewey was twenty years younger than FDR, but the age gap seemed even wider due to Dewey's robust health and Roosevelt's increasing frailty. The press had begun to pay attention to the President's worsening health, giving Dewey an opening to demonstrate that FDR was no longer up to the job.[113]

The centerpiece of Dewey's effort was his campaign against the "tired old men."[114] For a while, Roosevelt ignored him, conducting well-publicized inspections of military installations, conducting the war effort, and making "politics as usual" appear unseemly. The President maintained that posture for as long as it worked.[115] However, he could not sustain it for the entire campaign.

In 1944, Franklin Roosevelt was dying. In his oral history for the FDR Library, Jonathan Daniels, his Press Secretary, recounts the President's decline as it appeared in the months immediately prior to and after the 1944 election. Roosevelt's doctors had recommended a much-lightened workload for him.[116] With the war ongoing, the President could not relax to that degree, but he did take a month's rest that spring at financier Bernard Baruch's Hobcaw Barony estate in South Carolina.[117] Upon his return, Daniels reports, the President did not look much better. The Press Secretary was alarmed. Upon receiving press inquiries, he went to Roosevelt's attending physician, Ross McIntyre, only to be reassured that "It's all a bunch of crap. The President's in fine shape." Daniels suspected the truth was different, but played along. "I had, then, been going up to these morning conferences and noting the regularity with which the electrocardiograph machine was up near the President's quarters, but I, of course, was part of the protective mechanism."[118]

Roosevelt's deterioration worried the public. Whispers and rumors fed these concerns, buttressed by two events. One was a photograph of FDR in the train car delivering his acceptance speech. The President looked old and haggard.[119] The other was a speech Roosevelt gave on August 12, 1944, at a Bremerton, Washington, naval shipyard. Delivering his remarks standing up under windy weather conditions, FDR struggled with both his braces and his text. During his remarks, the President also suffered severe pain from angina.[120] The speech was rambling and ineffective.[121] Measured against the old campaigner, the 1944 version seemed a shadow. Americans had gotten used to magic. It seemed to be missing.

Dewey was pushing a narrative that Roosevelt and his Administration had run out of gas. After Bremerton, there were signs the public might be listening. Roosevelt's aide, Robert Sherwood, observes, "It was a significant fact that, after this speech, public opinion polls indicated a sudden and ominous slump for Roosevelt and a consequent rise in Dewey's stock."[122] At first, Roosevelt responded listlessly, almost with indifference.[123] If the situation persisted, victory in the election could not be assured. The President himself thought that Dewey might win. As his confidant, Daisy Suckley, noted in her diary of Wednesday, September 20, 1944, "The Pres. says he feels there is an excellent chance of his being defeated in the election—that Dewey is making a very good campaign. The Pres. is planning his life after he leaves the W.H."[124]

The White House concluded the erosion was such that FDR could not simply campaign as commander in chief, above the fray, but would have to engage in normal political combat. The President came around.[125]

Entering the arena, Roosevelt mapped out a fall schedule of speeches.[126] The President struck back on September 23, in Washington, DC's Statler Hotel with hard-hitting political remarks before the Teamsters Union. His prepared text started, "Well here we are together again after four years, and what years they have been! I am actually four years older, which seems to annoy some people. In fact, millions more of us are more than eleven years older than when we started in to clean up the mess that was dumped in our laps in 1933."[127] The friendly Teamsters audience was delighted.

Later in that speech, Roosevelt added a paragraph that he had handwritten himself. Faced with allegations that he had accidently left his dog behind during an inspection tour in the Aleutian Islands, and sent a Navy destroyer back to retrieve him, Roosevelt responded with buoyant and biting humor. "The Republican leaders have not been content to make personal attacks on me, or my wife, or my sons—they now include my little dog Fala." This became known as the "Fala Speech," and it rapidly became a fixture in American political folklore. FDR didn't seem tired anymore.[128]

When he first sought the presidency in 1932, Franklin Roosevelt had to battle against innuendos that depicted him as physically incapable to do the job. His flight that summer to the Democratic Convention, which he followed with a nation-spanning campaign trip by rail,[129] dispelled such concerns. Now, twelve years later, Roosevelt set out to prove the same thing again.

On October 21, 1944, the President journeyed by rail to New York for an address to the Foreign Policy Association. Unplanned for, but later added, was a 51-mile-long motorcade through four boroughs, including an appearance at Ebbets Field in Brooklyn. The weather turned out to be raw and nasty, with temperatures in the low fifties, feeling colder due to a substantial wind chill, and a steady downpour.[130] "It was raining when Mr. Roosevelt started his tour at the Brooklyn Army Base at the New York Port of Embarkation," reported the *New York Times*. "It was pouring—and the wind much colder—when the motorcade passed through Times Square and followed the blazed trail to the Washington Square apartment of Mrs. Roosevelt where the President rested for his night address."[131] FDR rode in a car with the top down, so bystanders could see him.[132] Estimates are that two million persons did.[133] The motorcade put sufficiently to rest the idea that Roosevelt did not have physical stamina for the job.[134]

Now on the campaign trail, the President appeared in major events in New Jersey, Pennsylvania, Delaware, Indiana, and Illinois.

As the campaign wound down, Dewey protested against the fourth term. Speaking in Buffalo, New York, on November 1, the candidate endorsed a two-term limit on presidential terms. As reported by the Associated Press, "He asserted that to keep one man in the White House for 16 years offered 'the most dangerous threat to our freedom ever posed by anybody.'" A crowd of 18,000 roared its approval, but in the country as a whole, his message did not resonate.[135]

In November, FDR prevailed with 53.4 percent of the popular vote, as against Dewey's 45.9 percent, or 25.6 million votes to just over 22 million. Of Roosevelt's four elections, it was his weakest performance.[136] Dewey did slightly better against FDR than had Willkie, both in the popular vote and in the Electoral College. Roosevelt won 432 electoral votes to Dewey's 99.

In 1940, Willkie's biggest electoral haul was in Michigan. Roosevelt won the State narrowly in 1944. Dewey was able to prevail by a sliver in Ohio, which Willkie lost in 1940. Apart from Michigan, Dewey also came close in Pennsylvania, Illinois, and New Jersey. However, even if he had carried all four states, it would have added 98 electoral votes to his total, still leaving him well short. Both Roosevelt and Dewey were from New York. The President carried it, and its 47 electoral votes. The South remained absolutely unbroken for Roosevelt, as it had in all his previous elections. The former Confederate States supplied FDR with 116 electoral votes, based on the allocation following the 1940 census. For the Democrats, that was a customary and significant head start to the 266 electoral votes then needed to win. After 1944, the South would never again be a solid Democratic bastion.[137]

Roosevelt did not live long enough to write memoirs, but Robert Jackson's book, *That Man*, contains a letter FDR sent on November 1944, after the fourth election. The recipient was Hamilton Holt, President of Rollins College in Winter Park, Florida. The letter describes FDR's attitude toward his third- and fourth-term candidacies, as close as one can find to the sort of reflection one would encounter in a memoir.

Third and fourth terms should not happen as a matter of course, the President wrote, but "I think I can well plead extenuating circumstances!" While there might be presidents who would seek to extend themselves in office because they loved power and could not bear to give it up, said Roosevelt, "I am not one of this type." He continued, "For as far as individual preference goes, I would, quite honestly, have retired to Hyde Park with infinite pleasure in 1941."

Whether it was reasonable to extend a president's term would require assessing the situation as a whole, not only existing conditions, but the capacity of other candidates to respond. "Then there is the other question of the alternative," Roosevelt mused, as he evaluated his 1940 and 1944 opponents. Willkie, he thought, was a well-intentioned man, but too inexperienced to deal with perilous times. "Willkie was an anomaly who improved greatly in his general thinking after 1940. But although I liked him personally, I did not feel he had much knowledge of the world and that he would have to have learned about the world in the school of hard experience. This would have been a rather dangerous experiment in 1940."

FDR had far less regard for Dewey. "As to the last gentleman who was the alternative, I say nothing."[138]

Beyond the circumstances that touched his own reelections, there was a matter of principle. Should restrictions be imposed on voter choice, either by tradition or by law? Roosevelt thought not. "The real meat of the question is not the length of the term, but the continued opportunity of the voters of the country freely to express themselves every four years," he told Holt.[139]

On January 20, 1945, in a brief ceremony on the South Portico of the White House, Franklin Roosevelt took the oath for a fourth term. Eighty-two days later, on April 12, he died from a cerebral hemorrhage at the Little White House in Warm Springs, Georgia. At the White House that evening, shortly after 7:00 PM, Harry S. Truman took the oath as the 33rd President of the United States.

Six weeks into his presidency, during which the San Francisco conference on forming the United Nations had convened, and General Eisenhower had accepted the German surrender, the Gallup Poll asked, "Do you approve or disapprove of the way Harry Truman is handling his job as President?" In this initial test, Truman scored breathtakingly well. On May 29, 1945, 86 percent of respondents indicated they approved, 2 percent disapproved, and 10 percent were undecided.[140]

Three months later, Truman did even better. In the interim, the United Nations conference successfully concluded, the President met with Churchill and Stalin at Potsdam, he authorized the bombing of Hiroshima and Nagasaki, and he announced the Japanese surrender. The good news further boosted Truman's popularity. On August 22, 1945, Gallup reported that his approval climbed to 91 percent. Merely 2 percent disapproved. Only 5 percent were undecided.[141]

No political figure could durably sustain such ratings, and Truman's decline from such artificial highs was dramatic. In the Gallup Poll announced on January 3, 1946, the President's approval had dropped nearly 30 points to 63 percent. By the end of May, he was treading water, with 45 percent approval and 42 percent disapproval. In the poll published on October 21, Truman had sunk to 27 percent approval, with 56 percent disapproving.[142]

At no point during the war had Roosevelt's approval rating scored below 65 percent.[143] But the war was a unifying factor, galvanizing support for the commander in chief. Truman's drop of 64 points in 14 months reflected the rising political divisions from dislocations associated with conversion to a peacetime economy. These involved a wave of strikes, the lifting of price controls, emerging shortages, and high inflation.[144] As well, stories surfaced about Communist espionage and potential infiltration, at a time when American attitudes toward the Soviet Union were turning hostile. These revelations also cost Truman public support.[145] By the time of the 1946 mid-terms, Truman was not a political asset. Hannegan told the President to stay off the campaign trail, fearing damage to Democratic candidates.[146]

With the war ended, and Roosevelt gone, circumstances that had stunted the Republican comeback and sustained Democratic political control, no longer existed. The GOP roared back in 1946, gaining 55 seats in the House and 12 in the Senate. When the 80th Congress convened on January 3, 1947, there were comfortable Republican majorities in both Houses, the strongest position for the Party since the pre-Depression election of 1928.[147]

As Truman's presidency unfolded, Congressional Republicans agitated for a constitutional amendment to ensure that no one would ever breach the two-term limit again. Although still in the minority, they were able to secure House and Senate hearings in 1945. Both were rather perfunctory, but nevertheless underscored Republicans' commitment to address term limits if they secured control of Congress in the foreseeable future, as they looked increasingly likely to do.

A TERM LIMITS HEARING IN THE SENATE

On September 27, 1945, Senator Carl Hatch (D-NM)[148] called to order a special subcommittee of the Senate Committee on the Judiciary. Subcommittee members along with Hatch were Senators Joseph C. O'Mahoney (D-WY),[149] Burton K. Wheeler (D-MT), Kenneth S. Wherry (R-NE),[150] and E.H. Moore (R-OK).[151] It was named the Subcommittee on S. J. Res. 1, 10, 12, 21, and 82. Each was a proposed constitutional amendment to restrict Presidential terms.

- S. J. Res. 1 made ineligible to be chosen as President a person who had been elected to or served as President for any part of two four-year terms, whether consecutive or not. It would allow anyone serving on the date of ratification to complete his term.
- S. J. Res 10 was identical, except without the clause that permitted a newly disqualified incumbent to complete his term. S. J. Res. 10 stated that no one could be chosen who had held, or even exercised the duties of the office of President during any part of two prior terms.[152] It would take effect on the first of February following ratification, and did not permit an incumbent to continue in office if the Amendment rendered him otherwise ineligible to serve.
- S. J. Res. 12 was much broader. In major part, it provided for national primaries, with States having voting power in party conventions that was equivalent to their strength in the Electoral College. The resolution abolished the Electoral College itself and provided for the winner of the general election to be determined by popular vote.
- S. J. Res. 21 created a single six-year term for both the President and the Vice President, and disqualified anyone who had previously served in those offices from being eligible for election to either of them.[153] The resolution also limited aggregate service in Congress to six years, and barred civil office appointments for Members of Congress until they had been out of office for five years. It would permit anyone disqualified from service by reason of ratification to complete his term.
- S. J. Res. 78 disqualified any person who had held the presidency during any part of two prior terms.

Four witnesses testified, each of them Senators. They were Hugh Butler (R-NE),[154] W. Lee O'Daniel (D-TX), Arthur Capper (R-KS),[155] and Wayne Morse (R-OR). No other witnesses were asked to appear, an apparent indication of public indifference.[156] Hatch made a point of noting this publicly, in this exchange with Calvin M. Cory, the Committee Clerk:

Hatch: So far as I know, there have been no requests to be heard—have there?
The Clerk: None at all.
Hatch: Neither for nor against?
The Clerk: That is right.
Hatch: It is strange that nobody wants to be heard on this. . . . There ought to be somebody for or against. . . . We have no request from anyone who wants to be heard.[157]

This state of affairs was vastly different from the situation in 1940, when Senator Edward Burke (D-NE) conducted his voluminous hearings before another Senate Judiciary subcommittee. During the five intervening years, Roosevelt won third and fourth terms, and then died in office. As well, American entry into the war had commenced and ended. By the time of the Hatch hearings, Truman had been President for five months, and the Japanese surrender was merely three weeks old. The public angst about breaking the two-term tradition, which animated the 1940 election, seemed to have dissipated. However, even without public demand, term limits advocates in Congress remained committed to the issue.

Senator Hugh Butler (R-NE) became a Senator in 1940 by defeating Democrat Roy L. Cochran, Burke's 1940 primary opponent. Butler shared Burke's affinity for term limits and, at the opening of the Seventy-ninth Congress,[158] sponsored S. J. Res. 1. Unable to be present, Butler submitted a statement.

The two-term tradition that Roosevelt had broken was unlikely to be revived voluntarily, Butler maintained. Instead, future presidents, perhaps younger and healthier than Roosevelt, were likely to continue what he had started.

> The Nation is now face to face with the unhappy fact that tradition is not sufficient to prevent the possible rise of a dictator in this country. . . . It becomes perfectly apparent that if a man young enough, brilliant enough, determined enough, and clever enough should get into the Presidency, he could cite precedent to run not only for a third term, and a fourth term, but a fifth and a sixth term.[159]

Entrenched in the White House and empowered by its trappings, such a President would be very difficult to dislodge. "Each term in the Presidency would make him stronger and more impregnable in his position," Butler warned, "so that after a matter of three terms he would not only have appointed nearly the whole of the judiciary, but he would have such a machine built up, he would have such power established, he would have such fear engendered, that no one would dare openly oppose him."[160]

The remedy was a constitutional amendment such as the one he proposed. It would, Butler argued, revitalize the now-discarded two-term tradition and make it "impregnable."[161]

Senator O'Daniel was the next witness. He authored S. J. Res 21, a constitutional amendment that would transform the system to nominate and elect presidential candidates, and that limited terms for president, vice president, and members of Congress. It was the only proposal pending before the subcommittee to address service in the Legislative Branch.

The Senator strongly believed in rotation in office. Without it, a president would command a patronage machine equivalent to ward politics at the federal level. Beyond that, such a president would dominate the judiciary. "Through our system of having the members of the judicial branch of the government appointed by the President, a judiciary lopsided in favor of whatever line of thought is taken by the head of the executive department can easily be established." Such overbearing influence would make a mockery of judicial independence and equal justice under law, he said.[162]

Rotation would also strengthen the independence of the Legislative Branch, O'Daniel claimed. Members of Congress seeking reelection become beholden to the executive for patronage and federal largesse, he observed. To secure such favors, Members have to support the President's program, setting aside contrarian views they might have. Term limits would free them from this burden and, as well, from interest group pressure. "If a Member of Congress was barred from reelection, I believe there would be far less opportunity for interest groups to influence legislation. A Member could not be threatened by defeat if he failed to support legislation which the group advocated."[163]

Mandatory replacement would bring fresh perspectives to Congress, O'Daniel continued, along with several other advantages. It would be useful if Members had to live under the laws they enacted. Furthermore, a former Member, out of government, but with experience in public office, could be "of service to the people of his community as a connecting link with government."[164]

Hatch challenged O'Daniel on term limits for Congress. It would needlessly sacrifice too much skill and expertise, the Chairman claimed. "I think the experience and wisdom that has developed here over a period of years defeats any adverse theory or situation. I think it would be a grievous mistake to deprive the Congress of the United States of the benefit of the experience of the men we have right now in the Senate, who are among the most valuable Senators we have, to compel the selection of young Members."[165]

Notwithstanding this criticism, O'Daniel remained committed to his idea. In 1947, during the debate on the Twenty-second Amendment, he would formally propose it, but would get no support.

Senator Arthur Capper (R-KS), author of S. J. Res. 10, testified next. The only way to fix the problem Roosevelt created was by an Amendment, Capper insisted. If the cure did not come, "that will be the end of representative government," he claimed. Presidents, being competitive, would seek to outdo their predecessors by extending in office for ever-longer tenure. "A mark has been set for any President who loves power to shoot at."[166]

Confronted with a perpetual President, the powers of Congress would diminish, he feared. Like so many others, Capper also predicted the erosion of judicial independence. Such would happen even after three terms, much less over a longer period. "In 12 years' time, a President who believes himself necessary to the continuance of the policies he believes best for the country also will be able to name such a preponderant majority of the judiciary that the third protection which the founders of our Republic created for the purpose of checking against autocratic personal rule will fail to provide that protection."[167]

Without rotation, Capper believed, dictatorship would emerge. It could be benevolent, but it would be a dictatorship, nonetheless. "The world is strewn with the wreckage of republics," he observed, a destruction that began with establishment of permanent chief executives.[168]

It was true that many term-limit amendments had surfaced over the years, he noted, and Congress had never seen fit to act on them. The public considered two-term tradition the unwritten law of the land, making a formal amendment unnecessary. "We know better now," the Senator commented.

Those who believed that the tradition was sacrosanct had fundamentally erred.

> We forgot human nature. Human beings love prominence and power. . . . Some love power so much they cannot surrender it voluntarily. . . . When one with that ambition holds power, he can always find some reason why he should not surrender that power, unless he knows he cannot continue to hold it.[169]

Presidents would seek to extend themselves in office, predicted Capper, even if they had to manufacture a justification to do so. "Some President, greedy for lifelong power, will create an emergency, that will not only justify himself in accepting a continuance of that power, but will justify his followers in insisting that he keep the power in his own hands."

Over the past decade, the Senator noted, the presidency had grown much bigger. A modern chief executive seeking to extend his tenure would greatly compound the problems that would have existed in earlier times. There was an urgent need for a cure. "I regard it as deeply important, vital, that we now set a definite, fixed, certain termination to the tenure of any man in the President's office."

After Capper came Senator Wayne Morse, sponsor of S. J. Res. 82.[170] He argued that the issue of presidential term limits was so fundamental to the structure of government, Congress had an obligation to submit it to the people for decision via ratification. Hatch inquired about whether the 1940 and 1944 elections did not constitute a referendum on extended tenure. Not so, replied Morse, because tenure was one of many topics at issue in those elections. "That specific issue has not been set out in signal relief, so that a decision was cast on that issue independent of all the other issues that were involved in the campaign." The ratification process would focus on term limits to the exclusion of other matters, he said.

Morse believed that a vibrant party system was fundamental to effective government. Perpetuated tenure weakened both the President's party and the opposition, he argued. In the former, politics would centralize around the incumbent. The Administration would fossilize. "I do not think it is helpful to any political philosophy, to have that philosophy become symbolized by just one individual," articulated Morse. "I think its strength is to be found in the fact that it is a party philosophy." Without turnover and refreshed leadership, even a dominant party would become stale. "I think it was a mistake of the Democratic Party to associate so closely a political philosophy with an individual. It weakened the party and prevented the development of other strong leaders."[171]

Morse concluded his statement. Change meant renewal. "I think that part of the dynamics of democracy is to be found in the concept of change itself." It was something to be welcomed, not feared. "Change does not mean the repudiation of policies already established, but the bringing in of new minds, and examination of old policies, keeping those that seemed to have performed well, and discarding those that have turned into abuses."[172]

Because the two-term tradition had been abandoned, change would have to be institutionalized through a constitutional amendment, Morse felt.

There were no additional witnesses, so Hatch gaveled the hearing to a close. It was 11:30 AM, merely one hour after the subcommittee had convened.

A TERM LIMITS HEARING IN THE HOUSE OF REPRESENTATIVES

Seven weeks later, on November 15, 1945, Representative Herbert C. Bonner (D-NC)[173] convened a hearing of the House Committee on the Election of president, vice president, and representatives in Congress.[174] Established in 1893 as a standing committee of the House, it existed until 1947, when the House folded the panel's jurisdiction into the House Administration Committee. At the request of House Minority Leader Joseph Martin, Jr. (R-MA), Bonner agreed to hear a series of joint resolutions intended to restrict presidential tenure by constitutional amendment. His first witness was Martin, one of the authors.[175]

Martin explained that the Framers' goal was to strengthen the National government and make it durable for future generations. They feared that imposing limits on service might make that government needlessly unstable. Therefore, they left that particular question open, to be considered in light of future experience.[176]

The Framers were staunch anti-monarchists, Martin noted. As such, they instituted an intricate web of checks and balances to prevent excessive concentration of power in any part of the government. The two-term tradition was a vital complement to these efforts. However, the modern presidency overwhelmed and distorted the constitutional balance, he alleged.

"As the American people in each generation became farther removed from those men who had personal experience with tyranny, the fear of tyranny lost its sharpness and, in time, Americans began to take for granted those personal liberties the price of which is eternal vigilance."[177] After unwritten restraints collapsed, they were unlikely to be restored. "The tradition against a third term is broken. There are no further restrictions upon the ambitious."[178]

Martin placed into the hearing record a letter from John W. Davis, the 1924 Democratic nominee for president, which included a statement made to a 1940 Senate hearing on the topic of term limits. "A tradition once broken ceases to have binding power," Davis had written. "Only law expressed in the Constitution can take its place. The basis of the tradition and the reason for your amendment is the sound principle sanctioned by all history that no free government can survive the coming of a permanent chief executive."[179]

Reinforcing Davis was a communication from Bainbridge Colby, Secretary of State under President Woodrow Wilson. Colby's letter stated, "We have seen that we require a greater protection that is afforded by a 'tradition' however sacred and vital to our survival as a nation. We have reached the time when the limitation of tenure of the presidential office must be safeguarded by express provision in our Constitution."[180]

The United States had just concluded a war against the Axis Powers, noted Martin. Each of them had been under a dictatorship. In every case, the dictatorship replaced a struggling democracy, proving to Martin that democratic systems could be vulnerable. "We have seen the factions supporting such leaders infiltrate into the governments of Europe and of Asia."[181]

A constitutional amendment would protect Americans from this decay, he said. Limiting tenure was not a partisan matter. He cited positions of Democratic and Republican presidents and the Democratic platforms of 1896 and 1912, all of which endorsed term limits. In addition, he cited the bipartisan Springer resolution of 1875 and its LaFollette clone of 1928.

The Amendment was necessary to preserve the American system of government, Martin concluded. He denied that Republican efforts were political retribution. "We are dealing with a fundamental principle and a deadly danger, and not with personalities."[182]

Representative Carter Manasco (D-AL),[183] a member of the committee, challenged Martin's premise that the best way to gauge public opinion was to submit an amendment for ratification. Was not a general election, such as the contests in 1940 and 1944, a more accurate test, he asked?[184]

Martin rejected the premise of Manasco's question. Elections involving entrenched incumbents had a built-in bias in their favor, especially with respect to renomination. "You cannot prevent the Chief Executive—and it is more so today than it was ever before—from dominating the nomination." As a practical matter, Martin observed, voters could only choose between general election candidates. "They do not have the opportunity to say who shall be the nominee."[185]

To neutralize incumbent dominance over the party apparatus, why not nominate candidates through primary elections, interjected Representative Jesse Combs (D-TX)?[186] If Martin's concerns were salient, would not direct voting mitigate the problem? Such a change would actually enhance voter engagement, rather than constrain it.

Martin deflected the query. The best possible election reform would be to submit the Amendment, he replied.[187]

The following witness was House Majority Leader John McCormack (D-MA).[188] Believing that Congress itself was the first line of defense against frivolous or unwise constitutional amendments, he rejected Republican logic that the House would serve the public interest by submitting the Amendment for ratification. "If we were to follow that line of reasoning alone, any proposed constitutional amendment should pass the Congress and be referred to the several states for ratification, and we would let every resolution calling for an amendment to the Constitution take that course," argued McCormack. "That reasoning is unsound."[189]

During 1940 and 1944 campaigns, he said, campaigns barraged voters with claims about the sanctity of the two-term tradition and the harms that breaching it would cause. They ignored the hyperbole and returned the President to office. If the people concluded that problems from extended tenure proved real, they were free to reimpose the two-term limit by defeating anyone who defied it and ran for a third term.[190]

During Roosevelt's campaigns, McCormack remarked, his opponents correlated extended tenure with a loss of political freedom. "We were warned against absolutism in government. We were threatened that a dictatorship would result."[191] But McCormack considered this demagogic. As anyone could observe, the country's actual experience was opposite. "The people of this nation today enjoy more freedom than any other people in the world," he claimed.[192] Americans could have no fear of dictatorship so long as they enjoyed freedom of speech, freedom of religion, a free press, and freedom of elections. Thus, there was no basis to impose external constraints, such as presidential term limits. Americans "have a right to resent, and will resent, any attempt to interfere with their constitutional right to vote for the man of their choice for the office of President."[193]

Congress should be especially wary of restrictive amendments, McCormack urged. Such cases justified extreme skepticism, he felt. Congress should not consider them unless there was strong and obvious public demand. However, seven months after Roosevelt's death, with the experience of his fourth election so fresh in their minds, voters were not demanding change. "Any amendment which would interfere with the unqualified right of freedom of voting choice should not be authoritatively suggested unless there is an inexorable demand for a limitation of such choice arising from the people. There is no evidence today that the people are asking to be saved from their own actions."[194]

If Representatives passed term limits anyway, they would be expressing only their personal views, not responding to public sentiment. This was a pernicious exercise in political paternalism, McCormack protested. He asserted that, were it attempted, the country would protest.

Facing the prospect of war in 1940 and actual conflict in 1944, Americans chose the pragmatic course of keeping Roosevelt in office, McCormack noted. "I think that the majority of the American people felt that there was a danger confronting our country, which prompted them to vote for him."[195] That doing so ended the two-term tradition did not trouble McCormack. "I prefer to be counted with those who believe that the third term question is an artificial, superficial contrivance designed to frustrate the will of the American people by preventing re-nomination of a popular President."[196]

As to what should happen next, McCormack was clear. "The reasons against limitations seem to me so logical and sound that the pending resolutions should receive nothing further than the dignity of a hearing."[197]

That the hearing was the end of the line was a very safe prediction. In the 79th Congress, Democrats were in control of both chambers, and he was House Majority Leader. He had much to say about scheduling House business. Republicans had been in the minority for a decade and a half.[198] The hearing was a courtesy, and nothing more, to Minority Leader Martin, who had decent relations with the Democratic Leadership. McCormack's biographer Garrison Nelson speaks about the extent to which Rayburn and McCormack would periodically accommodate Martin. "Joe Martin was close to Sam Rayburn and John McCormack, and it is likely that the two Democrats threw a victory at Martin every now and then as a way of keeping him on as Republican Leader rather than having him replaced by some of the more strident conservative and less reasonable Midwestern House Members such as Charles Halleck (R-IN) or Leslie Arends (R-IL)."[199]

However, with political conditions as they were in the House in 1945, prospects for resolution to advance beyond the hearing stage were nil.

Several additional witnesses appeared when the hearing resumed in the afternoon. The first was Representative Wat Arnold (R-MO),[200] sponsor of House Joint Resolution 229, which stipulated single six-year terms for president, vice president, and senators, and three two-year terms for Members of the House. Extended service rendered officeholders disconnected from the effects of the public policies they influenced, Arnold said. By removing the possibility of reelection entirely or, in case of Representatives, for the most part, public officials could focus on the public's business and not on their own perpetuation, he added.[201]

There was no sentiment in Congress to move forward with a proposal as stringent as Arnold's, but the Representative himself lived by its precepts. He retired at the end of 1948, having served in Congress for three terms.

Dr. Gleason L. Archer, President of Suffolk University in Massachusetts followed Arnold. The Framers erred in not putting a term limitation in the original Constitution, he began, but for most of the Nation's history, there was no urgency to fix the mistake. "No action was taken because for more than a century it was believed that Thomas Jefferson had settled the question, not as an organic law of the land, but as a custom that had the force of law."[202]

Archer noted that, after wrangling all summer over the presidential term, and never reaching a stable consensus, the Framers were exhausted. In September, "when they were sick and tired of everything," they accepted a committee recommendation and settled on a four-year uncapped term.[203] To James Madison, Jefferson expressed serious misgivings about the omission of term limits, predicting this condition would produce "cruel distress" to the United States.[204]

Once in office, Archer noted, Jefferson was able to act on his beliefs. Spurning calls that he run for a third term in 1808, Jefferson retired. "He knew that a benevolent ruler, if in office for more than a limited time, could become a menace to the people." As he expressed to supporters from Connecticut, "Having myself approved the example of an illustrious predecessor in voluntarily retiring from a trust which, if too long continued in the same hands might become a subject of reasonable uneasiness and apprehension, I could not mistake my own duty when placed in a similar situation."[205]

The problems Jefferson foresaw turned out to be valid, Archer stated. These included the concentration of executive power through a large and entrenched bureaucracy, and excessive influence on the courts through the sheer volume of judicial appointments. "The first eight years, Mr. Roosevelt had very little opportunity to do anything to the Supreme Court, but before the end of the third term he has changed the whole constitution of the Supreme Court."[206] The remedy, claimed Archer, was to limit tenure to two four-year terms.

The final witness was Dr. Frederic R. Coudert, a prominent New York lawyer who had appeared before the Senate in the 1940 Burke hearings (see Appendix One) to endorse term limitations. In the 1945 House hearings, he reaffirmed his position. Coudert spoke of alterations in the body politic that made it advisable to affix the two-term tradition firmly in the Constitution. Through immigration, America had experienced "enormous migrations of people who have not the American tradition of fear of power, of checks and balances, of desire to limit power."[207] Unmoored from traditional attitudes, voters could be susceptible to a leader wanting to perpetuate himself in office, especially when he could claim emergency conditions as justification. A constitutional amendment would mitigate against this danger, he believed.

Coudert's special concern was the undue influence of an extended presidency on the independence of federal courts.[208]

> I think it is a great misfortune that any President had an opportunity to appoint 80 or more percent of the Judiciary of the United States. . . . I do believe that the ultimate liberty of our people depends upon the complete impartiality and integrity of the Bench, and I think events in countries other than the English-speaking countries have indicated what a terrible thing political trials may be, and what a terrible thing a puppet bench might be, and I do not care how wise a perpetual President may be.[209]

After Coudert's appearance, the Committee adjourned without further action. No more would be done about presidential term limits for the remainder of the 79th Congress. In November 1946, mid-term elections returned Republican majorities in both Houses. This political earthquake was the foundation for acting on a constitutional amendment that Republicans had long advocated but been powerless to move.

NOTES

1. "The Republicans were in a fix in the summer of 1944 and knew it. The coming presidential election would be a referendum on the war, whether Roosevelt explicitly declared it one or not. And with the war going well, the incumbent would be nearly impossible to beat." Brands, *Traitor to His Class,* p. 767.
2. Geoffrey C. Ward, *Closest Companion: The Unknown Story of the Intimate Friendship between Franklin Roosevelt and Margaret Suckley* (New York: Simon & Schuster, 1995), p. 280.
3. For example, in a February 8, 1940, press conference, Roosevelt steadfastly refused to engage in a discussion about a fourth term candidacy. A story the following day in the *Washington Evening Star* under the byline of J.A. Fox, begins, "President Roosevelt's fourth term intentions are still a secret—hidden in a cloud of words. His news conference late yesterday made a second attempt to dispel the fog, without success." Roosevelt refused to answer a question about whether he would accept a fourth term nomination. J.A. Fox, "Fourth Term Inquiries Parried by President with Bible Reference," *Washington Evening Star,* February 9, 1944, p. A-3.
4. Hamilton, p. 255, citing Leahy's diaries.
5. Ward, *Closest Companion*, pp. 301–302.
6. *Washington Evening Star* (Washington, DC), March 3, 1944, Library of Congress, *Chronicling America: Historic American Newspapers*, www.chronicling-america.loc.gov.

7. David M. Jordan, *FDR, Dewey and the Election of 1944* (Bloomington: Indiana University Press, 2011), p. 16.

8. Jordan, p. 137. "Dewey could claim to be a new broom after eleven years of the Democracy, wherein the party of Roosevelt had worn itself out in meeting the challenges of the Great Depression and, now, World War II. Against those claims, in which there was more than a grain of truth, only 'the champ', the Democrats' greatest voter-getter since President Andrew Jackson a century and more before, could have assured victory. No other Democrat could have stood against Dewey and won." Robert H. Ferrell, *Choosing Truman: The Democratic Convention of 1944* (Columbia, Missouri: University of Missouri Press, 1994), pp. 1–2. Early in 1944, FDR was not sure that even he could win. In her dairy of March 10, 1944, Daisy Suckley writes, "At lunch yesterday, I asked one of my rare questions on the political situation—The P. said that without any question, if [the election] were tomorrow he would be beaten—by almost any Republican." Ward, *Closest Companion*, p. 284.

9. A May 20, 1944 column by *Washington Star* political writer Gould Lincoln noted a significant strain of anti-fourth term sentiment among Southern Democrats, as well as elsewhere, but that any such opposition proved ineffectual. Lincoln detailed three reasons this was so. "In the first place, even Democrats opposed to a fourth term for Mr. Roosevelt frankly admit that no other Democratic nominee would have a chance this year. Then too, all Democrats who hold office—and there is an army of job holders—feel that their future is bound up with Mr. Roosevelt. In the third place, Mr. Roosevelt has not lifted a finger or uttered a word to discourage his re-nomination or the election of Roosevelt-pledged delegates." Gould Lincoln, "The Political Mill," *Washington Evening Star*, May 20, 1944, p. A-6.

10. Jay Winik, *1944: FDR and the Year that Changed History* (New York: Simon and Schuster, 2015), p. 474.

11. Winik, p. 474.

12. Franklin D. Roosevelt, State of the Union Message to Congress, January 11, 1944, www.fdrlibrary.marist.edu/archives/address_text.html.

13. Nigel Hamilton, *War and Peace: FDR's Final Odyssey D-Day to Yalta, 1943–1945* (Boston: Houghton Mifflin Harcourt, 2019), p. 192.

14. "Willkie Declares GOP Victory Is Vital to Nation's Welfare," *Washington Evening Star,* February 9, 1944, p. A-3.

15. Robert H. Ferrell, *The Dying President: Franklin D. Roosevelt 1944–1945* (Columbia, Missouri: University of Missouri Press, 1998), pp. 37–40. To the contrary, the Surgeon General told reporters that the president's check-up was "satisfactory," except that Roosevelt suffered from respiratory ailments, for which he needed more sunshine and exercise. Ferrell, p. 39. To address this, doctors sent Roosevelt to the Hobcaw estate of Bernard Baruch in South Carolina, where he spent nearly a month, from early April to early May. Meanwhile, the alarming blood pressure readings from the Bethesda examination actually continued to worsen. Ferrell, pp. 67–70.

16. Jordan, pp. 131–133.

17. Victor Sebestyen, *1946: The Making of the Modern World* (New York: Pantheon Books, 2014), p. 17. Michael Korzi also argues that Roosevelt knew about the precariousness of his condition. "Notwithstanding his doctors attempts to keep

information from him, Roosevelt had, early on, discovered that Bruenn was a cardiologist and that he evidently had heart trouble. Given Roosevelt's legendary reputation for personal interaction and for 'reading' people, it is hard to believe that his advisers would have kept the seriousness of his illness from him had he not wanted it that way; and, in fact, the available evidence does not necessarily indicate that Roosevelt did not know the seriousness of his condition." Michael J. Korzi, "Theorizing Presidential Tenure: The Difficult Case of FDR's Fourth Term, Congress & the Presidency," *A Journal of Capital Studies*, Vol. 35, No. 2 (2008), pp. 39, 45, 54. DOI: 10.1080/07343460809507644.

18. Ferrell, pp. 76–77.

19. Ibid., p. 359.

20. Roosevelt's former ally had become a political pariah. "I did not roam around much during the convention. In the first place, I did not want my visits and conversations misunderstood, and I also did not want anyone punished for being seen with me. Many of my friends became marked men by the White House 'palace guard' just for being seen with me and for remaining loyal to me." Farley, p. 365.

21. Nigel Hamilton indicates that on July 8, Roosevelt reached a final decision to run. Hamilton, p. 281.

22. Winik, p. 476.

23. Hamilton, p. 284.

24. Jordan, p. 139.

25. David Lawrence, "Shift in Strategy with Roosevelt Move," *Washington Evening Star*, July 12, 1944, p. A-10.

26. "The showing made by anti-fourth-term Democrats was not as large as they had hoped, partly due to the fact that the convention had agreed to seat both the pro-Roosevelt and anti-Roosevelt delegations from Texas. "Divided Texans Air Views," *Washington Evening Star,* July 21, 1944, p. 5. The Southerners had a variety of complaints. Some did not like the party's platform, some were distressed that the party rebuffed their efforts to restore the two-thirds rule for nominations, and some vigorously opposed Wallace. Ibid.

27. Farley, p. 368.

28. David McCullough, *Truman* (New York: Simon & Schuster, 1992), p. 305.

29. McCullough asserts that if delegates to the 1944 Convention could have simply voted for their first choice, Wallace would have prevailed. McCullough, *Truman*, p. 305.

30. "Relations with the top echelon of the Democratic Party in early 1944 were reminiscent of the old description of the Massachusetts Democracy as the systematic organization of hatred." Burns, *Soldier of Freedom*, p. 503.

31. Farley, p. 368. "Pauley made a deal with Pa Watson, who was violently anti-Wallace, to arrange appointments with the President for anti-Wallace Democrats and to block pro-Wallace people. It was like dripping water on a stone. They came day after day, and said they didn't want Wallace. Roosevelt began to realize that he could not impose Wallace on the Convention, as he had done in 1940." Morgan, p. 726. Pauley is quoted in Korzi, "Theorizing," to say, "It was about a year before the convention that I proceeded to prevent his becoming the President. I say 'the President'

because, in my opinion, it was becoming obvious that the Vice President would become the President because of Roosevelt's health." Korzi, "Theorizing," p. 48.

32. Lacey, p. 443.

33. Ferrell, *Choosing Truman*, p. 18.

34. Jordan, p. 144.

35. Tully, p. 275.

36. "Byrnes wanted the nomination for the same reason that Wallace did: Roosevelt's ill health." Ferrell, p. 77. "A superlative politician, Jimmie Byrnes realized when FDR was seeking a fourth term in 1944, it was unlikely that incumbent Vice President Henry A. Wallace could be re-nominated. There were vehement objections by many party leaders and bosses across the country who felt Wallace would not only be a drag to the rest of the ticket, but might actually cost FDR votes. Franklin Roosevelt, distracted by the war, constitutionally averse to telling anyone 'no', and ailing, encouraged the prospective vice presidential candidacies of numerous ambitious Democrats, all while urging the hapless Henry Wallace to seek re-nomination. One of those Democrats encouraged to run for vice president was James F. Byrnes." "All in One Lifetime: James F. Byrnes of South Carolina," *Knoxville Focus,* October 26, 2014.

37. Jordan, pp. 144–145.

38. Lelyveld, p. 172. According to Robert Ferrell, Roosevelt had also considered Byrnes in 1940, but Catholic clergy dissuaded him from doing so. Ferrell, *Choosing Truman*, p. 19.

39. Ferrell, p. 13.

40. Jordan, p. 145.

41. Ibid., p. 146.

42. Ibid.

43. Morgan, p. 727.

44. Bell oral history, pp. 21–22.

45. In her diary of Wednesday, July 5, 1944, Daisy Suckley, reports, "He has to tell V.P. Wallace that the Dem. Party do not want him: another headache. The dear P. hates to hurt people's feelings, but he says the opposition to Wallace has become very strong & active in the last 6 weeks and something has to be done about it. He is sending two people out to the West Coast to meet Mr. Wallace & break it to him, when he arrives from China." (emphasis in the original) Ward, *Closest Companion*, p. 316. The two people were Roosevelt speechwriter Sam Rosenman and Secretary of the Interior Harold Ickes. They wound up not traveling to the West Coast but met with Wallace on July 10 in Washington. Wallace did not react well to their overture and said he would reserve the topic for a discussion he would shortly have with the president.

46. According to Robert Ferrell, both Wallace and James Byrnes "intensely" wanted the vice-presidential nomination. Both, says Ferrell, were mindful of Roosevelt's declining health. "They knew it meant the presidency, which they knew they could not hope to get on their own; each man could only come into it by what one might describe as an inheritance." Ferrell, *Choosing Truman*, pp. 14–15.

47. Lacey, p. 443.

48. "With the promise of a Roosevelt vote at the Convention, which Wallace wasn't going to get, and with the advice to the delegates to choose their own candidate, Wallace had to be satisfied." Ibid., pp. 25–26.

49. McCullough, *Truman*, p. 310. Roosevelt scholar Joseph Lelyveld has a somewhat different perspective, positing a subtle but activist Roosevelt who was determined to ease Wallace out. "It's a tribute to Franklin Roosevelt's wiliness that the notion has persisted over the years that he was only fleetingly engaged in the selection, that he was simply oblivious when it came to the larger issue of succession. . . . He never used the word 'succession' but cared enough about qualifications for the presidency to eliminate Wallace as a possibility." Joseph Lelyveld, *His Final Battle: The Last Months of Franklin Roosevelt* (New York: Alfred A. Knopf, 2016), p. 172.

50. Roosevelt told Wallace that Party leaders advised him that keeping the vice president would hurt the ticket. Wallace offered to withdraw. Roosevelt would not accept, then told Wallace, "While I cannot put it just that way in public, I hope it will be the same old team." Ferrell, *Choosing Truman*, pp. 24–25.

51. Ferrell, *Choosing Truman,* p. 25. "Roosevelt, of course, was being slightly disingenuous. He was always unable to deliver bad news face-to-face, and this trait was partially responsible for his assurances to Wallace, for whom he had personal affection." Jordan, p. 144.

52. Morgan, p. 728. Journalist Jack L. Bell, in an oral history for the Truman Library states, "that was the usual Roosevelt deception. Let the man down easy, don't kick him over the cliff, just say, 'oh, well, I'm a victim of circumstances, I have to do this.' Good-bye, Henry." Jack Bell oral history, p. 24.

53. Brands, *Traitor,* p. 768.

54. "Is Byrnes' Star Rising?" *The Wilmington Morning Star* (Wilmington, NC), July 18, 1944, p. 4.

55. Ferrell, p. 28.

56. Jordan, p. 149; Ferrell, pp. 29–30.

57. Ferrell, p. 29.

58. Ibid., p. 31.

59. Ibid., pp. 31–32.

60. Ibid., pp. 32–33.

61. Jordan, p. 151.

62. Lacey, p. 445.

63. Ibid.

64. The trip would allow the president to be away from the Convention during its deliberations, avoiding too many inferences that he was interfering in its deliberations. He left for Hawaii from California the day after the Convention ended. Hamilton, pp. 287, 303.

65. McCullough, *Truman,* p. 306.

66. Franklin Delano Roosevelt Library, Democratic National Conventions, Box 143, www.fdrlibrary.marist.edu/_resources/images/psf/psf000531.pdf (accessed July 21, 2018).

67. Tully, p. 276. Hannegan and Truman had Missouri connections and had been mutually helpful to each other politically. Ferrell, pp. 8–9.

68. According to Gould Lincoln, the *Washington Star's* political columnist, the CIO had three objectives for the 1944 convention. The first was to renominate Wallace. If that proved impossible, the second was to exercise a veto over any possible vice presidential nominee not acceptable to the union. Third, it insisted that the ultimate nominee be someone who had its blessing. Gould Lincoln, "The Political Mill," *Washington Evening Star*, July 20, 1944, p. A-10.

69. Jordan, p. 157.

70. Truman later wrote that he believed Byrnes knew about the July 11 White House meeting at which the South Carolinian had been edged out of consideration for the Vice Presidency. However, Byrnes mentioned nothing to Truman, who did not learn of the meeting until sometime later. Perhaps Byrnes felt he could generate sufficient support at the Convention to reverse the outcome of the White House meeting, so he enlisted Truman as if the meeting never took place. Harry S. Truman, undated longhand note, Truman Library (accessed July 28, 2018).

71. During the Convention, Byrnes encountered Jack L. Bell, a longtime political writer for the Associated Press. When asked about the Vice Presidency, Byrnes replied, "Labor has killed me. They won't take me." Jack L. Bell Oral History, Harry S. Truman Presidential Library and Museum, p. 19, www.trumanlibrary.org (accessed July 28, 2018).

72. Longhand Note of President Harry S. Truman, not dated. Truman Presidential Library, President's Secretary's Files, Longhand Notes, www.trumanlibrary.org (accessed July 28, 2018).

73. The pressure began on Tuesday July 18, 1944, the day before the Convention opened. Hannegan showed Truman a note in Roosevelt's handwriting. It said, "Bob, it's Truman. FDR." Harry S. Truman, undated longhand note, Harry S. Truman Presidential Library and Museum, www.trumanlibrary.org (accessed July 28, 2018).

74. Truman, *Years of Trial and Hope*, p. 204.

75. Although the note is undated, it had to have been prepared after 1948, because, at the end, it makes an oblique reference to that year. The note was written on a pad with a letterhead saying "From the Desk of Harry S. Truman" and is 18 pages long.

76. Longhand note of President Harry S. Truman. Not dated. Truman Papers—President's Secretary's Files, Harry S. Truman Presidential Library and Museum, www.trumanlibrary.org (accessed July 27, 2018).

77. "When Senator Jackson of Indiana, chairman of the convention, recognized David L. Lawrence, Pennsylvania's national committeeman, to move an adjournment of the session, there was a roar of protest from the Wallace demonstrators, most of them nondelegates. They thought the psychological moment to put Mr. Wallace across was at hand. "Wallace Gains as Balloting at Chicago Nears," *Washington Evening Star,* July 21, 1944, pp. 1, 5.

78. Ibid.

79. McCullough, *Truman*, pp. 316–317.

80. The result of the first ballot was Wallace 429.5, Truman 319. 5, with 427 votes divided among others.

81. When the second ballot roll call initially ended, Truman led 477.5 to 473, with 225.5 for others. Before the vote was announced, a massive amount of delegate switching put Truman over the top.

82. "Truman was referred to as 'the Missouri Compromise' and the 'Common Denominator,' surely not seizing upon his inherent fitness for the office but testifying to the mixture of qualities that made him most desirable to the various factions and leaders within the party." Korzi, "Theorizing," p. 49.

There were additional benefits, both political and substantive. According to Cold War chronicler Victor Sebestyen, the party selected Truman because, "in order to win a convincing victory in 1944, the Democrats needed to shore up votes in the Midwest and parts of the South." Sebestyen, p. 17. Dr. Milton Eisenhower, who was Dwight Eisenhower's brother, and who knew Truman well, also speculated that Roosevelt chose the senator in order to strengthen relations with Congress. For example, such connections could be crucial for the economic bill of rights agenda Roosevelt had outlined in his 1944 State of the Union Address. Dr. Eisenhower observes, "Although he had strong Democratic majorities in both houses of Congress, Roosevelt had not cultivated good relations with the Congress and he had bullied through the legislation he needed in recent years. That might be all right for fighting a war but it would not suffice for winning the peace that must follow. Roosevelt knew that he would need strong legislative support to make the United Nations an effective instrument. . . . He needed for his running mate and his successor a man who could win the Legislative Branch to his side." Eisenhower, p. 217.

83. Korzi, "Theorizing," p. 40.

84. Gould Lincoln, "Truman Victory Ends Turbulent Chicago Session," *Washington Evening Star*, July 22, 1944, pp. 1, 2.

85. Lincoln, pp. 1, 2.

86. Morgan, p. 729. Roosevelt's Press Secretary, Jonathan Daniels, reports that, after the Convention, Byrnes was aggravated over Truman's nomination, believing FDR had promised it to him, and remained bitter for years. Daniels Oral History, pp. 56, 62. Douglas, however, did not feel betrayed. While on a camping trip to Oregon, and on Supreme Court letterhead, he sent a July 27, 1944, handwritten note to FDR. Douglas was effusive, writing, "I learned of your letter to Hannegan saying that I would be acceptable as your running mate. That was a great compliment, Mr. President, and I want you to know it touched me deeply. . . . I thank you from the heart for your expression of confidence, Mr. President. I wish I could help you, but I doubt if you will need much help out here." Franklin Delano Roosevelt Library, Democratic National Conventions, Box 143, www.fdrlibrary.marist.edu/_resources/images/psf/psf000531.pdf (accessed July 20, 2018). It was, of course, a warm, personal note, but one from a member of a supposedly apolitical Branch that contained overt political references. Given worries often expressed in Congress about presidential influence on judicial independence, concerns exacerbated by extended presidential tenure, one wonders what Twenty-second Amendment advocates would have made of Douglas' letter if they had access to it.

87. Ibid. Ilo was Wallace's wife.

88. Franklin D. Roosevelt, "Address to the Democratic National Convention in Chicago," July 20, 1944. Online by Gerhard Peters and John T. Woolley, *The American Presidency Project*, http://www.presidency.ucsb.edu/ws/?pid=16537.

89. Republicans controlled the governorships and related political machinery in states with 339 electoral votes. Democrats governed states with 192 electoral votes. Ibid., p. 20.

90. "Republicans considered themselves the natural ruling party of the country," writes David Jordan. "They had established dominance during the Civil War and retained it until the Great Depression. During the 72-year period between Lincoln's election in 1860 and Hoover's defeat in 1932, Republicans had held the White House for all but 16 years (the two Cleveland and two Wilson Administrations). The Depression had led to the presidency of Franklin Roosevelt," continued Jordan, "and the threat of war had given him a third term in 1940. Republican partisans felt it was time to restore their party to its accustomed primacy, especially with the war nearing its close." Ibid.

91. In addition, there was support for General Douglas MacArthur and former Minnesota Governor Harold Stassen, but both were in military service, MacArthur in the Army and Stassen in the Navy; thus, neither campaigned or was an active candidate.

92. All major Republican leaders denounced Lend-Lease after Roosevelt proposed it in December 1940. This included Dewey, Taft, Vandenberg, Landon, and Hoover, all of whom alleged that the president was moving the United States closer into a war posture. Willkie was the exception, and quite vocally so, excoriating the Republicans who took the opposite view. "Appeasers, isolationists, or lip-service friends of Britain will seek to sabotage the program of aid to Britain and her allies behind the screen of opposition to this bill." Neal, p. 188.

93. Neal, p. 189.

94. "Isolationism has a long history in the Republican Party. Following World War I, in which over 100,000 Americans died, millions of citizens asked why the United States should remain entangled in world affairs. . . . Republican Presidents Warren Harding, Calvin Coolidge, and Herbert Hoover trimmed their sails to this isolationist sentiment and avoided entangling alliances with European nations. This scorn for the old world aligned with a growing chorus of domestic critics of U.S. foreign policy, which asserted that the Great War had only benefitted a small caste of arms manufacturers and bankers. . . . During the 1940s, the Republican Party seemed to abandon its isolationist policies. . . . But the strain of isolationism that animated the Republican Party in the interwar years never died." Jack Shafer, "How the GOP Embraced the World and Then Turned Away," *Politico Magazine*, www.politico.com/magazine/story/2018/07/13/gop-isolationism-trump-eisenhower-219003. (accessed July 13, 2018).

95. Republican reaction to Willkie's playing this role repeated in 2012, when party regulars castigated former Utah Governor Jon Huntsman for serving as President Barack Obama's Ambassador to China.

96. Shafer, "How the GOP Embraced."

97. Neal, p. 232.

98. When Willkie returned from his trip, he made a radio report to the country. Four networks carried it, and the broadcast secured more than 36 million listeners. Neal, p. 260.

99. In the 1920s, Willkie had strongly supported American entry into the League of Nations.

100. Neal, p. 264. This represented record sales of any political book in the history of publishing. Ibid., p. 280.

101. Lynne Olson, *Those Angry Days: Roosevelt, Lindbergh, and America's Fight Over World War II, 1939–1941* (New York: Random House, 2013), p. 448.

102. Neal, p. 279. "Willkie was a known quantity, with a strong following among international-minded Republicans. But the regulars hadn't liked him in 1940, when Roosevelt seemed at least a little vulnerable, and they liked him even less now, when Roosevelt looked unbeatable. They couldn't imagine letting him lead the party into the postwar era." Brands, p. 767. Nigel Hamilton notes that because Willkie's foreign policy positions were so similar to Roosevelt's, Adolf Hitler interpreted Willkie's poor showing in the primaries as evidence that the American people did not support the President's war strategy. Hamilton, p. 236, citing the diaries of Nazi Propaganda Minister Joseph Goebbels.

103. Even though they did not campaign, Stassen and MacArthur won several delegates each.

104. "Willkie Funeral to be Tomorrow; Son Still at Sea," *New York Times*, October 9, 1944, p. 1.

105. Ibid.

106. Dewey first tendered the spot to California Governor Earl Warren, who declined. Warren would run with Dewey in 1948. Richard Norton Smith, p. 396.

107. Angst about the fourth term was not entirely missing, however. David M. Jordan notes a series of editorials in the *New York Daily News* that predicted the demise of democracy if Roosevelt were permitted to continue in office and to use his continuity in the presidency to establish political foundations for his adult sons to perpetuate a political dynasty thereafter. Jordan, p. 233.

108. "Four more years of New Deal policy would centralize all power in the President, and would daily subject every act of every citizen to regulation by his henchmen; and this country could remain a Republic only in name." Republican Party Platforms, "Republican Party Platform of 1944," June 26, 1944. Online by Gerhard Peters and John T. Woolley, *The American Presidency Project*, http://www.presidency.ucsb.edu/ws/?pid=25835.

109. Ibid.

110. "Republican attempts to revive the third term issue again in 1944 proved to be 'decidedly anticlimactic and altogether a dismal failure.' Finally 'realizing that the popular appeal of the issue was gone, the proponents of the amendment never again tried to rouse public sentiment behind them.'" Stathis, p. 65.

111. Ibid. Dewey's own thinking was parallel. On June 6, 1944, he sent a letter to Governor Landon, in which he wrote, "Every day of successful war brings us closer to the time when our people will be thinking of the domestic future. . . . Certainly, if they can give their full attention to domestic problems, they will vote Roosevelt out unanimously." Richard Norton Smith, p. 397.

112. Michael Korzi writes, "According to a Gallup poll released in June of 1943, if the war were to be over before the election, 69% would be against Roosevelt's

reelection, whereas if it were still ongoing, only 44% would vote against his reelection." Korzi, "Theorizing," p. 41.

113. "By 1944, there were serious concerns about Roosevelt's health, reflected by 36 articles on his health in the *New York Times* by June of that year." Korzi, "Theorizing," p. 43. "There was one serious question in this campaign: Roosevelt's health. There were innumerable baseless and incredibly malicious rumors, but there was some visible support for them, for he was now truly crippled." Sherwood, p. 824. The White House physician, Admiral Ross McIntire, misled the public as to the President's condition. As a result of the President's visit on March 28, 1944, to Bethesda Naval Hospital, which included an examination by Lieutenant Commander Howard Bruenn, a cardiologist, McIntire knew that Roosevelt suffered from a serious heart ailment. Nigel Hamilton notes that before reporters later that day, "McIntire deliberately sought to bamboozle the press." It was, says Hamilton, "a model of what later would be called White House 'spin'." Hamilton, p. 226.

114. Korzi, "Theorizing," p. 42.

115. "The President's most effective electioneering technique, at least early in the campaign, had always been that of maintaining his presidential posture, above the battle. . . . Roosevelt continued just being President, offering as small a partisan flank as possible for the opposition to bombard." Burns, *Soldier of Freedom*, p. 509.

116. Hamilton, p. 223.

117. Resting was what the President did at Hobcaw, keeping as relaxed a schedule as one could imagine two months before D-Day. Citing Dr. Howard Bruenn, who attended Roosevelt at Hobcaw, Hamilton notes that the president worked approximately thirty minutes a day. Ibid., p. 246.

118. Oral history of Jonathan Daniels, pp. 52–56, Harry S. Truman Presidential Library and Museum, www.trumanlibrary.org (accessed July 25, 2018). Immediately following the Yalta Conference, which occurred some three months after the election, Roosevelt's daughter, Anna, hit Daniels with a further dose of reality. Anna had been with the president in the Crimea. She spoke of creating a *de facto* protectorate, much as Edith Wilson had done for her husband. "Anna Roosevelt took me aside and expressed her fears, not of the President's death but of his increasing incapacity. And there was a certain suggestion of something in the nature of a regency in which she and her husband, John Boettiger, would hold what would be dynastic positions. . . . I've often said that Roosevelt was blessed, and the country was blessed that when he got a cerebral hemorrhage, it was massive." Ibid.

119. Hamilton, p. 298.

120. Ibid., p. 328.

121. "When he delivered this speech, he wore his leg braces for, I believe, the first time since he returned from Cairo and Tehran [December 1943] and he was in such pain that he had to support himself by holding on to the lectern . . . which made it extremely difficult for him to turn the pages of his reading copy and made the speech sound faltering and uncertain to the listeners." Sherwood, p. 820.

122. Sherwood, pp. 820–821.

123. Hamilton, p. 338.

124. Ward, p. 328.

125. Nigel Hamilton surmises that a contributing factor in Roosevelt's change of attitude was the influence of Lucy Mercer Rutherfurd, with whom FDR had a romance in 1918, and with whom he remained in contact during the campaign. "Only one person could, arguably, inspire the President to fight for the presidency, given how deathly ill he often felt: Lucy Rutherfurd. Without her intercession, it seems doubtful he could make the effort, *or even possessed the will to do so*." Ibid., p. 339 (emphasis in the original).

126. Sherwood, p. 824.

127. Ibid., p. 820.

128. "Franklin Roosevelt's speech at the Statler in Washington on September 23 heartened the leaders of the Democratic Party as they recognized that 'the Champ,' as they liked to think of FDR, was in the fray at last." Ibid., p. 234.

129. His train, called the Roosevelt Special, left Albany on September 12, 1932, headed for the West Coast. FDR delivered fifty-six speeches over a period of twenty days. Houck and Kiewe, p. 97.

130. "For October 21 in New York City, the weather was bad. It was going to be rainy, cold, windy, and dreary all day, the tail end of a hurricane that had gone up the coast." Ibid., p. 272.

131. C.P. Trussell, "President Defies Rain, Wind to Let New York See Him," *New York Times*, October 22, 1944, p. 1.

132. "Through it all, the rain kept coming down, the wind blew, and Franklin Roosevelt kept smiling and waving to the thousands watching him, with Fala at his side." Ibid., p. 274.

133. "Most of Roosevelt's companions begged off, but the President didn't want to disappoint the millions of voters who lined the streets, and he wanted to bury the charges that he was on his deathbed. The cheering crowds didn't know that his car periodically darted into garages where he put on dry clothes and took warming shots of brandy." Brands, p. 784.

134. "President Roosevelt, openly campaigning for re-election in the usual partisan sense and bidding particularly for New York's forty-seven electoral votes, came from a rain-drench Washington to an equally wet and wind-swept New York City yesterday to let the people see him as he looked at the moment and judge his physical fitness with their own eyes." Trussell, p. 1.

135. "Remove Monarchy Threat," *Spokane Daily Chronicle*, November 2, 1944, p. 18.

136. In contrast to Roosevelt's landslide 58 percent in 1932 and 60.4 percent in 1936, his margin in 1944 was healthy, but not overwhelming. His win over Dewey was almost exactly parallel to George H.W. Bush's 1988 victory over Michael Dukakis, both in terms of the popular vote and Electoral College.

137. In 1948, the States Rights Democratic Party (otherwise called the Dixiecrats), headed by South Carolina Governor Strom Thurmond, won 39 electoral votes in the South, denying them to Harry Truman, the Democratic nominee.

138. Jackson, p. 45.

139. Ibid., p. 45.

140. Gerhard Peters and John T. Woolley, The American Presidency Project, www.presidency.ucsb.edu (accessed July 13, 2018).

141. Ibid.

142. Ibid. "Throughout 1946, Harry S. Truman was one of the most unpopular presidents in American history. Widely respected later as the leader who turned his country into the global colossus America has been since World War Two, he was dismissed as a lightweight for much of his first term in the White House." Sebestyen, p. 16.

143. Ibid.

144. McCullough, *Truman*, pp. 520–521. See Truman, *Years of Trial and Hope*, pp. 26–30.

145. Sebestyen, p. 65. The scandal involved revelations by Igor Gouzenko, employed at the USSR embassy in Ottawa, about Soviet efforts to steal atomic secrets. Ibid.

146. McCullough, *Truman,* p. 522.

147. Republicans controlled 246 of 435 seats in the House and 50 of 96 seats in the Senate.

148. Carl Hatch was a senator between 1933 and 1949.

149. Joseph O'Mahoney was a senator from 1933 to 1953 and, again, from 1954 to his death in 1962.

150. Kenneth S. Wherry served in the Senate from 1943 until his death in 1951.

151. E.H. Moore was a senator from 1943 to 1949.

152. The resolution seemingly disqualified a vice president who exercised the duties of president during a period of presidential disability without ever actually succeeding to the presidency itself.

153. Apparently, a person who had been vice president would be ineligible to run for president.

154. Hugh Butler served in the Senate from 1941 until his death in 1954.

155. Arthur Capper was a senator from 1919 to 1949.

156. One can speculate whether indifference existed because no one actually cared about the issue or because it was widely understood that the hearing was an exercise and Democrats would do nothing further.

157. "Term of President of the United States," Hearings before a subcommittee of the Committee on the Judiciary, United States Senate, Seventy-ninth Congress, First Session, September 27, 1945 (Washington, DC: United States Government Printing Office, 1945), p. 6.

158. The Seventy-ninth Congress sat from January 1945 to January 1947.

159. S. Hearings, 1945, p. 5.

160. Ibid.

161. Ibid.

162. Ibid., p. 7.

163. Ibid., p. 8.

164. Ibid., pp. 8–9.

165. Ibid., p. 9.

166. Ibid., p. 10.

167. Ibid., pp. 10–11.

168. Ibid., p. 11.

169. Ibid.

170. Dean of the University of Oregon School of Law, Wayne Morse was elected to the Senate in 1944 as a Republican and was reelected in 1950. In 1952, he was an early supporter of Dwight Eisenhower's bid for the Republican nomination, and may have entertained thoughts of being on Eisenhower's ticket, but in any case was prepared to nominate for Vice President the Senator from Massachusetts, Leverett Saltonstall. Charles Deemer, "American Gadfly: The Story of Wayne Morse," i.biblio.org (accessed June 2, 2018). However, Saltonstall was not under serious consideration for the ticket, and Eisenhower may not have considered him at all. His name does not appear on a recapitulation list in Eisenhower's memoirs. See Dwight D. Eisenhower, *Mandate for Change* (New York: Doubleday, 1963), p. 77. However, Morse was aghast at Eisenhower's actual choice, Senator Richard Nixon (R-CA). Morse was further distressed when Eisenhower and Senator Robert Taft (R-OH) reached a September 12, 1952, deal known as the Declaration of Morningside Heights. Taft had opposed Eisenhower at the party convention in July, and their Morningside Heights meeting was important in healing what could have been a bitter split. See Stephen Ambrose, *Eisenhower: Soldier, General, President-elect 1890–1952* (New York: Simon & Schuster, 1983), p. 553. To Morse, the deal looked like a sell-out to an element of the party with whom he had long tussled. For their part, Democrats emphasized the theme of betrayal. "Democrats labeled the meeting the 'Surrender at Morningside Heights' because Eisenhower had supposedly acceded to Taft's demands in exchange for the Senator's pledge to support the Ike-Nixon ticket." Irwin F. Gellman, *The President and the Apprentice* (New Haven: Yale University Press, 2015), p. 27. At the time, Eisenhower was president of Columbia University, a post he assumed in June 1948, but from which he was on leave since becoming Supreme Commander at NATO in the fall of 1950. For Eisenhower's experience at Columbia, see Dwight D. Eisenhower, *At Ease: Stories I Tell to Friends* (New York: Doubleday, 1967), pp. 336–364. Eisenhower resigned from Columbia before taking the oath as the 34th U.S. President in 1953. See Travis B. Jacobs, "Dwight D. Eisenhower's Presidency of Columbia University," *Presidential Studies Quarterly*, Vol. 15, No. 3 (Summer 1985), p. 553. In October, 1952, the alienated Morse endorsed Democratic nominee Adlai Stevenson. At the start of the 83rd Congress in 1953, Morse declared himself an independent and became increasingly outspoken against President Eisenhower. In 1955, he formally switched parties and became a Democrat. Morse was reelected in 1956 and 1962, but lost in 1968 to Robert W. Packwood (R-OR). Morse twice attempted to come back. He was the Democratic nominee in a losing 1972 campaign against Senator Mark O. Hatfield (R-OR). In 1974, Democrats nominated him for a re-match with Packwood, but Morse died during the general election campaign.

171. S. Hearings, p. 15.

172. Ibid., p. 16.

173. Herbert Bonner served in the House from 1940 until his death in 1965.

174. The hearing record is unprinted. Footnotes are derived from typewritten pages.

175. Joseph W. Martin was in the House from 1935 until 1967. He was Speaker in the 80th Congress (1947–1949) and in the 83rd Congress (1953–1955). Martin was also House Minority Leader from 1939 to 1947, from 1949 to 1953, and from 1955 to 1959, when Representative Charles W. Halleck (R-IN) deposed him.

176. H. Hearings, 1945, p. 3.
177. Ibid., p. 5.
178. Ibid., p. 6.
179. *Congressional Record*, September 19, 1940, Appendix, pp. 18712–18713.
180. H. Hearings (1945), pp. 23–24.
181. Ibid., p. 6.
182. Ibid., pp. 7–8.
183. Carter Manasco was in the House from 1941 to 1949.
184. H. Hearings, p. 10.
185. Ibid., p. 13.
186. Jesse Combs was a Congressman from 1945 to 1953.
187. H. Hearings (1945), p. 17.
188. John McCormack was elected to the House in 1928 and entered the Democratic Leadership in 1940, serving as number two to Speaker Sam Rayburn until the latter's death at the end of 1961. In 1962, McCormack became Speaker of the House. He held that post until his retirement in 1971.
189. H. Hearings (1945), pp. 20–21.
190. Ibid., p. 30.
191. Ibid., p. 37.
192. Ibid.
193. Ibid., p. 38.
194. Ibid., p. 42.
195. Ibid., p. 51.
196. Ibid., p. 45.
197. Ibid., p. 46.
198. In the 79th Congress, there were 242 Democrats and 191 Republicans. A majority of voting Members was 218. In their years in the political wilderness after the 1930 cycle, Republicans had reached a high of 209 after the 1942 election, their only time to break 200. They backslid in 1944, losing 18 seats. Prospects for a Republican majority seemed elusive.
199. Nelson, p. 342.
200. Wat Arnold served in the House from 1943 to 1949.
201. H. Hearings, 1945, pp. 3–4.
202. Ibid., p. 5.
203. Ibid., p. 6.
204. Ibid.
205. Ibid.
206. Ibid., p. 7.
207. Ibid., p. 8.
208. In 1937, Coudert was the president of the New York Bar Association. In that capacity, he testified before Congress in strenuous opposition to President Roosevelt's plan to enlarge the Supreme Court. Roosevelt's proposal, which would have greatly enlarged presidential authority, met with a crushing defeat in the Senate on July 20, 1937. The House did not act on it.
209. Ibid., p. 8.

Chapter 9

The Constitution Amended (1947–1951)

On November 5, 1946, Republicans finally scored the victory they had long awaited. The GOP won fifty-seven seats in the House. In so doing, they converted a 242-191 deficit into a 248-185 Republican majority. Thirteen new Republican senators were elected as well, transforming a chamber that had been 57-38 in favor of the Democrats into one controlled by Republicans, 51-46. There were multiple reasons for this turnabout, principally economic dislocation in converting from war to peace, but the president was the focus of blame, and had been a heavy liability to his party.[1]

Back in power on Capitol Hill, Republicans had a pent-up agenda to pursue. Nothing in their program took greater priority than redressing Roosevelt's destruction of the two-term tradition.

When the 80th Congress convened in January 1947, nine members of the House of Representatives introduced constitutional amendments to impose presidential term limits.[2] The Speaker referred these measures to the Committee on the Judiciary. In Judiciary, Chairman Earl Michener (R-MI)[3] sent them to Subcommittee Four, chaired by Representative Raymond S. Springer (R-IN).[4]

On Monday, February 3, at 10:00 AM, Springer gaveled in a markup on all the competing resolutions. Chief among them was H.J. Res. 27, proposed by Chairman Michener himself. The markup is the time when the committee drafts and reports legislation. Customarily, a hearing precedes a markup, but not in this case. As Michener explained to the subcommittee, in prior years there had been extensive hearings on presidential term limits, and to convene another would be superfluous.[5] Political scientist Stephen Stathis offers a further explanation for the accelerated schedule. "From the outset, the House Republican leadership sought to avoid public hearings that might arouse latent opposition. They hoped to secure quick passage in the House so that the amendment could reach state legislatures while they were still in session."[6]

Republican Members led off, advocating for one or the other proposals pending before the committee. These included ideas for a single six-year term as well as a ceiling of two four-year terms. Differences of opinion among these Members were modest and inconsequential. All Republicans in Congress supported presidential term limits and would quickly coalesce behind Michener's legislation.

As he had for several years, Minority Whip John W. McCormack (D-MA) spearheaded Democratic opposition to term limits. Even with his party in the minority, McCormack had a chance to prevail because passage of constitutional amendments requires two-thirds majority. However, while McCormack represented the views of most Democrats, a quarter of his membership would defect on the final tally.

McCormack asserted that the decision at the Constitutional Convention not to limit terms was deliberate, and not an omission. "The fact that the Constitution puts no limitation on the number of terms of the President is no oversight on the part of the Framers."[7]

From almost the start of the Convention until nearly its end, noted McCormack, delegates faced divisive questions of how to choose presidents, how long executives would serve, and whether they were eligible for another term. At first, the delegates provided for election by Congress, but feared that a president who could seek reelection might subordinate himself to legislators in order to win. To preserve executive independence, the Framers therefore barred reeligibility. Limiting the chief executive to a single term, they discussed caps of six or seven years. However, once they abandoned election by Congress in favor of the Electoral College, they shortened the president's term and eliminated the barrier to reeligibility.

This system afforded voters the flexibility to retain a president if circumstances warranted it. McCormack saw no reason to change that and, he added, neither did the American people. "I note in reading the last Gallup Poll that there were over 75 percent of the people . . . who were opposed to change."[8]

The impetus to amend the Constitution was not a response to public demand, McCormack charged, but was an act of political vengeance. "Congress has not, therefore, been mandated by the people to take any such action as is proposed by the resolutions under consideration. Any action taken by this Committee which would favor a restriction of term of service would be but the consensus of personal opinions of voting members uninstructed, in fact, by the American people who, at the last two presidential elections, decided against such limitation"[9]

Historically, Congress had shown scant interest in restricting voter choice, said McCormack. In the years since the Constitutional Convention, Members of Congress had introduced more than 150 proposals to restrict presidential terms. A few such ideas made a little progress, but none received bicameral support. Thus, McCormack could assert, "The entire history of Congress, since the ratification and adoption of the Constitution of the United States, has been against any interference by Congress with the right of the American people to elect the President."[10]

At that point, Chairman Springer interjected a question. Although McCormack opposed the legislation, would he acquiesce in having Congress pass it, and allow the people to speak through their state legislatures?

McCormack refused. Congress had an obligation, which it must not abdicate, to filter out unsound proposals. Otherwise, he reasoned, "Why stop any constitutional question from being submitted to the people?"[11] Thus, he insisted, Congress must carefully scrutinize every proposed amendment, and allow only the most essential to go forward. "I think that all of these amendments should be considered in light of the evidence of the necessity, and caution should be used—careful caution—and that no amendment should be submitted unless there is a demanding necessity for it, and a demand for it on the part of the people."[12]

He was sure that term limits failed both tests and that Congress should just reject the amendment outright.

McCormack reprised the theme of flexibility. Voters in 1940 and 1944 prioritized Roosevelt's leadership over the two-term tradition. He wondered why Congress should deny future voters similar rights. "I recognize the calculated risk that men honestly entertain about unlimited terms, but I recognize the calculated risk that will exist, too, to some generations in the future when we say, at the end of the term of a good President, with the country perhaps at war, with its back against the wall, that the dead hands of the past have determined their action."[13]

Custom was one thing McCormack argued, but formal barriers were another. "Prohibitions in the Constitution are dangerous," he exclaimed.[14]

McCormack concluded, "There is no such thing as an indispensable man, but there is a best man. . . . I cannot close the doors of my conscience to Americans of tomorrow . . . and cut them off from the opportunity, if there is a second-term President and if he is the man they want and need, of electing him."[15]

Representative George W. Gillie (R-IN)[16] spoke next. He observed that Democrats before Roosevelt had strongly advocated and faithfully observed term limits. Not only was Thomas Jefferson the philosophical godfather of the two-term tradition, said Gillie, but other prominent Democrats, such as James Madison, James Monroe, Andrew Jackson, and Grover Cleveland also advocated it.

Would sufficient numbers of Democrats return to their party's traditional moorings and join Republicans to impose term limits? An amendment could not move through Congress without significant bipartisan support. "Unless the Democrats, in goodly numbers, support it, a constitutional amendment is impossible. A division along straight party lines will doom this proposal to defeat," Gillie observed.[17]

Representative Karl Mundt (R-SD)[18] followed. On the opening day of the 80th Congress, he introduced a term limits' resolution providing that no person could be eligible to be a president, or to run for that office, if he had held the office of president for six consecutive years preceding the date of election. His objective was to avoid disqualifying a vice president who served for an incidental period as president during an unexpired term.[19] "I have used this particular language," Mundt explained, "because it seems to me that in those cases where a Vice President ascends to the Presidency during the last few months of a Presidential term it might not be wise to prevent such a President from running for a second full term."[20] Although the committee did not act on Mundt's legislation, the Twenty-second Amendment would address this problem much as Mundt did. Under its terms, a president who had served less than six years would be eligible to run again.[21]

Chairman Michener closed for the Republicans. He claimed that a failure to act would put at risk the core constitutional principle of co-equal Branches. The presidency had grown too strong, he asserted. Breaching the two-term tradition aggravated the problem. A constitutional amendment would correct the distortion. "The potential abuses and evils of more than two terms in office so far outweigh any conceivable advantages, that the people ought in self-protection to amend their Constitution to limit tenure to two terms," Michener proclaimed.[22]

Michener asserted there were three fundamental reasons Congress must act. First was the need to preserve judicial independence, which would erode over time by the over-representation of appointments by the same president over an extended time. Second, to a degree unprecedented in American history, power was centralized in the federal government, with the president as its singular figure. Mandating rotation in office would contain this enlarged authority within reasonable bounds. Third, perpetuation in office would counteract the staleness that comes from stagnant leadership. "Political apathy is a menace to democracy, and blind faith in a leader inevitably means an indifference to great issues and problems. Along with public apathy there is a stifling of other leaders, so that the capacity for political leadership is weakened."[23]

The Chairman disputed Democrats' claims that imposing term limits would betray the voters. Term limits would actually make elections fairer, he claimed. Due to a president's control over patronage and his dominance of the news, an incumbent had a lock on renomination and an upper hand in the general election campaign. "The longer a president remains in office, the more difficult it is for the people to remove him."[24] Michener claimed the amendment would neutralize these advantages.

Michener was unmoved by McCormack's complaint that mandatory rotation might deprive the country of strong leadership in a moment of crisis. "This is, in effect, an argument that a particular man is indispensable, an idea that should be completely alien to a democratic society."[25]

Insisting that the proposed amendment was apolitical, Michener urged the subcommittee approve it and advance the process. "All we are asking is that the people back home be permitted, through their legislatures, to express their views on the question with which they are entirely familiar."[26]

Later that day, the subcommittee favorably reported H.J. Res. 27, Michener's proposal. The full committee followed suit on February 5, 1947, sending it to the House Floor. Concurrent with the Judiciary Committee's action, the House Rules Committee reported H. Res. 91, which laid out the procedure that the House would follow in debating and amending Michener's resolution. On the following day, Floor proceedings would commence.

FLOOR PROCEEDINGS IN THE HOUSE OF REPRESENTATIVES

"Mr. Speaker," exclaimed Representative Leo Allen (R-IL),[27] "I call up House Resolution 91 and ask for its immediate consideration."[28] It was February 6, 1947, shortly after 11:00 A.M. On that frigid Thursday morning, the GOP would launch the first major initiative of the 80th Congress, a constitutional amendment to limit presidential terms. Doing so was an article of faith for the party, and it would command the allegiance of every Republican in Congress.[29]

Allen chaired the Committee on Rules, a principal mechanism for the majority party, whether Republican or Democratic, to control House proceedings.[30] The ability to structure process meant being able to shape substantive outcomes.

In the House, major legislation comes to the Floor accompanied by a procedural resolution specifying terms for the bill's consideration. The Rules Committee is responsible for drafting that resolution,[31] colloquially known as a rule.[32] Once presented by a Rules Committee member, the House debates the resolution for an hour, half of which, as a courtesy, the majority allocates to the minority for debate only.[33] While debate on a rule can focus on process, it often serves as a precursor for discussion of the accompanying legislation. Agreement to a rule needs only a majority of Representatives voting.[34] In this way, the majority party develops Floor procedure even if the minority is unhappy. Once the House approves the rule it proceeds under those terms to the pertinent legislation.

Allen's resolution concerned the procedures the House would follow to address H. J. Res. 27.[35] Written after a fifteen-minute Rules Committee hearing, at which the sole witness was Michener, the resolution provided that upon its adoption, the House would resolve into the Committee of the Whole, for consideration of the constitutional amendment.[36] There would be two hours of general debate,[37] following which Representatives could offer Floor amendments.

The committee proposed an open rule, a framework permitting an unlimited number of germane amendments. Although now rare, open rules were common in 1947. However, Republican leaders did not anticipate many amendments would be proposed.

Once the period for general debate and all amendments were exhausted, the Committee of the Whole would rise, reporting to the House on any action it had taken. After voting on the recommendations of the Committee of the Whole, it would be in order for the House to consider a motion to recommit.[38] Upon disposition of that motion, the House would vote on final passage of H. J. Res. 27, as and if amended.

Resolutions from the Rules Committee can be procedurally intricate. This one could not have been simpler.

"This resolution has but one purpose," Allen explained as he opened debate on the rule. "That purpose is to submit to the people, by and through their state legislatures, this very important problem of the Presidential tenure of office, and to let the people decide whether or not this limitation should be written into the Constitution."[39]

McCormack led Democrats in the Floor debate.[40] He argued that the public had exhaustively vetted term limits in the 1940 cycle, and spoken conclusively when returning Roosevelt to the White House then and in 1944. Democrats argued there was no better way to measure public sentiment than through those election outcomes.[41] Trusting the people meant respecting election results, said McCormack.

Republicans rejected that interpretation. They contended that those elections involved a complex and extenuating array of issues, not just a focus on term limits. The way to determine public sentiment was through state ratification of a constitutional amendment. In that way, the topic could receive undiluted attention.

Allen urged Congress to pass the amendment and submit it to the states. To bottle it up again on Capitol Hill would thwart a true expression of public opinion on this question.

He recounted the history. Since ratification of the Constitution in 1789, no subject for potential amendment had commanded more attention in Congress than term limits for the president. By 1947, more than 150 such amendments had been introduced.[42] Virtually all had died in committee. Almost none got through even a single chamber.

An exception came in 1824, when on a vote of 36 to 3, the Senate passed a joint resolution that no person elected twice could again be eligible. Senator Mahlon Dickerson (DR-NJ) sponsored it, just as James Monroe's presidency was drawing to a close.[43] Dickerson was the first Member of Congress to propose an amendment of this nature.[44] He argued that the examples of Washington, Jefferson, and Madison retiring after two terms was highly salutary and what was an accepted custom should be formalized into law.

Senator James Barbour (DR-VA) proposed an amendment, which the Senate defeated, to bar a president from serving more than two *consecutive* terms, allowing a president to return to the White House after a gap in service.[45] Although rejected by the Senate in 1824, Barbour's idea would resurface in subsequent decades, as supporters of Ulysses Grant and Theodore Roosevelt seized upon it to justify reinstatement of former presidents. After his amendment went down, Barbour supported the Dickerson resolution.

Notwithstanding this broad support in the Senate, the amendment died in the House.[46] Dickerson tried again in 1826. His proposal passed 32 to 7, but the House did not act.[47] Dickerson made one more attempt in 1830, but this time the Senate did not bring his legislation to a vote.[48] On February 1, 1913, the Senate passed a joint resolution that would have restricted the president to one six-year term. If ratified, the amendment would have applied to newly elected President Woodrow Wilson, potentially extending his term to 1919, then disqualifying him from reelection. The Senate expressly rejected a proposal that would have exempted Wilson from its coverage. Once again, the House failed to act.[49]

This time, Allen proclaimed, Congress must not be an impediment. It would send the amendment to the states, empowering the people to settle the long-standing and unresolved controversy over limits on presidential tenure.

Because a succession of presidents followed George Washington's example, Republicans said, self-restraint had been sufficient to safeguard Americans. However, once discarded, the tradition was unlikely to come back. Therefore, written limitation would have to replace it. "As the precedent no longer stands to protect them, the people should be given the opportunity to set a limit on the time an individual can serve as Chief Executive," declared Allen.[50]

Adolph Sabath (D-IL),[51] the Rules Committee's senior Democrat, took the Floor to complain about the rule. Even though the amendment was a matter of immense significance, deserving careful deliberation, he alleged that Republicans were ramrodding it through the House.[52] "This unseemly haste is due to the fact that the overwhelming majority of the American people are opposed to this Amendment, and the Republican leadership is hurrying to pass it through Congress before the public clamor grows too loud to be ignored." Sabath expressed confidence that the requisite three-fourths of state legislatures would never ratify it.[53]

As of 1947, the Constitution had been amended twenty-one times. Most of the amendments, especially recent ones, expanded political rights, Sabath noted. However, the thrust of H.J. Res. 27 was contrary. "This denies the longstanding principle of majority rule; it restricts and dilutes the rights reserved to the people under the Constitution. I cannot and will not concur in such a backward step."[54]

McCormack joined in, assailing the Republicans. Americans of a later generation would become familiar with John McCormack as an aged, cadaverous House Speaker who stood next in line for the presidency after the 1963 assassination of President John F. Kennedy. But the McCormack of 1947 was a vigorous presence on the House Floor, precise and pointed in debate.[55] His considerable advocacy skills were on full display during proceedings on H.J. Res. 27.[56]

In debate on the rule, McCormack reiterated the argument he made in the Judiciary Committee. The amendment would shackle future Americans to the political theories of past generations.[57] Doing that would render the Constitution dangerously rigid, preventing voters from choosing leadership they considered best suited to domestic and international conditions.[58]

McCormack agreed that, for the most part, the two-term tradition had served the country well. However, he sharply distinguished between following a tradition and fastening the principle into the Constitution.

Amendment advocates construed the two-term tradition as sacred doctrine, rooted in the wisdom and humility of George Washington. Folklore had it that he declined a third term as a matter of strict principle. But McCormack knew that was incorrect. Washington objected to serving a third term based on personal preference, not philosophy.

Washington had not wanted to assume the presidency at all, McCormack disclosed. "George Washington did not want a first term even. He accepted it reluctantly and as a patriotic duty. . . . He reluctantly served a second term because of the conditions abroad." McCormack was correct. Washington had hoped to leave after a single term and had prepared an address announcing his intention to do so.[59] At the time, instability in relations with Britain and France was such that he did not feel comfortable retiring. These conditions were no longer present as his second term was ending. Thus, in his Farewell Address, Washington stated, "I rejoice that the state of your concerns, external as well as internal, no longer renders the pursuit of inclination incompatible with the sentiment of duty or propriety."[60] Washington got his wish, and retired to Mount Vernon in his later years.

Nevertheless, Washington did not oppose the extended presidential tenure, if conditions justified it. McCormack quoted an April 28, 1788, letter that the president sent to the Marquis de Lafayette. Noting that delegates decided against term limits, Washington wrote,

> I confess, I differ widely myself from Mr. Jefferson and you, as to the necessity or expediency of rotation in that appointment. . . . There cannot, in my Judgment, be the least danger that the President will by any practicable intrigue ever be able to continue himself one moment in office, much less perpetuate himself in it—but in the last stage of corrupted morals and political depravity: and even then there is as much danger that any other species of domination would prevail. Though, when a people shall have become incapable of governing themselves and fit for a master, it is of little consequence from what quarter he comes.
>
> Under an extended view of this part of the subject, I can see no propriety in precluding ourselves from the service of any man who on some great emergency shall be deemed universally most capable of serving the public.[61]

The true philosophical father of term limitations was not Washington but Thomas Jefferson, McCormack reflected. However, even Jefferson could imagine a case to justify an exception. In 1808, as he was ending his second term, Jefferson remarked:

"There is, however, but one circumstance that could engage my acquiescence in another election; to wit, such a division about a successor as might bring in a monarchist. But this circumstance is impossible."[62]

The amendment was inconsistent with the philosophical thrust of the Constitution, McCormack proclaimed. "You will find limitations in the Constitution, but they are limitations upon Congress; and those limitations were imposed to protect the rights of individuals to assure that the legislative body would not take away the fundamental rights that our people believe in and for which the framers of our Constitution fought." H.J. Res. 27 was different. "This Amendment is a limitation upon the people."[63]

Majority Leader Charles Halleck (R-IN) countered. For many years, the amendment had been superfluous because tradition was strictly observed. "It is, of course, a common thing in American life to omit from the body of law those things which are accepted as commonplace in the habits, customs, and traditions of the people. Indeed, our whole system of law and government is reared on certain basic assumptions of morality and attitude which are not specifically enumerated in the *corpus juris,*" stated Halleck.[64] Rotation in the presidency was an essential part of the unwritten constitution, until Roosevelt disregarded it.[65] To provide the protections previously available by self-restraint, Halleck urged, the Constitution must be changed.

Representative Sam Rayburn (D-TX)[66] wrapped up debate on the rule. There was no justification for haste, exclaimed the Minority Leader.

Roosevelt's presidency was too recent. Better to take a longer view, allowing passions to subside, and then to weigh the amendment with greater care. "I believe it would be well for us to take just a minute more to consider this fundamental change in our fundamental law," he pleaded.[67]

Determined to mark their political legacy with this first major deed, the Republican majority would ignore Rayburn's advice.

Allen moved the previous question in order to close all further debate. The House agreed to the rule by voice vote.[68] Proceedings on the substance of the constitutional amendment would follow.

The House Takes Up H.J. Res. 27

Under the terms of the rule, Chairman Michener moved the House resolve itself into the Committee of the Whole to consider H.J. Res. 27. After the House did so, Michener was recognized to manage Floor proceedings for the Republicans. In turn, he yielded ten minutes to Springer[69] who chaired the Judiciary Subcommittee that favorably reported H. J. Res. 27, and who would explain its purpose and necessity.

Section one of the amendment declared ineligible for the presidency a person who had served for any portion of two presidential terms, but would allow an incumbent who would otherwise be disqualified to finish his term.

Section two provided a deadline for ratification by state legislatures within seven years of submission to the states; otherwise the amendment would fail.[70]

As reported from Committee, H.J. Res. 27 would have disqualified President Harry Truman from running for a third term, because he would have been president for a portion of President Roosevelt's fourth term plus a term of his own; however, he would not have been required to leave office midway through his term if he were still serving at the time the amendment was ratified.[71]

McCormack's strategy to frame the amendment as a partisan attack was crucial to the prospects for Democratic cohesion. However, he faced a significant party split, especially among Southerners. One such dissenter was Representative John Rankin (D-MS).[72] When the Confederate States of America formed in 1861, Rankin observed, its constitution permitted the Confederate President only one six-year term. At the time, the Confederacy faced an emergency of great severity and indeterminate length. If the Confederates saw fit to limit terms under these extreme conditions, argued Rankin, no circumstance would justify leaving tenure open-ended?[73]

Southerners like Rankin represented a very important segment of Congressional Democrats. So dominant was the Democratic Party in the old Confederacy, that, as the 80th Congress convened, they comprised 103 of 105

Representatives from the region. While 1946 was an exceptionally strong election for Republicans, yielding them fifty-seven House seats, the South was impervious to the trend. Of the 103 Southern Democrats, 59 ran unopposed. Opposition for most of the other 44 was token. Seven of them with opponents won with more than 90 percent of the vote. For many years, as in 1947, there were almost no Republican Members of Congress from the region.

From an ideological perspective, the Southerners were generally conservative. "Together with the Republicans, Southern and other conservative Democrats who wanted to block or weaken New Deal legislation had the votes in Congress to do so."[74] However, Southern Members were not a voting monolith. Some of the New Deal's ablest advocates and toughest enemies both came from Dixie. On the Twenty-second Amendment, Southerners divided. Their defections would prove critical in helping Republicans reach the supermajority necessary to pass the amendment.[75]

On behalf of Judiciary Committee Democrats, Representative Emanuel Celler (D-NY)[76] spoke next. He emphasized they would rather not amend the Constitution. However, if term limits were necessary, Democrats preferred a ceiling of one six-year term, instead of the two-term Republican proposal. A single term would permit a president to devote full attention to his job, Celler theorized, instead of being distracted by the demands of the next campaign. "It has always been natural for the incumbent President to have his eyes fixed on reelection, and all the acts of the first term, directly or indirectly, in some measure, are affected by the ambition for a second term."[77]

Celler noted that, in the past, the single term enjoyed prestigious support. During most of the Constitutional Convention, delegates supported a one-term presidency, limited to six or seven years. Although the Framers ultimately shortened the term and declined to limit reeligibility, the idea did not die. Discussion continued for much of the nineteenth century, and during that period, Presidents Andrew Jackson, William Henry Harrison, James Buchanan, Andrew Johnson, Rutherford Hayes, and Grover Cleveland endorsed the principle of a single term.

Celler added,

> Too often, the President, having his eye on the reelection possibilities, wants to be all things to all people at one time. . . . His efficiency thereby becomes greatly impaired. Not infrequently he has the overweening desire, in order that he may get the renomination, to punish his enemies unduly and to reward his friends too lavishly.[78]

Once the time allowed for general debate expired, Celler would propose his six-year, single-term amendment.

Another Judiciary Committee member, Representative Louis Graham (R-PA)[79] added historical context. Presidential tenure had been the most time-consuming issue at the Constitutional Convention. The Framers had discussed it on fourteen different days, never being able to settle on a conclusion. In frustration, they referred it to the Committee on Postponed Matters, otherwise known as the Third Committee of Eleven or the Brearley Committee, which reported on September 4, 1787, only two weeks before the end of the Convention.[80] The Brearley Committee recommended a four-year term without limit on reelection, Graham noted. While this concept was different from anything the delegates had previously endorsed, they accepted it.

The Constitution provided for a finely balanced government. However, Graham complained, the presidency was already outsized and growing more so. Of particular concern was Franklin Roosevelt's immense and disproportionate impact on shaping the federal courts. "I read a statement issued by the Attorney General of the United States," Graham noted, "that in the period from 1932 down to the present there have been appointed to the United States judiciary . . . a total of 231 judges. Of that number, 17 have been Republicans."[81] The process continued with Truman appointments during the remainder of what would have been Roosevelt's fourth term. Indeed, during the fourteen consecutive years of Democratic presidents immediately preceding this moment, Roosevelt made eight nominations to the Supreme Court and Truman added one more. These appointments fully remade the Supreme Court from the tribunal that Roosevelt had tried to enlarge and pack in 1937. As well, there had been a massive transformation of the judiciary at lower levels.[82]

The vast imbalance on the federal bench was striking and harmful, Graham complained. "This has now reached the point where the chairman of the Committee on the Judiciary of the United States Senate has taken this matter up and publicly declared through the press and through the medium of the *Congressional Record* that there must be a different division in the appointment of men to fill these great and high offices of our judiciary."[83]

It was, he concluded, "just one illustration of the case of a President having more than two terms and entrusting too much power to one man."[84]

Representative John Robsion (R-KY)[85] expanded upon this idea. Not only had Roosevelt overwhelmed the Judiciary, he also vastly enlarged the Executive Branch. "He created hundreds and hundreds of bureaus, commissions, and agencies, and at one time had more than 4,000,000 Federal civil officeholders in this country and in foreign countries, and through these agencies and officials, they attempted and did, to a large degree, control agriculture, industry, labor, and many of the normal activities of the American people."[86] Such power was inherently corrupting to elections, Robsion charged, because it generated vote buying through federal largesse and special favors. By such manipulation, it was possible to perpetuate an incumbency.

Representative John Jennings (R-TN)[87] forecast a dark future if the Constitution did not place checks on outsized presidential authority. A president who combined vast executive powers with "vaulting ambition," unchecked by a subservient Congress, "could well have in his hands the two mightiest instrumentalities of governmental power, the sword and the purse." Combined with the power of appointment to positions in the Executive and Judicial Branches, such a president could effectively remake the Constitution. Separation of powers as well as checks and balances would wither. Jennings saw a remedy. "Under the proposed Amendment, no President will have the power to perpetuate himself in office, to create a dynasty, and to substitute a succession for an assured rotation in the Presidential office."[88]

Democrats pushed back. In 1940, Roosevelt's opponents warned Americans about the claimed evils of extended tenure, including that of creeping dictatorship, but brushed those arguments aside. "Before 1940, the precedent for the President's tenure of office had been established by the Presidents themselves, notably Washington and Jefferson. But in 1940, the precedent was established by the people, and that is as it should be," said Representative Joseph Bryson (D-SC).[89]

Bryson would not accept that extended time in office represented an inherent threat to democratic institutions. "There can be no danger to democracy so long as the people may freely exercise the franchise," he emphasized, noting that "parliamentary governments have preserved their democracy with indefinite tenure for their prime ministers."[90]

Representative John Lyle (D-TX)[91] noted that in 1940 and 1944, voters resoundingly rejected claims of creeping dictatorship. "As I checked the *Congressional Record* for one week immediately preceding the 1940 election last night I found that more than 40 Members of the House made speeches similar, yes, almost identical, to the speeches made today predicting disaster to representative government. . . . Those predictions were made again in 1944. Both times the people of the United States repudiated the doctrine of this resolution." Roosevelt had carried thirty-eight states in 1940 and thirty-six in 1944. "The judgment of the people should be supreme," Lyle proclaimed, "over the judgment of this legislative body or that of any State of the Union."[92]

A rising figure in Tennessee politics, Representative Estes Kefauver (D-TN)[93] had no qualms if voters chose to extend a president in office. "I certainly believe it is more democratic to let the people of future generations, in view of the facts submitted to them and with which they may be confronted at that time, decide for themselves whether they want a President to carry on for one term, two terms, or three terms," Kefauver said.[94]

Kefauver hit again on a major Democratic theme. Almost all amendments enlarged liberty, but this one restricted it. He spoke of twentieth-century constitutional changes. The Sixteenth Amendment broadened and made more just the Nation's tax structure. The Seventeenth Amendment permitted election of senators by popular vote instead of by state legislatures. The Nineteenth Amendment provided for women's suffrage. The Twentieth Amendment moved the dates presidents were sworn in and Congress convened, making elections more meaningful. Only the Eighteenth Amendment on Prohibition had been restrictive, but that was widely understood to have been a mistake, and the Twenty-first Amendment swiftly repealed it. Kefauver criticized Republicans for seeming to reverse this trend. "I regret that the majority party in this Congress should show distrust of the majority of people and of future generations to govern themselves."[95]

Representative Frank Chelf (D-KY)[96] chastised Congress for interfering in the political process. "As I see it, the man selected and the number of times he is elected or reelected comes under the heading of the people's business."

In condemning the amendment, Chelf was unsparing. The joint resolution was a patronizing insult to the intelligence of the American voter, he declared. Congress was appointing itself as a People's Committee, but one unwanted by the public. "Yes, a committee of the people, by the people, for the people, with malice toward none, but with a straightjacket for all."[97]

Republicans continued to assert that congressional action was merely a preliminary step to put the issue before voters via state legislature ratification. Democrats countered with two arguments. One of these deferred entirely to the legislatures; another totally bypassed them. While contradictory to each other, they served a common goal: to kill the amendment by whatever strategy possible.

The first argument was that Congress need not act at all, because the Constitution permitted states to initiate the amendment process. If sentiment truly was strong for term limits, such petitions would materialize. If two-thirds of states petitioned for a constitutional convention to consider the issue, Congress would call one.[98] Congress should defer the question, they said, and await such a demand.

The second contention involved bypassing state legislatures altogether, in favor of ratification by special conventions. Advocates of this approach claimed that debate in such conventions would better reflect public opinion than in legislatures, because legislatures had a multifaceted agenda and conventions would address a single issue only.

"Members of State legislatures now in session or in existence were not elected on this specific issue only, they were elected on many other issues," noted Representative John Murdock (D-AZ).[99] The Constitution expressly permitted the use of conventions as mechanisms of ratification. Murdock considered them a superior way of proceeding, at least in this instance. "The proposed constitutional amendment should not be adopted except by affirmative action by conventions chosen for the purpose in three-fourths of the States."[100]

Murdock's comments previewed an amendment Democrats would offer after time for general debate expired. Even though it was customary to ratify constitutional amendments through the action of state legislatures, ratification by conventions had two important precedents. The Framers arranged for conventions to ratify the original Constitution.[101] Furthermore, conventions had ratified the most recent amendment, the Twenty-first, which repealed prohibition.

The use of the convention mechanism was not actually controversial in 1932–1933, when Congress proposed the Twenty-first Amendment. Indeed, the 1932 Democratic platform, which called for repeal, specifically called for ratification by conventions. "To effect such repeal," the platform stated, "we demand that the Congress immediately propose a constitutional amendment to truly representative conventions in the States called to act solely on that proposal." Republicans concurred. In their 1932 platform, they asked for an amendment to be "promptly submitted to the States by Congress, to be acted upon by State conventions called for that sole purpose."[102]

As passed by Congress in February 1933, the Twenty-first Amendment contained the convention directive. "This article shall be inoperative unless it shall have been ratified as an amendment to the Constitution by conventions in the several States, as provided in the Constitution, within seven years from the date of the submission hereof to the States by the Congress."

During the period in which the Twenty-second Amendment would be ratified (1947–1951), Republicans dominated many state legislatures outside the South. Thus, Democrats reasoned there might be a better chance to defeat ratification in conventions than would be possible in legislatures.

Conversely, Republicans believed that the convention proposal, as well as one providing for limiting presidents to single six-year term, was a killer amendment. Chairman Michener spotlighted the problem. "The opponents of the bill are driving for the 6-year limitation, and when the roll is called, if I do not miss my guess, every Member who is opposed to any limitation will vote for the 6-year term. You who are familiar with the procedure here, and are acquainted with strategy of one kind or another to defeat a bill, know that the best way to kill a bill or to injure it is to vote for all amendments offered regardless of their merits."[103]

Neither party forgot that the amendment fight would occur on two battlefields: Capitol Hill and in the states. Republicans wanted something to emerge that could survive ratification. Democrats looked to kill the amendment in any way feasible.

Without term limitation, Michener predicted, lasting damage to the American system was likely. He predicted overconcentration of power in the Executive Branch, stifling the development of future leaders, and instilling deadening apathy in the voting public. The amendment would mitigate those evils. "For 150 years, the sanction of tradition proved sufficient," said Michener. "Now that the two-term tradition has been broken, however, a longer tenure may well become the practice unless constitutionally forbidden."[104]

With that, the two hours of general debate provided for by the Rule ended. Amendments were then in order, with any Representative who wished to speak on an amendment having five minutes to do so under House rules.

Celler proposed the first amendment, providing for a single term of six years. If, during mid-passage, a vice president succeeded to the presidency, he could only serve the balance of the term and could not succeed himself. Celler's proposal stipulated that it would not affect the term of a president or a vice president who was serving at the time of ratification, meaning that ratification would not oust someone from office.

Celler claimed his proposal would enhance the quality of presidential service. "Under the two-term rule, the last 18 months of the first term are primarily given over to the coming campaign. A President cannot do both and do both well; that is, conduct a successful campaign for reelection and at the same time conduct the affairs of the Chief Executive for the good of all."[105]

Springer opposed him. The Judiciary Committee was familiar with a range of proposals to limit terms and all the supporting arguments. Ultimately, it had concluded the Framers were correct: six years was too long to leave a mediocre president in office without chance for removal except by impeachment. Moreover, a single term left disaffected citizens without political redress. Better, he argued, to allow voters to render a verdict on presidential performance.[106]

Representative Kenneth Keating (R-NY)[107] added that cloistering a president from politics was inherently undesirable. A chief executive subject to reelection would be sensitive to public opinion, and would serve voters better than one more politically aloof from them.[108]

Keating also contended that the single-term amendment would damage the chance for ratification. "The four-year term of President is firmly embedded in the finest traditions of our great country. It is my considered judgment that there is a very much greater likelihood that the people, when they finally pass upon this question through their elected representatives on their home grounds, will support a limitation which retains the four-year tradition and gives them a more frequent voice in the selection of their President than is likely to be the case if the six-year proposition is submitted to them."[109]

As Keating had deciphered, this appeared to be the true motive of the single-term amendment. Many of the strongest opponents of amending the Constitution at all proved to be the ones proposing the most stringent term limitations.

Once debate on the Celler amendment concluded, the Committee of the Whole voted on it. Notwithstanding the spirited exchange, there was no roll call. By voice vote, the amendment was rejected.[110]

Also, by voice vote, the Committee of the Whole agreed to a technical Judiciary Committee amendment, which perfected the wording, but not the terms, of H.J. Res. 27.[111]

Representative William Colmer (D-MS)[112] followed with his proposal to substitute ratification by state conventions instead of legislatures. "The objective of the amendment is to give the people of the United States the opportunity to pass upon this momentous question without any extraneous matters entering into the discussion," Colmer stated. He stipulated that, "This amendment offers the only vehicle through which we can get a clear-cut and unequivocal decision of the people on the question before the House." Colmer promised that if the House accepted his proposal, he would vote on final passage to submit the amendment, but not otherwise.[113]

No one spoke in opposition to Colmer's amendment. On a division vote, in which proponents and opponents record their position by standing, the amendment lost by 74 ayes to 134 nays.[114]

Even though further amendments were permissible, none was proposed. Under terms of the rule, the Committee of the Whole rose and reported H. J. Res. 27 to the House, with the single technical amendment it adopted. By voice vote, the full House agreed to the committee recommendation. In this form, the Joint Resolution was engrossed and read a third time.[115]

Speaker Joseph Martin (R-MA)[116] announced, "The question is on the passage of the Joint Resolution." Minority Leader Sam Rayburn (D-TX) requested a roll call.

By a vote of 285 ayes to 121 nays, the Joint Resolution passed. Every Republican voted in favor as did 47 Democrats, mainly Southerners and those from Border States.[117] Thus, advocates reached the two-thirds threshold constitutionally necessary for passage. The conservative Democrats who joined the Republicans were part of a bipartisan coalition that had been active and powerful in Congress for roughly a decade.[118]

House proceedings had taken about three hours. After passage, H.J. Res. 27 moved to the Senate, where deliberations would be considerably longer.

THE SENATE ACTS

The Senate referred H. J. Res. 27 to its Judiciary Committee, chaired by Senator Alexander Wiley (R-WI).[119] By 1947, senators were well acquainted with issues involved in presidential term limits. As with the House, Wiley's committee did not conduct fresh hearings. It held a markup and affirmatively reported the joint resolution to the Senate with several amendments. The accompanying committee report was only three pages long. "Much public discussion has taken place on this subject," it stated, "and it would be repetitious and cumulative for the committee to attempt to condense it for this report or outline it for the information of the Members of the Senate."[120]

The Committee proposed two major changes to the House-passed measure. While the House stated that no person could again be president who had served any portion of two presidential terms, the Senate committee amendment stipulated that the disqualification would attach to anyone who had served 365 days or more in each of two terms. For example, an individual who succeeded to office in the final year of a presidency could theoretically serve more than eight years by completing the balance of that term and winning two full terms of his own. The second committee proposal provided for ratification by conventions, a Democratic-inspired idea that the House rejected when it voted down the Colmer amendment. Like the House version, the committee-reported legislation would not end the term, and cause removal from office, of anyone holding the presidency at the time the amendment became operative.[121]

On Monday morning, March 3, 1947, Wiley moved that the Senate consider H.J. Res. 27.[122] Without debate and by voice vote, the Senate agreed. No further consideration occurred that day, as the Senate dealt with a series of unrelated measures. It returned to H.J. Res. 27 on March 5.

Wiley stressed six reasons why the Senate should approve the amendment:

First, a two-term limit had been a venerated custom for most of American history. The amendment would memorialize it in writing.

Second, overextended tenure would create conditions conducive to corruption and dictatorship. Wiley quoted a 1932 speech from Governor Franklin Roosevelt, who was trying to end a three-consecutive-term Republican lock on the White House. "Even a wisely led political party, given a long enough tenure of office, finally fails to express any longer the will of the people; and when it does so fail to express the will of the people, it ceases to be an effective instrument of government," Roosevelt proclaimed at the time.

Third, now that custom was breached, future presidents would be tempted to lengthen their terms, no longer burdened by political stigma.

Fourth, an incumbent president would control the political machinery in a way that stifles intra-party competition, a condition likely to worsen the longer he remained in office. "It is the President, of course, who is the head of his party, and who, through disposition of a large number of jobs, can win the allegiance of many members of the party."

Fifth, and very much related, a semi-permanent presidency would suffocate the development of fresh political figures. "Through this resolution, we will be helping to assure a full supply of constantly new talent for leadership of the Nation."

Sixth, presidents would be tempted to generate or identify emergencies to justify remaining in office. Wiley was skeptical about such claims, and quoted Thomas Jefferson about the need to maintain rotation in office, regardless of potential calamities. "No pretext should ever be permitted to dispense with it," Jefferson had said, "because there will never be a time when real difficulties will not exist and furnish a plausible pretext for dispensation."

Wiley noted that during the Constitutional Convention, the Framers had explored at length the idea of limiting the president to a single term, but could not reach a durable consensus to do so. "There were few subjects in the Convention that caused more controversy than the tenure and re-eligibility of the Presidential office," he noted. Ultimately, delegates decided to permit reelection without limitation.

For a century and a half, America had been able to depend on custom and practice to limit presidential terms. Roosevelt's third and fourth elections established that such reliance was no longer reasonable. That being the case, Wiley argued, Congress must settle the fundamental question the Framers left open. "That issue is whether or not the principle of long-time continuance in office by so called indispensable leaders . . . is compatible with our republican form of government."[123]

The matter was urgent, agreed Senator John Overton (D-LA).[124] The Framers' decision to leave things open may have made sense in 1787, but no longer did in the context of the modern presidency. Without express term limits, Overton feared, "we are likely to drift into an undemocratic form of government."[125]

After a modest amount of additional debate, the Senate set H. J. Res. 27 aside. On Friday, March 7, it resumed proceedings, beginning with consideration of the two committee amendments.

Senator Lister Hill (D-AL)[126] took the Floor. In 1940, Hill gave the principal nominating speech for Franklin Roosevelt at the Democratic Convention. An ardent New Dealer, Hill emerged as the Senate's most outspoken opponent of H.J Res. 27. Hill claimed to agree in principle with the two-term tradition, but refused to codify it. "There is a vast difference between a rigid prohibition in the Constitution, absolutely denying a right to the people, and a custom under which the people ordinarily do not exercise that right."[127]

History proved that voters must have the capacity to respond nimbly to current events, he maintained. "When we contemplate the world today and recall what it was like ten years ago, we can readily realize how violent and revolutionary have been the changes. . . . Many of the old moorings and landmarks seem to have disappeared. No one can know what may lie ahead of us or what danger or emergency may confront our nation in the days ahead. Why then should we suggest writing into the Constitution of the United States a rigid prohibition which might prevent the American people from meeting a danger or an emergency as they in their wisdom may think best?"[128]

Hill and Minority Whip Scott Lucas (D-IL)[129] engaged in a colloquy to explore the origins and meaning of the two-term tradition. They agreed that while George Washington was the first to observe it, his position was misunderstood.

"The fact that George Washington refused a third term has been referred to as evidence that Washington was opposed to anyone serving a third term," stated Lucas. "I think the able Senator will agree with me that is an inaccurate conclusion."[130]

Hill concurred. He quoted Washington's 1788 letter to the Marquis de Lafayette. There was no propriety, Washington wrote, in forcing someone from office in the face of an emergency.[131]

Washington stepped down after two terms simply because he wished to retire, Hill remarked. After tenure in the Continental Army, the Constitutional Convention, and the Presidency, Washington had spent decades in public life. It was enough for him. "The desire closest to his heart was to retire from public service, to be relieved of the burdens and labors of public office, and return to his beautiful acres at Mount Vernon."[132]

In fact, Washington would have preferred to retire even sooner, interjected Senator John Sparkman (D-AL).[133] However, international turmoil at the end of Washington's first term did not permit that, so the president remained in office. Hill responded, "He accepted a second term only because of what he felt was the compulsion of duty to his country." Sparkman surmised, "Certainly it is fair to draw the inference that had those conditions continued to exist at the end of his second term, he would have accepted a third term." Hill concurred. "He practically said as much in his letter to the Marquis de Lafayette."[134]

Senator Raymond Baldwin (R-CT)[135] asked why Hill preferred to bottle up the proposal in Congress, and impede further action by the states. "A great many people think this would be a good constitutional change. Why not let them decide that question for themselves?"[136]

Hill retorted that the people had already spoken. A majority of voters in 1940 and 1944 decided to keep Roosevelt in office, notwithstanding vigorous objections opponents raised to the third and fourth terms.

Moreover, Lucas added, there was negligible evidence of voter remorse or clamor to change the Constitution. "The Senator from Illinois has received exactly eight letters from his constituents on this question. That is a pretty fair indication that the people of Illinois and of the Nation are not very much excited about the constitutional limitation which is sought to be written into the Constitution."[137]

Senator Overton claimed that tenure restrictions were fully compatible with popular democracy. He cited the model of state constitutions. By 1947, eighteen states had imposed term limits on governors, including Overton's own state of Louisiana.[138] Most of these had come into state constitutions as a result of referenda. He asked Hill, "Am I to be told that the people of such states which have adopted such a provision have no confidence in themselves?"[139]

Hill declared that gubernatorial comparisons did not hold water.

> I can see no analogy whatever between the Governor's office and the office of the President of the United States. With all due respect to the Governor and to his office . . . that office in respect to the problems which may or may not confront it, is not in any way whatever comparable to the office of President of the United States.[140]

It was ironic that Republicans were so eager for the amendment, continued Hill. On the subject of the third term, their own party history was complicated. In the 1880 Republican Convention, Ulysses Grant sought nomination to a third term. Although Grant ultimately lost on the 36th ballot, he was the candidate of the party regulars and the leading contender until the last moment, when delegates broke a deadlock in favor of James Garfield. "The roll was called 36 times and on each and every one of those 36 roll calls the faithful Old Guard of Republicans held out for a third-term nomination for General Grant."[141]

As well, many Republicans did not seem to have qualms in 1912, when Theodore Roosevelt pursued return to the White House for a third term. As Hill pointed out, more Republicans voting in primaries supported Roosevelt than backed the incumbent, President Taft. "The majority of Republicans voting in the election of 1912 felt that the situation was such that a former President should be put back in office for a third term."[142]

Thus, Hill alleged that the amendment was an act of political retribution rather than a matter of constitutional principle. "There are legitimate reasons why one might support this resolution; but surely there are some who would support it in an effort to repudiate the memory, the work, and the immortal services of Franklin D. Roosevelt."[143]

Senator W. Lee (Pappy) O'Daniel (D-TX)[144] took the Floor. He had been outspoken in support of efforts to limit tenure, more so than any other Senate Democrat. In 1943 and 1945, O'Daniel introduced constitutional amendment resolutions providing for a six-year cap, applicable to the president, vice president, senators, and representatives. Both of those resolutions went to committee, without further action. On January 8, 1947, O'Daniel introduced his resolution again. It was designated as S.J. Res. 18. The senator announced he would offer it as a substitute amendment for H.J. Res. 27.

"I see no reason why we should confine our discussions and actions solely to the question of the tenure of the office of the President," O'Daniel stated. "In my judgment, we should discuss the subject fully and act on it fully, rather than have the legislative branch of government pick on the President and take the position that while great harm may result to the Nation from long tenure in the Presidential office, the same objections cannot be raised by long tenure by those who serve in the Senate and the House of Representatives."[145]

O'Daniel placed in the *Congressional Record* a lengthy and greatly detailed article he prepared about the history of term-limitation efforts, beginning with debates in the Constitutional Convention.[146]

Senator John McClellan (D-AR)[147] was a skeptic about ratification by conventions, and questioned Wiley as to why the Judiciary Committee recommended it. State legislators, McClellan felt, could better speak for the voters.[148]

The Chairman responded. The proposal was the work of Democrats, who won a vote in markup by claiming that conventions would have the sole mandate to consider the constitutional amendment. This would not be true of state legislators, who were elected on diverse issues and had a more cluttered agenda. Thus, the Committee Report stated, "The committee was of the opinion that although many of the state legislatures are now in session and might be able to act on the proposed Amendment, the members of such legislatures in many instances had no direct mandate from their constituencies on which to base a vote for or against the measure. The method of constitutional convention provides the only adequate and expeditious manner of registering the sentiment of the citizen directly."[149]

Wiley personally disliked the idea of conventions, and had opposed it in committee but lost. As Chairman, he said he felt obligated to support the committee's position on the Floor, and potentially in conference, even though he disagreed with it.[150]

Senator Chapman Revercomb (R-WV)[151] wanted to know whether the Senate needed to establish the terms and conditions for holding the conventions or if those were questions reserved for state legislatures.[152]

The text and history of the Constitution were silent on this subject, Wiley answered, so the responsibility would fall to the states. "It seems to me that the machinery of the several States would go into operation without further direction from Congress. In other words, power is conferred on the states to organize conventions."[153]

This question was not actually new to Congress. Members explored it at some length during deliberations on the Twenty-first Amendment. At the time, Representative James Beck (R-PA),[154] a leader in prohibition repeal efforts and a former U.S. Solicitor General, argued that amending the Constitution is fundamentally a federal responsibility. Accordingly, Congress could not only decide whether ratification should occur by conventions, but if it wished could specify the terms and conditions under which such conventions would be arranged. If Congress were silent, the states would act as they saw fit.

In Senate debate on February 22, 1933, Senator Henry Ashurst (D-AZ)[155] took an opposite view. "It would be offensive, unconstitutional, almost insulting to the States for the Federal Government to attempt in any way to dictate to the States how or in what manner they should choose delegates or hold the conventions. That is left to the respective states."

However, many states recognized that Congress could exercise preemption power if it so chose. As constitutional scholar Philip L. Martin notes, at the time of the Twenty-first Amendment, "twenty states explicitly recognized in their enabling acts that any future national law governing this subject would supersede their provisions. Only New Mexico absolutely denied Congress any regulatory power over state ratifying conventions."[156]

Revercomb inquired whether legislatures could simply resolve themselves into conventions. Lucas responded that while such an arrangement might theoretically be legal, legislators would never misappropriate such power. "The legislature of Illinois would not dare, under the laws of our state or under the Constitution of the United States, to attempt to sit as a convention on a serious question of this kind. . . . In my opinion, it is mandatory that the legislature call a convention. So much for that."[157]

Other senators reinforced Lucas. "If a legislature attempted to do so, it would nullify the action of Congress in declaring that conventions should be called." Majority Leader Alben Barkley exclaimed.[158]

Senator Forrest Donnel (R-MO)[159] was even more emphatic. "If a legislature of a state can resolve itself into a convention, obviously . . . it would thus directly undertake to nullify the clear distinction stated in the constitutional provision to which I referred," stated Donnel.[160] The senator was certain that no legislature had the moral or even legal right to make itself a convention.

Donnel observed that Congress could direct states on how to constitute a convention, or leave such details for determination by individual legislatures. He quoted from a 1933 judicial opinion of the Ohio Supreme Court. In *Donnelly v. Myers, Secretary of State* (186 Northeastern 918), the Ohio court stated, "The action of the legislature in performing this function rests upon the authority of Article V of the Constitution of the United States. It is a Federal function, which in the absence of action by the Congress, the state legislature is authorized to perform."[161]

Senator Tom Connelly (D-TX)[162] mentioned a potential deterrent to such usurpation. At the time, state ratifications were filed with the U.S. Secretary of State.[163] It was he who certified to Congress that a sufficient number of states had ratified and that the Constitution had been amended. If the

Secretary deemed that a state's procedure was not lawful, he could reject the ratification and it would not count.[164]

As in the House, many Republicans saw mischief in ratification by conventions and staunchly opposed it. One of them was Senate Majority Leader Wallace White (R-ME).[165] "If the convention system is adopted," White noted, "it must go through the legislative process of submission, and then subsequent legislation by the several states. Then comes a new obstacle, namely that of holding a convention."[166] According to White, this introduced needless complexity to a process that, by the amendment's own terms, had to conclude within seven years.[167]

White pointed out that advocates for conventions tended to be the same people who opposed amending the Constitution in the first place. At a minimum, he noted, there could be delays in constituting the conventions. Some states might refuse to appoint conventions at all. The conventions presented an opportunity for focused and targeted lobbying, particularly in states where delegates were uninstructed and had full discretion to vote as they pleased. While many state legislatures seemed favorably disposed to the amendment, conventions might see it differently. White asserted that was the precise reason Democrats promoted it.[168]

Debate for March 7 was winding down, but senators were not ready to vote. The Majority Leader moved that the Senate adjourn for the day, to reconvene at noon on Monday, March 10.

When the Senate resumed proceedings on the 10th, it voted on adoption of the committee amendment calling for ratification by conventions. The provision proved to be highly unpopular. On a roll call, twenty senators supported convention ratification, including Wiley and four other Republicans. Sixty-three senators opposed it, among them twenty-two Democrats.[169]

Next pending was the committee amendment that provided that no one could be president who had served 365 or more days in each of 2 terms. This formula would not only affect someone twice elected to the presidency, but also one who had succeeded to office for a partial term. The latter circumstance had already occurred twice in the twentieth century.

Theodore Roosevelt became president on September 14, 1901, after the assassination of President William McKinley. He then completed 42 months of McKinley's term, won in 1904, sat out the 1908 election, and wanted to come back for a nonconsecutive second election in the 1912. Had he won, Roosevelt could have been president for eleven years and six months.

Within the decade, the issue recurred. Calvin Coolidge succeeded to office on August 2, 1923, upon President Harding's death, finished the remaining 19 months of Harding's term, won in 1924. If nominated in 1928, he would have been seeking a second consecutive election. If successful, he could have served for nine years and seven months.

This history presented several crucial questions to the Senate Judiciary Committee. Was it important how long a vice president served once elevated to the presidency? The House-passed version said no, disqualifying for future service someone who had been president for any portion of two terms. The Committee thought to draw the line elsewhere, and was more lenient. Under its version, someone who had served fewer than 365 days of another person's term would not be disqualified from serving two full terms of their own.

Thus, the Judiciary Committee Report stated, "The section also, in effect, defines a 'term' as being in excess of 364 calendar days. The committee felt that simply because a man might hold office or act as President for a few days or months, he should not arbitrarily be foreclosed from serving two further terms of four years each. At most, such a person could not serve more than nine years."[170]

Either the House version or the Judiciary Committee proposal would have disqualified both Theodore Roosevelt and Calvin Coolidge from seeking a second elected term.

The presiding officer recognized Senator Warren Magnuson (D-WA)[171] to offer a substitute, which read, "No person shall be elected to the office of the President more than twice."[172] Under this proposal, Roosevelt and Coolidge could both have run for a second elected term because each had been elected president only once.

"We might as well get down to brass tacks," the senator began. Proponents were concerned about a president using the power of his office to entrench and perpetuate himself indefinitely. Such concerns applied with considerably less force to an accidental president, a person who "through circumstances beyond his control, and with no deliberation on his part, might because of some unfortunate circumstances, be required to assume the Presidential office." It made little sense to apply a mathematical test that took no account of how someone came to office, Magnuson suggested.[173]

Senator McClellan agreed. A president who succeeded to office would feel bound to continue the policies of his predecessor, he conceded. However, after election in his own right, he would pursue a distinctive program. McClellan contended that such a president should be allowed to seek public approval by running for reelection on his own record. It was unfair to deny someone that chance, simply because he had completed someone else's term. "Every man is entitled to have an endorsement term of his own policy," McClellan concluded. "Having been elected, and having served for a term, he is entitled to an endorsement term. That is democracy."[174]

However, Magnuson's amendment would generate an unintended and unfair consequence, complained Senator Bourke Hickenlooper (R-IA).[175] The only person who could serve longer than eight years was someone who began as an accidental president, with no mandate in the first place. "Instead of giving the preference and the privilege to a man or a woman who has been affirmatively voted into the Presidential office by the people, the advantage is given to someone who has never been voted into the particular office by the people."[176]

However, Senator Harley Kilgore (D-WV)[177] had the opposite take on what was unfair. "Does it not discriminate against the man who, as the Senator from Iowa says, accidentally gets into office and while he is accidentally holding the office does such a good job that he is elected to that office?" The House-passed proposal, and the committee-reported version, both discriminated against the accidental president, observed Kilgore. The effect was to punish someone who succeeded to office for a partial term. He preferred to eliminate the 365-day stipulation and impose no disability for partial-term service of whatever length.[178]

Senator Robert Taft (R-OH)[179] joined in. Under the committee amendment, the longest an elected president could serve was eight years, but a presidency could be limited to as few as five years, one elected term plus 365 days of another person's term. That struck Taft as unreasonably short, but he thought Magnuson's proposal was far too expansive. It would allow someone to serve as long as twelve years minus one day. Taft did not think an amendment permitting a term that long was worth passing in the first place.

The dispute between Taft and Magnuson over the appropriate length of presidential service roused Hill to criticize the amendment yet again. Their disagreement proved how difficult and unwise it was to place arbitrary tenure limits into the Constitution. Only voters could properly resolve it. "The question of who should be elected President and how long he should serve should remain where it has been for the past 150 years, that is, in the sound judgment and the wisdom of the people of the United States."[180]

Further debate that afternoon did not resolve the impasse. Magnuson stressed that he was hoping to vote on his amendment that day, but it became apparent that the mood of the Senate was too unsettled for a vote to occur. Taft suggested a recess, giving time to explore a solution.[181]

On motion of Majority Leader White, the Senate stood in recess until noon the next day, Wednesday, March 12, 1947.

After the Senate opened on the 12th, Taft announced a compromise he planned to offer as a substitute for the Judiciary Committee amendment. The senator's draft provided that a person could serve as a president for up to ten years, two years of a term to which he had not been elected as well as two elected four-year terms.[182] To enhance the prospect that his compromise would gain bipartisan support, Taft provided that the amendment would not apply to President Truman.[183] As Taft explained the exemption, "In the case of President Truman, when he ran for Vice President there was no limitation, and it seems to me that differentiates him from a man who knows when he runs for Vice President that if the President dies in the first two years of his term he can serve for only six years. In other words, as to President Truman, the law would be retroactive except for this amendment."

Meanwhile, Magnuson had modified his proposal, making it even less restrictive. The senator's original idea was that no one be eligible to be elected more than twice. However, Magnuson accepted the recommendation of Senator Spessard Holland (D-FL)[184] and changed it to say that no one could be elected to more than two *consecutive* terms.[185] That would allow a president to complete two terms (or even longer if he had succeeded to office), sit out a term, and then run twice again. As Magnuson explained, "The modification suggested by the Senator from Florida merely breaks the line of succession."[186]

Holland referred to Theodore Roosevelt's case. Taft's proposal would disqualify Roosevelt from running in 1912, because he would already have served most of McKinley's 1901–1905 term and his own 1905–1909 term. However, if the modified Magnuson amendment applied to Roosevelt, he could have run in 1912 because he would have sat out the term of the Taft presidency, and been able to seek a consecutive reelection in 1916.[187]

After forty minutes of debate, the Senate stood in recess to attend a joint meeting in the House chamber. Its purpose was to hear President Truman speak about foreign assistance to Greece and Turkey. Both those nations were facing Communist-supported insurgencies. Truman proposed the United States help them resist. Known as the Truman Doctrine speech, the president's address was one of the watershed moments in the emerging Cold War.[188]

The Senate reconvened at 1:30. Holland resumed his argument. Unless the Senate agreed to the modified Magnuson proposal, the Florida senator would oppose changing the Constitution. Holland criticized both the committee's amendment and Taft's. Either version was potentially prejudicial to an accidental president. And either of those versions would disqualify an eight-year president from ever running for a nonconsecutive term, which might prejudice the country. "The result of this amendment as offered by the committee and of the substitute amendment offered by the distinguished Senator from Ohio would be to render persons of experience, of high, proven qualities, ability, and courage wholly ineligible, regardless of conditions and regardless of their age and strength."[189]

The ostensible purpose of H. J. Res. 27 was to prevent the accrual of entrenched power. Holland contended that permitting reeligibility after a break in service would satisfy that objective without unduly infringing on voter choice.[190]

Late in the afternoon, the Senate rejected the modified Magnuson amendment by a vote of 34 ayes and 50 nays. No Republican supported Magnuson. Five Democrats opposed him.[191]

Taft offered his substitute. He reported that after the previous day's stalemate, he worked with Senator Carl Hatch (D-NM)[192] to find middle ground Democrats who could support it. "It seems to me that my amendment represents a perfectly fair compromise of the differences of opinion which have developed during the debate," said Taft.[193]

Lucas disdained such a compromise, and took the Floor to oppose the whole effort. "Here in a moment of emotionalism, a moment of power, a moment of prejudice, resulting from the 1946 Republican victory, we are called upon to enact for the first time a dangerous and far-reaching piece of legislation which strikes at the very heart of our democracy."

It should be up to the people to choose the government without artificial barriers, argued Lucas. "What omnipotent power do we possess which gives us the right to deny the citizens of tomorrow freedom of choice and freedom of action."[194]

Lucas quoted from a 1939 editorial by Senator Arthur Vandenberg (R-MI),[195] titled "Mr. Roosevelt and the Third Term Dictatorship." In it, Vandenberg framed a choice between Roosevelt seeking a third term and an opponent committed to running only once, a concept he promoted. Vandenberg was confident the public would be sensitive to the potential for dictatorship and reject the third-term. So, he proposed to leave the Constitution alone. "Who shall say that a tradition and a habit against a prolonged Presidency on the one hand, or freedom of action on behalf of a shorter pre-pledged Presidency on the other hand, is not better and safer than a constitutional stricture which could not be changed to fit one emergency or another?" Best to leave the choice to voters, wrote Vandenberg, without artificial constraints. "In the presence of 1940, the people are free to elect Mr. Roosevelt for a third term if they wish. They are equally free to choose a pre-pledged one-term successor to him—or an unpledged two-term successor—if they wish. And since this is their Government, it is illogical to tie their freedom of action."[196]

Notwithstanding this argument, the Senate agreed to the Taft substitute by voice vote, then to the committee amendment as amended by Taft.[197] Under Senate rules, that action should have ended the amendment process. However, Senator William Langer (R-ND)[198] secured unanimous consent to offer a further amendment, adding a requirement that nominees for president and vice president be chosen in national primary elections. The individual receiving the greatest number of votes would be designated as the party nominee. Langer's amendment also proposed to abolish the Electoral College in favor of election by direct popular vote.[199]

Langer alleged that, for the most part, party bosses and special interests controlled nominations. The system needed to democratize. "It seems to me that if the people of this country are fit to elect the mayors of their towns, if they are fit to select the governors of their states, if they are considered competent to select Members of Congress and United States Senators, certainly the people can be trusted to select the candidates of the Republican Party as well as of the Democratic Party, or any other party, for President."[200]

Langer's message on the Electoral College was similarly populist. He contended that the existing system distorted the will of the voters, creating apparent landslides when none existed. For example, Langer noted, in 1940 Roosevelt received 27 million votes as against 22 million for Willkie. However, the president's margin in the Electoral College was 449 to 82. Had the electoral vote been proportional to the popular vote, Roosevelt would have prevailed 286 to 245. "Thus, we see," Langer commented, "that the Electoral College is not bound by any precept of the Constitution to reflect with any degree of accuracy the will of the people as expressed by the popular vote."[201]

Chairman Wiley responded that Langer's proposal was premature for Floor consideration. At no point in the Judiciary Committee discussions on term limits was either the direct primary or abolition of the Electoral College addressed. He urged the amendment's defeat.[202]

On a roll call, the Senate rejected the Langer amendment by 14 ayes to 66 nays.[203]

Senator O'Daniel followed by offering his amendment to limit the service of the president, vice president, senators, and representatives to six years. Wiley urged its defeat. On a roll call, O'Daniel was the sole supporter. The amendment went down by a vote of 1 aye and 82 nays. O'Daniel quipped, "I hope the Senate will give me credit for one thing, and that is getting the Democrats and the Republicans together."[204]

It was 5:30 PM. Having disposed of all amendments, the Senate was nearly ready to vote on final passage. However, Senator Claude Pepper (D-FL)[205] notified colleagues that he wished to offer additional remarks. Not seeing a way to wrap up proceedings in a few minutes' time. Majority Leader White moved that the Senate stand in recess until 7:00 PM, when it would return for an evening session.

The Senate reconvened at 7:00 PM to continue the debate. Hours earlier, it had agreed to the Taft substitute, and defeated the Langer and O'Daniel amendments, leaving only the question of whether two-thirds of senators would pass H.J. Res. 27 as amended by Taft.

The presiding officer recognized Pepper. The Senator stressed that the American people were justified in electing FDR to third and fourth terms, and argued strenuously that an amendment precluding that outcome would have damaged the country.

The President sought a third term at a time of national emergency, Pepper noted. The Senator reminded colleagues of the world situation. England was in extreme danger in 1940, especially after the British Expeditionary Force had narrowly escaped disaster at Dunkirk, and the country was under

Luftwaffe air assault. In response to the crisis, Roosevelt first dispatched armaments, and then concluded a September 1940 deal to transfer 50 destroyers to Britain in exchange for 99-year leases on strategic bases in the Western Atlantic.

Roosevelt's critics claimed that, in taking these steps, the President exceeded his authority. Pepper acknowledged these charges may have had some basis, but he justified Roosevelt's actions in light of the crisis at hand. "We do not always remember that had we not a courageous President at that time, who dared to risk impeachment, Britain might not have survived. President Roosevelt had no congressional authority either to transfer light arms to Britain after Dunkirk or the 50 destroyers; nor had he any congressional authority to start the wheels of our factories moving in America in order that a trickle, at least, of supplies might start toward Britain in the moment of her severest trial."[206]

In September 1940, the President successfully moved through Congress the Selective Service Act. Then, after the election, at Roosevelt's urging, Congress passed the Lend-Lease Act. That program proved immensely beneficial to Britain as well as to the Soviet Union. By bolstering their resistance, the program saved American lives and enhanced prospects for allied victory. "In the dangerous and difficult path which President Roosevelt for America had to tread, what would any inexperienced man have done," Pepper asked.[207]

Voters did not have to be coddled or saved from themselves, the senator concluded. They could assess circumstances and choose suitable leadership, in peacetime as well as wartime. "I think our people are to be safely trusted with their own destiny. . . . We do not need to protect the American people with a prohibition against a President whom they do not wish to elect; and if they wanted to elect him, have we the right to deny them that power?"[208]

Once Pepper finished, debate ended. It was time to vote. On the question of passage of H.J. Res. 27, as amended, fifty-nine senators were affirmative and twenty-three opposed, giving the amendment four more votes than the two-thirds majority necessary for passage. All twenty-three opponents were Democrats. Of the 59 ayes, 46 were Republicans and 13 were Democrats, mostly Southerners.[209] Republican unanimity in the Senate matched that of the House, which is to say that no Republican in either body stood against the amendment.[210] As in the House, approximately 25 percent of Democrats broke with their Party on the vote.

On the final roll call, fourteen senators were absent. One of them was Minority Leader Alben Barkley. As would soon become apparent, Republicans considered themselves fortunate that such a potentially effective opponent was not there.

Taft successfully moved that the Senate insist on its amendment to H.J. Res. 27 and request a conference with the House. The presiding office appointed Senate conferees.[211] However, a conference would not occur.

Although he had taken the necessary procedural steps to arrange a conference, Taft worried that changes potentially necessary to reach a compromise with the House could erode support among Senate Democrats for the conference report. Barkley was a skilled strategist, who would avail himself of any opportunity to peel away votes. The Senate and House versions were fundamentally similar. Knowing it would be better for his side if the Senate never got another crack at the amendment, Taft decided he must get the House to agree to the Senate amendment as it stood.

On March 15, the senator sent a letter to House Majority Leader Charley Halleck in which he urged that the House concur in the Senate amendment. Taft's letter stated:

"Dear Charley:

"I enclose a copy of the constitutional amendment as adopted by the Senate. The only difference between our amendment and that of the House lies in the treatment of men who, as Vice Presidents, succeed to the office of President, and the exception of President Truman from the effect of the amendment. In my opinion, it was necessary to make these concessions to get the bill through the Senate, and a material change might endanger our position here. We were lucky in that Barkley was away, but we have to hold about thirteen Democrats. It is about the only measure on which we have had a unanimous Republican vote.

"If it were possible for the House to accept our language without a conference, I would feel much safer, and it seems to me the Republican Party would get just as much credit."[212]

Halleck discussed Taft's request with Chairman Michener, who assessed sentiment on the Judiciary Committee. The committee was willing to cooperate.

On March 21, Michener brought the amended joint resolution to the House Floor, and moved that the House concur in the Senate amendment.[213]

Michener laid out the situation. "More than two-thirds of each House is agreed that the people should be permitted to vote on limiting the term which a President of the United States may serve," Michener explained.

> There is a difference among those two-thirds as to the length of that term. There is a difference as to the best language to be used in a constitutional amendment. Those differences have not been composed in precise accordance with the views of any individual in Congress. There is some language I would like to change. . . . However, this is the composite view of the people's representatives in Congress, and I hope my motion will prevail, that this Senate amendment will

> be agreed to, and that state legislatures will be advised at once and permitted to pass on this important question in their respective current sessions.[214]

Minority Whip McCormack replied. The Democrats did not object to Michener's procedural motion, but wanted to clarify that their absence of protest did not equate with support for the amendment itself. "I am very much disturbed by the inflexibility of this Amendment in binding the Americans of tomorrow," McCormack insisted. He again implored Congress to defeat the amendment. If that proved impossible, he urged its rejection during state ratification.[215]

By a vote of 81-29, the House approved Michener's motion to concur in the Senate amendment. No one pursued a point of order that a quorum was lacking.[216] Congressional proceedings on the amendment thus ended. The ratification process in state legislatures would soon commence.

RATIFICATION IN THE STATES

Under the amendment's terms, there was a seven-year window of opportunity for ratification. It would expire in 1954.

Twenty-seven state legislatures were in session when Congress submitted the amendment for ratification.[217] Maine and Michigan were the first states to act. Both ratified on March 31, 1947, just over two weeks after the amendment cleared Congress. By late spring, the time most legislatures adjourned for the year, sixteen additional states had followed suit. The eighth was Oregon, which ratified on April 3. In 1940, its legislature petitioned Congress to pass a term limitation amendment, the only one of the forty-eight states to have done so at the time of Roosevelt's third-term bid.[218] Each of those 1947 legislatures had overwhelming Republican majorities, with the exception of Nebraska, which was unicameral and non-partisan. For example, in the Maine Senate, the ratio was thirty Republicans to three Democrats. In the Michigan House, there were ninety-five Republicans and five Democrats. Controlled by Democrats, Texas and Oklahoma rejected the amendment in 1947.

Only three more states ratified in 1948. However, two of those legislatures were ones in which Democrats dominated, Mississippi and Virginia, reflecting a fraying of bonds between Southern Democrats and the rest of the party.[219] New York also approved. Republican South Dakota and North Dakota joined them in 1949, bringing the total to twenty-three. In 1950, one more state was added, when Louisiana ratified. No Republican sat in its legislature.[220]

Throughout this process, ratification met with determined resistance from the National Committee against Limiting the Presidency. Formed by journalist Daniel F. Clancy[221] during the third-term controversy of 1940, and abetted by former Secretary of the Interior Harold Ickes, former Representative Maury Maverick (D-TX), and other Democrats, the Ohio-based Committee worked ceaselessly to defeat it.[222] Ickes was Clancy's highest profile recruit, joining the Committee in 1949.[223]

The earliest Cabinet member to endorse a third-term for Roosevelt, Ickes was characteristically forthright. "It seems to me nothing short of absurd to limit the right of the people to select their own President, regardless of the length of tenure," Ickes wrote when accepting Clancy's invitation to join the Committee. "In fact, I consider it a dangerous device. If the time should ever come when we had a critical domestic or international situation, and the people thought that the President ending his second term was, beyond all doubt, the one man to lead the country, they might ignore any constitutional limitation as to terms and thus, effect a revolution."[224]

Ickes went full steam in January 1951, with a piece he authored for the *New Republic*. He noted that as the year began, the amendment was still thirteen states short of ratification. While the amendment had gotten off to a fast start in 1947, after Congress had submitted it, progress had become glacial. If momentum did not revive, Ickes hoped, the amendment might fail to have enough states by the time the seven-year ratification deadline expired in March 1954.

Ickes insisted that "the people know Roosevelt left our democratic processes stronger than he found them," and continued, "the people can look back and realize that the attempt to stampede them into adopting the proposed Twenty-second Amendment was a sinister plot on the part of anti-social agencies to frighten them into mutilating their own precious democracy to the advantage of those who have exploited the people and always will."[225]

However, even as Ickes published, the pace of ratifications sharply accelerated. In early 1951, following a strong Republican showing in the 1950 mid-terms, there was a breakthrough.[226] Montana approved on January 25. Ten additional states ratified by late February.[227] Alarmed as this cavalcade developed, Clancy reached out to Truman, hoping that last minute presidential intervention might change momentum. Truman remained eligible to run and had not yet withdrawn, Clancy argued that a failure to prevent ratification would damage the president's chances. "Although specifically exempted from the limitations of the Amendment, ratification by the required 36 states would be used by your opponents as a compelling argument when no President should be permitted to break the provisions of the Amendment, even though exempted from them."[228] Although Truman would later go on record as favoring repeal of the amendment, he did not respond to Clancy.

On February 27, Minnesota became the thirty-sixth state to ratify.[229] Well inside the seven-year deadline, three-fourths of the legislatures had approved the amendment.[230] On March 1, 1951, the head of the General

Services Administration proclaimed the Twenty-second Amendment duly ratified.[231]

After Minnesota's ratification, Clancy denounced the new amendment in a press release. "The Twenty-second 'Sour Grapes' Amendment was ratified to taunt Truman, repudiate Roosevelt, and discredit the Democratic Party. For such poor, partisan, and inglorious purposes, our Constitution has been amended by a diversity of demagogues to protect us from an imaginary menace."[232]

Ratification continued after the amendment became part of the Constitution. Five additional states, all situated in the South and each with a Democratic-controlled legislature, approved it in 1951. The last of these was Alabama on May 4, bringing the total number of ratifying states to forty-one. Two states expressly rejected it, Oklahoma in 1947 and Massachusetts in 1949. Five states did not act on the amendment at all.[233]

As ratified, the Twenty-second Amendment clearly erects a barrier to the *election* of a person who has served as president for two terms plus more than two years of someone else's term, a maximum of ten years. But because of the way the Senate redrafted it, confusion exists. Would the amendment also prohibit *service* as president of an individual who had been president, who was barred from further election, but who subsequently assumed a place within the line of succession to the presidency? For example, imagine that the House of Representatives elected a former two-term president as speaker. Further imagine that the sitting president died with more than two years remaining in his term, and there was no vice president. The speaker would be next in line to assume the office. Is he eligible to serve, even though barred from seeking further election? The Twenty-second Amendment leaves this question unanswered.[234]

A similar situation arises if the person succeeding to the office was a vice president who had previously been president and who would otherwise be disqualified from running again. The Twelfth Amendment to the Constitution provides that, "no person constitutionally ineligible to the office of President shall be eligible to that of Vice President of the United States." For example, that means a person cannot be foreign-born or underage and be vice president, because presidents must be native-born and at least thirty-five years old. However, the interrelationship of the Twenty-second and Twelfth Amendments on eligibility on *service* of a former two-term president succeeding from the vice presidency is murky.

As originally passed in the House of Representatives, the amendment would not have been unclear. The House barred someone from serving as president who had served in that office for more than 365 days in any two previous terms. The Senate created the ambiguity when it amended H.R. 27 to address barriers to election rather than barriers to service. Nothing in the

Senate proceedings illuminates the reason for this change. The possibility of clarification went away when the House simply accepted the Senate amendment, rather than working through differences in conference.

SPECIAL NOTE: LEGISLATING IN A DIFFERENT TIME

Looking back at the process by which Congress considered H.J. Res. 27 in 1947, one marvels at differences between legislating then and legislating now. A high degree of polarization, combined with growing ideological homogeneity within each party, has caused modern senators and representatives to be increasingly aggressive in asserting procedural rights. Significant variations would be:

- Open rules were common in 1947, particularly on significant measures. That is no longer true. In current practice, it is likely that the Rules Committee would propose a resolution that limited possible amendments to the ones it expressly designated. Members who hoped to offer amendments would testify, seeking to have their amendments made in order.
- The Rules Committee hearing in 1947 to grant a rule for H.J. Res. 27 was perfunctory. Today, a measure as significant as a constitutional amendment would receive a hearing that was much lengthier and very likely more contentious.
- In 1947, Chairman of the Senate Judiciary Committee Alexander Wiley, and not Majority Leader Wallace White, made the motion to proceed to H. J. Res. 27. In the present day, the Majority Leader would offer the motion to proceed and exert a greater measure of control over Floor proceedings generally.
- Although the amendment was controversial in the Senate, there was no effort to filibuster Senator Wiley's motion to proceed to its consideration. In the current Senate, filibusters on motions to proceed are common. Cloture motions to shut down filibusters were possible under Senate rules but almost unheard of then; now many of the Senate's roll call votes are on cloture motions.
- There also was no effort to filibuster the joint resolution itself; therefore, no cloture motion was ever filed to end debate on the merits. Today, it is highly likely that a cloture process would be needed to conclude proceedings on the substance of the measure, in addition to one on the motion to proceed, even though the approval threshold for cloture (sixty votes) is lower than that for constitutional amendments (two-thirds of senators voting).
- In 1947, senators often resorted to an accommodation process called "pairing." For example, if a senator in favor of a measure had to be absent, and

did not want his absence to affect the ratio of yea to nay votes, he would pair with a senator on the other side of the issue. The second senator, who could be present, would announce his position as well as that of the absentee, and then indicates he would withhold his vote. In another variation, absentees from one side would be paired with absentees from the other, as a mechanism for making a public declaration of their position. For either purpose, the pairing process was usually bipartisan. In a supermajority situation, such as a constitutional amendment, a pair would consist of two affirmative senators and one negative senator. Indeed, on final passage of H.J. Res.27, three sets of pairs were announced.[235] Pairing was common in the more genteel Senate of 1947. In current times, this kind of accommodation has almost entirely disappeared.[236]

- Thirteen senators missed the final roll call vote. In the present day, few, if any, senators would be absent for such a consequential vote.

NOTES

1. "Throughout 1946, Harry S. Truman was one of the most unpopular presidents in American history. Widely respected later as the leader who turned his country into the global colossus America has been since World War II, he was dismissed as a lightweight for much of his first two terms in the White House. . . . Bumper stickers on cars read 'To err is Truman.' A recording was made using a play on the lyrics of a popular song: 'I'm just mild [wild] about Harry.' In a Gallup Poll at the start of 1946, only nine percent of the public thought a Democrat could win the presidential election in two years' time." Victor Sebesteyn, *1946: The Making of the Modern World* (New York: Pantheon Books, 2014), p. 16.

2. Several of them called for a limit of two four-year terms. The others proposed a single six-year term. Eugene W. Hickok, Jr., "Pique Over Principle: Partisan Politics and the Twenty-second Amendment" in *Restoring the Presidency: Reconsidering the Twenty-second Amendment* (Washington, DC: The National Legal Center for the Public Interest, 1990), p. 36.

3. Earl C. Michener served in the House from 1919 to 1933 and again from 1935 to 1951.

4. Raymond S. Springer served in the House from 1939 until his death in August 1947.

5. Markup before Subcommittee Number Four, House Committee on the Judiciary, February 3, 1947, p. 61.

6. Stephen W. Stathis, "The Twenty-second Amendment: A Practical Remedy or a Partisan Maneuver," *Constitutional Commentary* (1990), p. 66. https://scholarship.law.umn.edu/concomm/1018 (accessed October 17, 2018).

7. H. Markup, 1947, p. 16.

8. Ibid., pp. 20–21.

9. Ibid., p. 19.

10. Ibid., p. 22.
11. Ibid., p. 27.
12. Ibid., p. 28.
13. Ibid., pp. 31–32.
14. Ibid., p. 33.
15. Ibid., p. 36.
16. George W. Gillie was in the House of Representatives between 1939 and 1949.
17. Prepared statement by Representative George W. Gillie, February 3, 1947, and inserted into H. Markup, 1947, following p. 37.
18. Karl Mundt served in the House of Representatives from 1939 to 1948, and then in the Senate from the end of 1948 until 1972.
19. For example, Calvin Coolidge completed the last 19 months of Warren Harding's term, following the president's death on August 2, 1923.
20. Prepared statement of Representative Karl Mundt, February 3, 1947, and inserted into H. Markup, 1947, after p. 39.
21. For example, Lyndon Johnson served 14 months of John F. Kennedy's term. In 1964, Johnson was elected to a full term. Under the Mundt resolution as well as the Twenty-second Amendment, Johnson could have sought reelection in 1968. Had he won, and completed his term, Johnson would have been president for nine years and two months.
22. H. Markup, 1947, p. 66.
23. Ibid., p. 64.
24. Ibid. At the time Michener spoke, only two twentieth-century presidents had been defeated for reelection. Both had lost in extraordinary circumstances. Taft went down in a three-way race in 1912 that saw his party hopelessly divided; however, he survived a bitter renomination fight despite Theodore Roosevelt's popular appeal. Hoover lost in 1932 due to the Great Depression.
25. Ibid., p. 65.
26. Ibid., p. 66.
27. Leo Allen served in the House of Representatives between 1933 and 1961.
28. *Congressional Record,* February 6, 1947, p. 841.
29. Author's note: Reading the Congressional proceedings on the Twenty-second Amendment, one is reminded of the fervor with which later generations of Democrats pursued health care reform, and Republicans sought Obamacare repeal.
30. In 1947, the Rules Committee was composed of eight Republicans and four Democrats, exactly the opposite ratio than which existed in the previous Congress, when the Democrats had control. This two-to-one balance between Majority and Minority was customary for the House in that era. In 1961, Speaker Sam Rayburn fought to expand the Committee's size to fifteen, so he could control a working majority on the Committee and report out legislation favorable to the Kennedy Administration. In a close vote, Rayburn prevailed over Rules Committee Chairman Howard Smith (D-VA). In the late 1960s, the fifteen became thirteen, with a nine to four ratio favoring the Majority. This ratio still operates today.
31. The Rules Committee prepares such resolutions in consultation with the majority party leadership and the House Parliamentarian. Late nineteenth- and early

twentieth-century speakers such as Thomas Reed (R-ME) and Joseph Cannon (R-IL) actually chaired the Rules Committee, a circumstance that significantly enhanced their power over the House. After an anti-Cannon revolt in 1910 by Republican backbenchers and minority Democrats, the House removed the Speaker from the Rules Committee. Nevertheless, for most of the time since then, the Speaker has strongly influenced the Committee's work. In the present day, the speaker appoints the majority party members of the Committee and the Minority Leader appoints the minority party members.

32. Officially, the term is a "special rule."

33. When the majority yields time for debate only, it prevents the minority from proposing amendments to the rule.

34. The same thing could not happen in the Senate, because overriding Senate rules with a procedure tailored to a specific circumstance needs unanimous consent. An unhappy minority, or even a discontented dissident, will simply object.

35. The Judiciary Committee reported H.J. Res. 27 by a vote of 20-5. Garrison Nelson, *John William McCormack* (New York: Bloomsbury Academic, 2017), p. 365.

36. The Committee of the Whole is a device to facilitate consideration of major legislation. Quorum requirements are reduced, as is the number of members needed to request a roll call. The speaker appoints a member to preside. Once the amendment process is completed, the committee rises and reports the outcome of its proceedings to the House. Having been constituted for this purpose, the Committee of the Whole is thereafter extinguished until it is once again organized for other legislation.

37. At the Rules Committee, Michener indicated that the two-hour debate limit he requested reflected the wishes of the Majority leadership. Then, as now, the leadership has immense influence as to how a rule is constructed.

38. Under House rules, the motion to recommit is debated for ten minutes, if someone chooses to offer it. It can take the form of a straight motion to return a measure to committee, which, if agreed to, would take the measure off the Floor with no obvious path back. Ordinarily, however, the form is a motion to recommit with instructions to report back with an amendment. If the motion carries, the measure remains on the Floor, as amended. By long-standing House practice, the motion to recommit is reserved for the minority. When a member seeks recognition to offer a motion to recommit, the presiding officer will inquire whether the member is opposed to the bill. When the member answers that he is opposed in its current form, the presiding officer will announce that the member qualifies to make the motion.

39. *Congressional Record*, February 6, 1947, p. 841.

40. Minority Leader Sam Rayburn assigned McCormack the task of leading opposition to the Amendment. See Nelson, p. 365.

41. *Congressional Record*, February 6, 1947, p. 842.

42. Most of them involved limiting a president to a single six-year term. Between 1826 and 1971, for example, 131 such amendments were introduced. Paul B. Davis, "The Future of Presidential Tenure," *Presidential Studies Quarterly*, Vol. 10, No. 3 (Summer 1980), pp. 469–475, 470–472. http://www.jstor.org/stable/27547601 (accessed October 10, 2018).

43. James Q. Howard, "Duration of the Executive Term," *The Galaxy*, Volume XVIII (New York: Sheldon & Company, 1874), p. 818. Mahlon Dickerson was a senator from 1817 to 1833.

44. Herman Ames, *The Proposed Amendments to the Constitution of the United States* (New York: Burt Franklin, 1896), p. 124.

45. James Barbour served in the Senate from 1815 to 1825.

46. Alan P. Grimes, *Democracy and the Amendments to the Constitution* (Lanham, Maryland: University Press of America, 1987), p. 115.

47. Charles Lingley, *Texas Review*, Vol 1, No. 4 (April 1916), p. 310, https://www.jstor.org./stable/43465717 (accessed August 10, 2018).

48. Ames, p. 125.

49. See 1945 unprinted testimony of John W. McCormack in hearings before the House Committee on the Election of the President, Vice President, and Representatives in Congress, p. 33.

50. *Congressional Record*, February 6, 1947, p. 841.

51. Adolph Sabath served in the House from 1907 to 1952. He rose to be Dean of the House (the longest serving member in the chamber) in 1934 and remained so until his retirement. During 1937 to 1952, except for the 80th Congress (1947–1949), Sabath chaired the House Rules Committee.

52. During the Rules Committee hearing, Sabath asked Michener how many days the Judiciary Committee would need on the Floor. "Those opposed to it, like my distinguished friend (referring to Sabath) want a week. Others who are for it want it right away." House Rules Committee Hearing (unprinted), February 5, 1947, p. 4.

53. *Congressional Record*, February 6, 1947, p. 842.

54. Ibid.

55. Representative Carl M. Vinson's (D-GA) biographer describes McCormack's presence on the House Floor. "The fighting Irishman's quick mind, acid tongue, and zest for a good fight superbly equipped him to advance his party's agenda in legislative combat." James F. Cook, *Carl Vinson: Patriarch of the Armed Forces* (Macon, Georgia: Mercer University Press, 2004), p. 162, quoted in Nelson, p. 275.

56. McCormack was born in 1891. As a young lawyer in Boston during the 1920s, he was a notably successful defense attorney. He maintained his legal practice while serving in the Massachusetts legislature, giving it up when he entered Congress in 1928. Nelson, p. 121.

57. McCormack's remarks are in the *Congressional Record*, February 6, 1947, pp. 842–843.

58. Harold J. Laski, the eminent political scientist, had made a similar point in his 1940 study of the presidency. "It is indeed true that no man is indispensable," said Laski. In general, rotation in office is what distinguished democracies from dictatorial systems, he added. However, Laski was not in principle against a third term. There could be great benefit to extending an incumbency, even if there were no looming emergency. "If, patently, he seems superior to any alternative, it must seem to the outsider a grievous waste of human resources to put a president on the shelf." Harold J. Laski, *The American Presidency, An Interpretation* (New York: Harper & Brothers Publishers, 1940), p. 69.

59. "Washington was personally resistant to serving as president at all, and he originally indicated he would retire after his first term; he reversed himself only after Hamilton, Thomas Jefferson, and James Madison all pleaded with him to run for a second term and his own fears about the increasingly partisan air of national politics coalesced." Bruce G. Peabody, "George Washington, Presidential Term Limits, and the Problem of Reluctant Leadership," *Presidential Studies Quarterly*, Vol. 31, No. 3 (September 2001), pp. 439–453, 442. http://www.jstor.org/stable/27552322.

60. Washington's Farewell Address, 1796. The Avalon Project, www.law.yale.edu (accessed October 8, 2018).

61. *Congressional Record*, February 6, 1947, pp. 842–843.

62. Ibid. As Jefferson's biographer, Jon Meacham, put it, "Visions of a crown worried him still." Meacham, p. 409.

63. Ibid., February 6, 1947, pp. 843–844.

64. Ibid., February 6, 1947, p. 844.

65. For example, former President John Quincy Adams, by then back in Congress, stated in 1839 that the two-term custom, "has become a tacit subsidiary constitutional law." Lingley, p. 311.

66. Sam Rayburn came to the House in 1913 and served until his death in 1961. He was speaker of the House during the periods September 16, 1940, to January 3, 1947; January 3, 1949, to January 3, 1953, and January 3 1955, to November 16, 1961. He also served as Minority Leader from January 3, 1947, to January 3, 1949, and from January 3, 1953, to January 3, 1955.

67. *Congressional Record*, February 6, 1947, p. 845.

68. Ibid.

69. Raymond Springer was a member from 1939 until his death in August 1947.

70. Many constitutional amendments have been proposed without ratification deadlines. For example, the Twenty-seventh Amendment was originally sent to the states in 1789 and did not become part of the Constitution until 1992. However, the Equal Rights Amendment failed because the ratification deadline expired. Congress proposed it in 1972. By 1979, thirty-five states had ratified it, three fewer than necessary to incorporate it in the Constitution. That year, Congress extended the deadline until 1982, but no additional states ratified. Therefore, the amendment died.

71. The final version of the Twenty-second Amendment explicitly "grandfathered" Truman, meaning it exempted him. Thus, he would have been able to seek another term in 1952.

72. Rankin was in the House from 1921 to 1953.

73. *Congressional Record*, February 6, 1947, p. 846.

74. John W. Jeffries, *A Third Term for FDR: The Election of 1940* (Lawrence: University Press of Kansas, 2017), p. 24. Failure of the court-packing plan and entrenchment of the Neutrality laws were the work of such coalitions. After the 1946 election, the South remained a bastion for Congressional Democrats, while Republicans replaced Democrats in northern states. As a result, Southerners increased their strength as a percentage of the Democratic caucus. See Nelson, p. 350. Furthermore, with the exception of the five states in the Hoover-Smith presidential election of 1928,

and the State of Tennessee during the 1920 Harding-Cox election, Republicans could not win an electoral vote anywhere in the South. The political philosophy of Southern Democrats differed from their Northern counterparts on certain matters, most obviously civil rights. By 1947 the highly diverse Democratic coalition was still intact, although fraying.

75. During the ascendancy of the New Deal, Southern strength within the Democratic Party as a whole diminished. This was true because of the rise of big-city machines, heavily influenced by big labor and enhanced by a physical and political migration of African-American voters. As well, Roosevelt had engineered an amendment to party convention rules in 1936 to allow for nomination only by a majority, instead of two-thirds. In four elections, Franklin Roosevelt did not lose a single electoral vote in the region.

76. Emanuel Celler was in Congress nearly 50 years, from March 1923 to January 1973. He was dean of the House from 1965, and served as chairman of the House Judiciary Committee from 1949 to 1973.

77. *Congressional Record*, February 6, 1947, p. 846. These arguments would precisely reprise those of Senator John D. Works (R-CA), who made them while pushing a six-year single term amendment through the Senate in 1913. The amendment died in the House.

78. Ibid.

79. Louis Graham was in the House from 1939 to 1955.

80. The committee was composed of one member from each state in attendance.

81. Ibid.

82. McCormack biographer Garrison Nelson writes about Roosevelt prevailing in his tussle with the Court. "With the opportunity to name eight new Justices and elevate Harlan Fiske Stone to Chief over that period, the conflict abated. The Senate defeated none of his appointments, with seven confirmed by voice vote, and only Hugo Black (63 to 16) and William O. Douglas (62 to four) faced nominal roll call opposition." Nelson, p. 238.

83. *Congressional Record,* February 6, 1947, p. 847.

84. Ibid.

85. John Robsion was an appointed U.S. senator in 1930 and returned to service in the House of Representatives from 1935 until his death in 1948.

86. *Congressional Record*, February 6, 1947, p. 849.

87. John Jennings was in the House from 1939 to 1951.

88. *Congressional Record,* February 6, 1947, pp. 852–853.

89. *Congressional Record*, February 6, 1947, p. 848. Joseph Bryson served in Congress from 1939 until his death in 1953.

90. Ibid. For example, Canadian Prime Minister Mackenzie King served for 13 consecutive years between 1935 and 1948.

91. John Lyle was a Member of the House from 1945 to 1955.

92. *Congressional Record*, February 6, 1947, p. 854.

93. Estes Kefauver was one of the most prominent Congressional Democrats in the twentieth century. He served in the House from 1939 to 1949 and in the Senate from 1949 until his death in 1963. Kefauver ran for the Democratic nomination for

president in 1952 and 1956. He defeated President Truman in the 1952 New Hampshire primary, but lost the nomination to Governor Adlai Stevenson of Illinois. In 1956, he was again unsuccessful in his effort to secure the nomination, but the Democratic Convention selected him to run for vice president on a ticket that Stevenson headed. Stevenson-Kefauver lost to Eisenhower-Nixon in the 1956 general election.

94. *Congressional Record,* February 6, 1947, p. 867.

95. Ibid.

96. Frank Chelf was in the House from 1945 to 1967.

97. *Congressional Record*, February 6, 1947, p. 851.

98. It is unclear whether, in calling the Convention, Congress could limit the agenda. Fear of a runaway Convention is one deterrent to using this mechanism, and a problem that does not exist if Congress takes the initiative to amend the Constitution. As former Chief Justice Warren Burger wrote in 1988, "There is no way to effectively limit or muzzle the actions of a Constitutional Convention. The Convention could make its own rules and set its own agenda. Congress might try to limit the Convention to one amendment or one issue, but there is no way to assure that the Convention would obey. After a Convention is convened, it will be too late to stop the Convention if we don't like its agenda." Letter from Chief Justice Warren Burger to Phyllis Schlafly, June 22, 1988, http://constitution.i2i.org/files/2013/11/Burger-letter2.pdf.

99. John Murdock served in the House from 1937–1953.

100. *Congressional Record*, February 6, 1947, p. 853.

101. During the Constitutional Convention, on July 23, 1787, delegates rejected by a vote of seven to three a proposal for ratification by legislatures and agreed by nine to one for convention ratification.

102. Republican Party Platform, adopted June 14, 1932, www.presidency.ucsb.edu (accessed March 8, 2018). Republicans were quite specific that they did not want the question presented to be limited to simple repeal of the Eighteenth Amendment. Their platform proposal closely resembled the framework of the Twenty-first Amendment, which grants states unique regulatory powers over alcohol. The platform stated, "We therefore believe that the people should have an opportunity to pass upon a proposed amendment the provision of which, while retaining in the Federal Government power to preserve the gains already made in dealing with the evils inherent in the liquor traffic, shall allow the States to deal with the problem as their citizens may determine, but subject always to the power of the Federal Government to protect those States where prohibition may exist and safeguard our citizens everywhere from the return of the saloon and attendant abuses."

103. *Congressional Record*, February 6, 1947, p. 847.

104. Michener's full closing statement appears at *Congressional Record*, February 6, 1947, pp. 862–863.

105. *Congressional Record*, February 6, 1947, p. 863. Many advocates of a single six-year term offered this kind of justification. One of them was Milton Eisenhower, a distinguished academic and President Dwight Eisenhower's brother, who wrote, "My reason for favoring a single term for the president is based on my conviction that we should expect the president to foster only those programs and policies which he is convinced are in the interest of the nation as a whole—that he should have no

incentive to propose and fight for measures conceived mainly to enhance his chances for re-election, or merely to confound the political opposition. . . . The incentive to spend or take any other action for sheer political advantage should not exist. It would not if the president were limited to one six-year term. . . . Presumably, even such a president would still act politically, to benefit his Party, including perhaps to influence the election of his successor. Continuity of policies is a powerful incentive for a president not to 'stand above' politics, even if he is not a direct political beneficiary of his actions." Milton Eisenhower, *The President is Calling* (Garden City, New York: Doubleday & Company, Inc., 1974), pp. 233–236.

106. *Congressional Record*, February 6, 1947, pp. 863–865.

107. Kenneth B. Keating was in the House from 1947 to 1959, and was a senator from 1959 to 1965.

108. Presidential scholar Thomas Cronin strongly concurs. "Presidents should be guided by how the voters will judge them at the next election," he writes. "Supporters of the six-year single term somehow think this is improper. In most instances, it is preferable to have a president who is guided by the voters' appraisal at the end of four years than by what a president alone thinks is best or by what he or she alone thinks will look good in the history texts." Thomas E. Cronin, "Presidential Term, Tenure, and Re-eligibility," *Inventing the American Presidency* (Lawrence, Kansas: University Press of Kansas, 1989), p, 80.

109. *Congressional Record*, February 6, 1947, pp. 864–865.

110. *Congressional Record*, February 6, 1947, p. 870.

111. Ibid.

112. William Colmer served in the House from 1933 to 1973.

113. *Congressional Record*, February 6, 1947, pp. 870–871.

114. *Congressional Record*, February 6, 1947, p. 871.

115. *Congressional Record,* February 6, 1947, p. 872.

116. Joseph W. Martin, Jr. served in the House from 1925 to 1967. He was speaker from 1947 to 1949 and again from 1953 to 1955.

117. Of the forty-seven Democrats, forty-one came from the South or Border States. One of the six Northern Democrats to support the amendment was freshman Representative John F. Kennedy (D-MA). Nelson, p. 365. The forty-seven Democrats represented approximately 25 percent of the Democratic Caucus, a fairly sizeable rate of defection, but much lower than the 50 percent of Judiciary Committee Democrats who supported the amendment in committee. Paul G. Willis and George L. Willis, "The Politics of the Twenty-second Amendment," *The Western Political Science Quarterly*, Vol. 5, No. 3 (September 1952), pp. 469–482, 481, https://www.jstor.org/stable/442606 (accessed October 12, 2018).

118. Constitutional scholar David Kyvig theorizes that, by supporting the amendment, Southerners hoped to mitigate presidential leadership on civil rights. "Abetted by southern Democrats concerned that stronger presidents might enhance African-American civil rights, Republicans quickly obtained the necessary two-thirds majority, first in the House and shortly thereafter in the Senate." David E. Kyvig, "Everett Dirksen's Constitutional Charades," *Journal of the Illinois State Historical Society*, Vol. 25 (Spring 2002), p. 71. The southern Democrats who defected to join with the

Republicans on the amendment vote supported their party just under 70 percent of the time on House votes—giving statistical evidence of their willingness to coalesce with Republicans. Southern Democrats who did not defect on this vote remained loyal to their party over 80 percent of the time. Research quoted in Stathis, p. 67.

119. Alexander Wiley was a senator from 1939 to 1963.

120. United States Senate Committee on the Judiciary, "Presidential Terms of Office," Rept. No. 80–34, p. 2.

121. *Congressional Record*, March 5, 1947, p. 1680.

122. *Congressional Record*, March 3, 1947, p. 1611.

123. Wiley's full statement appears at *Congressional Record*, March 5, 1947, pp. 1680–1681.

124. John Overton served in the House from 1931 to 1933 and in the Senate from 1933 until his death in 1948.

125. *Congressional Record*, March 5, 1947, p. 1681.

126. Lister Hill was in the House of Representatives from 1923 to 1938 and in the Senate from 1938 to 1969.

127. *Congressional Record*, March 7, 1947, p. 1771.

128. Ibid.

129. Scott Lucas served in the House from 1935 to 1939 and in the Senate from 1939 to 1951. During the 81st Congress (1949–1951), Lucas was the Majority Leader.

130. *Congressional Record*, March 7, 1947, p. 1711.

131. Ibid.

132. Ibid.

133. John Sparkman was a Congressman from 1937 to 1946 and a senator from 1946 to 1979. In 1952, he ran unsuccessfully for vice president on the Democratic ticket headed by Governor Adlai Stevenson.

134. This exchange appears at Congressional Record, March 7, 1947, p. 1772.

135. Raymond Baldwin was a senator from late 1946 until his resignation from the Senate in 1949.

136. *Congressional Record*, March 7, 1947, p. 1773.

137. Ibid.

138. Seven of the thirteen original state constitutions also had executive term limits. These occurred in states in which the legislature elected the governor, and not in ones where the governor was chosen by popular vote. "Prevention of intrigue and bargaining with the legislature by a governor intent on his own continuance in office seems to have been a major objective of these early state constitutional restrictions on re-eligibility." Joseph E. Kallenbach, "Constitutional Limitations on Re-eligibility of National and State Chief Executives," *American Political Science Review*, Vol. 26, No. 2 (June 1952), pp. 438–439.

139. Ibid.

140. Ibid.

141. Ibid.

142. Ibid.

143. Ibid.

144. "Pappy" O'Daniel was a senator from 1941 to 1949.

145. *Congressional Record*, March 7, 1947, p. 1799.

146. This article appears at *Congressional Record*, March 7, 1947, pp. 1794–1799.

147. John McClellan served in the House from 1935 to 1939 and was a senator from 1943 to 1977.

148. *Congressional Record*, March 7, 1947, p. 1800.

149. Senate Rept. No. 80–34, p. 2.

150. *Congressional Record*, March 7, 1947, p. 1800.

151. Chapman Revercomb served in the Senate from 1943 to 1949 and again from 1956 to 1959.

152. *Congressional Record*, March 7, 1947, p. 1800.

153. Ibid.

154. James Beck served in the House from 1927 to 1934.

155. Henry Ashurst was a senator from 1912 to 1941, and was one of Arizona's original two U.S. senators.

156. Philip L. Martin, "Convention Ratification of Federal Constitutional Amendments," *Political Science Quarterly*, Vol. 82 No. 1 (March 1967), pp. 61–71, 69. https://www.jstor.org/stable/2147300 (accessed October 13, 2018). In any case, when the amendment was sent out for ratification, operational details for the conventions were omitted.

157. *Congressional Record*, March 7, 1947, p. 1801.

158. Ibid., p. 1804. Alben Barkley served in the House from 1913 to 1927. He was a senator from 1927 to 1949, after which he became vice president from 1949 to 1953. Barkley returned to the Senate in 1955, and died in office on April 30, 1956.

159. Forrest Donnel was a senator from 1945 to 1951.

160. *Congressional Record*, March 7, 1947, p. 1804.

161. *Congressional Record*, March 7, 1947, p. 1805.

162. Tom Connally served in the House from 1917 to 1929 and was a senator from 1929 to 1953.

163. Presently, the Administrator of the General Services Administration performs this function.

164. *Congressional Record*, March 7, 1947, p. 1806.

165. Wallace White was a representative from 1917 to 1931 and a senator from 1931 to 1949. In the 80th Congress (1947–1949) he was Majority Leader. "In view of the fact that the two-term tradition had been repudiated by the voters of the nation by the reelection of President Roosevelt in 1940 and 1944, supporters of the proposal in Congress had good reason to mistrust a ratification method which would have, in effect, permitted a popular referendum, state-by-state, on the issue." Kallenbach, p. 450.

166. *Congressional Record*, March 7, 1947, p. 1803.

167. Similar concerns about slowdowns were voiced during Congress' consideration of the Twenty-first Amendment. Many state legislatures were already in session and could act immediately, convention opponents argued. Worried about delays, the Senate Judiciary Committee provided that legislatures ratify Prohibition repeal. However, mindful that both party platforms had endorsed ratification by conventions,

the full Senate reversed the committee, and the House accepted the Senate version. In fact, convention ratification by sufficient states was swift, occurring by December 5, 1933, only ten months after Congress submitted the amendment. Martin, p. 68.

168. Political scientist Joseph Kallenbach concurs, stating, "In view of the fact that the two-term tradition had been repudiated by the voters of the nation by the reelection of President Roosevelt in 1940 and 1944, supporters of the proposal in Congress had good reason to mistrust a ratification method which would have, in effect, permitted a popular referendum, state-by-state, on the issue." Kallenbach, p. 450.

169. *Congressional Record*, March 7, 1947, p. 1862.

170. Senate Committee Report No. 80-34, p. 3.

171. Warren Magnuson was in the House from 1937 to 1944 and was a senator from 1944 to 1980.

172. *Congressional Record*, March 7, 1947, p. 1863.

173. Ibid.

174. Ibid.

175. Bourke Hickenlooper was a senator from 1945 to 1969.

176. *Congressional Record*, March 10, 1947, p. 1864.

177. Harley Kilgore served in the senate from 1941 until his death in 1956.

178. *Congressional Record*, March 10, 1947, p. 1864.

179. Robert A. Taft was a senator from 1939 until his death in 1953. Between January and July 1953, Taft was Senate Majority Leader.

180. Ibid.

181. *Congressional Record*, March 10, 1947, p. 1867.

182. Twenty years earlier, in 1927, Congressman Benjamin J. Fairchild (R-NY) proposed a nearly identical amendment in the final days of the Congress. No action was taken before adjournment, and when Congress next convened, Fairchild was no longer a member.

183. "The amendment specifically excluded Truman as an attempt by the Republican leadership of Congress to show that it was a non-partisan measure." Paul B. Davis, "The Results and Implications for Enactment of the Twenty-second Amendment," *Presidential Studies Quarterly*, Vol. 9, No. 3 (Summer, 1979), pp. 289–303, https://www.jstor.org/stable/27547484 (accessed October 12, 2018).

184. Spessard Holland was a senator from 1945 to 1971.

185. In 1803, by a vote of four to 25, the Senate rejected a similar idea. That resolution provided that a president could serve for four years, then after sitting out for four years, could run for one additional four-year term. See 1945 testimony from House Majority Whip John W. McCormack, House Hearings before the Committee on the Election of the President, Vice President, and Representatives in Congress, p. 3. See also, Stathis, pp. 62–63.

186. *Congressional Record*, March 12, 1947, p. 1939.

187. Ibid. Senator Robert A. Taft was the son of President William Howard Taft.

188. "Somberly clad in a dark suit and dark tie, Truman strode into the packed House chamber just after 1:00 PM on March 12, 1947. . . . Speaking for nineteen minutes—clearly, slowly, with a measured forcefulness—he laid out a sweeping new doctrine of American global engagement." Benn Steil, *The Marshall Plan: Dawn of the Cold War* (New York: Simon & Schuster, 2018), p. 44.

189. *Congressional Record*, March 12, 1947, pp. 1939–1941.
190. Ibid., p. 1941.
191. Ibid., p. 1955.
192. Carl Hatch served in the Senate from 1933 to 1949.
193. *Congressional Record*, March 12, 1947, p. 1956.
194. Ibid.
195. Arthur Vandenberg served in the Senate from 1928 until his death in 1951.
196. *Congressional Record*, March 12, 1947, pp. 1957–1959, depicting Vandenberg's article in full.
197. Ibid., p. 1959.
198. William Langer was a senator from 1941 until his death in 1959.
199. *Congressional Record*, March 12, 1947, p. 1959.
200. Ibid., pp. 1960–1961.
201. Ibid., p. 1961.
202. Ibid.
203. Ibid., p. 1962.
204. Ibid., p. 1963.
205. Claude Pepper served in the senate from 1936 until 1951, having been defeated in the 1950 Democratic primary by Representative George Smathers. Pepper attempted to return to the senate in 1958, but lost in the Democratic primary to Senator Spessard Holland. When the Miami, Florida, area gained an additional seat in reapportionment, Pepper ran for the House. He was elected in 1963 and remained in the House until his death in 1989.
206. Ibid.
207. Ibid., pp. 1966–1967.
208. Ibid., p. 1971.
209. Ibid., p. 1978.
210. "This is not to say that the Republican Party in Congress did not feel the thrust of intra-party tensions in this matter. It is to say, however, that the requirements of newly acquired power in the legislature, reinforced by the historically conservative party position, did not permit its membership, *at that time*, the luxury of openly-expressed dissensions." Willis and Willis, p. 481. (emphasis in the original).
211. *Congressional Record,* March 12, 1947, p. 1978.
212. Charles E. Wunderlin, Jr., ed., *Papers of Senator Robert A. Taft, Volume 3, 1945–1948* (The Kent State University Press), pp. 261–262.
213. *Congressional Record*, March 21, 1947, p. 2389.
214. Ibid., p. 2390.
215. Ibid., p. 2391.
216. Ibid., p. 2392.
217. Willis and Willis, p. 481.
218. The list of concerned legislatures grew longer after the third term became a reality and a fourth term was possible. Between March 1940 and September 1943, eight legislatures passed resolutions on the topic. Stathis, p. 65.
219. Stathis, p. 70. Democratic dominance of Southern legislatures was profound. As they rejected the amendment in 1947, all members of the Texas legislature, 31 senators and 150 representatives, were Democrats. Their votes and those in Oklahoma

occurred in the year prior to the moment President Truman's Commission on Civil Rights recommended civil rights initiatives. Those proposals ultimately split the party at the 1948 Democratic Convention, and precipitated the Dixiecrat walkout. As the split materialized, Democratic-controlled legislatures in Southern states could no longer be depended on to withhold support for ratification. Ibid., p, 72.

220. Like Mississippi, Louisiana defected from Truman in 1948 to support the Dixiecrat candidate, Governor Strom Thurmond.

221. In 1940, Clancy wrote a pamphlet titled, "The Two-term Tradition," and spent the next decade campaigning to ensure that it never became part of the Constitution.

222. For example, Clancy proposed that ratification be limited to a single session of state legislatures, so that all legislatures could act contemporaneously. Such a plan would have been significantly more restrictive, even than the seven-year ratification limit Congress imposed on the Twenty-second Amendment.

223. Ickes left the Government in 1946, after 13 years of service as Secretary of the Interior.

224. Letter from Harold L. Ickes to Daniel F. Clancy, February 2, 1949, National Committee Against Limiting the Presidency subject file, Harry S. Truman Presidential Library and Museum, www.trumanlibrary.org, accessed July 26, 2018.

225. Letter from Harold L. Ickes to Daniel F. Clancy (with attachment), January 16, 1951, Ibid.

226. In 1950, Republicans gained twenty-eight seats in the House and five in the Senate.

227. One of these was Texas, which, on February 22, 1951, reversed its earlier rejection of the amendment.

228. Letter from Daniel F. Clancy to Harry S. Truman, National Committee files, Ibid.

229. At the time Minnesota acted, twenty-seven states did not limit their own governors. Of these, twenty-two nevertheless ratified the amendment. Kallenbach, p. 447.

230. Republican support among state legislators was nearly as strong as the unanimity within Congress. Of 3,272 Republican state legislators to cast votes on ratification, only twenty-five state senators and fifty-nine representatives opposed it. That meant 97.75 of Republicans in state legislatures voted to ratify. Stathis, p. 70. Many of the Republican state legislators hoped their vote would discourage President Truman from running in 1952, even though he was legally eligible. Ibid., p. 71. After the 1948 Dixiecrat split, Southern Democrats also found that strategy useful. Ibid., p. 72. Such an approach mimicked the Springer Resolution against Grant, adopted in the House in 1875, and the LaFollette Resolution against Coolidge, adopted in the Senate in 1928.

231. From 1950 to 1985, the GSA Administrator certified constitutional amendments. Since then, the Archivist of the United States has had that responsibility.

232. Statement by Daniel F. Clancy, ca. 1951, National Committee files, Ibid.

233. Shortly after the Twenty-second Amendment became part of the Constitution, University of Michigan political scientist Joseph A. Kallenbach wrote, "The fact that this proposal came so soon after the two-term tradition had been successfully challenged by a Democratic President gave it the character of a pro-Roosevelt,

anti-Roosevelt partisan issue in much the same sense that earlier actions of Congress had reflected anti-Grant, anti-Theodore Roosevelt, anti-Coolidge partisan sentiment. . . . Only after political developments in the post-war period had begun to raise increasing doubts in Democratic ranks concerning the soundness of President Roosevelt's judgment as a policymaker did Democratic-dominated state legislatures display in any numbers a favorable attitude toward the Amendment." Kallenbach, p. 446.

234. Neale.

235. For example, the *Congressional Record* reflects, "The Senator from New Mexico (Mr. Hatch) and the Senator from Washington (Mr. Cain), who would vote 'yea' if present are paired with the Senator from Kentucky (Mr. Barkley), who would vote 'nay' if present." *Congressional Record*, March 12, 1947, p. 1977.

236. During the October 6, 2018, confirmation vote on the nomination of Brett Kavanaugh to be an Associate Justice of the Supreme Court, Senator Lisa Murkowski (R-AK) paired with Senator Steve Daines (R-MT). Senator Daines did not vote. Senator Murkowski withheld her vote, so that Daines' absence would not affect the outcome. By the time of that vote, pairing had become so uncommon that the press was largely unfamiliar with it and senior Senate staff had to tutor reporters.

Chapter 10

The Last Unlimited President

Harry S. Truman (1952)

KEFAUVER DEFEATS TRUMAN

Perhaps the most iconic photograph and misleading headline in American political history appeared on the front page of the November 3, 1948 *Chicago Tribune*. "Dewey Defeats Truman," it proclaimed. Standing in the St. Louis rail station on his way back to Washington, Truman was pictured gleefully holding the paper aloft. Conventional wisdom, based on polling and reflected in the erroneous headline, held that Dewey victory was certain. For example, the lead story in *Time's* November 1, 1948, issue was about the impending election and implicitly forecast Truman's defeat. Of Truman's feverish "Give 'em Hell, Harry, whistle stop" campaign, it wrote, "The key figure in the campaign was President Harry Truman—though his role was essentially a negative one. The man who was not wanted by his party before convention time had provided most of the campaign's real color and life. Few Presidents had traveled so far, spoken so rashly, or attracted such big, good-humored crowds. But if the polls were right, a majority of the voters continued, gently though firmly, to oppose him."[1]

Not so. Truman won the popular vote by just over two million votes out of 46 million ballots cast for major party candidates,[2] and he prevailed in the Electoral College 303-189-39. The thirty-nine electoral votes were for Governor Strom Thurmond of South Carolina, who led a splinter ticket of Dixiecrats. All thirty-nine electoral votes came from the South. Thurmond received the electoral votes of South Carolina, Alabama, Mississippi, and Louisiana, plus one from a "faithless elector" in Tennessee, notwithstanding Truman's popular vote majority in that state.

In 1948, Democrats also roared back to power on Capitol Hill, winning nine seats in the Senate and seventy-five in the House.

Truman's full term was beset with controversy, as Cold War tensions grew more severe. In October 1949, Mao Zedong proclaimed the People's Republic of China, setting off a wave of recrimination over "who lost China?" In June 1950, the Korean War began. After initial North Korean successes, United Nations' forces under General Douglas MacArthur struck back, and pushed all the way to the Chinese border. By October of that year, China joined the fighting, leading to a vicious and debilitating military stalemate. In April 1951, convinced of MacArthur's insubordination, Truman fired him. The president's action generated immense political discord in the United States. At the same time, McCarthy-era allegations of Communist infiltration in government and private industry roiled domestic politics.[3] These problems took their toll on Truman's popularity. During the period 1945–1949, the president enjoyed average popularity of 55.6 percent. However, within the period 1949 to 1953, that sunk to 36.5 percent. A president who enjoyed peak ratings of 87 percent in June 1945 was down to 22 percent by February 1952.[4]

On March 11, 1952, almost five years to the day of Truman's pivotal Cold War speech to Congress on aid to Greece and Turkey, it was the President's turn to be flummoxed. Tennessee Senator Estes Kefauver soundly defeated Truman in New Hampshire's Democratic primary, capturing 19,800 votes to 15,927 for the president, and won all the state's convention delegates.[5]

Truman's home state newspaper, *The Southeast Missourian*, assessed the upset. "In terms of pre-election forecasts, Kefauver's victory over the President was even more stunning. The Tennessean made modest claims—but not for a victory—in the popular vote, and said he believed he would win 'some delegates.'" As the paper described it, Kefauver "smashed the Democratic state party organization."[6]

The *Spirit of Jefferson Farmer's Advocate*, published in West Virginia's panhandle, took stock on the Thursday following the primary. "We hope the President will give careful consideration to the New Hampshire vote in making his decision regarding another term. Undoubtedly, politics being what they are, Mr. Truman can get the nomination if he wants it. But we hope that he will see in the New Hampshire results some evidence that many Democrats do not want him to run again."[7]

One political professional, who knew Truman well, believed the president would have the opposite reaction. Stung by the primary outcome, Truman might hunker down and fight back. So thought Senator George Aiken (R-VT)[8] in the immediate election aftermath. "Say what you want about Harry Truman," Aiken remarked, "he's a fighter, especially when he's hurt, and he'll fight now."[9]

Nevertheless, the primary proved to be an action-forcing mechanism. Facing an unraveling and potentially untenable political situation, Truman soon withdrew from the race.[10] On March 29, 1952, he spoke to 5,300 Democrats at Washington's National Guard Armory, an event broadcast nationwide over radio. The occasion was the annual Jefferson-Jackson dinner, a major event for the party. At the end of his strongly partisan prepared remarks, Truman made an impromptu announcement. "I shall not be a candidate for re-election. I have served my country long, and I think efficiently and honestly. I shall not accept a re-nomination. I do not feel that it is my duty to spend another four years in the White House."[11]

Although the Twenty-second Amendment was ratified the previous year, Truman was eligible to run in 1952 because Congress had specifically exempted him. Truman had permitted his name to appear on the New Hampshire primary ballot, because he did not want to be a premature lame duck and because he had not found someone he believed to be an acceptable successor. Nevertheless, Truman later wrote in his memoirs that he had never intended to seek reelection. "My decision not to be a candidate for reelection in 1952 goes back to the day of my inauguration in 1949. On this day, facing four more years of the Presidency, I kept reviewing the many grave problems facing the nation and the world. And I found myself thinking about my own future, and how long a man ought to stay in the Presidency, and a nation's need for a constant renewal of leadership. I was now certain that I would not run again."[12]

Truman wrote that, at the time, he could not share the decision with anyone. Instead, he prepared a memorandum on April 16, 1950, which he filed away and did not then disclose. The memo stated, "I am not a candidate for nomination by the Democratic Convention." Recounting his service in local office, the army, the Senate, the Vice Presidency, and the Presidency, Truman added, "I have been in public office well over thirty years, having been President of the United States almost two complete terms."

Truman recounted the history of the two-term tradition. "By then, seven Presidents had adhered to it," Truman wrote. "Three attempted to break it. Grant and Theodore Roosevelt had tried but failed. Only FDR was successful."[13]

In 1940, Truman had gone public with his opposition to the third term for FDR. However, he did not follow Senator Ed Burke and engineer a complete break with Roosevelt. Instead, Truman endorsed Missouri Senator Bennett Clark for president, while promising to support Roosevelt if FDR won nomination by the Democratic Convention.[14] "I hope he will not run again, but if he does, I will support him," indicated Truman.[15]

In his memoirs, Truman illuminated his reasoning in support of presidential term limits. "There is a lure in power," he observed. "It can get into a man's blood just as gambling and lust for money have been known to do." Therefore, Truman saw great importance in the custom of term limits by self-restraint. "In my opinion, eight years as President is enough and sometimes too much for any man to serve in that capacity."[16]

Truman continued, "When we forget the examples of such men as Washington, Jefferson, and Andrew Jackson, then we will start down the road to dictatorship and ruin."

When Truman wrote his 1950 memo, the Twenty-second Amendment had gone through Congress but the state ratification process was still underway. The president supported the policy but disagreed with amending the Constitution. He intended to bring back term limits by restoring the two-term custom personally. "I know I could be elected again and continue to break the old precedent as it was broken by FDR. It should not be done. *That precedent should continue not to be a Constitutional Amendment, but by custom based on the honor of the man in the office.*" (Emphasis added)

Truman concluded, "Therefore, to re-establish that custom, although by a quibble I could say I've had only one term,[17] I am not a candidate and will not accept the nomination for another term."[18]

In March 1951, eleven months after he prepared the memo, Truman revealed its contents to his staff. They reacted negatively. "The staff responded with deep emotion and expressions of protest and disappointment," wrote the president. Perhaps fearing that publicizing the memo would make the decision irrevocable, and worried about Truman becoming a lame duck, the staff urged him not to reveal its contents.[19]

Truman did not need much persuasion. "By the very nature of his office, this is one secret a President must keep to himself until the last possible moment."[20]

Having taken himself out of the running, Truman still felt responsible for promoting the worthiest possible candidate to succeed him. His first choice would not have seemed obvious to most Americans. The president preferred Chief Justice Fred M. Vinson of the United States Supreme Court.[21]

Vinson had a distinguished career in all three branches of government. He served in the House from 1924 to 1929 and again from 1933 to 1937. Thereafter, he was a member of the U.S. Court of Appeals for the District of Columbia from 1938 to 1943. Vinson resigned from the appellate bench to become Roosevelt's Director of Economic Stabilization, where he served until Truman made him Secretary of the Treasury. Vinson spent eleven months in that position. Following the death of Chief Justice Harlan Fiske Stone on April 22, 1946, Truman nominated Vinson to be the 13th Chief Justice.[22]

Searching for a suitable successor as president, Truman made overtures to Vinson, in 1950 and again in 1951. Vinson declined, believing that the Court was not an appropriate launching pad for the White House. In addition, the Chief Justice cited reasons of health.[23]

With Vinson out of consideration, Truman focused on Governor Adlai Stevenson of Illinois. On May 8, 1951, the president wrote a pertinent memorandum.

> I've said that no third term appeals to me. . . . Now if we can find a man who will take over and continue the Fair Deal, Point IV, Fair Employment, parity for farmers and a consumers-protective policy, the Democratic Party can win from now on. It seems to me now that the governor of Illinois has the background and what it takes. Think I'll talk to him.[24]

Truman and Stevenson met in January 1952 at Blair House.[25] If Stevenson were willing, Truman offered to pull the necessary political levers. Truman wrote, "I told him that a President in the White House always controlled the National Convention."[26] However, at the Blair House meeting, Stevenson declined to run.

The conversation renewed in March. Stevenson called on Truman and told the President of a commitment to run that year for reelection as governor of Illinois. In addition, Stevenson also opined that Truman was the only Democrat who could defeat the Republican ticket in November, regardless of who ultimately was the GOP nominee.[27]

McCullough observes that following his second unsatisfactory discussion with Stevenson, Truman had considered openly declaring for renomination. "For several weeks, Truman toyed with the prospect of running again. Some of the staff felt sure he had changed his mind and was about to announce his candidacy."[28] Leading those who had been lobbying Truman to reconsider was Vinson himself.[29]

Truman was conflicted. Philosophically, he was against a third term and thought he should retire. But he was eligible to run, and the question of leadership succession was unsettled. For the time being, the President made no definitive moves, neither declaring his candidacy nor disclaiming a run.

Meanwhile, the March 11, 1952, New Hampshire primary loomed. On January 29, 1952, acting without the President's consent, J.H. McPhail, a New Hampshire Democrat, entered Truman's name. At a news conference on January 31, Truman indicated he would ask to be removed from the ballot, while reserving the right to enter the race later.[30] At that point, Democratic National Chairman Frank McKinney intervened, holding a February 2 press conference to advise reporters that he would urge Truman not to withdraw from the primary.[31]

Truman decided to comply.[32] On February 5, 1952, the president sent a letter to Enoch D. Fuller, the Secretary of State for New Hampshire, saying that while he considered it preferable not to appear on any primary ballots until he decided for certain about his reelection plans, "the Chairman of the

Democratic National Committee and many good Democrats of New Hampshire are of the opinion that my name should be left on the ballot." Truman went on, "At their suggestion, therefore, I shall not ask you to take my name off the list."[33]

While Truman did not campaign, he remained in contention. Then, Kefauver won the primary.

Speculation abounded about how Truman would respond. As reported from New Hampshire in the March 12, 1953, *New York Times,* "It was also felt that President Truman's disappointing showing here today might have an important bearing on Democratic campaign strategy. Some of the Democratic leaders here believe that it may influence Mr. Truman to reach a decision one way or the other—and fairly soon—on whether or not he intends to run again."[34]

A few days later, Truman had dinner at the Blair House with Democratic National Chairman Frank McKinney and others, including his counsel, Clark Clifford. These advisors tried to discourage him, but Truman deferred a decision.

On March 21, 1952, in Key West, Florida, he met with Clifford alone. Testing a basis to be an active candidate, Truman brought up the conflict in Korea. Clifford reports that "President Truman was concerned about the effect his withdrawal would have on the war in Korea—to which I pointed out that the war's course had long been established."[35] Instead, Clifford argued for Truman's unambiguous and prompt public withdrawal. "I warned him that the longer he waited, the harder it would be for any other Democrat to mount an effective effort against Kefauver, whom the President neither liked nor respected. And the longer he waited, the weaker the party would be—whomever they nominated—in the November election."[36]

The president made up his mind, telling Clifford that he would announce withdrawal at the next suitable moment.[37] By the time of the Armory dinner, Truman's position was clear. "There was no chance I would change, and at this point, I was even more certain that under the circumstances, it would be better for me, for the party, and for the country to have a change in leadership."[38]

Meanwhile, on March 11, 1952, New Hampshire Republicans had given General Dwight Eisenhower a nudge toward the White House, choosing him over Senator Robert Taft. On the Republican side, General Eisenhower defeated Senator Taft by 46,661 to 35,838 and captured every New Hampshire GOP delegate.

Eisenhower had been a reluctant candidate. Several years earlier, Truman had actually cultivated Eisenhower as a potential Democratic nominee for president. In his memoirs, Clark Clifford, writes, "In great secrecy, he sent word to General Eisenhower that he would step aside if Eisenhower wanted the Democratic nomination."[39] Eisenhower refused, disclaiming any interest in electoral politics.[40] Truman renewed the effort on November 5, 1951. McCullough states, "The first week in November, on a brief visit to Washington, the General had lunch with Truman at Blair House and reportedly Truman again offered his full support if Eisenhower would accept the Democratic nomination."[41] Again, Eisenhower declined.

Ironically, the possibility Truman might seek another term may have motivated Eisenhower to reconsider and enter elective politics. In 1959, near the end of Eisenhower's presidency, Associated Press reporter James Marlow filed a story that began, "Why did President Eisenhower decide to seek the presidency in 1952? One main reason was to beat President Truman whose re-election, he felt, would be bad for the country." Marlow continued, "Two of Eisenhower's chief political advisors—while he was still commander of the NATO forces in Europe—were New York's Governor Thomas E. Dewey and Senator Henry Cabot Lodge (R-MA). They told him Truman would try for a second full term and that only he, Eisenhower, could beat him."[42]

In July, Democrats nominated Governor Stevenson, with Alabama Senator John Sparkman as his running mate. Truman campaigned vigorously for the ticket, visiting nineteen states on a coast-to-coast rail whistle-stop tour between September 27 and October 12, 1952.[43] And the president wasn't done. He made a second rail tour that left Washington on October 27, and took him through six states, dropping him in Missouri just prior to the election, so he could be home to vote.

On November 4, 1952, the nation elected Dwight D. Eisenhower the 34th President of the United States, ending a twenty-year drought for the Republican Party. Eisenhower won the popular vote by 55 to 44 percent over Adlai Stevenson, and prevailed in the Electoral College 442-89.

After Eisenhower's Inauguration, Truman went to lunch at the home of his Secretary of State, Dean Acheson, and then proceeded to Union Station for the train ride home to Independence, Missouri. That morning, departing from the White House, Truman quipped, "If I had known how much packing I would have to do, I would have run again."

NOTES

1. "The Nation: View from a Polling Booth," *Time*, Vol. LII, No. 18, November 1, 1948, p. 21.
2. Truman received 24,179,347 to Dewey's 21,991,292.
3. Joseph R. McCarthy was a senator from Wisconsin between 1947 and his death in office in 1957.
4. "Presidential Approval Ratings: Gallup Historical Statistics and Trends," https://news.gallup.com/poll/116677/presidential-approval-ratings-gallup-historical-statistics-trends.aspx.

5. Former Senate Majority Leader Bill Frist (R-TN) writes of Kefauver's 1952 effort, "Neither he nor anyone else could be certain whether Truman would seek another term, but he did know that his appeal lay among the grassroots of his party and not its leadership. If he were to win, he had to take his case to the people and not concern himself with Truman's intentions. He announced his candidacy on January 23, then practically moved to New Hampshire for the next six weeks to campaign in the Democratic primary there . . . Truman, by contrast, stayed away, sending Scott Lucas as a replacement. New Hampshire is known for its surprises and Kefauver tallied a full 55 percent and all of its delegates." Senator William H. Frist with J. Lee Annis, Jr., *Tennessee Senators 1911–2001* (Lanham, Maryland: Madison Books, 1999), p. 88.

6. "Kefauver Win in New Hampshire," *The Southeast Missourian*, March 12, 1947, p. 1.

7. *Spirit of Jefferson Farmer's Advocate*, March 13, 1952.

8. George Aiken was a senator from 1941 to 1975. During Aiken's first term, he had been Truman's colleague in the Senate.

9. Associated Press, "Truman, Taft Opponents Not Belittling Them," *Lewiston Evening Journal*, March 13, 1952.

10. Eisenhower scholar William I. Hitchcock writes of Truman's crumbling political situation after the New Hampshire primary coupled with the entry of Georgia Senator Richard Russell into the race. "The double blows of New Hampshire—the Eisenhower and Kefauver victories—had concentrated his mind: if he were to run for re-election, he would not only face a wildly popular war hero and political superstar, but he would also have to lead a badly divided Democratic Party into the campaign. Kefauver's win in New Hampshire had shown the northern liberals and labor supporters were ready for a change in leadership, and down in Dixie just a few weeks earlier, Senator Richard Russell of Georgia, an opponent of Truman's civil rights policies, had announced his own candidacy. The segregationists in the Democratic Party were once again threatening to secede, as they had under the Dixiecrat Strom Thurmond in 1948." William Hitchcock, *The Age of Eisenhower* (New York: Simon & Schuster, 2018), p. 64.

11. Harry S. Truman, "Address at the Jefferson-Jackson Day Dinner," March 29, 1952. Online by Gerhard Peters and John T. Woolley, *The American Presidency Project*. http://www.presidency.ucsb.edu/ws/?pid=14439.

12. Harry S Truman, *Years of Trial and Hope 1946–1952* (Garden City, New York: Doubleday & Company, 1956), p. 488.

13. Truman did not mention Woodrow Wilson's effort to secure the 1920 Democratic nomination via draft. Wilson engaged in surreptitious maneuvering that quickly amounted to nothing. Theodore Roosevelt and Grant, however, were declared candidates who mounted substantial efforts to win.

14. McCullough, *Truman*, p. 244.

15. Davis, p. 289.

16. Truman's views on the maximum tenure for a president were not quite that fixed. Political scientist Paul Davis has written about an undated memorandum that he speculates Truman wrote in 1947. In it, Truman postulates a constitutional amendment in which senators would be limited to two six-year terms, and Representatives

would have three four-year terms. The four-year term would be coterminous with the presidential term. Such a system would potentially enhance prospects the president would have a working majority in the House throughout his service. "The House of Representatives should be elected with the president for a four-year term of service," Truman wrote. Quoted in Davis, p. 290.

17. Truman was referring to the fact that Roosevelt served eighty-two days into the fourth term, and therefore, Truman had only a partial term during the January 1945 to January 1949 period.

18. The memo is recounted in full in Truman, *Years of Trial and Hope*, pp. 488–489. In 1959, during hearings before the House Judiciary Committee on repeal of the Twenty-second Amendment, Truman offered a similar opinion to Congress. His telegram to the Committee is set out in chapter 11 of this book.

19. Ibid., p. 489.

20. Ibid., p. 488.

21. Clark Clifford, Truman's counsel, observed, "Few others shared the President's extraordinarily high assessment of the Chief Justice. Fred Vinson was a decent and amusing person whose friendship I valued greatly, but he had hardly shown special leadership qualities as Secretary of the Treasury or as Chief Justice. In addition, at age sixty-two, he was not in good health." Clark Clifford, *Counsel to the President: A Memoir* (New York: Doubleday, 1991), p. 282.

22. https://www.oyez.org/justices/fred_m_vinson.

23. Truman, *Years of Trial and Hope*, p. 490. Vinson's health was more precarious than perhaps even he knew. The Chief Justice died of a heart attack on September 8, 1953, only eight months after Truman left office.

24. Ibid., p. 491.

25. At the time, Truman was living at Blair House because the White House mansion was under a massive renovation.

26. Truman, *Years of Trial and Hope*, p. 492.

27. In his notes from the meeting, Truman records that his wife and daughter gave him the same advice. Wanting to retire, Truman felt conflicted. "What the hell am I to do," wrote Truman. "I'll know when the time comes, because I am sure God Almighty will guide me." McCullough, *Truman,* p. 891.

28. Ibid., p. 891.

29. Clifford reports on a dinner Truman held on February 18, 1952, with six advisors. Vinson was present, as was Clifford. "Vinson began with a strong statement that the President should run again, while he did not believe in the theory of the indispensable man. Vinson said he did not see how he could refuse another term." Clifford, p. 283.

30. Joseph A. Fox, "Truman Balks at Vote Test in New Hampshire: Will Withdraw Name. Says This Is No Sign He Won't Run Again, "*Washington Evening Star* (Washington, DC) January 31, 1952, Library of Congress. *Chronicling America: Historic American Newspapers,* https://chroniclingamerica.loc.gov (accessed June 15, 2019).

31. Joseph A. Fox, "Truman Changes Mind, Remains in New Hampshire Primary Race, Says McKinney Persuaded Him," *Washington Evening Star* (Washington, DC), February 5, 1952, Library of Congress, *Chronicling America: Historic American Newspapers,* https://chroniclingamerica.loc.gov (accessed June 15, 2019).

32. David McCullough notes that, "Truman had allowed his name to be entered, but he did not campaign. He thought primaries were a lot of 'eye-wash.'" McCullough, *Truman*, p. 892. By the time of the New Hampshire primary, Kefauver had entered other forthcoming contests. But Truman, who had not removed himself from the New Hampshire ballot, had not taken affirmative steps to enter any of the other primaries. James Marlow, "The World Today," *Gadsen Times Daily*, March 13, 1952.

33. "Letter to the Secretary of State of New Hampshire Concerning the Presidential Preference Primary," *Public Papers Harry S. Truman, 1945–1953,* www.trumanlibrary.org (accessed July 21, 2018).

34. "Move Gains to Get Eisenhower Home," *New York Times*, March 12, 1953, p. 1.

35. Ibid.

36. Ibid.

37. Ibid.

38. Truman, *Years of Trial and Hope*, p. 892.

39. Clifford, p.188.

40. McCullough, *Truman*, p. 584.

41. Ibid., p. 587.

42. James Marlow, "Truman Main Reason Ike Sought Presidency," *Gadsden Times*, August 4, 1959.

43. "Trip of the President: September 27–October 12, 1952, The Old President as Campaigner: 1952–1972, Itinerary for Campaign Trip," Harry S. Truman Presidential Library and Museum, www.trumanlibrary.org (accessed July 25, 1972).

Chapter 11

The Question of Repeal

The Twenty-second Amendment remained deeply unpopular with Democrats, who had opposed it in heavy, but insufficient, numbers when it passed Congress in 1947. Repeal proposals surfaced in the years immediately thereafter, but none got much attention. However, in 1959, the issue seemed to get more traction. As the 86th Congress began, Democratic Members introduced resolutions in both the House and Senate to repeal it and proceeded to hold high visibility hearings.

Republicans continued to defend the Twenty-second Amendment, even though it seemed to work to their immediate political disadvantage. Running without Eisenhower at the top of their ticket in 1960 was rather like Democrats running someone besides Roosevelt in 1940. Prospects for victory looked dimmer without a popular incumbent heading the campaign. But Eisenhower was nearing the end of his second term, the first president whose tenure the Twenty-second Amendment restricted.[1]

However, it seemed unlikely that even if the Democrats' repeal effort had succeeded, Eisenhower would have sought a third term. As early as a 1957 news conference, he disclaimed interest. Responding to a press inquiry, the president stated, "Look, I will give you people a piece of news. They can repeal it (the Twenty-second Amendment) if they want to. I shall not run again."[2]

By the time he completed his second term, Eisenhower was 70 and not in robust health. The president had suffered three significant illnesses during his presidency,[3] and may not have been physically able to serve another term, even had he been willing to run.

Nevertheless, it was impossible to conceive of a stronger Republican candidate. In his absence, the probable Republican nominee in 1960 was his Vice President Richard Nixon. At that point, there was no record of a vice president successfully running to extend a party's tenure, since Vice President Martin Van Buren prevailed in the 1836 election to succeed President Andrew Jackson.[4]

Notwithstanding big GOP setbacks in the 1958 mid-term elections, Eisenhower remained well-liked by American voters.[5] Although his approval rating had declined to 52 percent at the time of the mid-terms, he had rebounded to 64 percent by August 1959.[6] Had he been eligible and willing, Eisenhower might well have won a third term.

As it was, the amendment disqualified a popular president from further election. Surely, Republicans could not have imagined these circumstances when they marched in unison to amend the Constitution. Was it possible that GOP "buyer's remorse" might generate broad bipartisan support for repeal?

At the start of January 1959, six House Democrats introduced repeal proposals.[7] Prime among them were those by House Judiciary Committee Chairman Emanuel Celler (D-NY), who sponsored H.J. Res. 139, and Representative Stewart Udall (D-AZ), who wrote H.J. Res. 124.[8]

On February 19, 1959, Celler convened a hearing before Subcommittee Five of the House Judiciary Committee. The subcommittee had "catch-all" jurisdiction. Celler used it for all legislation on which he wanted to take personal charge.[9]

In 1947, Celler had offered an amendment to H.J.Res. 527 to provide for a single six-year term. His proposal was a tactic to complicate passage, either in Congress or during state ratification, and it was soundly defeated. By the 1959 hearing, Celler dropped any pretense and simply announced openly his opposition to term limits. Referring to 1947, he stated, "Of course I did at that time advocate a one-term Presidency but I said it should be for a period of six years. Since then I have however, shall I say, grown a little intellectually. . . . I think many men of stature and importance have on one occasion advocated one side of an issue and then subsequently, when light has dawned, advocated the opposite, so I feel today that the Twenty-second Amendment should be cast into limbo."[10]

"I would be less frank not to make note of this point," Celler added "that the 80th Congress, controlled by the Republican Party, gave expression to its violence of feeling against Franklin Delano Roosevelt."[11]

Celler disparaged the 1947 proceedings. Congress acted "in haste," he noted, producing only "desultory debate" in both the House and the Senate, leading to "a conviction that this was not a matter of deliberate judgment but a verdict on a personality which dominated his age."[12]

The Chairman repeated the often-expressed argument that Americans had settled the term limit issue in 1940 and 1944, and that there had been no demand to revisit it when the Republicans moved ahead. "The Twenty-second Amendment bespeaks a distrust of the people," he charged.[13]

Celler construed that omitting term limits in the original Constitution was an act of great foresight, because the Framers understood that time and experience would demonstrate whether rotation or continuation better served the country.[14]

Americans had promptly grasped that Prohibition was an unworkable and unreasonable policy, and repealed it in little more than a decade. Might similar retrospection doom the Twenty-second Amendment, and within a like timeframe? Reprising the theme that it was motivated mostly by political vengeance, the Chairman concluded, "I believe it is time to recognize that animosity dictated this proposal and that good sense dictates its repeal."[15]

Two witnesses would appear that day before Subcommittee Five. They were Representatives Udall and Chester Merrow (R-NH). Before they testified, however, Celler read into the hearing record a telegram from former President Harry Truman. It stated, "February 16, 1959. Honorable Emanuel Celler, Chairman of the House Judiciary Committee. I just don't see how it will be possible for me to be present with you tomorrow or the next day. I regret it very much. I have never thought well of the Twenty-second Amendment. It seems to me that it ranks along with the Eighteenth and one or two others that have not been thoroughly considered when the public interest is at stake. Signed Harry S. Truman."[16]

Representative Udall was the first witness. Entering Congress in 1955, Udall had already emerged as a leading advocate for repeal. To build a case, he had worked with the American Political Science Association and the American Historical Association to survey eminent scholars on whether the country should retain or scrap the Twenty-second Amendment. Udall had solicited the views of thirty-seven professors. Of that group, twenty-six responded substantively. Within academic circles, the amendment did not sit well. Twenty-one of the professors favored repeal and five opposed it.[17]

Udall placed their responses in the hearing record. Here quoted is a representative sample, beginning with scholars who supported repeal. They saw the amendment as diminishing the presidency by imposing, as a matter of certainty, lame-duck status on a second-term incumbent.[18] As well, they considered it a repudiation of democracy, an ill-considered effort to save voters from themselves, and an unnecessary artifact to protect the country from dictatorship.

Opponents of repeal worried that doing so could be construed as approving of future third term bids, rather than just removing a barrier to them. They worried about presidents manipulating or exaggerating conditions to justify continuity in office. They were not much concerned that lame-duck status would unduly hamstring a term-limited president. Some presidents, such as Polk or Hayes, had declared early in their term that they would not seek reelection, and others, such as McKinley or Theodore Roosevelt, openly disclaimed a third term. All these presidents were openly lame ducks, but none seemed to have been diminished in office. Repeal opponents went on to note that other important variables affected the success of a president in his final term. These include factors such as the makeup of Congress, the political environment, international conditions, and characteristics of the person serving as president.[19]

PROFESSORS SUPPORTING REPEAL

Clinton Rossiter, Chairman of the Department of Government, Cornell University:

> Although it is still too early to make this point with certainty, it very probably has weakened the office of the Presidency permanently. Everything in our history tells us that a President who does not or cannot seek reelection loses much of his grip in his last couple of years, and we no longer can afford Presidents who lose their grip. Although we may have to wait many years, and I hope the wait is even longer, we may live to regret this amendment bitterly in a time of severe national emergency.

James McGregor Burns, Department of Political Science, Williams College.[20]

> The Amendment is an artificial and dangerous interference with the basic principles of our constitutional system. That system . . . assumes that the President . . . will serve as the integrating and energizing force in Government. This was the plan of the Framers of the Constitution and the system has worked well. . . . Any attempt artificially to limit Presidential tenure is to weaken the great role that the Framers planned for the President.

Henry Steele Commager, Department of History, Amherst College.

> I opposed the Twenty-second amendment when it was proposed and I have been a consistent critic of it since it was ratified. It was, as President Eisenhower said, an act of retroactive vindictiveness. . . . The fundamental, and to my mind, irrefutable criticism of the Twenty-second Amendment is that it represents a vote of no confidence in democracy. . . . The only time the American people have ever had a chance to vote on the question, namely in 1940 and 1944, they voted overwhelmingly in favor of more than two terms. The vote of the state legislatures, therefore, is an act of defiance of the American public.

Arthur M. Schlesinger, Jr., Harvard University.

The notion that unlimited Presidential re-eligibility threatens dictatorship is in my judgment chimerical. It did not do so in the 150 years of American history before the adoption of the Twenty-second Amendment. It should be noted that our northern neighbor, Canada, has had the same man as Prime Minister for a total of more than 20 years without suffering any notable diminution in the rights and freedoms of the people. If we get dictatorship in the United States it will come not because public officials can be re-elected to office, but because of far more fundamental breakdowns of Government. To suppose that the Twenty-second Amendment has blocked up what otherwise might be an invitation to totalitarianism is to accept a most superficial view of the origins of totalitarianism.

Cortes A.M. Ewing, Department of Government, University of Oklahoma.

Against this traditional American fear of tyranny stands the equally desirable principle that a President ought to be the first leader of the American people throughout his term as Chief Executive. After a President's second election, everyone knows that he cannot be elected for a third time and the inevitable jockeying among presidential aspirants occurs. Real leadership passes from the President. Politically, he becomes an elder statesman while still occupying the Presidential office. This situation unquestionably handicaps the Administration in its plain responsibility to secure the adoption of its legislative program. . . . The prime desideratum is to achieve optimum leadership throughout the term for which the President is elected.

PROFESSORS OPPOSING REPEAL:

Carl B. Swisher, Department of Political Science, Johns Hopkins University.

While I think it is unfortunate that the political power of President Eisenhower should be currently limited by the knowledge that he cannot constitutionally be re-elected for a third term . . . the price is one that we may have to pay for the unwise abandonment of the third term tradition in 1940. . . . Now that we have the Twenty-second Amendment, the repeal of which would imply much more in the way of approval of multiple terms than many of us would wish to give, I am inclined to believe we should live with the Amendment and make the best of it. . . . The theory of indispensability is always suspect, and I doubt the advisability of taking now a step that would be interpreted as giving far more than I believe the people want to give in the way of approval of re-election for multiple consecutive terms.

Thomas S. Barkley, Professor Emeritus, Department of Political Science, Stanford University.

> The experience under the operation of the Twenty-second Amendment has not been of sufficient length to supply conclusive evidence of either the necessity or desirability of repealing it. . . . A President can create or utilize emergencies in order to maintain that it is necessary to keep himself and his party in power. . . . It is true that a President . . . must face during the last two years of his administration a waning of his influence over Congress and elsewhere. If permitted to seek a third or a fourth or a fifth term, he would face the same difficulty at a later time. . . . The assertion that the people should be permitted to retain in office for more than two terms a President seems singularly unconvincing. . . . Constitutional restrictions on governmental power, and most statutory law, prevent people from doing what they might wish to do.[21]

Udall resumed his testimony. While Americans agreed in principle with the two-term limit, it was an artifice that voters should have flexibility to sidestep if circumstances dictated. It was exactly what happened in 1940, Udall observed. He cited a Gallup Poll taken in May of that year that gave Roosevelt only 37 percent of the vote against a generic Republican candidate. Then, conditions in Europe markedly worsened and public opinion reversed. Particularly disconcerting was the surrender of France.[22] "My opinion is that except for the world crisis, Mr. Roosevelt would have been defeated in 1940," Udall opined.[23] It should be the people's right to size up the situation and decide who was best to lead, Udall insisted.

"The only way under our system that the people can express their view on the third term question is at a national election," he said.[24] The Roosevelt elections altered the unwritten constitution, that body of custom and practice that provides mortar between the legal bricks. But that is how the public wanted it. When amending the Constitution, Members of Congress and state legislators purported to represent constituents, but it seemed obvious to Udall that they did not.

Udall referred to Truman's 1952 retirement announcement. It was obvious, Udall said, that Truman wanted to defer lame-duck status for the maximum time. He could do so because the Twenty-second Amendment grandfathered him, but successor presidents would suffer. "Under the Twenty-second Amendment, the powers of the Presidency are permanently weakened. I think the President is a political eunuch as a result of this Amendment."[25]

Diminution of the presidency was not something to celebrate, Udall insisted. While some in Congress might welcome it, believing their power would grow proportionately, he was not among them. "I do not happen to think we are living in a time when we can afford Congressional governance. I am in favor of strong Presidents at this time."[26]

Representative George Meader (R-MI)[27] asked Udall whether the Amendment was beneficial as a barrier to dictatorship. Udall thought not, believing that such claims relied on fearmongering. "It seems to me we have three great checks against dictatorship that make us almost impregnable," he replied. "First is the Congress, second is the Constitution as expounded by the Supreme Court, and third and most importantly is the power of the people speaking at elections. I think these checks were designed to give us several avenues whereby we might combat excesses, and I think the people have done a pretty good job at checking 'dictators' by exercising these powers."[28]

Representative Merrow was the day's final witness. He argued that the Twenty-second Amendment inherently damaged the presidency. "After his election for a second term, a President's prestige, influence, and political power have a tendency to decline, not because of his fault but because under the Constitution, as amended, he cannot be a candidate for the Presidency again."[29]

Several times, Merrow stressed, President Eisenhower expressed his displeasure with the amendment. In a 1956 press conference, Eisenhower indicated that it was "not wholly wise." Merrow explained the president's thinking. "The reason he gave at that time was that the people are restricted in the choice of a leader and it was his feeling that they should elect or select anyone for President they want, no matter what the terms may be."[30]

Three years later, in a 1959 press conference, reporters again asked Eisenhower about this subject. Merrow recounted the president's remark. "If I were asked to give an opinion officially on this now," said the president, "I would say I would rather see it repealed than be kept."[31]

Merrow continued, "In your opening remarks, Mr. Chairman, you read a telegram from former President Truman. So now with President Eisenhower on the record this would seem to be a bipartisan effort to make this needed correction in the Constitution."[32]

Continuing his questioning, Meader noted that a number of presidents declared early in their first term that they did not expect to stand for a second. Had such declarations weakened them in office? Merrow responded that such history was not especially instructive. The Twenty-second Amendment presented a different situation, because a president had no ability to reverse and seek reelection, and because it converted second term incumbents into instant and irretrievable lame ducks. "There was no prohibition, even though the president said he was not going to run, there was nothing to prevent him from changing his mind if the people wished to select him to run again."[33]

Merrow concluded his testimony by reinforcing Udall on the imperative to have a strong president, because Congress was institutionally incapable of providing sustained, unified leadership in his stead. "The Congress particularly, and the state legislatures, as you well know, have a leadership which is splintered . . . and I have oftentimes felt that the Executive who makes the most outstanding record is the one who exercises strong leadership. I do not fear the system we have. I do not entertain the fear that the Executive would become too powerful under our system."[34]

Celler gaveled the hearing to a close. His Committee took no further action on this subject during the 86th Congress.

On the morning of Monday, May 4, 1959, in the Senate Caucus Room, Senator Estes Kefauver convened companion proceedings before the Subcommittee on Constitutional Amendments of the Senate Judiciary Committee. The subject was S.J.Res. 11, a repeal resolution Senator Thomas Hennings (D-MO)[35] introduced, and which Kefauver cosponsored along with Senators John Pastore (D-RI) and Philip Hart (D-MI).[36]

The Hennings resolution amended the Constitution to repeal the Twenty-second Amendment, and allowed seven years for ratification. Present at the hearings were senators Kefauver, Hennings, Langer, and Dirksen.

"Although adoption of the Twenty-second Amendment may have had some partisan overtones," Kefauver began, "its repeal has none."[37] He claimed that both presidents Truman and Eisenhower endorsed repeal.[38] Truman was already on record with his statement to the House committee, so Kefauver properly characterized the former president's views. But what about Eisenhower?

In public comments early in 1959, the sitting president had also been skeptical about the Amendment. At a press conference on January 21, 1959, Pat Munroe of the *Chicago American* asked Eisenhower about the Twenty-second Amendment. "Mr. President, we know that the anti-third-term amendment can't be repealed in time to change your plans for retiring next year, but you have described it as being perhaps not wholly wise. I wonder if you favor current efforts in Congress to repeal this Amendment?" Eisenhower answered, "I would rather see it repealed than be kept."[39]

However, during press conferences on May 5 and 13, 1959, Eisenhower shifted from endorsing repeal in principle to emphasizing that Congress should take no action.[40] This coalesced with his Administration's view that the Amendment had been in effect too briefly to evaluate whether or not the country should retain it.[41]

Attorney General William Rogers reinforced that wait-and-see perspective in a June 5, 1959, letter to Kefauver. "Without now discussing the intrinsic merits of either the Twenty-second Amendment or the instant resolution, it is to be noted that the Amendment has been in effect during the term of only one President—too short a period of time fairly to test its efficacy. It would seem wise, therefore, to defer any legislative action in regard to the Amendment to permit further experience thereunder. Accordingly, the Department of Justice is unable to recommend adoption of the joint resolution."[42]

Kefauver was disappointed. In a June 12, 1959, reply to the Attorney General, the senator stated, "A few months ago, it seemed that the President favored repeal of the two-term limitation, although he made perfectly clear that the Amendment's possible repeal would have no bearing on his personal plans for retirement. The President's position at the time coincided with mine, and, naturally, I was quite pleased with his several expressions on the subject. Needless to say, I regret that he has changed his mind."[43]

Continuing his opening statement, Kefauver condemned the 1947 effort as hasty and ill-conceived. "There was an indecent amount of debate on it in both Houses,"[44] he claimed, citing in particular the rule limited general debate in the House to two hours.

It was correct, said the senator, that a number of state constitutions limited terms for Governors. However, they restricted the number of consecutive terms a chief executive could serve, rather than imposing an absolute limit. "No state constitution is as inflexible as the Twenty-second Amendment," he charged.[45]

A president is leader of his party, Kefauver noted. This important role was diminished when the incumbent became an automatic lame duck. "Although Franklin Roosevelt was the first President to win a third term, several Presidents, including Ulysses Grant and Theodore Roosevelt tried and were unsuccessful.[46] A number of others held back the announcement of their decision not to run until very near election time. It was the possibility that they might seek another term than left them in control of their party during their second term."[47]

Eisenhower was the first president to govern under the new constitutional restrictions. The amendment had weakened him, Kefauver alleged. The possibility of renomination "would have given him much needed strength—both at home and abroad—during his current term of office."[48]

Critics of repeal argued that it was premature, because it was too early to know if it had been harmful. Kefauver strongly disagreed. The country could not afford to wait for a crisis to find out. The process of fixing a constitutional mistake was too slow. "If the Amendment's pernicious effects became obvious only in a crisis, it would then be too late to remedy the situation."[49]

Kefauver's witness that morning was former President Harry S. Truman. "My position on this question is a very simple one," Truman began. "This is a bad amendment and it ought to be repealed."[50]

The Framers declined to impose term limits, said Truman, because they wanted to retain flexibility to respond to emergencies. He quoted a 1788 speech before the South Carolina House of Representatives by Charles Cotesworth Pinckney, a delegate to the Constitutional Convention. "His term of service might expire during the raging of a war, when he might, perhaps, be the most capable man in America to conduct it," Pinckney stated, "and would it be wise and prudent to declare in our Constitution that such a man should not again direct our military operations, though our success might be owing to his abilities?"[51]

Term limits had only been considered as a way to promote executive independence. Once the Framers settled on the device of the Electoral College to choose a president, they had found a better way, and dispensed with them. Truman quoted Pinckney, "The mode of electing the President rendered undue influence almost impossible; and it would be imprudent of us to have put it out of our power to re-elect a man whose talents, abilities, and integrity were such as to render him the object of the general choice of his country."[52]

Truman continued that the two-term tradition had served the country well for most of American history, but the Constitution had permitted custom to be set aside when the situation dictated. The value of that flexibility was vivid when Americans retained Roosevelt in 1940 and 1944. "To me, his re-election, which made it possible for him to lead us to victory in World War II, proves more than ever how wise the Framers of the Constitution were in 1787."[53]

According to Truman, during the 80th Congress "the Roosevelt haters got busy and sold the country a bill of goods." What they accomplished, however, "instead of hurting Roosevelt, was to make a 'lame duck' out of every second-term President for all time in the future."[54]

The Presidency is an immense and almost impossible job, Truman noted. To perform effectively, the incumbent "needs all the prestige, all the position of leadership, that it is possible for him to have."[55] Converting a second-term president into a lame duck from the moment of his reelection was utterly counterproductive, Truman insisted.

> "You do not have to be very smart to know that an officeholder who is not eligible for re-election loses a lot of influence. . . . You have sent him out to fight with one hand tied behind his back, because everyone knows he cannot run for re-election."[56]

Truman's position did not actually contradict his philosophical support for an eight-year limit. However, he considered rotation should be voluntary, not mandated. To avoid the debilitating effects of lame-duck status, he also believed in holding open the prospect of a third-term candidacy as long as possible. It is what he had done in 1952.

The former president had an exchange with Senator Everett Dirksen (R-IL).[57] As a Congressman in 1947, Dirksen had sponsored an amendment providing for a single six-year term. By 1959, he appeared to have changed his mind. He told Truman, "Mr. President, it has occurred to me that when we write into the Constitution restrictions upon the people instead of upon government, it isn't very long before we get around to taking them out of the Constitution again."[58]

Dirksen asked if Truman believed there was sufficient public support for repeal. The volume and content of Congressional mail didn't seem to disclose it, the senator noted. Truman responded that there was latent public concern that could stir if repeal advocates would launch a broad and persistent education program, "That is all you need to do with the repeal of the Twenty-second Amendment. You may not get it repealed at this time, but you should keep working on it." If Congress approved repeal, Truman believed the states would shortly concur.[59]

As the hearing was ending, Senator Langer interjected, "Summing up your testimony, it amounts to this: that you believe that in any emergency, you can always trust the people." Truman replied, "I do; I do; I always believed that, and you can."[60]

Truman's appearance before the subcommittee lasted thirty-five minutes. When the president was finished, Kefauver recessed the committee indefinitely.

On September 1, 1959, the subcommittee approved Kefauver's legislation,[61] but there was no further action in that Congress in full committee or on the floor, notwithstanding lots of activity during that Congress on other constitutional issues.[62] Opposition from the Eisenhower Administration, and disinterest from full Judiciary Committee Chairman James O. Eastland (D-MS)[63] served to sidetrack the 1959 repeal effort on the Twenty-second Amendment. For advocates of repeal, the 86th Congress (1959–1960) was the high water mark. Never again would repeal get even so much as a hearing.

As a follow-up, and parallel to Representative Udall's work, Kefauver sent a July 30, 1959, letter to some 350 heads of political science departments affiliated with the American Political Science Association. By December 8, 1959, sixty-two professors responded to the Senator. Of these, fifty-three favored repeal, eight opposed it, and one respondent was neutral. The committee printed responses in Part 2 of the 1959 hearings.[64]

Scholars favoring repeal focused on what the amendment had done to upend the unwritten Constitution. Custom and usage were a crucial aspect of self-governance. To provide for the Nation in a time of emergency, the public had seen fit to depart from tradition. The amendment would deny future generations that privilege, regardless of conditions. Moreover, the professors claimed, the role of the president as a party leader was central to the political system, but the amendment diluted it. The amendment, they observed, made the presidency smaller at a moment when the country needed strong executive leadership.

Opponents claimed that the Twenty-second Amendment enshrined vital principles from the now-discarded two-term tradition, helped restore proper balance between the three branches of government, and diminished the likelihood of Executive overreach.

PROFESSORS SUPPORTING REPEAL

Rowland Egger, Chairman, University of Virginia Department of Political Science.

> It is said that the Twenty-second Amendment merely enacts a tradition that prevailed inviolate until the time of President Franklin D. Roosevelt. That is true and that is the Amendment's fatal weakness. The two-term tradition, as a usage of the Constitution is an admirable component of our system of government. The two-term rule, as a constitutional amendment, is a monstrosity. . . . The traditions are strong precisely because their sanctions rest on a higher law than the Constitution—the instinct of the people for national survival. They can be departed from when survival is threatened and returned to when security is restored.[65]

Joseph LaPolombara, Department Head, Department of Political Science, Michigan State University.

> The distrust of democracy injected in the Amendment is dangerous because it assumes that the purpose of the Constitution is that of restricting or denying the rights of American citizens rather than extending rights and privileges to them. . . . The Amendment seriously impedes the effectiveness of an American party system. . . . A President who is serving in his second (and last) term is not likely to be able to exercise the kind of leadership over his party that he should if there is going to be any coordination at all between the programs of the Executive Branch and legislative enactments. . . .The Amendment weakens the Chief Executive in an age when strong and vigorous executives tend to be the rule rather than the exception around the world. . . . Constitutional provisions in and of themselves are not likely to prevent a democratic system from falling to dictatorial sources. Rather, we must trust in the strength of our basic democratic values and in the willingness of the people to be sufficiently flexible to assure the survival of the Nation.[66]

Morton Tenzer, Department of Government, Wesleyan University.

> The President is the leader of his political party. While the Constitution does not mention this function, it is at the present time perhaps the most important aspect of the Presidential office. The Twenty-second Amendment, vindictively and foolishly aimed at the career of President Franklin D. Roosevelt, has the effect of weakening the President in this most important function of party leadership. . . . It is remarkable that so many years after the Congress and the people eliminated the notorious "lame-duck" aspect of Congressional service through a constitutional amendment, that an amendment was added which in effect makes a President in his second term of office a "lame-duck."[67]

Edgar W. Waugh, Professor of Political Science, Eastern Michigan University.

> The Twenty-second Amendment is a dead hand ever threatening to fall athwart of the Nation with its ghastly and chilling effect. It cannot recognize crisis. . . . It would reach equally a Neville Chamberlain and a Winston Churchill. It would cut off the service of the one as arbitrarily and as precipitately as that of the other, in time of peace and war, victory or defeat, national well-being or catastrophe alike. . . . The proposed Amendment was submitted to state legislatures rather than state conventions for ratification. Thus, ratification took place with hardly a modicum of public notice and little pretense at discussion among the people. . . . Many thought we were making sort of a posthumous apology to George Washington for disregarding his warning and, of course, nothing could be further from the truth. The Twenty-second Amendment is a patent repudiation of the views of Washington and a permanent injunction against the judgment of the American people.[68]

Arguments against repeal focused on the importance of the two-term limit, when imposed by tradition or by Amendment. Before Roosevelt, that tradition was so well entrenched that there was no expectation that a president would seek a third term. Therefore, the second termer was effectively a lame duck, even if the held the public in some measure of suspense by formally declaring it. "Trust in democracy" was a nice-sounding concept, said Waugh, that did not reflect the structures or values of the American system. Not only was the United States a republic and not a democracy, but the Constitution contained express limitations on the capacity of majorities simply to impose their will or infringe on the rights of others.

PROFESSORS OPPOSING REPEAL

Avery Leiserson, Chairman, Department of Political Science, Vanderbilt University.

> I favor the two-term tradition, which, as I understand it, is almost completely incorporated in article XXII. Whether or not we were mistaken to adopt the Twenty-second Amendment, as I believe we were, now that it is part of the written document, we must face the question of the effect of the repeal on that constitutional expectation. . . . It seems to me highly problematical as to whether the Amendment is any more weakening than was the unwritten understanding before its adoption.[69]

Gilbert L. Lycan, Chairman, Department of History and Political Science, Stetson University.

> Our system of government is endangered if any man holds the Presidency for more than eight years. His appointment of federal judges may warp the courts. Similar damage may result from his influence on other Federal departments, commissions, boards, and bureaus. . . . I see little substance in Commager's reported statement that the Twenty-second Amendment 'represents a vote of no confidence in democracy.' One of the basic principles of a Constitution is to establish fundamental rules and principles that are hard for people to change—principles that with withstand a temporary—or faddish—demand of the people.

Repeal went nowhere in 1959, but the issue would periodically resurface in the years that followed. Gradually, the public seemed to view it more as a device to strengthen presidential power than one to expand voter choice.[70] Recast that way, it was less alluring. Proponents such as Celler and Kefauver left Congress, as did other veterans of the 1947 Amendment fight, and no strong advocates replaced them. Discussion of repeal became rare and theoretical, not exciting very much interest in Congress or in the general public.

Beginning in the middle 1980s, Representative Guy VanderJagt (R-MI)[71] led the one more high-profile attempt at repeal. It built off the political popularity of Ronald Reagan, who was set to become the first president since Dwight Eisenhower to retire based on the amendment. In July 1986, VanderJagt sent a letter to some 300,000 Reagan supporters. "Ronald Reagan is one of the greatest Presidents of all time and I want to keep him on the job," VanderJagt wrote.[72] The letter was a fundraising appeal, which he augmented by introducing repeal legislation in the House. He renewed such legislation several times thereafter. VanderJagt's efforts inside Congress never got off the ground.

President Reagan forswore interest in a third term for himself, but he otherwise supported repeal. In a November 1987 interview with British television personality David Frost, he denounced the amendment as an infringement on voter choice. The President indicated he would lead a repeal movement as soon as he left office. "I would like to start a movement to eliminate the constitutional amendment that was passed a few years ago that limits a president to two terms. Now I say I wouldn't do that for myself but for Presidents from here on."[73]

Reagan returned to this theme in a January 18, 1989, interview with Tom Brokaw of NBC News. The president would be leaving office in two days, and was contemplating one of the purposes to which he would dedicate his post-presidential years. Reagan said, "This is the only office that is elected by all the people. I think that is an infringement on the democratic rights of the people. And now that I'm out of office, so that they can't accuse me of wanting to do it for myself, I'm going to see if I can't mobilize the people to demand the repeal of that Amendment. It is an invasion of their democratic rights to vote for whomever they want to vote for and for however long."[74]

In 1990, Reagan contributed to a set of essays prepared at the National Legal Center for the Public Interest. They were collated into a book titled, *Restoring the Presidency: Reconsidering the Twenty Second Amendment.* Reagan's was the lead article.

Reagan stood the main premise of the Twenty-second Amendment on its head. While amendment advocates claimed it would restrain a dominant presidency, Reagan argued it went too far in the other direction. Before 1951, elections would influence the balance of power between the Branches. Voters would elect strong leaders or lesser ones. They would return incumbents or pick someone new. But the amendment introduced the new element of mandatory rotation in office, cutting voters out of the decision and making every second-term president an automatic lame-duck. Reagan considered these outcomes both antidemocratic and an impairment of the office. "It had undermined necessary presidential power to conduct the great public business assigned to that office, while simultaneously denying the people their most hallowed democratic right of having whomever they desire hold their offices for as long as the people desire."[75]

National emergencies would periodically arise, Reagan pointed out. When they did, as happened in 1940, Americans must be able to rely on an experienced executive. The Twenty-second Amendment cut off this possibility. In 1947, John McCormack inveighed against the amendment's inflexibility. In 1990, Reagan echoed him.[76]

Although Republicans of the Eightieth Congress denied political motivation when they passed the Amendment, Reagan labeled it an "act of partisan pique." The consequences, observed Reagan, were to stifle voter choice and to impair the effectiveness of whomever they happened to elect.[77]

A term-limited president was inherently disadvantaged when doing battle with legislators who were not term-limited, Reagan argued. Presidents spoke for the country as a whole; Congress acted more parochially. This tension could be resolved in the public interest if the duration of a presidency was not artificially constrained. Otherwise, Members of Congress would be tempted just to wait a president out. The problem was particularly manifest on budget issues, Reagan said from experience. "From the moment of his second inauguration, a two-term president is increasingly a lame duck. Where Congress might yield on certain budget particulars if the president might hold his office indefinitely, there is not much incentive to yield to someone who is on his way out. As a result, the dialogue between the two Branches becomes strained, the politics grow ever more vituperative, and consensus more difficult."[78]

The presidency must be fortified, Reagan asserted, so that the Framers' vision for the office might be realized. "As it stands with the Twenty-second

Amendment, the constitutional field has been tipped and the president faces nothing but an uphill struggle. Repealing the Twenty-second Amendment would go far in restoring the political balance between the two Branches charged with policymaking under our Constitution."[79]

Reagan was never able to mount an effective attack on the Twenty-second Amendment. In November 1994, he disclosed that he had been diagnosed with Alzheimer's disease. Early that year, he ceased making public appearances. The former president died on June 5, 2004.

Over the years, the public grew as accustomed to the Twenty-second Amendment as they had the two-term tradition. Indeed, they seemed to view it as restoring a custom they abandoned for an emergency, but with which they otherwise felt innately comfortable. Opinion polls showed this; so did the absence of serious repeal efforts in Congress.

In 1964, the *Midwest Journal of Political Science* published an opinion survey about the Twenty-second Amendment. Pollsters conducted it just before the 1960 election with a sample of 1350 respondents in Detroit. The authors, Roberta S. Sigel and David J. Butler, chose that city because it was a Democratic stronghold, which had a tradition of reelecting mayors and governors. A survey there would test whether respondents considered the amendment partisan overreach, or construed it as reinforcing sound constitutional principles. The authors found no major differences between Republicans and Democrats. However, there were major distinctions between academic views, as expressed in the hearings, and those of the general public. Two-thirds of respondents favored retention of the amendment, and only 11 percent opposed a two-term restriction. This outcome closely correlated with a 1959 Gallup Poll in which 60 percent of respondents supported such term limits.[80]

While political and academic opponents of the Twenty-second Amendment complained about restricting voter choice, survey respondents believed that the Amendment actually protected voters. "The fear which is expressed is the fear of power and its abuse. . . . The fear is overwhelming that a President would become too powerful if continuously re-elected, that such concentration of power might lead to monopoly of power and possible dictatorship."[81]

With the public generally accepting the "term limits principle," Congress has put the issue to rest. Although Members have introduced in recent years many resolutions proposing constitutional amendments, these do not concern the Twenty-second Amendment. A review of activity over the past three Congresses bears this out. In the 113th Congress (2013–2015) there were eighty-nine joint resolutions about constitutional amendments. Several would have imposed congressional term limits; others would have abolished the Electoral College. However, only one, H.J.Res. 15 by Representative Jose Serrano (D-CA), would have repealed the Twenty-second Amendment. The 114th met from 2015 to 2017. There were seventy-nine proposals for constitutional amendments. None concerned the Twenty-second Amendment. In the 115th

Congress (2017–2019), Members made seventy proposals for constitutional amendments. Again, none touched the Twenty-second Amendment.

The amendment still sparks opposition in some quarters, but it has not been the focus of systemic reform in Congress. On Capitol Hill, attention is turned elsewhere, such as abolishing the Electoral College.[82]

In parliamentary systems, there is a ruling party, whether that party has an absolute majority in the legislature or governs by coalition. From within the legislature, the dominant party leader forms a government. It may serve for a term fixed by law but, in some structures, may fall sooner on a vote of no-confidence or due to an election that the executive calls within the term to maximize the chances that the ruling party may remain in power. There are no term limitations.

Presidential systems, like that of the United States, are different. The executive has independent constitutional authority and serves a fixed term. Countries with variants of this system have thought to contain executive power by restricting tenure. However, limits on executive power have not always withstood pressure to weaken or dispense with them. There are familiar rationales to do so. The nation is in crisis, the revolution is incomplete, the country is developing, no more experienced or able person is available; and thus, the leader must be retained.[83]

Once Franklin Roosevelt breached the two-term tradition, it would only be a matter of time before another unrestricted president sought to extend his tenure. It was tempting even for Harry Truman, himself a believer in the custom, because he could not identify a worthy successor. The Constitution was amended to constrain the ambitions of even the most honorable figures.

The two-term tradition lasted for 150 years. It was part of the unwritten constitution, a practice not commanded by law but embedded in how both candidates and voters conceived of the presidency. Trying to breach it, Ulysses Grant in 1880, Theodore Roosevelt in 1912, and even Calvin Coolidge in 1928 faced major political obstacles. They proffered rationales for why it did not apply or concocted the appearance of inescapable public demand for their candidacies. Without a genuine national emergency to justify their renewed or continued service, they failed. Franklin Roosevelt was also worried. Even after he settled upon a theory for a third term, he still felt the need to manufacture a Convention draft. Without the extraordinary conditions that existed in 1940, it is questionable that Roosevelt would have even sought a third term, much less been elected to one.

It is difficult to restore customs once discarded.[84] We may say this of the two-term tradition, if the principle were not written into law. Since ratification of the Twenty-second Amendment, America has had five two-term presidents. Perhaps Eisenhower and Reagan would have been too old to run again. However, that was not true of Bill Clinton, George W. Bush, and Barack Obama. Both Clinton and Obama were only fifty-four years old when they left the presidency. Bush was aged sixty-two. All were in good health. Each of those presidents took office knowing in advance of the Constitutional limits on their tenure. Suppose those restrictions did not exist? What might they have done?

Had any of them run again, would they have needed to argue extraordinary circumstances to justify it? That seems doubtful. The two-term tradition might have seemed like a political relic, perhaps useful in an earlier day, but long ago abandoned.

Franklin Roosevelt was a great leader and an outstanding wartime president. One could conclude that arguments against the third term, including warnings of dictatorship, proved exaggerated and hollow in his time. One could further surmise that the third term brought far greater benefits than harm to the country. As the *New York Times* editorialized on the day after the president died, "Men will thank God on their knees, a hundred years from now, that Franklin D. Roosevelt was in the White House, in a position to give leadership to the thought of the American people and direction to the activities of their government."[85]

FDR was a singular personality in a unique moment. But the exception does not necessarily prove the rule. Without the guardrails later imposed by the Twenty-second Amendment, Roosevelt's success in wartime may have opened the way to extended tenures that would be much less benign.

The presidency is an institution of extraordinary scope. Although the three branches of government are balanced within the Constitution, in many ways the president is first among equals. If permitted limitless tenure, a president's capacity to dominate policymaking would grow even more disproportional. Congress speaks with hundreds of voices; the president speaks with one. And in time, most of the judiciary would be his appointees, potentially weakening an essential check on his authority.

The Framers of the Constitution structured a government that no single part could dominate. A presidency unrestrained by term limits would put their theories under severe stress.

The foundation of the United States Constitution is robust checks and balances. Separation of powers prevents any one part of the government from becoming excessively dominant. By restricting accrual of authority in the presidency, and curbing his or her capacity to overshadow the other Branches, the Twenty-second Amendment undergirds this bedrock principle.

NOTES

1. In his book about the presidency, Reedy writes, "There arose a widespread, popular impression that presidents generally serve two terms. This concept is so

deeply ingrained that it was finally written into the Constitution, under the impression that it was a 'norm . . .' The Republican leadership of the Eightieth Congress lived to regret this constitutional amendment when it prevented Dwight D. Eisenhower from running for a third term, which he obviously could have won with ease." Reedy, p. 62.

2. W.H. Lawrence, "President Bars a 3d-Term Race Even if 'They Repeal' Ban on It," *New York Times*, January 31, 1957, p. 14. Eisenhower's view may not have been so rigid. Four years later, after Vice President Richard Nixon's defeat, Eisenhower mused that he would have considered a third term if he had been constitutionally eligible and had been able to foresee that Nixon would lose. Stathis, p. 77.

3. These included a heart attack in 1955, a bout of ileitis (intestinal inflammation) in 1956, and a stroke in 1957. "It should be mentioned that Eisenhower was re-elected under circumstances that led some to question his physical fitness to withstand the rigors even of a second term of office." Davis, p. 290.

4. Nixon lost in 1960, and there was not to be another until George H.W. Bush's victory in the 1988 election to follow President Ronald Reagan.

5. As a result of the 1958 mid-terms, Republicans declined from 201 members in the House of Representatives to 153, and from 47 senators to 34. However, one can look at Bill Clinton's reelection in 1996 and Barack Obama's in 2012 to see how a president can easily secure reelection only two years after devastating off-year elections for his party. In 1994, Democrats lost control of both the Senate and the House, and not a single Republican incumbent seeking reelection to Congress was defeated. In 2010, Democrats lost sixty-three seats and control of the House.

6. The public was especially approving of Eisenhower's August 3, 1959, announcement that Soviet Premier Nikita Khrushchev would be coming to the United States the following month at the President's invitation, and that Eisenhower himself planned to reciprocate with a 1960 visit to the USSR. Hitchcock, p. 451. Indeed, between 1951 and 1960, according to the Gallup Poll, Eisenhower was the most admired man in America. His average approval rating as president was 65 percent. Ibid., p. 244.

7. Davis, pp. 469–475. Two such proposals were introduced near the end of the 84th Congress in 1956, but were not considered. Five more were introduced in the 85th Congress (1957–1958). None received action, but Representative Stewart Udall (D-AZ), one such author, claimed he had initiated the process in order to have a focal point for discussion about the desirability of repeal. Stathis, p. 73.

8. Stewart Udall served as a Representative from 1955 to 1961 and then Secretary of the Interior from 1961 to 1969.

9. For example, when President Kennedy proposed civil rights legislation in 1963, Celler introduced it in the House. The speaker referred the bill, H.R. 7152, to the Judiciary Committee. Celler sent it to Subcommittee 5, where he undertook to strengthen it.

10. House Hearings 1959, p. 20. At the time Celler proposed his 1947 amendment, he had been in Congress for twenty-four years.

11. "Proposing an Amendment to the Constitution of the United States to Repeal the Twenty-second Amendment Thereto," Hearings before Subcommittee 5 of the House Committee on the Judiciary, February 19, 1959, pp. 3–4.

12. Ibid., p. 4.
13. Ibid.
14. Ibid., p. 5.
15. Ibid.
16. Ibid., p. 7. The Eighteenth Amendment prohibited the production, sale, and transport of alcohol in the United States. It passed Congress by the end of 1917 and was ratified in 1919. It took effect in 1920 after passage of implementing legislation, the Volstead Act. The Twenty-first Amendment repealed it in 1933.
17. Ibid., p. 8.
18. Professor David Crockett notes the anomaly that a president has maximum influence at the beginning of his first term, with a long tenure ahead, but at a time when he is least experienced to benefit from it. As the president's experience lengthens, his remaining time in office grows briefer. As well, attention begins to shift from the incumbent to the question of who might succeed him. Thus, a lame-duck president, "does not lack incentives to pursue bold projects—his desire to establish a legacy and reputation overrides the dampening effect of term limits—but the structure of the system works against that desire." Crockett, p. 713. Without the Twenty-second Amendment, these influence-robbing effects could be mitigated if there was a credible possibility an incumbent would seek a third term. It is impossible to know whether the public would by now be willing to accept that as normal, or whether Roosevelt would have been seen as an outlier, under peculiar circumstances unlikely to repeat. In any case, Crockett argues that diminution is more likely to occur on domestic issues, and that lame-duck presidents have exerted substantial force in foreign policy. Crockett, p. 714.
19. For example, Lyndon Johnson was a forceful personality with an ambitious program, and could have run again in 1968. Although unhampered by lame-duck status, Johnson was distracted by rampant divisions over the Vietnam War and was weakened by reduced Democratic majorities in Congress after the 1966 mid-term election. See also, Davis, p. 292.
20. Burns wrote two books on Franklin Roosevelt. These were *Roosevelt: The Lion and the Fox (1956*) and *Roosevelt: The Soldier of Freedom* (1971). The latter won the Pulitzer Prize as well as the National Book Award in History and Biography.
21. In 1979, Paul Davis looked at this hearing testimony and comments from additional scholars on both sides of the question. One expert he cited was James Hagerty, Eisenhower's Press Secretary, who testified in a 1971 hearing that the Twenty-second Amendment actually worked to the president's *advantage* because it diminished the political overtones that might otherwise have colored Administration actions. "Indeed," wrote Hagerty, "the President himself, in his second term, in reports to the people, pointed out many times that he was not a candidate for re-election, that what he was referring to were programs that were for the good of the country." Quoted in Davis, p. 295. Having reviewed the scholarship, Davis concluded, "there appears to be no unanimity of scholarly opinion as to whether the Twenty-second Amendment impeded, helped, or had no effect whatsoever on the Administration of Dwight Eisenhower." Ibid.
22. These same conditions helped propel the internationalist Wendell Willkie to the Republican nomination over isolationists like Taft, and, at the time, Dewey and

Vandenberg. It is said that Adolph Hitler nominated Willkie and elected Roosevelt, meaning that only that kind of extraordinary pressure could have provided incentive to breach the two-term tradition or to defy the isolationist bent of the Republican Party.

23. House Hearings, 1959, p. 13.

24. Ibid.

25. Ibid., p. 16.

26. Ibid., p. 18. As Udall spoke, the United States was in an existential struggle with the Soviet Union. That struggle would intensify during the Kennedy and Johnson years, during which Udall was in the cabinet as Secretary of the Interior. Regardless of one's views about term limits, and no matter how constructive Congress can be as a check and balance, Udall was surely right about the need for Executive leadership. Later in the hearing, in response to a question, Udall clarified that he did not mean for the strong presidency to come at Congress' expense. He was really making an argument for functional government, with the president at its head. "I think the stronger the President and the stronger the Congress the better. I am speaking in terms of leadership. But the President is the only person elected by all the people." Ibid., p. 28.

27. George Meader served in Congress from 1951 to 1965. In 1948, he lost a Republican primary to Representative Earl Michener, the Chairman of the House Judiciary Committee who managed House Floor proceedings on the Twenty-second Amendment.

28. House Hearings, 1959, p. 29.

29. Ibid., pp. 33–34.

30. Ibid., p. 34.

31. Ibid.

32. Ibid.

33. Ibid.

34. Ibid., p. 42.

35. Thomas Hennings served in the House from 1935 to 1940, and in the Senate from 1951 until his death in 1960.

36. John Pastore was a senator from 1950 to 1976. Philip Hart served in the Senate from 1959 until his death in 1976.

37. United States Senate Committee on the Judiciary, "Presidential Terms of Office," Hearings before a Subcommittee of the Committee on the Judiciary United States Senate, Eighty-sixth Congress, First Session, on S.J. Res. 11, Proposing an Amendment to the Constitution to Repeal the Twenty-second Article of Amendment to the Constitution, Part 1, Washington, DC, United States Government Printing Office, 1960, p. 2.

38. Indeed, during Eisenhower's reelection campaign in 1956, he opined that the public "ought to be able to choose for its president anybody it wants, regardless of the number of terms he has served." Quoted in Kyvig, p. 73.

39. Ibid., Appendix C, pp. 14–15.

40. Notwithstanding his earlier remarks, by May 5, 1959, the president was expressing a different position. Asked at a news conference about Truman's view that the amendment tied one hand behind an incumbent's back, Eisenhower said, "Well, I haven't sensed that particular feeling." He added, "on balance, the amendment gives

greater assurance to America than its repeal would." Ibid., p. 20. Asked again at a May 13, 1959, press conference, Eisenhower expanded on his revised views. "I think the Constitution is something that ought to be amended only after careful thought . . . so, as of now, I would say, let's let it lay on the shelf for a while and see how it works." Ibid., p. 21.

41. In his memoirs, Eisenhower wrote that he had, "come to believe, on balance, that the Amendment was good for the nation." Quoted in Stathis, p. 75. However, that is not exactly what Eisenhower told the press. He never expressed that the amendment was beneficial; rather, that it had not been in effect long enough to determine its effects.

42. Ibid.

43. Ibid., p. 22.

44. Ibid.

45. Ibid.

46. Neither Grant in 1880 nor Theodore Roosevelt in 1912 was seeking three consecutive terms.

47. S. Hearings, p. 2.

48. Ibid., p. 3.

49. Ibid., p. 3.

50. Ibid., p. 5.

51. Ibid., p. 6.

52. Ibid.

53. Ibid. Truman said this without equivocation of any kind. He apparently came to this conclusion in hindsight. In 1940, he opposed a third term for Roosevelt and endorsed Senator Bennett Clark (D-MO) for the Democratic nomination. Once the party convention nominated Roosevelt, Truman supported him in the general election.

54. Ibid.

55. Ibid., p. 7.

56. Ibid.

57. Everett Dirksen served in the House from 1933 to 1949, and in the Senate from 1951 to his death in 1969.

58. S. Hearings, p. 10. Dirksen was known for his willingness to change positions over time. "Life is not a static thing. The only people who do not change their minds are incompetents in asylums, who can't, and those in cemeteries. I try to be a realist and appreciative of what you have to do in the world in light of changing conditions." Interview with E.W. Kenworthy, *New York Times*, January 2, 1965, Dirksen Information File. In a similar vein, he noted, "I am a man of principle, and one of my principles is flexibility." Byron Hulsey, "Everett Dirksen on Record," The Dirksen Congressional Center. "Dirksen, who had voted for the amendment in 1947, was one of several members of the Senate Judiciary Committee who listened to Truman and then hurried to agree with him that term limits, like national prohibition, represented an undemocratic restriction on voters who could be trusted to make wise choices." Kyvig, p. 74.

59. Ibid., p. 11.

60. Ibid., p. 12.

61. The repeal proposal was packaged with a second constitutional amendment, which would have abolished the poll tax as a voting requirement in federal elections. The margin in the Kefauver subcommittee was five in favor, with only Senator James O. Eastland (D-MS) opposed. One member of the subcommittee, William Langer (R-ND), indicated that he actually was against repeal, but voted to report out the package so that the matter might be advanced for full Senate consideration. Inasmuch as Eastland chaired the full Judiciary Committee, the prospect for further proceedings on the repealer seemed dim. "Senate Unit Clears a Bill to Repeal 2-Term Rule," *New York Herald Tribune*, September 2, 1959, p. 12.

62. Kefauver's subcommittee reported S. J. Res. 39, a proposal he had authorized to empower Governors to appoint members of the House in the event of national disasters. On the Senate Floor, two other amendments were added. One, by Senator Spessard Holland, abolished use of the poll tax in national elections. A second, by Senator Kenneth Keating (R-NY) extended voting rights for District of Columbia residents in elections for president, vice president, and delegates to Congress. It passed the Senate on February 2, 1959. President Eisenhower endorsed this package and recommended two ideas of his own. One was to increase the term of House members from two to four years, the other was a presidential line-item veto for appropriations bills. "Ike Supports Senate Move for Suffrage: Urges Amendment to Increase Terms of House Members," *Washington Post Times Herald*, February 4, 1960, p. A1. Reaction in the House to the Senate-passed joint resolution was muted. For example, House Judiciary Committee chairman, Emanuel Celler, observed, "The Senate has just dumped this in our laps. They want to take the credit for doing something and leave us the hard work of unraveling all this and doing what is best for the country." In addition, Rules Committee Chairman Howard Smith (D-VA), whose committee had the power to advance or halt the package, strenuously opposed the poll tax amendment. Ibid. Accordingly, the House passed Celler's resolution, H.J. Res. 757, dealing solely with DC voting rights, then amended S. J. Res. 39 with the House proposal, and returned the measure to the Senate for further action. On June 16, 1960, the Senate agreed to the House amendment, ending legislative action on DC suffrage, and submitting such for ratification. The ratification process took slightly more than nine months. John R. Vile, *Encyclopedia of Constitutional Amendments, Proposed Amendments, and Amending Issues, 1789–2002*, 2nd ed. (Santa Barbara, California: ABC-CLIO, Inc., 2003), p. 480.

63. James O. Eastland served as a senator for three months in 1941, and then again between 1943 and 1978.

64. United States Senate Committee on the Judiciary, "Presidential Terms of Office," Hearings before a Subcommittee of the Committee on the Judiciary, United States Senate, Eighty-sixth Congress, First Session, on S.J. Res. 11, Proposing an Amendment to the Constitution to Repeal the Twenty-second Article of Amendment to the Constitution, Part 2, Washington, DC, United States Government Printing Office, 1960.

65. S. Hearings, 1959, Part 2, p. 9.

66. Ibid., pp. 17–19.

67. Ibid., pp. 23–24. Professor Tenzer was referring to the Twentieth Amendment, which adjusted the date of the presidential inauguration and the convening time for Congress. The Amendment was ratified in 1933. Under it, presidents are sworn in for the full four year term on January 20 following the election. Previously, the Inauguration was sworn on March 4. Congress convenes on January 3 (unless it appoints a different day). Previously, it convened on December 5 in the year after the election (unless it appointed a different day). The term of Congress expires at noon on January 3 following the election. Previously, it expired on March 4. Under the old system, Congress would return after the election for a "short session." In reality, it was not so short. Lame-duck lawmakers from the not-yet-expired Congress would sit for around four months, the period between the election and March 4. Professor Tenzer applauded the Twentieth Amendment for eliminating this lengthy interval.

68. Ibid., pp. 26–30.

69. Ibid., pp. 32–33.

70. Davis, p. 474.

71. Guy VanderJagt served in the House of Representatives from 1966 to 1993.

72. "Promoting Reagan for a Third Term," *New York Times*, July 22, 1986, p. A16, www.timesmachine.nytimes.com (accessed November 16, 2018).

73. Irvin Molotsky, "Reagan Wants End of Two-Term Limit," *New York Times*, November 28, 1987, p. 31, www.timesmachine.nytimes.com (accessed November 16, 2018).

74. "President Reagan Says He Will Fight to Repeal 22nd Amendment," *NBC Nightly News*, New York, NY: NBC Universal, January 18, 1989. NBC Learn: https://archives.nbclearn.com/portal/site/k-12/browse/?cuecard=3066 (accessed November 16, 2018).

75. Ronald W. Reagan, "Introduction," *Restoring the Presidency: Reconsidering the Twenty-second Amendment* (Washington, DC: The National Legal Center for the Public Interest, 1990), p. 1.

76. Reagan, p. 4.

77. Ibid.

78. Ibid., p. 13.

79. Ibid.

80. Roberta S. Sigel and David J. Butler, "The Public and the No Third Term Tradition: Inquiry into Attitudes Toward Power," *Midwest Journal of Political Science*, Vol. 8. No. 1 (Feb. 1964), pp. 39–54, http://www.jstor.org/stable/2108652 (accessed May 22, 2018).

81. Ibid., p. 44. Across party lines, approximately two-thirds of respondents approving the Amendment did so because they feared power being monopolized or because they believed in the benefits of change. Not even five percent of Republicans said they supported the amendment because Roosevelt was in office too long, and among Democrats that number was barely ½ of 1 percent. Among those who disapproved, two-thirds believed that voters should have the choice to elect a president as often as they pleased, or because the skills and experience of a president might be needed as his term expired. Again, this was a minority view. Ibid., pp. 46–47.

82. For example, in the first four months of 2019, three joint resolutions were introduced proposing to abolish the Electoral College.

83. For example, in 2018, China abolished outright its limit of two five-year terms for president, put in place after the Cultural Revolution. In 2008, Russia extended the presidential term from four to six years. While Russia limits a president to two consecutive terms, the change means twelve continuous years are possible, instead of eight. As well, Russia allows for a person to return to office after sitting out a term. It was the arrangement that Vladimir Putin exploited to return to the presidency in 2012 after serving as prime minister for four years under his hand-picked successor, Dmitry Medvedev. Under this system, Putin will have been Russia's elected leader for twenty of twenty-four years by the time he is due to step down in 2024. Since the time of the Russian Revolution a century ago, only Josef Stalin will have held power longer, and barely so. By referendum, Venezuela abolished presidential term limits in 2009, allowing Hugo Chavez to extend his rule indefinitely. In power since 1999, Chavez attempted in 2007 to perpetuate himself in office by changing the constitution. In a referendum held that year, he failed. Chavez conceded defeat, but made clear the setback was merely temporary. He persisted, pulling all necessary strings to prevail in the 2009 referendum. Freed of constitutional limitations, Chavez could have remained in office indefinitely. As matters turned out, he died on March 5, 2013, two months into his fourth term. He had ruled the country for fourteen years. See, generally, John Fund, "Scrapping Term Limits Fits the 'Dictator Forever' Model," *National Review* (February 25, 2018).

84. It is difficult to restore customs once abandoned. This is apparent to the author from decades of observing Congress. For nearly a half century after the Senate adopted the cloture rule to curtail filibusters, simple obstruction was uncommon, and cloture votes were rare. In recent years, filibusters have mushroomed, and cloture votes to combat them happen all the time. Until the twenty-first century, filibusters of judicial and executive nominees were essentially nonexistent. In the early 2000s, they emerged. Changes did not occur in the text of rules, but in the implementation and exploitation of those rules. Within a few years, the right to stop nominees by filibuster disappeared. In the House of Representatives, it used to be common for major legislation to come up under procedures called "open rules." This practice allowed for an unlimited number of germane amendments. Member self-restraint limited the quantity of amendments offered. Then, self-restraint began to slip away. In response, the number of "open rules" dwindled to nothing, and the House imposes amendment restrictions on major bills. None of the old practices, which long were reverently observed on Capitol Hill, is coming back.

85. "Franklin D. Roosevelt," *New York Times,* April 13, 1945, p. 16.

Appendix A

Hearings in the Senate Judiciary Committee (1940)

Edward Burke was a Nebraska Democrat. Voters sent the Harvard-educated lawyer to the Senate in 1934, after one term in the House. Burke stood fast for the New Deal, but he broke sharply with Roosevelt in 1937 on the president's effort to pack the Supreme Court. "I believe President Roosevelt, in 1932, was chosen by God to lead this people out of the Depression," said the senator, "but I believe that this (court) proposal strikes at the heart of democratic institutions"[1]

Frustrated by several court rulings against New Deal programs, FDR unveiled his court-packing idea on February 5, 1937. Roosevelt proposed that a president could appoint one additional justice for any justice over the age of 70 who refused to retire. The plan would permit the court to expand to a maximum of sixteen members.[2]

In a March 9, 1937, Fireside Chat, Roosevelt laid out his case. The president told listeners, "Last Thursday I described the American form of Government as a three-horse team provided by the Constitution to the American people so that their field might be plowed. The three horses are, of course, the three branches of government—the Congress, the Executive and the Courts. Two of the horses are pulling in unison today; the third is not. Those who have intimated that the President of the United States is trying to drive that team, overlook the simple fact that the President, as Chief Executive, is himself one of the three horses. It is the American people themselves who are in the driver's seat. It is the American people themselves who want the furrow plowed. It is the American people themselves who expect the third horse to pull in unison with the other two."[3] Many in Congress considered the president's plan as an attack on separation of powers and a weakening of checks and balances.

Although the Senate was overwhelmingly Democratic at that time, court-packing was deeply controversial on Capitol Hill. The general public shared this unease.[4] Industrious and indefatigable, Burke attacked the plan relentlessly. A newspaper profile at the time described the intensity of the senator's commitment. "He has had an important part in the selection of witnesses who have testified against the proposal and in the planning of the opposition's moves. He had frequently taken the lead in questioning witnesses who supported the President's plan. And he has shown marked industry in preparing for these examinations so that on several occasions he has produced magazine articles and books, written by the witnesses, which indicated that their past beliefs and statements on the Supreme Court were in complete disagreement with their present testimony."[5]

At the time of court-packing fight, Burke was midway through his freshman term in the Senate. In 1937, it was highly unusual for new senators to be so outspoken.[6]

In July, the Senate handed the resident a decisive rebuke, with many Democrats joining Burke's position.[7] Following a negative report from the Democratic-dominated Senate Judiciary Committee, Senator Burton Wheeler (D-MT)[8] led the opposition on the Floor. The tiny Republican caucus unified to oppose the plan, but was essentially helpless until sufficient Democrats, like Burke, coalesced against it.[9]

Notwithstanding extensive administration lobbying, including by the president himself, Roosevelt's reform collapsed on the Senate Floor on July 22, 1937. A successful motion was made to recommit the bill to the Senate Judiciary Committee with instructions to strip out the court-packing provisions. Only twenty senators opposed the motion. The seventy favorable votes included all the Republicans and conservative Democrats, but also a fair smattering of customary New Deal loyalists.[10] The reproach came notwithstanding immense Democratic majorities in both the Houses. After the 1936 election, there were seventy-six Democrats, sixteen Republicans, and four independents in the Senate. In the House, there were 333 Democrats, only eighty-nine Republicans, and thirteen Independents.

Shortly thereafter, FDR's executive reorganization proposal met its demise. Members opposed to both the court-packing and reorganization plans tied them together and condemned both as examples of gross presidential overreach.[11] Later, opponents of the third-term would reprise these themes.

Roosevelt stewed about his losses. He was livid, and remained upset for months.[12] When James Farley, Chairman of the Democratic National Committee, prepared a statement disclaiming administration or DNC intent to intervene in 1938 party primaries, Roosevelt disregarded him.[13] Angered by Democratic defections, and ignoring the advice of some of his top political advisers, the president wanted a purge so he could politically restructure the Democratic Party.[14] As Roosevelt scholar Susan Dunn notes, there was another side to the sunny, optimistic, ebullient FDR with which the public was well acquainted. It included a large capacity for vindictiveness.[15] Professor Arthur Schlesinger also comments on this aspect of Roosevelt's complex personality. "Beyond the screen, the real Roosevelt existed in mystery, even to himself. . . . Underneath, there remained the other man – tougher than the public man, harder, more ambitious, more calculating, more petty, more puckish, more selfish, more ambitious, more profound, more complex, more interesting. Only intimate friends saw Roosevelt in these aspects, and then in enigmatic and sometimes terrifying glimpses."[16]

Preferring a system in which there would be two highly distinctive and ideologically divergent parties, rather than one of diversity within both parties,[17] Roosevelt campaigned in 1938 to rid Congress of Democratic dissidents in the House and Senate.[18] Apart from his success in ousting House Rules Committee Chairman John O'Connor, FDR mostly came up short.[19] For example, the president failed to remove men such as Senators Walter George (D-GA), Guy Gillette (D-IA), Ed Smith (D-SC), and Millard Tydings (D-MD).[20]

Senator Burke was not up for reelection in 1938, but FDR loyalists set their sights on him in 1940. In the Nebraska Democratic primary, held on April 9, three-term Governor Roy L. Cochran defeated Burke.[21] The count was not close. Cochran received 84,869 votes to Burke's 60,400.[22]

More overtly than any other Congressional Democrat, Burke opposed a third term for Franklin Roosevelt. Freed from having to stand for reelection, and in contrast to other disgruntled Democrats,[23] Burke endorsed Republican Wendell Willkie for president.[24] However, that endorsement was only Burke's opening move.

Burke served on the Senate Judiciary Committee, which gave him a forum to explore the question of presidential term limitations. Reprising the persistence he exhibited during the court-packing fight, Burke exploited his position to the fullest. During September 1940, after the Senate returned from its summer recess, Burke convened the astounding number of 16 days of hearings, mostly held in a hearing room on the fourth floor of the Senate Office Building.[25] Altogether, forty-seven witnesses appeared.

The Senator was determined to prove that many Democrats believed, as he did, that the third term was anathema. Exposing fissures within the party, Burke generated a detailed, if imbalanced, record. Testimony was overwhelmingly from Democrats, some quite prominent, who shared his views. However, none was an incumbent officeholder. Near the end of the hearings, Burke extended an invitation to several third-term supporters, including his colleague, Senator George Norris (R-NE), but they declined to appear.

The Burke hearings present the fullest available array of arguments in favor of term limits. Witnesses voiced concerns that checks and balances were badly distorted, vital traditions were being discarded, or even that the country was on a path toward dictatorship. These fears can seem exaggerated today, but their expression should be considered in the context of the domestic and international situation prevailing in 1940. The hearings also laid a foundation for the bipartisan support needed to amend the Constitution after Republicans took control in 1947.

Pending before the subcommittee were two resolutions. S. J. Res. 15 provided for a single six-year presidential term, and would have barred anyone serving at the time of ratification from seeking reelection. Burke was its sponsor. It was subject to a seven-year ratification deadline. S. J. Res. 289, authored by Senator Styles Bridges (R-NH),[26] allowed for a maximum of two terms, and would have barred anyone from remaining president after ratification if he had served all or any part of two separate terms. It did not have a ratification deadline.[27]

HEARINGS COMMENCE: DAY ONE

At 10:30 AM on a blistering late summer Wednesday, Burke gaveled in the first of his hearings.[28] The site was the stately and imposing Caucus Room of the Senate Office Building.[29] It was September 4, 1940. Attending for the subcommittee were senators Burke, Frederick Van Nuys (D-IN),[30] Warren Austin (R-VT),[31] and Alexander Wiley (R-WI).[32] On questions such as the third term or the court-packing plan, none of those senators was Roosevelt's friend.

Burke delivered opening remarks, intended to establish him as a longstanding advocate for presidential term limits. The Senator noted that as far back as January 1937, the same month as the second Roosevelt inauguration, he introduced a constitutional amendment that provided for one six-year presidential term. The Judiciary Committee did not act at the time, because it was preoccupied with the court-packing plan. When the next Congress opened in 1939, Burke introduced the identical resolution. This time, full Committee Chairman Henry Ashurst (D-AZ)[33] appointed a special subcommittee, with Burke as Chair, to consider the issue. The subcommittee had five members, the four senators present at that morning's hearing plus Senator Tom Connally (D-TX).[34]

In July 1939, Burke's subcommittee favorably reported S.J. Res. 15, his resolution for a single six-year term. However, the full committee did not act on it.[35] A year later, the Democratic Convention put Roosevelt up for a third term, training intense public focus on the issue of term limits.

"We meet, therefore, to consider the views of witnesses on any side of the question of limitation on the tenure of office of the President of the United States," Burke announced. The subcommittee would review "limitation to one term of any specified duration, limitation to two terms, or no limitation at all; limitation by constitutional amendment, by tradition, or in any other manner."

Burke's first witness was Thomas Jefferson Coolidge, a lineal descendent of President Thomas Jefferson.[36] Coolidge served as Under Secretary of the Treasury during FDR's first term. He noted that during much of the Constitutional Convention, the Framers were committed to a system in which Congress elected the president once, to a single seven-year term. However, delegates worried that in a system in which one branch elected another, there would not be sufficient separation between them. This problem would be worse if a president was dependent on Congress for reelection. To safeguard against subordination of the executive to the legislature, they would bar a president from eligibility to a second term.

Ultimately, the Framers decided to eliminate election by Congress and instead to entrust it to a group of independent and eminent electors, designated by state legislatures.[37] Having assured executive independence, delegates shortened the president's term and permitted his reelection.

However, the emergence of political parties, with the president in command of one of them, undermined the independence of the Electoral College. "The president, instead of being apart from the Congress, became the leader of a Party with necessarily great influence over the members of his Party in Congress," Coolidge noted. "Had this result been foreseen, it would seem reasonable to suppose that the same limitation of one term, as made when the election was to be by Congress, would have been placed in the Constitution."[38]

To mitigate this unforeseen problem of presidential dominance, Coolidge asserted, the Constitution must be amended. "We see the power of the President magnified out of all resemblance to what was originally intended. He has become the leader of the dominant party. His Government has taken over the duties of local and state governments. The Executive Branch has been given enormous sums to spend directly on individual citizens. To offset this great increase in power, which itself may be used to perpetuate the ruler, it certainly would seem wise to limit the time one man may exercise it by constitutional amendment."[39]

The next witness was James Truslow Adams, a Pulitzer Prize-winning scholar. Unable to attend in person, Adams submitted a statement for the record. During colonial times, Adams wrote, the Crown appointed governors, fomenting significant distrust of Executive power. This sentiment permeated in the Constitutional Convention. The Framers worried that an executive invested with too much authority or too long a tenure might become a *de facto* monarch.[40] "It was for that reason that many of the most important powers of government were given to the Congress and not to the President," Adams explained.[41] As a further check, the Framers created the Electoral

College. "His powers were not only to be well limited, but he was not to be elected directly by the people."[42]

However, this careful balance had gone awry. The executive had become a Goliath in proportion to the other branches. It was improbable that the Framers would be pleased. Had they been able to foresee it, Adams speculated, the Constitutional Convention "would undoubtedly have taken a very different turn and both his powers and length of service would have been further curtailed."[43]

In the United States and elsewhere, there had been a disturbing trend to one-man government, claimed Adams. "It is a tide which has gained amazing speed and momentum and threatens to engulf the entire world." In such a climate, restraints on power would not occur naturally. More likely, the opposite would occur. "If we break with usage and tradition and allow a man to retain such powers for 12 years instead of eight, why not for 16, 20, or for life?" Adams added wistfully, "Our world is changing fast and it can always be said that there is a crisis."[44]

Believing that old bulwarks needed reinforcement, and that no leader was indispensable, Adams endorsed a limit of two four-year terms.

The day's final witness was William Alfred Eddy, president of Hobart, and William Smith Colleges in Geneva, New York. Eddy supported Burke's single-term resolution, on the basis that a single term would divorce a president from politics, and lend dignity and majesty to the office. "No President while in office should be the leader of his political party as well as the leader of the Nation. The solemn responsibilities to which he is elected, to promote the general welfare, demand all the time and energy of which he can dispose, and they are incompatible with the party purpose of wresting power from the opposition."[45]

The senators on Burke's committee were skeptical that a president could or should be separate from active politics. Even a lame-duck president, whether serving one term or the last of two terms, would need to marshal forces in Congress and the country to bolster his policies.

Believing Eddy naïve, they preferred a solution that acknowledged the inherently political nature of the presidency, but also capped service to prevent undue accumulation of power. The Bridges' two-term limit resolution appeared to serve the purpose. "I think when you come to the end of the second term, we must make a change or else we are really changing our form of government right at that juncture," said Senator Warren Austin. "Regardless of what the emergency is, I want to see it stopped there."[46]

Senator Van Nuys added that imposing term limits was not inconsistent with freedom of franchise. His remarks contradicted a core Democratic argument that restrictions unreasonably burdened voter choice. Many states had imposed caps for Governors and other top officials, noted the senator.[47] These arrangements proved successful and durable, without being anti-democratic.

"I have yet to find a single state that has done away or repealed or changed that constitutional limitation."[48] At the time Van Nuys spoke, thirty-four states had some form of term limitations.

At 11:45 AM, the hearing adjourned. Additional hearings would follow the pattern of the first day, beginning at 10:30 AM and lasting until daily sessions of the Senate opened at noon.

DAY TWO

On the morning of Thursday, September 5, 1940, the subcommittee convened for a second time in the Senate Caucus Room. There was one witness, William Mather Lewis, president of Lafayette College in Easton, Pennsylvania.

Lewis claimed the single-term amendment would preserve republican principles in a world increasingly dominated by dictators. Totalitarian governments were at their zenith in the 1930s. Democracies seemed ill-equipped to confront them. America itself had experienced demagogues, such as Senator Huey Long[49] and Father Charles Coughlin.[50] Would the country embrace them?[51] Lewis worried that Americans might be susceptible to their appeal. "Our people, I believe, are no less emotional, are no more difficult to lead, than some of those across the water."[52]

In uneasy times, one could not comfortably rely on the unwritten constitution, Lewis asserted. Preservation of the Republic required more formal protection.

It is useful to give context to Lewis' testimony. The Burke hearings occurred at a time of severe crisis in Europe. In 1938, a democratic regime fell in Austria. Early in 1939, the same happened in Czechoslovakia. Both had been absorbed into the Hitler dictatorship. War began in September of that year, as Germany invaded Poland and compelled its surrender within the month. In 1940, the onslaught continued. Germany overran France, Norway, and the Low Countries.

As Burke convened his subcommittee, the Battle of Britain raged. Convinced that an emergency was at hand, during which it was too risky to change leaders, Democrats stuck with Roosevelt.

Such turbulent conditions did not cause Lewis to reconsider his argument. "Civilization is always on trial," he remarked. "There are not many times in the life of a republic when there is not a crisis of this or that nature, so I would suggest that, in the first place, clever men around a President could create a crisis in order to keep that man in office."[53]

Lewis was also unpersuaded that rotation in office would destabilize American leadership. To the contrary, military and civilian agencies would continue to run, notwithstanding a change at the top. "Periods of transition are not as critical as the country believes them to be."[54]

If the Constitution were to be amended, Lewis insisted that single-term tenure was the best approach. "A single six-year term for the President of the United States is of the utmost importance."[55] At least six presidents had advocated for it, he noted, including some who wound up seeking reelection.[56] Moreover, the Senate itself had endorsed the single term. In 1913, senators passed a Constitutional Amendment, which stated: "The term of office of the President shall be six years, and no person who has held office by election and discharged its power or duties, or acted as President under the Constitution and laws made in pursuance thereof, shall be eligible to hold again the office by election."[57]

While the House did not follow suit in 1913, Lewis thought the Senate had offered a useful roadmap to maintaining constitutional government. Such an amendment would avert the possibility that authoritarianism would infect the United States, Lewis averred.

Today, the fears of dictatorship that Lewis and other witness expressed may appear paranoid. However, such is the comfort of retrospection. Considered not only against the ominous international conditions of 1940, as well as domestic concerns about executive overreach, such as court-packing and a politicized mega-bureaucracy, the anxiety in context seems less overwrought.[58]

DAY THREE

Burke's subcommittee resumed its hearings, moved this time and for the remainder of such proceedings to room 457 of the Senate Office Building.[59] The day's first witness was Bishop Edward H. Hughes of the Methodist Church. It was unfortunate, the bishop said, that Congress had to consider the third-term issue in the heat of a presidential campaign. Under such circumstances, constitutional theory could not be separated from politics. But Hughes was a realist. He was sure Congress would never address the topic unless the two-term tradition was in grave jeopardy.[60]

Such situations had presented themselves twice in the past. Each was grave enough to generate congressional intervention to preserve the two-term tradition. These occurred via the Springer Resolution in the House in 1875[61] and the LaFollette Resolution in the Senate in 1928.[62] Hughes laid out the record.

Alarmed at the possibility that President Ulysses Grant might seek the Republican nomination for a third term, Representative William Springer (D-IL)[63] sponsored a resolution urging Grant to desist. It read: "That in the opinion of this House, the precedent established by Washington and other Presidents of the United States in retiring from the Presidential office after their second term, has become by universal concurrence a part of our republican system of government, and that any departure from this time-honored custom would be unwise, unpatriotic, and fraught with peril to our free institutions."[64]

Proposed on December 15, 1875, the Springer resolution passed without debate in a Democratic-controlled House.[65] The vote was 233 to 18. Hughes recounted that all Democrats voted for it as did 70 of 88 Republicans.[66] Although it is impossible to assess for certain how influential the resolution may have been, Grant did not go forward. Chroniclers of the period considered it impactful.[67]

In 1928, contemplating the possibility that President Calvin Coolidge would seek another term, Senator Robert M. LaFollette, Jr. (R-WI) revived the 1875 language in a resolution that passed 56 to 26. At the time, Coolidge's Party controlled the Senate. The resolution's supporters included eighteen Republicans, thirty-seven Democrats and one independent. Twenty-two Republicans and four Democrats opposed it. Congressional sentiment was clear and helped shut the door on another Coolidge run.[68]

Although nonbinding, those resolutions reinforced the two-term custom. But in the lead up to the 1940 nominating convention, the prospect of another Congressional intervention was nonexistent. In firm control of Congress, loyal to FDR, and wanting him to head their national ticket, Democrats would never have fomented or tolerated such an insurrection. Thus, while the 1940 Republican platform expressly endorsed the two-term limit, Democrats outright abandoned it.

Therefore, Americans could no longer safely rely upon old traditions and standards. Hughes concluded that law must replace custom.

Burke's next witness was Samuel B. Pettengill, who represented Indiana in the House of Representatives from 1931 to 1939 and who was Chairman of the National Committee to Uphold Constitutional Government. Pettengill had been an early Roosevelt man, the first prominent Indiana Democrat to endorse FDR in 1932. In 1936, he backed the president for a second term. However, in 1937, in opposition to Roosevelt's court-packing plan, Pettengill was instrumental in forming the National Committee. Victorious in that fight, the National Committee took up the term limits issue. Prominently arrayed against his president, Pettengill did not seek reelection in 1938.

The first constitution in the United States was in Fundamental Orders of Connecticut, noted Pettengill. Written in 1639, it limited the term of the chief executive to one year. That was the harbinger of many similar provisions, he said. "In 1787, when the Constitution of the United States was written, the great majority of states had charters, which prevented the Chief Executive from holding office longer than for a short-named term."[69]

Initially favorable to presidential term limits, Pettengill noted, delegates abandoned them when they settled upon election by independent electors.

As originally conceived, the Electoral College was ingenious. Successive layers of political filtration would mitigate the danger of corrupted elections. As Pettengill explained, "the people voted for state legislatures; the latter chose Presidential electors; the electors were to choose the President. . . . And as the electors, chosen in each state, are to assemble and vote in the state in which they are chosen, this detached and divided situation will expose them much less to heat and ferment."[70]

There was an additional safeguard as well, one against self-dealing, he continued. Members of Congress or other federal officeholders cannot be electors.[71] "This was clearly designed to prevent a sitting President from influencing his own reelection in the Electoral College by packing it with his own employees."[72]

Due to the rise of political parties and broadening of the popular vote franchise, the Electoral College did not serve the independent purpose the Framers intended.[73] "By 1820, the people were voting directly for members of the Electoral College, and parties were nominating candidates whom the electors were morally bound to vote for, thus destroying their independence of choice originally intended," Pettengill stated.[74]

Americans of the present day comprehend little, if anything, about why an Electoral College exists. Many see it only a constitutional relic that has commanded public attention mainly because in the 2000 and 2016 elections, it produced presidents that lost the popular vote. However, it is likely that, in 1940, voters understood the Electoral College even less; no president had lost the popular vote but won the presidency since Benjamin Harrison defeated Grover Cleveland 52 years earlier.[75]

One can speculate whether the Framers would have written term limits into the Constitution if they had foreseen that the Electoral College would evolve in this manner. Instead, restraint on power wound up depending much more on the unwritten two-term tradition than on the constitutional apparatus. Pettengill called the custom a "postscript to the Constitution."[76]

In 1940, that postscript was about to be voided. Democrats, who had expressly endorsed term limits in 1896 and 1912, had abandoned them. Pettengill was perplexed, convinced that his Party had forsaken a core tenet. "In view of the vast extension of Presidential powers, it is vastly more important now that the principle be maintained than at any other time, not only in the history of America but in the history of mankind."[77]

Pettengill referred to the international situation. Dictatorships were overwhelming democratic systems. "Look abroad where the dikes erected by free men have broken down and where power, absolute and unrestrained, is raging through the world like an uncaged beast." Amending the Constitution would help cushion the United States from this evil, he asserted.

Extended tenure was rife with potential for patronage abuse, Pettengill argued. Congress had also grasped the problem, when passing the Hatch Act in 1939 to curtail political activity in the federal bureaucracy. Named for its sponsor, Senator Carl Hatch (D-NM), it was officially named An Act to Prevent Pernicious Political Activities.[78] The statute prohibits all but a handful of federal employees from engaging in most forms of politics. According to Pettengill, it represented "clear recognition in the judgment of Congress that public policy requires some effort be made to protect the disinterestedness of office." He added, "corruption and government seem to have an almost magnetic attraction to each other."[79]

Pettengill believed that the Hatch Act and an Amendment limiting the term of the chief executive served similar objectives. Both were attempts to ensure public integrity and preserve the balance of power between political institutions.

His testimony concluded, the hearing adjourned. The subcommittee would resume the following Monday.

DAY 4

September 9, 1940, was a beautiful late summer day in Washington. At 10:30 that morning, Burke's subcommittee convened for its fourth day of hearings. The initial witness was Dr. Jacob Gould Schurman, formerly president of Cornell University, head of the First Philippine Commission,[80] and U.S. Ambassador to Greece (1912–1913), to China (1921–1925), and to Germany (1925–1930).

Schurman spoke of the difference between term limits applied to the Legislative Branch as against restricting tenure for the executive. One was pointless and the other was essential, he claimed.

Because authority within Congress was diffuse, Schurman said, term limits were not needed there to curb accumulation of power. However, the presidency was distinct. "The Executive Department is vested absolutely and in its entirety in one man only." The concentration of great and expanding power in a single place required restriction. "A limit of the term and the entire duration of tenure of the office of the Chief Executive is an indispensable condition of the safety and perpetuity of democratic government," he urged.[81]

Schurman observed that the informal two-term tradition had been sufficient to rein in the executive, but would not remain so. Even though the outcome of the 1940 election was yet uncertain, Roosevelt's nomination left only one major party on record for the custom. If left to political discretion, further erosion rather than restoration was likely. Schurman saw no alternative to a constitutional amendment. "The nature of the menace to our entire system of democratic government indicates the character of the remedy to be applied," he avowed.[82]

Schurman acknowledged that discarding tradition to respond to crisis could be appealing. However, he did not believe custom would revive once the crisis abated. "Gentlemen, if there is one law revealed to us in the history of government it is this – that any departure from constitutional prescription or long established and unbroken custom makes a precedent which in the course of time becomes general practice."[83]

Schurman had been ambassador to Germany at the time of the Weimar Republic.[84] When he arrived in Berlin, Germany enjoyed a democratic system, however fractious. It also confronted dire economic conditions. Schurman recounted how a dictatorship emerged. Although the rise of National Socialism seemed almost inevitable in hindsight, most Germans did not foresee it, said Schurman. As an ambassador, he had canvassed the country, asking people what would happen if the inflation-ridden Republic collapsed. "I was of the opinion it would be replaced, not by any member of the Hohenzollern Dynasty[85] – a general expectation at the time – but by a German Mussolini." His interlocutors had been skeptical. "The reaction of my German friends to this expression of opinion was almost invariably, 'but where is our Mussolini.'"[86]

Nevertheless, Hitler emerged, initially through democratic means. By the time of the Burke hearings, the Fuhrer was near the apex of his dominance. Drawing upon the German example, Schurman set out a roadmap for how a dictator might similarly acquire power in the United States:

- A leader with inordinate political gifts, and unbounded ambition arrives on the scene. "Let us imagine an American political leader of Bryan's gifts but with Hitler's love of power."[87] The leader is elected.
- Over a period of eight years, he exerts control, not only over the Executive Branch but over Congress and his party. "The reelected President, as leader of his party, would be in a position to dictate all important congressional legislation. The bills he desired to become laws would be marked as 'must' legislation, and any Congressman who opposed them would be apt to be driven by the President into the political wilderness."[88]
- If ordinary tools of influence were inadequate, such a president might proclaim an "emergency," or something of the type, to justify exercise of extraordinary authority. It would be possible to do so legally. For instance, Schurman observed, Hitler relied upon powers in the Weimar Constitution to bypass the Reichstag and issue decrees that would have the force of law.[89]
- The president, who perpetuated himself in office, could control the judiciary by exercising the power of appointment for an extended period of

time. "It is not impossible that he would nominate as judges citizens who were in full sympathy with his own political views." And there was a further threat—domination by enlargement, as Roosevelt attempted in his court-packing plan. "As the Constitution sets no limit to the number of judges on the Supreme Court, Congress acting under the leadership of the President might enlarge that Court so that the President's nominees or supporters should be in the majority."[90]

- The president would naturally dominate the military and the conduct of the Nation's foreign policy. Even though the Constitution grants the Senate the power to advise and consent to treaties, and thus makes foreign policy a domain of overlapping powers, the president could bypass the Senate and govern through Executive Agreements.[91]

Schurman endorsed Wiley's two-term resolution because he thought capping tenure was less radical than limiting a president to just one term.[92]

Shortly thereafter, the hearing adjourned.

DAY 5

The fifth day of hearings commenced on Wednesday, September 11, 1940. The lead witness was Fredric R. Coudert, a prominent New York attorney. While he supported Roosevelt in 1932 and 1936, Coudert steadfastly opposed a third term for anyone.

Relying on tradition served the country well, but was no longer useful. The country could not fall back on self-restraint, so a constitutional amendment was urgent. If it did not happen, Coudert predicted, republican institutions would disintegrate. Similar trends were evident in other countries.

Coudert lamented the "complete, abject, and humiliating failure of nearly every democracy among the nations of the world."[93] These systems had collapsed because "democracy had taken the direct or plebiscitary form, which has led to the destruction of democracy itself and the exalting of one individual who is supposed to typify an omnipotent and infallible state."[94]

In 1940 and later, opponents of a constitutional amendment complained that it represented a muzzling of the popular will. But Coudert approached the issue from exactly the opposite perspective. He equated unfiltered, direct democracy to rule by the mob.

With the neutering of the Electoral College, quadrennial elections had become tantamount to, in Coudert's words, "election by plebiscite," the equivalent of mob rule. Napoleon rose under such conditions, Coudert warned, as did Hitler and Mussolini. "They have had themselves sanctioned by direct vote of the people completely organized and impelled and compelled through the central power they possess."[95] Indeed, Coudert continued, the danger was inherent in popular democracy itself. "In the Hellenic world, a direct democracy voting directly and not through representatives, had led to dictatorship."[96]

A constitutional amendment could control these impulses, although such barriers had not proven insurmountable elsewhere. In countries that had tenure limitations, such as Mexico, Cuba, and Panama, plebiscites had lifted them, allowing leaders to perpetuate themselves in office. These examples greatly alarmed Coudert.

The same thing might happen in America, but Coudert was confident it would not. Because term limits were long a part of the unwritten constitution, incorporating them formally would likely prove durable. In any case, it was the best the country could do. "If our electorate so changes its nature as to revere neither the tradition nor the constitutional amendment which would embody it, then the Constitution itself ceases to be of any value."[97]

Therefore, Coudert endorsed the Wiley proposal for two four-year terms, as against Burke's single-term amendment. Coudert believed Wiley's legislation reflected a practice to which Americans had become accustomed and would therefore win greater public acceptance.[98]

In a later exchange with the witnesses, and notwithstanding his own single-term proposal, Senator Burke signaled openness to Coudert's approach. "If it is decided that there should be a limitation, then it is a matter more of detail and not of commanding importance whether this limitation take the form of a proposal for a single six-year term . . . or whether it should be a limitation upon the tenure of two terms of four years each," the senator said. "But as a practical matter . . . since we have operated 150 years already under the idea of two terms of four years each, it may well be argued that we should not try to change that now and go to what theoretically at least would have been a better system."[99]

Representative Donald McLean (R-NJ),[100] one of the very few Republican witnesses to come before the subcommittee, gave the final testimony of the day. He was long a proponent of term limitations, having endorsed it as a private citizen, even at a time of Republican presidents. When he arrived in Congress in 1933, McLean introduced H. J. Res. 96, a constitutional amendment providing for one six-year term. His legislation would have permitted Roosevelt to run for a second term in 1936, because the restriction was to take effect on January 20, 1941.[101] Congress never acted on McLean's proposal.

McLean spoke to the difficulties the Framers' experienced on fixing a presidential term. By the end of the Convention, the delegates were exhausted, he said. Fatigue was a factor in delegates agreeing to the Brearly Committee recommendations, said McLean. As evidence, he quoted an 1823 letter from James Madison to George Hay, in which the former president remarked that resolution of the issue "took place in the latter stage of the session, and it was not exempt from a degree of hurrying influence produced by fatigue and impatience."[102]

Agreement was also facilitated because members of the Convention knew who the first president was likely to be, said McLean. "The delegates to the Constitutional Convention were willing to leave some part of their work unfinished in the confidence they had in George Washington . . . and that by precedent he would supply the elements to give the Constitution the meaning intended."[103]

McLean reinforced a theme already heard in prior testimony. The Constitutional balance the Framers hoped to strike was already fraying, and would become even weaker with abandonment of the two-term tradition. To mitigate this trend, the Constitution must strictly cap Presidential tenure. "We are a government of principles and not of individuals, and we must provide these principles which will restrain the ambitious individual from dominating our habit of life."[104]

DAY 6

The subcommittee convened again at 10:00 AM on Thursday, September 12. Walter F. Dodd, a prominent Chicago attorney and academician, testified first. Dodd was familiar to the Senate Judiciary Committee. Three years earlier, he had appeared as a witness against Roosevelt's court-packing plan.

Returning to Capitol Hill, Dodd described a disturbing pattern. "A short time ago the Judiciary Committee of the United States Senate was holding hearings upon a proposal by the present National Executive to assume control of the United States Supreme Court. The hearings now conducted by this Committee relate to the proposal of the same National Executive to extend the occupancy of that position to 12 years."

Dodd acknowledged that neither court-packing nor the third term violated the Constitution's text, but he was sure they contradicted its spirit. "These are fundamentals of our Government, and to abandon them directly or indirectly is to make the written Constitution but a scrap of paper."[105]

Dodd feared that the third term would permit domination of the federal judiciary, neutralizing the benefit of defeating the court-packing plan. Perpetuation in office meant a President could fill the bench just as decisively over time. "We fought out a battle for the freedom of the courts several years ago," Dodd recalled. "We now have presented very much the same type of problem, except that the attack, or possible attack, upon the courts is more indirect."[106]

Dodd noted that, a half century earlier, President Grover Cleveland identified the corrupting effects of entrenched power. In Cleveland's words, "When we consider the patronage of this great office, allurements of power, the temptation to retain public office once gained, and, more than all, the availability a party finds in an incumbent whom a horde of officeholders stand ready to aid with money and trained political assistance, we recognize in the re-eligibility of the President for reelection the most serious danger to that calm, deliberate action which must characterize a government by the people."[107] Since Cleveland's time, such patronage and allurements had vastly expanded, as had the dependency of people on federal programs. Abandonment of the two-term tradition was likely to exacerbate these antidemocratic effects, Dodd felt.

While assertion of crisis might tempt voters to discard tradition, Dodd insisted the benefits were illusory, while the harm was durable. "A free people must often surrender power to a temporary dictatorship in time of war," he concluded, "but freedom is gone if they are unable to recapture power when the emergency is over."[108]

Clarence J. Hand, a New York lawyer and executive secretary of the Anti-Third Term Association, was the next witness. He also focused on the potential extended tenure had for corruption. "The most compelling argument today against allowing any President more than two terms is an argument Jefferson never used," Hand noted. "It is the patronage argument, the fear that the vast appointive and appropriation-directing power in a modern President's hands may be used to secure first his re-nomination and then his re-election."[109]

Such abuses were not new, Hand recounted. During Andrew Jackson's Presidency (1829–1837), the "spoils system" was pervasive and cemented Jackson's hold on the Democratic Party. The problem worsened in the following decades, to the point that in 1866, Senate President Pro Tempore Ben Wade[110] (R-OH) proposed a term limits amendment. In justifying it, Wade stated that the absence of such a restriction was "among the most glaring defects" of the original Constitution.[111] The amendment did not pass, and difficulties continued.

Hand quoted Senator George Norris (R-NE), who warned in 1928 that, "When this influence (patronage) is combined and used for the perpetuation in office of the head of our Government, it is a danger to free institutions and strikes at the very root of democracy. . . . It exists now to a greater extent than it did because Federal offices have been multiplied many fold and partisan machines . . . are now enthroned in power greater than ever in our history."[112]

Patronage enabled a president to maintain ironclad control of party machinery. Even a beleaguered president could secure renomination in the face of popular opposition. William Howard Taft's victory over Theodore Roosevelt at the 1912 Republican Convention proved this, said Hand.

Although he advocated rotation in office, Hand saw a major difference between seeking a third successive term and a third nonsuccessive term. He did not oppose a president sitting out a term and attempting to come back, as Theodore Roosevelt had done in 1912. The interruption of service would dissipate the problem of patronage, he claimed. "If objection to a third term is put on practical rather than on traditional grounds, the argument that patronage can be used to grab off a re-nomination obviously does not apply to a man who has been out of office for four years."[113]

Hand was encouraged that Roosevelt's opponent, Wendell Willkie, was emphasizing the term limits issue. Quoting Willkie from that day's *New York Times*, "The third term is one of the great issues of the campaign, and it is not only the third term, but the continuation of a group with great power, which is destructive of democracy."[114]

Hand concluded by noting the potency of the issue. "Democrat after Democrat, prominent Democrats throughout the country, are coming out not for Willkie, but against the third term."[115]

The hearing adjourned until Friday, September 13.

DAY 7

The principal witness at Friday's session was Dr. William E. Masterson, professor of law at Temple University. Rotation in office had very significant antecedents in American history, Masterson observed. It was a feature of the earliest days of American self-governance. Under the Articles of Confederation, Members of Congress could serve no more than three years in any six-year period. "From the beginning of their independence, the constant aim and desire of the people was to devise a system that would ensure periodic elections and prevent indefinite tenure."[116]

These concepts carried forward to the Constitutional Convention, at least with respect to executive tenure. While the Virginia Plan did not initially specify the number of years in the president's term, nor even necessarily if the executive should be one person or several, it was explicit that he would be "ineligible a second time."[117] Within three days, the delegates voted for a single, seven-year term, a concept that survived almost until the end of the Convention.

Ultimately, delegates opted to shorten the term and remove the barrier to reelection. Masterson believed they felt comfortable doing so because they had created the Electoral College, which was supposed to separate election of the president from the impulses of popular democracy. "This procedure was designed to prevent a President's perpetuating himself in office by direct appeals to the four 'P's' – the Passions, Prejudices, Patronage, and Purses of the voters," Masterson explained.[118]

Partisan politics overtook the Electoral College, and it never succeeded in bringing dispassion to Presidential elections. Accordingly, the country had to rely on usage and custom rather than on written law. Said Masterson,

"A two-term precedent – if there was to be one – was left to… the sagacity of statesmen who were the first to launch the new ship of state and steer its course past the shallows and shoals that lay ahead."[119]

James Buchanan, later president, but a Congressman in 1829, told the House of Representatives about the impact of early leadership precedents on shaping the unwritten Constitution. Masterson quoted him. "The example of Washington, which has been followed by Jefferson, Madison, and Monroe, has forever determined that no President shall be more than once reelected. The principle is now become as sacred as if it were written in the Constitution."[120]

"During these 150 years of our national history," Masterson continued, "Democratic and Republican Presidents alike have unfailingly and unfalteringly championed the precedent set by Washington . . . It has transcended party politics. Whatever other changes may have taken place in the fundamental law of the land . . . this precedent has doggedly persisted."[121] Masterson pondered what might have happened under less stalwart leaders. "Washington and Jefferson could have had third terms for the asking. Had they sought or accepted them, others less scrupulous and more ambitious might have done so. No one knows what the course of our history might have been."[122]

Democratic platforms in 1896 and 1912 explicitly endorsed rotation. Masterson was distressed that Democrats in 1940 did not follow suit. He called the repudiation "striking proof of Senator Dickerson's observation in 1826 that 'it is unsafe to rely upon a law sanctioned only by precept and example,' and that as great an authority as was Jefferson will have but little weight when opposed to the views of ambition and power."[123]

Masterson observed that at the time of ratification, three state conventions called for an amendment to limit presidential terms. Virginia and North Carolina proposed adoption of language that would restrict a president from serving more than eight years in any 16-year period. As George Mason stated during proceedings at the Virginia Convention, "Nothing is so essential to the preservation of a republican government as a periodical rotation."[124]At the same time, New York recommended an amendment to bar presidents from election more than twice.[125]

Periodically, Congress would try to resurrect the term limits issue. Masterson noted that, in 1824, the Senate by a vote of 36 to 3 passed a constitutional amendment establishing a two-term restriction. It died in the House. In 1826, there was another failure in the House of a Senate-generated constitutional amendment for a single six-year term. In 1912, the Senate once more took up term limits. It passed another single six-year term amendment, by 47 to 23, just over the necessary two-thirds. It disqualified from future service anyone who had previously served as president by the time of ratification.[126] Working through Representative A. Mitchell Palmer, a member of the House Judiciary

Committee, President-elect Wilson killed chances for House action. Notwithstanding these failures in Congress, it was possible for the country to fall back on the unwritten Constitution.

Now, in 1940, the two-term tradition was in jeopardy. Masterson predicted, "A third term in our day might open the way for a fourth in the next generation, a fifth in the following until finally life tenure might not seem unnatural but indispensable."[127]

Masterson finished his testimony by rebutting a key argument against the amendment. Critics claimed that the right to serve as president should be wholly a matter of voter discretion. "It is said that the decision should be left to the people, to sound policy and educated public opinion, and that the anti-third term tradition will be better sustained by their free choice than by an enforced limitation placed in the Constitution."[128]

However, Masterson noted that the Constitution already restricted what citizens could do, safeguarding against abridgement of speech, religion, and assembly. "Such constitutional provisions as these are to protect the liberties of minorities against invasion by temporary majorities."[129] Masterson was comfortable with restricting voter choice in order to preserve essential checks and balances.[130]

DAYS 8 AND 9

Minor testimony consumed the hearing on Wednesday, September 18, 1940. However, when the Subcommittee reconvened on the following day, the principal witness was John W. Davis, a New York attorney who was the unsuccessful Democratic nominee for president in 1924.[131] Now, two months after his party fostered a third term for Roosevelt, Davis appeared before Congress to denounce the decision taken in the Democratic Convention.

Davis had long opposed the leftward trend of the party. In 1924, he was a compromise candidate in a convention divided between supporters of former Treasury Secretary William G. McAdoo and New York Governor Alfred E. Smith. By 1940, Davis was a full-fledged Roosevelt opponent. Four years earlier, he joined the American Liberty League, an organization devoted to opposing New Deal legislation. As a former Solicitor General, Davis litigated to invalidate several major bills of that era.[132]

Davis endorsed Burke's proposal for a single six-year term. He understood the argument that Bridges' resolution for two four-year terms reflected "national habit," and that to continue with it might be easier than doing something new. However, Davis wanted to remove from a president "the temptation to play for his own reelection." Thus, he stated, "If we are to go through the process of amendment, as I clearly think we must, I would prefer to do the best rather than the expedient thing." Six years was long enough for any President to realize all the major goals of his program, proclaimed Davis. He was skeptical that longer service would produce better results. "If his conscience and zeal do not stir him to his utmost effort in that length of time, the hope that he will do better on a second trial is a vain illusion."[133]

Across many decades, the principle of rotation was nearly a universal value, said Davis. "The one thing upon which those who founded this Government and those who have carried it on have all agreed, is that we should never risk the permanent control of our Government by a single man."[134]

The two-term tradition animated this principle. Proposals to write it into the Constitution went nowhere because adherence to the principle seemed immune from serious challenge. "When one reflects . . . upon the canons of conduct that control men in their personal affairs, it is amazing to find out how many of them are rooted in tradition and tradition alone."[135]

Davis feared that if custom fell away, and if the system were not stabilized by Constitutional Amendment, "we have every reason to dread a future occupancy of the White House limited only by the ambition or life of the tenant."[136]

Witnesses throughout the hearings referred to the prospect of dictatorship. Many reflected that dictators usually came to power through legal means, then aggrandized authority to make their rule absolute. It being 1940, Hitler in Germany and Mussolini in Italy were most often cited, but they were by no means the only cases. Davis offered an older example, that of Porfirio Diaz in Mexico.

Diaz won the presidency in a legitimate election in 1876, Davis told the committee. The Mexican Constitution provided for a term of four years with no chance for reelection. The system meant to promote rotation, but Diaz fashioned a work-around. In 1880, he surrendered his office to a hand-picked placeholder, and then returned to the Presidency in 1884. By that time, Diaz had dominated Mexican politics for a long time. Officially back in charge, he had a sufficient grip to intimidate and neuter the opposition.[137] In 1887, Diaz secured a constitutional amendment dispensing with term limits altogether.[138] He then ruled without interruption until the Mexican revolution of 1911 removed him.

From this troubled history, Davis drew a lesson. "Power too long continued is always abused, for it works queer changes in the minds and morals of those who wield it. The only prophylactic is a wholesome and cleansing rotation in office."[139] He added, "If this cannot be compelled by custom, it must be forced by law."[140]

Advocates of the third term claimed that 1940 was an inconvenient and inappropriate time to shed seasoned leadership for new. But Davis felt any president could make such an argument as he was concluding a term. If voters reelected Roosevelt, the president could reprise the same argument at the end of year twelve. "To fall in with this line of reasoning is to abandon altogether the principle of rotation in office, and calmly contemplate the possibility of a permanent President. There is no stopping place."[141]

Davis concluded. "Free government is under challenge throughout the world." As important as it would have been to codify the rotation principle in earlier times, the expansion of the presidency and the international events of the 1930s generated a special urgency. "I think the whole attempt at personal government by individuals has risen to a height none of us 30 years ago had thought possible," he lamented.

"If there was ever a time for the American people to stand fast against those doctrines, certainly this is the time."[142]

DAY 10

On Friday, September 20, as the subcommittee resumed its hearings, the lead witness was Vance McCormick, a newspaper publisher from Harrisburg, Pennsylvania, and former chairman of the Democratic National Committee.[143]

A self-proclaimed Woodrow Wilson Democrat, McCormick had strongly opposed Roosevelt's 1940 renomination, believing that modern Democratic leaders had abandoned the party's core ideals. "I am eager to do what I can to try to save that great party from the errors into which it is being led by its present leaders and to help restore the principles of democracy as taught by its founders."[144] He set out four major objections to the third term:

- The two-term tradition was deeply rooted in Americans' "fear of perpetuation of one-man government."[145]
- Once the two-term barrier was exceeded, there was no limiting principle. A third term could lead to a fourth, he surmised.
- The theory behind a third term was the need for stable leadership in a time of crisis. However, no leader was indispensable.
- By 1940, federal largesse had grown so profoundly that its control should not be entrusted to anyone for extended time. "The power over the ballot which could be exercised by the beneficiaries of these enormous funds along with their friends and relatives is too tremendous to be left in the hands of any President for more than two terms. It would constitute a bureaucracy of such voting strength that it could perpetuate itself in office and leave the citizens of the Nation helpless to correct it."[146]

McCormick worried about the effects of perpetuation on the Nation's image overseas. He paid special attention to the Good Neighbor Policy, a hallmark initiative of Roosevelt's international program. McCormick supported this policy, which bound the Americas closer together after decades of Latin American estrangement from the United States. However, he thought its benefits would be eroded by Roosevelt's quest for a third term. "It will be a vindication of the actions of the dictators of Central and South America and a disappointment to the real democrats of those lands who have been looking to this Nation for leadership in the process of free government."[147]

Later that morning, the subcommittee heard from Stanley I. Stuber, editor of a religious journal, *United States Baptist*. He claimed that perpetuation in office would lead to the establishment of a permanent party in power, and impinge on religious freedom. "I fear that any third-term administration will . . . establish here a dictatorship in principle, if not in fact, and this would mean the end of religious liberty and individual conscience."[148]

Stuber did not think the controversy over the third term would be a conclusive factor in the 1940 election. Instead, voting would in effect be a referendum on Roosevelt. "The majority of voters will not be voting directly for or against the third term," Stuber declared. "Millions will vote the straight party ticket even though the devil himself were candidate. And millions of United States citizens will think first of the candidate best suited to meet the international situation."[149]

To demonstrate this, Stuber quoted a series of *New York Times* correspondents about the central issues in the campaign. One such writer, reporting from the Midwest, stated, "The third-term tradition rather languishes as a matter of sustained interest. It may be the subject of desultory sniping throughout the campaign and it furnishes the objective for the organization of bipartisan Willkie clubs as a rallying point for deserting Democrats."[150]

The *Times* writers dismissed the importance of the third term as a voting determinant. Democrats who deserted their ticket were likely to have other complaints against the administration. "It turns out almost invariably that these Democrats are more outraged by the New Deal, Mr. Roosevelt, and the New Dealers, than by the violence done to the third-term tradition."[151] Reporters from other regions offered similar conclusions.

Thus, Stuber concluded that a majority of Americans were willing to rely on Roosevelt as a known quantity, especially in view of world developments. While the third term would be an issue in the 1940 election, other topics, especially related to the president's stewardship of foreign policy would supersede it.[152]

Stuber expressed confidence that public sentiment backed the principle of term limits, if election year politics did not complicate the question.[153] The way to test this would be to submit a constitutional amendment for ratification, he argued.[154]

Following Stuber was Jefferson Hayes-Davis, grandson of Jefferson Davis, President of the Confederate States of America. The witness discussed a provision in the Confederate Constitution limiting its president to one six-year term.[155] As Hayes-Davis noted, the Confederates closely modeled their document on the U.S. Constitution. Nevertheless, there were some differences. One was a cap on presidential service. To explain the rationale for this, Stuber quoted Alexander Stephens, vice president of the Confederacy. "It will remove from the incumbent the temptation to use his office or exert the powers confided to him for any objects of personal ambition. The only incentive to that higher ambition which should move and actuate one holding such high trusts in his hands will be the good of the people, the advancement, prosperity, safety, honor, and true glory of the Confederacy."[156]

Hayes-Davis stated that when the Confederate Government formed, its founders had 80 years of hindsight that were not available to the Framers in Philadelphia. Political realities that Madison and others could not anticipate were by then manifest. The principal one was emergence of an electoral system built around party politics. "It was obvious that our particular form of democracy could not operate except through the party system, and that the President would of necessity be at the head of the party in power – the more power that was vested in the National Government, the more power an ambitious President would have to strengthen his own political party."[157]

Strongly committed to states' rights, Confederates found this trend ominous. By limiting the presidential term, they hoped to remove incentives to entrench authority and expand national power.[158]

The final witness was Edward T. Lee, Dean of the John Marshall Law School in Chicago. A lifelong Democrat, he condemned Roosevelt for distracting the public by introducing the third term issue into a debate that should be focused on "the whirlpool of cataclysm that has engulfed Europe."[159] The president had done so because he decided he was the best suited person to meet those challenges. As the witness described it, "on the nominating night of the recent Democratic Convention in Chicago, the President announced, in what was probably a closed conference with his conscience lasting several years, that he had become persuaded it was his duty to run for a third term."

If Roosevelt was moved by this, Lee was not. In his view, Roosevelt's decision had brought the country to crisis. If either variation of the pending constitutional amendments had been adopted, the crisis could not have materialized. Therefore, moving an amendment through ratification was imperative. Lee endorsed the single six-year term.[160]

Lee argued that if the Framers could foresee how the presidency would evolve, they would have limited tenure. "It is reasonable to believe that they would have hedged in that great office, curtailed its powers, and made its occupant what Mr. Bryan declared was the intention of the founders 'the people's hired man' and not their boss."[161]

The original Constitution contained many imperfections, Lee conceded. In the century and a half following ratification, the process of amendment had rectified many of them. Capping tenure was a piece of unfinished business that Congress should not leave undone.[162]

Following Lee's testimony, the subcommittee adjourned for the weekend, to resume work on September 23.

DAY 11

On a warm and sunny Monday morning, the subcommittee began its last full week of hearings. Its first witness was Irene Tinsley Washington, whose husband was a descendent of President George Washington.[163]

"Until recently, I was of the opinion that the unwritten third term tradition was as strong as the Constitution itself," she began. The politics of 1940 had disabused her of that belief and instilled in her the determination that Congress must amend the Constitution. "The time has now come for the strongest written law against a third term that the human mind is capable of drafting."[164]

Mrs. Washington was unpersuaded that the international situation made it too risky to change presidents. However grave circumstances might be, the United States was not even at war. Other countries had actually grown stronger by substituting leaders notwithstanding wartime conditions.[165] For example, Britain was already at war for eight months, with its Expeditionary Force stranded in France, when it replaced Prime Minister Neville Chamberlain with Winston Churchill. The witness concluded, "If Great Britain could change Prime Ministers in the midst of the worst war and crisis the world has ever known, and to an advantage, why should America hesitate to change Presidents?"[166]

John F. Voight, former president of the Illinois Bar Association, submitted testimony for the record. He noted that the principle of rotation in office had its roots in a tempestuous era, early in the Nation's history. The presidency passed from George Washington to John Adams notwithstanding war between Great Britain and France and efforts on the part of the French Government to draw America into the conflict.[167] "Even in those critical times, Washington did not regard it necessary for him to be continued in office for the safety of the young Republic," said Voight.[168]

In 1808, at the end of Thomas Jefferson's second term, turmoil in Europe imperiled the Nation's economy, and even its independence. Under these conditions, Jefferson could have argued a case for stability and sought to remain in office. However, he was strongly committed to the principle of rotation, and refused to consider a third term. The eight-year presidencies of James Madison and James Monroe followed, firmly establishing the two-term tradition as part of America's political code. As Voight captured it, "In the same manner as the unwritten Constitution of England is based upon the practices and customs of the English Government since the barons of Runnymede wrested from King John the fundamental rights of Englishmen, just so Americans regard the custom and practice of never permitting any President to serve more than two terms as part of the unwritten Constitution of the United States."[169]

Maintaining equilibrium between the Branches was fundamental to constitutional governance, Voight stated. He quoted Madison, "The accumulation of all powers, legislative, executive, and judicial in the same hands, whether of one, a few, or many, and whether hereditary or appointed or elected may justly be pronounced the very essence of tyranny."[170]

Voight believed the third term presented the perilous aggrandizement of power that Madison decried. A president too long in office would overbear on the other branches. "When all three departments of government are under the control of the Executive, no matter how great or good or experienced he may be, you have arbitrary government," Voight opined.

In a world in which authoritarianism was growing stronger, the American system had thus far held fast. Voight attributed this to the two-term tradition, and the self-restraint that led Presidents to forego accumulating power. Much was at stake in keeping things that way, he claimed. "The advice and practice of the Fathers of the Republic are before us. For 151 years our beloved Republic has followed their advice and their example, and the rights and liberties of Americans have been preserved when nearly all the world has either been persuaded or compelled to adopt, and has succumbed to, dictatorships."[171]

The hearing adjourned until the following morning.

DAY 12

When the subcommittee reconvened on Tuesday, September 24, the first witness was Richard Cleveland, a Baltimore attorney and son of former President Grover Cleveland. Echoing the voices of the people who testified before him, Cleveland characterized the two-term tradition as essential to preventing a slide toward dictatorship. "There is no doubt," Cleveland began, "that if the voters of the United States in 1940 sanction a third Presidential term, they will remove our most effective check against the world's present tendency toward concentration of political power."[172]

Roosevelt was justifying his bid on grounds of national emergency, Cleveland noted. However, Cleveland asserted the sword of emergency was doubled-edged. Such a stage was when American freedoms were most imperiled, he felt, presenting a premise for a power grab. To Cleveland, this was actually a time to resist rather than enable breaching the unwritten Constitution. "An emergency is therefore the basic argument against a third term, not in favor of it," he claimed.[173]

Cleveland recalled for the committee a moment in 1896 when his father was completing a second term in office. Democrats in that year nominated William Jennings Bryan for the first of his three bids for the White House. Bryan represented a faction that favored easing the money supply. An opposing faction of Gold Standard Democrats wired President Cleveland and proposed to nominate him for a third term, feeling confident that if the president were open to the idea, the nomination could have been his for the asking.[174] Cleveland would have none of it, and responded, "My judgment and personal inclination are so unalterably opposed to your suggestion that I cannot for a moment entertain it."[175]

Now, in 1940, it seemed probable that such self-restraint would be scrapped. Richard Cleveland considered the change ominous. "I solemnly believe that unless a third term for any man is forestalled by the voters in a free election or by suitable legislative action, we shall pass the great divide between democratic process and power government."[176]

A further witness that Tuesday was William Strite McDowell, a Michigan attorney and constitutional scholar. As proceedings in Philadelphia concluded, McDowell noted, Benjamin Franklin was asked what form of government the Framers thought best suited the young Nation. "A republic, if you can keep it," was Franklin's response.

Structured with filtered and restricted powers, the republic constrained majoritarian impulses. McDowell explained, "The framers of our national charter had learned from the pages of history that a pure democracy quickly gravitates into a violent mobocracy, where the rights of the few are trampled or destroyed by the temporary majority."[177]

The two-term tradition, although informal, was one of those essential constraints, McDowell felt. Custom and tradition had added layers of meaning to the actual Constitution. The document needed to be considered as a whole, both in its textual and unwritten forms, and scrupulously observed. "Disrespect for the constitutional limits on the powers of executives and their individual power and on terms of office is the first step toward unlimited power."[178]

The Framers built a republican form of government to control the destructive passions of the mob, he added. Faithful adherence to that system required self-restraint by presidents unwilling to perpetuate themselves. McDowell considered departure from that tradition to be a cataclysm for the American system of government. He demanded a constitutional amendment to fasten down a principle otherwise abandoned. "With ability now possessed by a national administration to continue itself in office, there is now a need for limitation that our liberties as a Republic can survive."[179]

The Subcommittee adjourned, to resume the following day.

DAY 13

On a rainy Wednesday morning, the subcommittee met for its thirteenth day of hearings. Its first witness was Bainbridge Colby, President Woodrow Wilson's third and last Secretary of State.[180]

Colby recounted warnings from Washington and Jefferson about presidents seeking to perpetuate themselves. In his Farewell Address, Washington held that only "corrupted morals and political depravity" would motivate a president to attempt extending tenure.[181] Jefferson went even further, Colby noted, proclaiming that the failure to include presidential term limits was a defect in the written Constitution. Notwithstanding this omission, Jefferson had written, should a president "consent to be a candidate for a third term, I trust he would be rejected on this demonstration of ambitious views."[182]

Roosevelt had done more than consent to a nomination, remarked Colby. The president had actively conspired to get it. "By his course as a President-candidate prior to the nominating convention at Chicago, his direction of its proceedings, and his subsequent actions as its third-term candidate, he has contributed a perfect illustration of every danger and evil which Jefferson foresaw so clearly and against which he warned his countrymen so earnestly."[183]

It was true, Colby acknowledged, that voters could reject the third term and, in doing so, preserve tradition. But he opined that was unlikely because the power of incumbency would give the President nearly insurmountable advantages. Colby quoted Alexis De Tocqueville. "A candidate who is not the President, seeking the Presidency, is but an individual, while the President seeking re-nomination is the state itself, intriguing and corrupting with its immense resources."[184]

The upcoming election seemed destined to jettison protective traditions. Colby called for an amendment, preferably for a single six-year term.

Colby's role in trying to engineer a third-term nomination for Woodrow Wilson in 1920 went unmentioned at the hearing, because committee members did not know about it and Colby obviously did not advertise it. It was not until Jonathan Daniels' 1946 memoir that the story of Colby's work on Wilson's behalf was revealed.

Oswald Garrison Villard followed Colby to the witness table. Grandson of the Civil War–era abolitionist William Lloyd Garrison, Villard was the publisher and editor of the *New York Evening Post* as well as *The Nation.* Although a liberal, committed to New Deal programs as well as to civil rights, and Roosevelt's professed friend, Villard broke with the president on three major initiatives. He favored neutrality legislation, opposed the court-packing plan, and rejected the third term.

"With democracy collapsing everywhere, with the totalitarian idea spreading rapidly and to a considerable degree in the United States, it is a primary consideration with me that the attempt to violate the no-third-term tradition shall be rebuked at the polls, since otherwise the road to a dictatorship is open,"[185] Villard began. Moreover, once the barrier was out of the way, Villard saw no limits to indefinite tenure. "If there is a sound reason for a third term, then similar reasons will be found for a fourth and a fifth."[186]

Villard favored limiting a president to a single term of not more than five years duration. Such an amendment would "save the President from himself," Villard held, adding that Roosevelt may have been the first president to seek a third term, but was not the first tempted to do so. Villard recalled the example of Woodrow Wilson, who had run in 1912 on a platform calling for one six-year term. Almost from the moment of his inauguration, Villard noted, Wilson sought to be relieved of that commitment. "Mr. Wilson, the scholar and historian, was determined from the start to be among the two-term Presidents."[187] Even that was not enough, Villard continued. "In Mr. Wilson's case, he not only sought and obtained a second nomination, using patronage if not coercion and all the power of the Presidential office to achieve it, but he actually desired a third term when he was a complete physical wreck and a politically discredited man."[188]

Calvin Coolidge also had such ambitions, Villard claimed. Notwithstanding Coolidge's announcement that he would not seek reelection in 1928, there remained the possibility Republicans would nominate him anyway. When that did not occur, noted Villard, Coolidge was distraught. "We know from an eyewitness that despite President Coolidge's having told the country 'I do not choose to run,' he threw himself on his bed in the White House in an agony of disappointment and was unapproachable two days after the telegraph reported to him that Mr. Hoover had been nominated in Kansas City."[189]

Villard believed such cases shed light on a political axiom. "It is the complete truth that no man ever willingly leaves the White House."[190]

Constitutional checks and balances were insufficient to restrain presidential power, Villard argued, because Congress was too quick to cede authority. No better example existed than the New Deal, he said. "In the first 100 days of Mr. Roosevelt's service as President, 77 new powers and authorities were conferred upon him by a terrified Congress."[191] And in foreign policy, where a president enjoyed natural dominance, the situation was yet worse. Roosevelt's war preparations, which the isolationist Villard strenuously opposed,[192] illustrated the problem. "If one examines what the present President is doing in the field of foreign relations, accepting foreign territory,[193] entering into close foreign relations and alliances with belligerents in the middle of a war in which the country is supposed to be neutral, it is impossible to deny that he has in this field at least practically dictatorial powers, since the Congress will put no curb on him."[194]

The sole meaningful curb on presidential rule was an amendment limiting tenure in office, Villard concluded. He exclaimed, "Three terms seem nothing short of treason to the Republic," adding, "I have weighed these words carefully."[195]

DAY 14

The principal witness on Thursday, September 26, was J.W. Creighton, the president of Hastings College in Hastings, Nebraska. He worried about the corrosive effect that the third term would have on the nation's political system. "Each party checks the other and this keeps politics relatively decent," Creighton remarked. "Unlimited tenure would tend to destroy the parties as they now exist." Dynamism would die in both parties, he claimed. A small cadre would dominate the President's inner circle, blocking rising leaders. Within the opposition, the effect would be even worse. "Each period of long and continuous lack of responsibility produces atrophy. Party machinery functions when it gears into real national responsibility. The power of protest weakens when protests are of no avail. Leadership emerges only with the opportunity."[196]

Such conditions would produce "mental sloth and the atrophy of patriotism," Creighton predicted. As politics lost vigor, the perpetual president would expand his power. This trend would not be benign. "We may recognize the blessings from one benevolent despot, but we know that the price is too great because the next dictator will not be benevolent."[197]

John McSparran, former Secretary of Agriculture for Pennsylvania, followed Creighton.[198] He noted that, during its history, Pennsylvania had four constitutions. The first three did not limit reeligibility for the Governor. However, in 1873, the state adopted a fourth constitution, which did not permit a Governor to be reelected to a second consecutive term. A Governor who had left office could return after an intervening period. Term limits for state chief executives were common, noted McSparran. In 1940, Pennsylvania and thirteen other states restricted the Governor to a single term. Four other states capped service at two terms.

Advocating the Pennsylvania arrangement be applied to the presidency, McSparran quoted De Tocqueville. "Intrigue and corruption are the natural defects of elective government; but when the head of state can be reelected these evils rise to a great height and compromise the very existence of the country."[199]

McSparran recounted that, in 1913, the Senate passed a joint resolution to amend the Constitution and provided for one six-year term. Although the full House did not act, the House Judiciary Committee reported favorably on it. The fundamental rationale was to depoliticize the office and to diminish time a president wasted on reelection campaigns. The committee report stated that making a president ineligible for a second term would improve the "non-partisan and businesslike efficiency" of the Executive Branch. As well, extending the term to six years without reelection pressures, "would give sufficient opportunity for the President properly to organize his administration and bring about real accomplishments within the bounds of his duties and powers under the Constitution."[200]

DAY 15

Burke convened the subcommittee's fifteenth day of hearings on Friday, September 27. The first witness was former Virginia Governor George C. Peery.[201] He explained that at no point in Virginia's history had a governor been eligible for reelection. In a few cases, such as those of Patrick Henry or James Monroe, term-limited governors had returned to service, but only after intervening terms of other governors. Peery advocated applying the Virginia system nationally.

Supporters of the third term took comfort in the concept that dictatorships could not take root in the face of free elections.[202] Peery disagreed. Perpetuated tenure would have a corrupting influence on elections, making them less free and less of a barrier to dictatorship. "It may be true that dictators do not arise where free elections exist," said Peery, "but one may question whether elections are entirely free and untrammeled where the Executive, or his partisans without his knowledge, use the lever of power and patronage to bring about a reelection. The great office of President of the United States should be entirely free of any such suspicion."[203]

DAY 16

The final day of Senator Burke's hearings was Monday, September 30. The opening witness was Bishop A.W. Leonard of the Methodist Church, Washington, D.C. area. He observed that in April 1938, an opinion survey produced by the American Institute of Public Opinion showed that more than 70 percent of American voters were against a third term.[204] Yet, slightly more than a month before the election, there was the serious prospect Roosevelt might be reelected. Did the change in international conditions justify this transformation?

Leonard conjectured not. "If a third term is essential, then a fourth term and a fifth and on and on until American democracy is destroyed," he predicted. "All that is needed in the event of such a change is to lead the people to believe there is an 'emergency.'"[205] He submitted for the record a September 19, 1940, editorial from *New York Times*.

The *Times* had endorsed Roosevelt in 1932 and 1936, but in 1940, it supported Willkie. The third term issue was central to that endorsement, which stated, "As the situation created by the war developed, the President came to regard his own personal leadership as indispensable and to believe that there was no other member of his party, however trusted, however close to him, however deeply in accord with his own convictions about the war or about domestic issues, who could safely take his place. The doctrine of one man's indispensability is a new doctrine for this country. It is a doctrine which less scrupulous men in Europe have used to root themselves in power. It is a doctrine which we in the United States have good reason to question, particularly when we consider how the powers of the Presidency have grown, what immense patronage, what gigantic expenditures, what enormous power to perpetuate himself in office is now within the grasp of any President of the United States."[206]

The *Times* editorial summarized, "At a time when the traditional safeguards of democracy are failing everywhere, it is particularly important to honor and preserve the American tradition against vesting the enormous powers of the Presidency in the hands of any man for three consecutive terms of office . . .. In the defeat of Mr. Roosevelt and the election of Mr. Willkie, there is an opportunity to safeguard a tradition with the wisdom of long experience behind it."[207]

Next to testify was Dr. Young B. Smith, Dean of Columbia Law School. He endorsed the Bridges' resolution calling for a limit of two four-year terms. Six years was too long to leave a weak president in office, Smith said, and was too short a time for a good president to serve.

Smith urged Congress to declare its commitment to term limits before the 1940 election. If, instead, Roosevelt secured a third term, there was low probability that a constitutional amendment could ever pass. "If this principle is abandoned by the people in November, efforts to restrict the President's tenure by constitutional amendment would be futile and its further discussion would be academic."[208]

Smith's principal objection to the third term was that extended tenure would destroy essential checks and balances because it would allow a president to dominate the other branches. For example, "a President might, and probably would, in 12 to 16 years have the opportunity to appoint all the members of the Supreme Court – to appoint, in effect, his own Court."[209] This threat to judicial independence corresponded to similar pressure on the Legislative Branch, Smith observed. "No realistic student of government can deny the power which a President has over Congress through his control over patronage and the distribution of federal funds."[210]

Such domination, actual or attempted, had been much in evidence during Roosevelt's second term, said Smith. The 1937 court-packing attempt, the futile 1938 reorganization bill,[211] and the 1938 party purge were all manifestations of an attempt, it was alleged, to foster a burgeoning dictatorship.[212] That such efforts had failed mattered little to the witness. Far more important was that Roosevelt had tried. Continuity in office would exaggerate Roosevelt's strengths, especially as Federal expenditures grew in response to foreign crisis.[213]

Smith's additional concern was degradation of the integrity of elections. Roosevelt partisans claimed systemic damage would not occur from extended tenure, because regular elections were the ultimate corrective. Like previous witnesses, Smith thought elections held in the face of such presidential supremacy were not really free. "If a President is permitted to remain in office for more than two terms, he can, through patronage and the use of federal funds, achieve such personal power and build up such a political machine that freedom of nomination and freedom of election will disappear and the ultimate power of the people will be lost."[214]

Smith believed prolonging one-party control would cause grievous damage to the political system. Perpetually in the minority, the opposition party would atrophy. "A vigilant and fearless opposition is one of the essential differences between our form of government and the Nazi, Fascist, or Soviet form which permits only the government party to exist."[215]

The final witness of the hearings was Dean Ignatius M. Wilkinson of the Fordham College of Law. As the 1940 election approached, he warned, fundamental constitutional principles were at risk. Wilkinson quoted Justice Louis Brandeis' 1926 dissent in *Myers v. United States* (272 U.S. 52, 292). Brandeis wrote, "Checks and balances were established in order that this should be 'a government of laws and not of men.' The doctrine of the separation of powers was adopted at the Convention of 1787 not to promote efficiency but to preclude the exercise of arbitrary power."[216]

If this carefully balanced arrangement were to fail, Wilkinson continued, it would be because executive authority would grow disproportionately. The judiciary had not the power of the sword or the purse. Congress controlled the purse and, to some degree the sword, but power within it dissipated. However, "it was in the executive department that the danger of an overgrowth or overextension of power was inherently greatest, because here you had a single head with the power of the sword and to a degree the purse also."[217]

These potential problems very much worried the Framers, noted Wilkinson. Having considered limiting the president to one term of six or seven years, they ultimately shortened it to four years without fixing a cap. The abbreviated term coupled with election via the Electoral College, seemed safeguard enough in a system in which no other official's term was limited. But Wilkinson added, "The important point, however, is not so much the form in which Article II, section 1 of the Constitution as it finally appeared and was ratified was drawn, but the fact that a considerable number of delegates at the Constitutional Convention were in favor of a definite disqualification for reelection."[218]

Wilkinson stated that Jefferson regarded the absence of presidential term limits in the Constitution as a grave omission. "I confess there are some things in it which stagger all my disposition," he wrote to John Adams in the fall of 1787. Later that year, he corresponded with James Madison. "Experience concurs with reason in concluding that the first magistrate will always be reelected, if the Constitution permits it. He is then an officer for life." In May 1788, while generally praising the new Constitution, Jefferson complained by letter to Washington about the absence of a declaration of rights and "the perpetual re-eligibility of the President." In that same correspondence, Jefferson cited his abject alienation from the principle of monarchy and his fear that unlimited tenure would make the president tantamount to a king. "I hope that before there is danger of this change taking place in the office of the President," Jefferson stated, "the good sense and free spirit of our countrymen will make the changes necessary to prevent it."[219]

Soon after ratification, the first Congress proposed ten amendments encompassing the Bill of Rights. But Jefferson's ardent wish for presidential term limits went unrequited, with custom and tradition standing in for a formal amendment. By 1940, Wilkinson remarked, Jefferson's apprehension about descent into monarchy was far-fetched, but something more pernicious had taken its place. "In our day and generation, kings as such are a vanishing race. But we need only look about us in the world today at the chaos and destruction in Europe to realize that kings have been succeeded by something worse, the totalitarian state and absolute dictators."[220]

To cope with such challenges, Roosevelt supporters argued, the United States needed stability of governance. They warned about uncertain leadership Americans would suffer if the Constitution were amended to prohibit continuity in office. Wilkinson was prepared to assume that risk. "To my mind, it is safer to hazard the remote contingency of a future emergency and to close the door for all time on the real possibility of life tenure in the Presidential office with its inevitable trend to dictatorship."[221]

Congress must close the gap in the Constitution, Wilkinson concluded.

On that Monday, September 30, Senator Burke wrapped up the hearings. He hoped they shed light on the benefits of a venerable custom and the damage that would flow from abandoning it. The Senator considered the November 5, 1940, election crucial. If the country repudiated Roosevelt, it would reaffirm its faith in the two-term tradition, making a constitutional amendment unnecessary.

Although his and Bridges' resolutions had been the focal point of the hearings, and brought additional attention to the third-term issue, Burke questioned whether either proposal would ever really go forward. Before gaveling the proceedings to an end, he remarked, "I am inclined myself to believe that we will probably never reach the point of submitting a constitutional amendment to the States, unless it is decided that the single term is very much more desirable than two terms and that we want to amend it in that respect."[222]

Senator Burke proved to be an inaccurate prophet. Propelled by Roosevelt's four elections and the Republicans' 1946 mid-term success, a two-term limitation passed Congress in 1947 and went to the states for ratification. By that time, Burke was in the private sector, heading a trade association.[223]

Through his hearings, Senator Burke tried to illuminate the dangers he saw from ending the two-term tradition. While he failed to derail Roosevelt's third term bid, Burke made an important contribution to the arguments of senators who would soon validate his vision for the necessity of term limits.

NOTES

1. Burke, quoted in Gerald Griffin, "A New Voice in the Senate," *The Baltimore Sun,* April 11, 1937, p. 85, ProQuest Historical Newspapers: *The Baltimore Sun,* p. 85.

2. The plan germinated from the president's frustration when the Supreme Court ruled as unconstitutional key New Deal legislation, the National Industrial Recovery Act in *A.L.A. Schechter Poultry Corp. v. United States*, 295 U.S. 495 (1935), and the Agricultural Adjustment Act in *United States v. Butler*, 297 U.S. 1 (1936). "Roosevelt considered it an ominous failure in American government that nine, unelected elderly men could thwart the New Deal and block the will of the popular majority. Nowhere in the Constitution did the founders give the Supreme Court the power to veto legislation and act as a policy-making body." Dunn, *Purge*, p. 13.

3. https://www.presidency.ucsb.edu/documents/fireside-chat-17.

4. "Public opinion reacted with considerable energy to the plan, viewing it as an unwise attempt at 'politicizing' the Supreme Court." Hickock, p. 38. In early 1938, 70 percent of respondents told pollsters they opposed a third-term for Roosevelt. Ibid., p. 39. How much of that sentiment represented fealty to the two-term tradition and how much related to sourness over Court-packing is difficult to gauge.

5. Ibid.

6. "In the Senatorial scheme of things, the younger members of the upper house of Congress ordinarily are seen but not heard – at least very much. Those who

transgress are eyed with curiosity, and are this called upon to present their case rather well if they are to spring from state leadership to national prominence. One Senator who is now making that jump. With the issue of the Supreme Court reorganization as his springboard, is Edward R. Burke. He has given many observers the impression that he has made a promising start." Griffin, op. cit.

7. "Opposition to what quickly became known as the 'Court-packing' bill was widespread. Republicans denounced it and conservative, especially Southern, Democrats gave it lukewarm lip service at best and often outright opposition. Many liberals worried about Roosevelt's tactics and what a future, illiberal President might do." Jeffries, p. 26. Vice President Garner and House Judiciary Committee Chairman Hatton Summers (D-TX) were openly skeptical. Ibid. "In later years, Roosevelt would claim that although he had lost the battle, he had won the war. The Supreme Court no longer presented a barrier against reform legislation. On the other hand, the fight over the Court was thc catalyst for emergence of a bipartisan conservative bloc in Congress to resist such legislation." Levy and Fischer, p. 1322.

8. Burton K. Wheeler was a senator from 1923 to 1947.

9. "Something was happening to the Grand Coalition that had carried Roosevelt to his election triumph. Something was happening to the Republicans too. Knowing that their little band in Congress could not overcome the President in a straight party fight, they resolved to stay silent and let the Democrats fight one another. When Hoover, Landon, and other national leaders wanted to rush to the microphone and make the court plan a party issue, congressional Republicans McNary, Borah, and Vandenberg, acting quickly, headed them off." James McGregor Burns, *Roosevelt: The Lion and the Fox* (New York: Harcourt, Brace, & World, Inc., 1956), p. 299.

10. The plan's collapse followed the July 14, 1937, death of Senate Majority Leader Joseph Robinson. A possible appointee to one of the vacancies the plan would create, Robinson led the Floor fight on the Administration's behalf. "Robinson found it hard going, and often he had to resort to a personal plea to embarrassed Senators for help in realizing his life ambition." Burns, p. 308. According to Farley, Roosevelt had for some time declined to commit to the appointment, wanting to avoid the appearance of a *quid pro quo*. However, several days before Robinson's death, authorized Farley to tell the senator confidentially that the appointment would be made. Farley, pp. 86–90.

11. "The President's request for expanded Executive Branch reorganization authority was viewed by some as another effort to expand the President's power, in this case at the expense of the Legislative Branch." Henry B. Hogue, "Presidential Reorganization Authority: History, Recent Initiatives, and Options for Congress," Congressional Research Service, Report R42852 (2012), p. 11.

12. "Late that January (1938) I got a definite indication of what I had long feared – that the President's hate for the members of the party who had opposed him on the Court fight had not cooled by the lapse of time but glowed as fierce as ever under the ashes of the past six months." Farley, p. 120. On July 23, 1939, Farley met with Roosevelt at Hyde Park, and heard the president explain the purge. "He talked about the purge, explaining that he started it because conservatives were hamstringing his program and he felt the Democratic Party must be liberal to be successful." Farley, p. 181.

13. FDR personally struck from the statement the following two sentences: "These nominations are entirely the affair of the States or the Congressional districts, and however these early battles may result, the National Committee will be behind every candidate that the people themselves choose. This goes for every state and Congressional district." Farley, pp. 120–121.

14. "With a few of his closest, and most combative advisors, termed by some the 'elimination committee' – including Secretary of the Interior Harold Ickes, Works Progress Administration head Harry Hopkins, and White House advisor and political operative Thomas (Tommy the Cork) Corcoran . . . he sought to address the problem by trying to deny re-nomination to key conservative Democrats in 1938, particularly in the Senate." Jeffries, p. 30. Farley assessed the purge as a disaster. In addition to failing in its purpose, it instigated a breach between Farley and the president that never fully healed. "I knew from the beginning that the purge could lead to nothing but misfortune, because in pursuing his course of vengeance, Roosevelt violated a cardinal political creed which demanded that he keep out of local matters. Sound doctrine is sound politics. When Roosevelt began neglecting the rules of the game, I began to have doubts. When he persisted in violating the rules, I lost faith in him." Farley, pp. 146–147.

15. "The people in Roosevelt's inner circle were already acquainted with his taste for crushing his opponents and enemies . . . His easy-going affability was only a mask." Dunn, *Purge*, p. 21.

16. Arthur Schlesinger, *The Age of Roosevelt: The Crisis of the Old Order 1919–1933* (Boston: Houghton Mifflin Company, 1957), p. 410.

17. Ibid. p. 6. "His long-term goal was to *highlight* the conflict between conservatives and liberals within the Democratic Party and then eliminate that conflict – by banishing conservatives and creating a unified, solidly liberal Democratic Party . . .. If the Democrats succeeded in ejecting conservatives from their ranks and if the Republicans absorbed those conservatives, the result, FDR hoped, would be party realignment and healthy, principled conflict between Republicans and Democrats." Ibid., p. 31.

18. The Great Depression caused a tremendous upswing of support for Democrats, and produced wide ideological diversity among politicians glad to gather under that party's umbrella. In a fireside chat on June 24, 1938, Roosevelt signaled his intent to identify candidates who ran under the Democratic label but were insufficiently committed to the party platform. "As the head of the Democratic Party, however, charged with the responsibility of carrying out the definitely liberal declaration of principles set forth in the 1936 Democratic platform, I feel that I have every right to speak in those few instances where there may be a clear-cut issue between candidates for a Democratic nomination involving these principles, or involving a clear misuse of my own name. Do not misunderstand me. I certainly would not indicate a preference in a state primary merely because a candidate, otherwise liberal in outlook, had conscientiously differed with me on any single issue. I should be far more concerned about the general attitude of a candidate towards present day problems and his own inward desire to get practical needs attended to in a practical way. You and I all know that progress may be blocked by outspoken reactionaries, but we also know that

progress can be blocked by those who say "yes" to a progressive objective, but who always find some reason to oppose any special specific proposal to gain that objective. I call that type of candidate a 'yes, but' fellow." See presidential speeches, Franklin D. Roosevelt, June 24, 1938, www.millercenter.org.

19. An eight-term Member of the House, O'Connor, lost the 1938 primary to James H. Fay, who went on to win the general election.

20. Fed by an economic downturn, the 1938 mid-terms were disastrous for Democrats. They lost seventy-two seats in the House and seven in the Senate. In the face of such losses, Democrats were able to retain control of both chambers only because of the overwhelming majorities they secured in the 1936 cycle and their inherent strength in Southern States. Indeed, outside of the South, Republicans won about half of the vote. After the election, Southern Democrats made up a majority of Democratic membership in the House and nearly a majority of Democratic Senators. Jeffries, pp. 33–35. The 1938 election was the beginning of the comeback that led to Republicans capturing Congress in 1946 and their successful efforts to advance the Twenty-second Amendment. While Roosevelt never confronted a Republican majority in Congress, immense ideological diversity among Democrats meant problems for the president on Capitol Hill. The president was not on the ballot in 1938, which may have been fortunate for him. "As economic conditions deteriorated during early 1938, so did Roosevelt's popularity. By the summer months of that year, barely half the people questioned in a nationwide survey said they would vote for Roosevelt if they were going to the polls at that time." Burns, p. 337.

21. Cochran never made it to the Senate. In the 1940 general election, he lost to Hugh Butler (R-NE).

22. Official Report of the Nebraska State Canvassing Board, Primary Election April 9, 1940, compiled by Harry R. Swanson, Secretary of State.

23. For example, although James Farley had opposed the third term, contested Roosevelt for the nomination, and disdained Roosevelt's insistence that Henry Wallace be nominated for vice president, he was a Democrat through and through. However uncomfortably, once the Convention made its choice, he rallied behind the party. "I had made my fight within my party. I had lost that fight. It therefore became incumbent upon me to go along with a majority of my party." Farley, p. 334. Senator Harry Truman, who also opposed the third term, followed the same course. See United States Senate Committee on the Judiciary, "Presidential Terms of Office," Hearings before a Subcommittee of the Committee on the Judiciary, United States Senate, Eighty-sixth Congress, First Session, on S.J. Res. 11, Proposing an Amendment to the Constitution to Repeal the Twenty-second Article of Amendment to the Constitution, Part 1, Washington, DC: United States Government Printing Office, 1960, p. 2.

24. Burke did so via a telegram to Willkie on July 18, 1940, and made public that same day. See "Burke Bolts Party Over Third Term." In his wire, Burke stated, "I disclaim the leadership of those of my party who but a few years ago put themselves on record that any departure from the two-term tradition would be unwise, unpatriotic, and fraught with peril to our free institutions, and who today take the very action that they then denounced. A fitting rebuke to their apostasy will be administered by an

aroused people. In that program of education, I volunteer my services for the duration of the campaign." *New York Times*, July 19, 1940, p. 1. Among Democratic senators, Burke did not stand alone in his public defection. His Nebraska colleague, Edward Walsh, joined him. West Virginia's Rush Holt, who had introduced a resolution opposing a third term, openly and futilely pressed for the Senate to vote on it. Peters, p. 153.

25. The hearing room is now designated as Room 485 of the Russell Senate Office Building, named in 1972 for Senator Richard B. Russell (D-GA).

26. Styles Bridges was a senator from 1937 until his death in office in 1961.

27. In addition to the Burke and Bridges resolutions, eight constitutional amendments dealing with presidential tenure were also introduced in the House of Representatives during the 76th Congress. Furthermore, on November 19, 1940, following Roosevelt's reelection, Senator Arthur Capper (R-KS) introduced a resolution to limit a president to two terms. Capper's proposal was referred to the Senate Judiciary Committee and died along with the Burke and Bridges resolutions. "Proposed Amendments to the Constitution of the United States Introduced in Congress from December 6, 1926 to January 3, 1941," Compiled for use by the Office of the Secretary of the Senate, Government Printing Office, 1941.

28. "Third Term for President" Hearings before the United States Senate Subcommittee on the Judiciary, September 4, 1940.

29. Presently known as the Kennedy Caucus Room, it is the grandest location in the Senate office complex. The Russell Building in which it sits opened in 1909. The Caucus Room has seen events of great moment and drama, such as the hearing into the Titanic sinking, the Teapot Dome Investigation, Army-McCarthy, the Fulbright hearings on conduct of the Vietnam War, the Ervin Committee investigating Watergate, the Clarence Thomas nomination, and many more. It is also the place where senators John F. Kennedy and Robert F. Kennedy announced their presidential candidacies.

30. Fred Van Nuys was a senator from Indiana from 1933 until his death in 1944.

31. Warren Austin served in the Senate from 1931 until his resignation in 1946. After leaving Congress, he was the first American ambassador to the United Nations.

32. Alexander Wiley served as a senator from 1939 to 1963.

33. Henry Ashurst was Arizona's first senator. He served from the advent of statehood in 1912 until his death in 1941.

34. Tom Connally was in the House from 1917 to 1929 and served in the Senate from 1929 to 1953. He was often absent from the hearings.

35. Burke's statement outlining this background appears in S. Hearings (1940), pp. 1–3.

36. Mr. Coolidge was President Jefferson's great, great, great grandson.

37. This is known as the Electoral College.

38. S. Hearings, p. 5.

39. Ibid., p. 5.

40. "In response to perceived abuses of executive power by the king and his royal governors, state constitutions of the revolutionary era generally provided for eviscerated executive branches, which were made largely subordinate to state legislatures." Klarman, p. 213.

41. Ibid., p. 7. Presidential scholar Thomas Cronin reinforces this point. Colonial governors were appointed and mistrusted. Legislatures were seen as protectors of the people's liberties. Once the revolution was over, these attitudes carried forward. Thus, in the formative years of the republic, it was customary for state legislatures to elect governors. Short terms were common, as were restrictions on reeligibility. Both were thought necessary to protect the people. Cronin, pp. 62–63.

42. Ibid. As Adams noted, "There was also a fear of the people, or the mob as it was then called, and not without reason . . . They (the Framers) never intended to establish an almost pure democracy but a representative form of government."

43. Ibid., p. 8.

44. Ibid.

45. Ibid., p. 12.

46. Ibid., p. 15.

47. This circumstance has been further reinforced over time. By 2018, 37 of 50 states had imposed term limits on their Governors.

48. Ibid., p. 16.

49. Huey Long was governor of Louisiana from 1928 to 1932 and a senator from 1932 until his assassination in Baton Rouge in 1935. Running on a populist agenda of income redistribution, he intended to challenge Roosevelt in 1936 for the Democratic nomination. A witness on the third day of hearings, former Representative Samuel Pettengill (D-IN) testified that Long was a "small-scale dictator." Pettengill continued, "His will became the law of a great State. He held in the hollow of his hand the legislature, the judiciary, and the machinery to nominate and elect all candidates for public office, including himself." S. Hearings, p. 36. Franklin Roosevelt had the same estimation of Long. As he told his son, Elliott, "That man is an influence for evil in the entire structure of our country." Roosevelt and Brough, p. 289.

50. Father Charles Coughlin (1891–1979), pastor of the National Shrine of the Little Flower in Royal Oak, Michigan, was known as the "radio priest." He was famed for stridently anti-Semitic, anti-New Deal, and pro-Fascist commentary on widely syndicated radio broadcasts during the 1930s.

51. According to James Farley, Long might have been impactful as a third-party candidate in 1936. "The Democratic National Committee conducted a secret poll on Long's bid for national power which disclosed, to our surprise, that he might poll between 3,000,000 to 4,000,000 votes as the head of a third party. His support was not confined to Louisiana and nearby states, but his 'share the wealth' program was attracting strength in the industrial and farm areas of the north . . . It was conceivable that his third-party movement might constitute a balance of power in the 1936 election, although indications were that he would cost us no more than the electoral votes of a few states . . . I am firmly convinced Long would have been a source of annoyance rather than a threat in 1936." Farley, p. 51.

52. S. Hearings, p. 20.

53. Ibid., p. 22.

54. Ibid.

55. Ibid.

56. These were Thomas Jefferson, Andrew Jackson, James Buchanan, Andrew Johnson, Grover Cleveland, and William Howard Taft. Jefferson ran for a second

term in 1804, Jackson, in 1832, Cleveland in 1888, and after his defeat in that year, in 1892, and Taft in 1912.

57. Ibid., p. 24. In 1913, Democrats were the majority party in both Houses. Notwithstanding the Senate's action, the amendment was not brought to a vote in the House of Representatives. The 1896 Democratic platform contained a provision stating that, "We declare it to be the unwritten law of this Republic, established by custom and usage of 100 years, and sanctioned by the examples of the greatest and wisest of those who founded and have maintained our Government that no man should be eligible for a third term of the Presidential office." The American Presidency Project, 1986 Democratic Party Platform, www.presidency.ucsb.edu (accessed October 11, 2018).

58. In 1939, Congress passed the Hatch Act to respond to documented use of federal workers for political purposes.

59. It is presently designated as Room 485 of the Russell Senate Office Building. At the time, it was the hearing room of the Senate Committee on Claims, which Burke also chaired.

60. S. Hearings, p. 29.

61. The 44th Congress had a Democratic majority in the House and a Republican majority in the Senate.

62. The 70th Congress had Republican majorities in both Houses.

63. William Springer served in the House from 1875 to 1895.

64. S. Hearings, p. 30.

65. Springer was recognized to offer his resolution, did so, and immediately moved the previous question. The motion is a device to cut off debate. The House agreed to it by a vote of 144 to 2. To forestall a final vote, Representative Clinton D. MacDougall (R-NY) moved to adjourn. By voice vote, the House refused to do so. Then, the House votes 223 to 18 to adopt the resolution itself. A Civil War veteran, MacDougall served in the House from 1873 to 1877. He was one of the eighteen members who opposed the resolution.

66. *Congressional Record*, December 15, 1875, p. 228.

67. A contemporary account of the Springer Resolution and its impact may be found in an 1880 article by Timothy O. Howe in the *North American Review*. Howe wrote, "That reiterated vociferation accomplished the purpose for which it was designed. It defeated the re-nomination of General Grant in 1876." Having reviewed the record of the Constitutional Convention, Howe was deeply offended by Springer's resolution, which he believed distorted the Framers' vision of the presidency. He also found Springer's logic ridiculous. "To tell rational creatures that 'free institutions' are imperiled by the reelection of one who for eight years has proved a faithful magistrate, but are insured by the election of one who has never been proved at all, seems to be the extreme of audacity." Timothy O. Howe, "The Third Term," *The North American Review*, Vol. 130, No. 279 (February 1880), pp. 116–129, Published by: University of Northern Iowa. Stable URL: http://www.jstor.org/stable/25100831 (accessed April 21, 2018).

68. *New York Times*, "Senate Declares Against Third Term by 56 to 26 Vote: LaFollette Resolution Adopted Viewing Departure from Precedent as 'Fraught with Peril,'" February 11, 1928, p. 1.

69. Ibid., p. 37.

70. Ibid.

71. U.S. Constitution, Article II, section 2.

72. H. Hearings, p. 37.

73. There is an unresolved constitutional question as to whether electors can act independently of the will expressed by the popular vote in their states. Thirty states purport to bind their electors, some with pledges, threats of removal of "faithless electors" or imposition of fines and even criminal penalties. Twenty-one states make no such effort. "The Electoral College," www.nscl.org (accessed August 22, 2018).

74. H. Hearings, p. 38.

75. Harrison won 233 of 401 electoral votes, even though Cleveland won the popular vote by 90,000, or .8%. Results were exceedingly close in many states that Harrison won, such as in New York, Ohio, and Indiana. As Cleveland's biographer, Allan Nevins, observes, "A slight shift in the distribution of this popular plurality would have given him what all the political wiseacres would have called a 'sweeping victory.'" Allan Nevins, *Grover Cleveland: A Study in Courage* (Newtown, Connecticut: American Political Biography Press, 1932), p. 439. Cleveland was able to prevail in the popular vote by running landslide percentages in former Confederate states such as South Carolina, Mississippi, Louisiana, and Georgia. In 1892, with Harrison hampered by public dissatisfaction over high tariffs, Cleveland roared back into the White House, prevailing by more than a half million popular votes and by 277 to 145 in the Electoral College. Until the vote, the election was imagined to be close. "Yet the magnitude of Cleveland's victory astonished everyone, for it was the most decisive since the re-election of Lincoln in 1864." Ibid., p. 507.

76. H. Hearings, p. 38.

77. Ibid.

78. The Act grew out of allegations of political activities by employees in the Works Progress Administration, and specifically by the intervention of its Administrator, Harry Hopkins, in the 1938 Democratic primary for the U.S. Senate. Hopkins openly endorsed Representative Otha Wearin against incumbent Senator Guy Gillette. Iowa Democratic leaders protested loudly about interference in the primary and leading newspapers inveighed against the alleged or apparent use of federal relief dollars for political purposes. Inasmuch as such intervention could be interpreted as payback for Gillette's independence from Roosevelt, the idea sunk in on Capitol Hill that federal legislation could provide protection against such political retribution. See Dunn, *Purge*, pp. 115–116. In an October 14, 1940, address in Syracuse, Willkie excoriated the administration for politicizing federal workers. "Under the third-term candidate, men on WPA have been forced to contribute New Deal campaign funds. They have been forced to sign pledges to vote for the New Deal candidates. In some sections of the country, allegiance to the party in power has been made a test of eligibility to a WPA job." "Text of Willkie's Address at a Rally in Syracuse," *New York Times*, October 15, 1940, p. 12.

79. S. Hearings, p. 39.

80. The United States established the Commission to govern the Philippines in the aftermath of the Spanish-American War.

81. S. Hearings, p. 46.

82. Ibid., p. 47.
83. S. Hearings, p. 54.
84. The era of Weimar Republic governance was 1919 to 1933.
85. The last of the Hohenzollern Kaisers was Wilhelm II, who abdicated in November 1918. The family was prominent in Prussia, and ruled the entire country after the unification of Germany in 1871.
86. S. Hearings, p. 50.
87. Ibid., p. 52. Schurman referenced William Jennings Bryan. Known as "The Great Commoner," Bryan was a stunning orator whose "Cross of Gold" speech at the 1896 Democratic Convention propelled him from being a little known Congressman from Nebraska to that year's Democratic nominee. At the time, Bryan was 36 years old, barely eligible to serve as president and the youngest person ever nominated for president. In the years since, no one else so young has been a major party nominee. Although he lost to Republican William McKinley, Bryan again headed the Democratic ticket in 1900 and 1908.
88. S. Hearings, p. 52. Although he did not say so, Schurman might have mentioned Roosevelt's 1938 efforts to purge conservative Democrats, and even the ousting of Senator Burke in the 1940 Democratic primary.
89. Ibid., pp. 52–53. According to Schurman, the Weimar Constitution contained this provision because political parties in the Reichstag were so susceptible to fragmentation that it became impossible to form a cabinet. The result was that "free recourse was had to this constitutional provision, which was intended for use only in a great emergency, by President Von Hindenburg and his later chancellors. They paved the way which Hitler followed."
90. Ibid., p. 53.
91. In questioning, Senator Wiley asserted that the 1940 Bases for Destroyers arrangement that Roosevelt made with Churchill represented precisely this kind of situation. To assist the British war effort, FDR transferred fifty destroyers to Britain in exchange for basing rights on British-held territory.
92. Ibid., p.57.
93. Ibid., p. 63.
94. Ibid.
95. Ibid., pp. 63–64.
96. Ibid., p. 64.
97. Ibid., p. 65.
98. Ibid., p. 63.
99. Ibid., p. 77.
100. Donald H. McLean served in the House of Representatives from 1933 to 1945.
101. The text of the amendment appears at S. Hearings, p. 89. This grandfathering concept is not dissimilar to the way President Harry Truman was exempted from the Twenty-second Amendment and could have sought another term in 1952.
102. Ibid., p. 74.
103. Ibid.
104. Ibid., p. 76.
105. Ibid., p. 92.

106. Ibid.
107. Ibid.
108. Ibid., p. 95.
109. Ibid., p. 101.
110. Benjamin F. Wade served in the Senate from 1851 to 1869. Had Congress impeached Andrew Johnson in 1868, Wade would have succeeded to the presidency.
111. Ames, p. 128.
112. Ibid., pp. 101–102. George Norris served in the House from 1903 to 1913, and was the leader of a successful 1910 effort to restrict the power of Speaker Joseph Cannon (R-IL). Elected to the Senate, he served from 1913 to 1943. Notwithstanding these sentiments, which Norris expressed when opposing the possibility of a 1928 Coolidge candidacy, Norris endorsed many New Deal initiatives, and backed Roosevelt for a third term in 1940.
113. Ibid., p. 102. During 1947 Senate proceedings on H.J. Res. 27, which became the Twenty-second Amendment, Senator Warren Magnuson (D-WA) proposed that the term limits apply to two *consecutive* terms and that a person could become eligible again if he sat out a term. However, the Senate did not agree to Magnuson's amendment.
114. Ibid., pp. 105–106.
115. Ibid., p. 105.
116. Ibid., p. 126. The Articles of Confederation Congress was a unicameral legislature with each State having one vote. State delegations ranged in size from two to seven persons, but voted as a unit. Executive-type functions were performed by a president of the United States in Congress Assembled. Elected from within the Congress, he could serve no more than one year in any three-year period.
117. Klarman, p. 214.
118. Ibid., p.127.
119. Ibid.
120. Ibid., p. 128.
121. S. Hearings, p. 129.
122. Ibid., p. 133.
123. Ibid., p. 130. Reference is made to Mahlon Dickerson of New Jersey, who served in the Senate from 1817 to 1833.
124. S. Hearings, p. 133.
125. Ibid., pp. 130–131.
126. Democrats and regular Republicans supported it, while progressives opposed it. Lingley, p. 317.
127. Ibid., p. 133.
128. Ibid., p. 137.
129. Ibid.
130. Professor Judith A. Best has argued that constitutional provisions undergirding the federal system also afford vital protections for political minorities. The division of authority between various units and layers of government allows for minorities overall to constitute majorities somewhere. In political science terms, it is the theory of concurrent majorities. "To allow minorities to be part of a majority, it is necessary to divide both society and government in multiple and complex ways,"

she writes. "Majorities must be formed in each of the fifty states and each of the 435 congressional districts in order to fill our national elective offices." Best, pp. 5–6.

131. In a long and highly distinguished career, Davis served in the House of Representatives from 1911 to 1913, as Solicitor General from 1913 to 1918, and as ambassador to the United Kingdom from 1918 to 1921. During his time as an attorney both in public office and in the private sector, Davis appeared more than 150 times before the United States Supreme Court.

132. William Harbaugh, "Davis, John W." *Encyclopedia of the American Presidency,* (New York: Simon & Schuster, 1994), pp. 347–348.

133. S. Hearing, p. 149.

134. Ibid.

135. Ibid.

136. Ibid., p. 147.

137. The parallels to the Russian presidencies of Vladimir Putin and Dmitri Medvedev are inescapable.

138. Manipulating constitutions to expand a leader's power is a tactic appealing to modern autocrats. It rearranges the political system while maintaining the veneer of legality. The experiences of presidents Xi Jinping in China and Recip Tayyip Erdogen in Turkey illustrate this.

139. Ibid., p. 148.

140. Ibid.

141. Ibid.

142. Ibid., p. 150.

143. McCormick chaired the DNC from 1916 to 1919, after which President Woodrow Wilson made him chairman of the American delegation to the Paris Peace Conference, which convened that year and produced the Treaty of Versailles.

144. S. Hearings, p. 156.

145. Ibid.

146. Ibid. Contrasting what was available to Roosevelt in 1940 with what Wilson could use in 1916, when McCormick chaired the DNC, the witness lamented, "I only wish we had had it in 1916. We would have had an easy fight." Ibid.

147. Ibid., p. 157.

148. Ibid., p. 173.

149. Ibid., pp. 173–174.

150. Ibid., p. 174.

151. Ibid.

152. In 1940, and certainly during the pivotal debate of 1947, Republicans would claim that there was broad public demand that Congress do something to preserve the two-term tradition. For reasons here outlined, it was difficult to discern that sentiment in 1940. Even in 1947, Democrats would scoff at such claims, plausibly so.

153. S. Hearings, p. 175.

154. Ibid., p. 178.

155. The provision read, "The executive power shall be vested in a President of the Confederate States of America. He and the Vice President shall hold their offices for the term of six years; but the President shall not be reeligible."

156. S. Hearings, p. 181, citing an address Stephens made in Savannah, Georgia, reported in Richard Malcolm Johnston and William Hand Browne, *The Life of Alexander H. Stephens*. (Philadelphia: J.B. Lippincott & Co., 1878), p. 396.

157. S. Hearings, p. 181.

158. Ibid.

159. Ibid., p.188.

160. Ibid.

161. Ibid., p. 189.

162. Ibid.

163. Her testimony appears at S. Hearings, pp. 198–201.

164. S. Hearings, pp. 198–199.

165. For example, Georges Clemenceau did not become Prime Minister of France until November 1917, more than three years into World War I. David Lloyd George succeeded Henry Asquith as Prime Minister of the United Kingdom in December 1916, 28 months into the war. Both of the new leaders prosecuted the war to a successful conclusion. In the United States, Roosevelt's death on April 12, 1945, with World War II ongoing, elevated Harry Truman to the presidency. Under Truman's leadership, the war ended in both the European and Pacific Theaters.

166. Ibid., p. 199.

167. This was known as the Citizen Genet Affair, named for Edmond-Charles Genet, the French Ambassador.

168. S. Hearings, p. 212.

169. Ibid.

170. Ibid., p. 215.

171. Ibid.

172. Ibid., p. 217.

173. Ibid., p. 219.

174. A faction of Gold-Democrats met in Indianapolis on September 2, 1896, in opposition to Bryan's candidacy. After Cleveland spurned their overtures for what would have been a third-term candidacy, they nominated Senator John M. Palmer (D-IL) and named themselves the National Democrats. Palmer got less than 1% of the vote in an election in which William McKinley commanded an absolute majority and beat Bryan by five points. Cleveland knew that Palmer would not win any states, but supported the mission of the National Democrats to ensure Bryan's defeat. "He never believed for an instant that the Chicago ticket was Democratic at all, and as between Bryan and McKinley, he unquestionably preferred the latter." Nevins, p. 708.

175. S. Hearings, p. 218.

176. Ibid., p. 220.

177. Ibid., p. 238.

178. Ibid., p. 239.

179. Ibid., p. 243.

180. Colby served during Wilson's last year as president, March 1920 to March 1921, succeeding Robert Lansing as Secretary of State after the Senate, for the second time, defeated the Treaty of Versailles.

181. S. Hearings, p. 248.

182. Ibid.
183. Ibid., p. 249.
184. Ibid., p. 250.
185. Ibid., pp. 251–252.
186. Ibid., p. 252.
187. Ibid., p. 253.
188. Ibid.
189. Ibid.
190. Ibid.
191. Ibid., p. 254.
192. Villard was active in the America First Committee, at the time, the leading isolationist organization. Charles Lindbergh played a prominent role in this group.
193. In September 1940, the United States and Great Britain agreed to exchange British bases for American destroyers.
194. S. Hearings, p. 254.
195. Ibid.
196. Ibid., p. 266.
197. Ibid., p. 267.
198. McSparran served as Pennsylvania's Secretary of Agriculture from 1931 to 1935.
199. S. Hearings, p. 270.
200. Ibid.
201. George C. Peery was governor of Virginia from 1934 to 1938.
202. Indeed, in 1947, when the Twenty-second Amendment was before Congress, Democrats made this same point.
203. S. Hearings, p. 278.
204. S. Hearings, p. 314.
205. Ibid., p. 315.
206. Ibid.
207. *New York Times*, "The Choice of a Candidate," September 19, 1940.
208. S. Hearings, p. 316.
209. Ibid., p. 317.
210. Ibid.
211. Roosevelt's reorganization bill would have allowed for major realignments within the Executive Branch. It proved very controversial. After extensive debate, it passed the Senate in March 1938 by a vote of 48 to 42, with major Democratic defections, but the House in a floor vote shelved it later that year, again with major Democratic defections. *New York Times*, "The Summary of the Reorganization Bill," March 29, 1938, p. 4. "In the late 1930s – an epoch famous for power-driven dictators erecting their miserable totalitarian regimes – some Americans were frightened by the idea of increasing executive power." Dunn, *Purge*, p. 8.
212. "In the spring, Congress rejected the President's attempt to reorganize government agencies. This was little more than an administrative reform designed to increase efficiency. But having sown suspicion with his Court-packing plan, Roosevelt now reaped a harvest of distrust. No fewer than 108 Democrats helped to vote down the reorganization scheme in the House of Representatives." Brendon, p. 436.

213. Ibid., p. 319.
214. Ibid., p. 317.
215. Ibid.
216. Ibid., p. 335.
217. Ibid.
218. Ibid., p. 336.
219. Ibid., p. 337.
220. Ibid., pp. 338–339.
221. Ibid., p. 340.
222. Ibid., p. 341.
223. Burke served from 1942 to 1947 as the head of the Southern Coal Producers Association, after which he was General Counsel to the Hawaiian Statehood Commission. He retired in 1950, a year before ratification of the Twenty-second Amendment. Burke passed away in 1968, just short of his 86th birthday. See "Edward Raymond Burke" in bioguide.congress.gov.

Appendix B

Texts of the House and Senate Versions of the Twenty-Second Amendment (1947)

The text of H.J. Res. 27, as reported by the House Judiciary Committee and passed by the House in 1947:

Section 1: Any person who has served as a president of the United States during all, or any portions, of any two terms, shall hereafter be ineligible to hold the office of president, but this Article shall not prevent any person who may hold the office of president during the term within which this Article is ratified from holding such office for the remainder of such term.

Section 2. This Article shall be inoperative unless it shall have been ratified as an amendment to the Constitution by the legislatures of three-fourths of the several states within seven years from the date of its submission to the states by the Congress.

The text of H.J. Res. 27, as reported in amended form by the Senate Judiciary Committee:

Section 1: A person who has held the office of president, or acted as president, on three hundred and sixty-five calendar days or more in each of two terms shall not be eligible to hold the office of president or act as president, for any part of another term, but this Article shall not prevent any person who may be holding the office of president or acting as president during the term within which this Article becomes operative from holding the office of president or acting as president during the remainder of such term.

Section 2: This Article shall be inoperative unless it shall have been ratified as an amendment to the Constitution by conventions in the several states, as provided in the Constitution, within seven years from the date of its submission to the states by the Congress.

The text of H.J. Res. 27, as passed by the senate, agreed to by the House, in 1947, and finally ratified by the states as the Twenty-second Amendment to the United States Constitution in 1951:

Section 1: No person shall be elected to the office of the president more than twice, and no person who has held the office of president, or acted as president for more than 2 years of a term to which some other person was elected president shall be elected to the office of president more than once. But this Article shall not apply to any person holding the office of president when this Article was proposed by the Congress, and shall not prevent any person who may be holding the office of president, or acting as president, during the term within which this Article becomes operative from holding the office of president or acting as president during the remainder of such term.

Section 2: This Article shall be inoperative unless it shall have been ratified as an amendment to the Constitution by the legislatures of three-fourths of the several states within seven years from the date of its submission to the states by the Congress.

Bibliography

Abbott, Lawrence F., ed. *The Letters of Archie Butt*. Garden City, New York: Doubleday, Page and Company, 1924.

Ackerman, Kenneth D. D*ark Horse: The Surprise Election and Political Murder of President James A. Garfield.* New York: Carroll & Graf Publishers, 2003.

Adams, Henry. *History of the United States of America During the Administrations of Thomas Jefferson.* New York: Literary Classics of the United States, 1986.

"A Great Nation in Grief." *New York Times*, July 3, 1881.

"Alienists to Quiz Man Who Shot T.R." *Journal Gazette* (Mattoon, Illinois), November 13, 1912.

Ambrose, Stephen A. *Eisenhower: Soldier, Statesman, General, President-elect 1890–1952*. New York: Simon & Schuster, 1983.

Ames, Herman. *The Proposed Amendments to the Constitution of the United States*. New York: Burt Franklin, 1896.

"Asks Taft to Withdraw." *The Topeka State Journal* (Topeka, Kan.), May 22, 1912.

"A Victory that is a Defeat." *Lancaster Daily Intelligencer* (Lancaster, Pa.), February 26, 1880.

Badeau, Adam. *Grant in Peace: From Appomattox to Mount McGregor, a Personal Memoir*. Hartford: S.S. Scranton & Co., 1887.

Bailey, Thomas. *Wilson and the Peacemakers*. New York: The MacMillan Company, 1947.

Balch, William Ralston. *The Life of James Abram Garfield*. Philadelphia: Hubbard Brothers, 1881.

Bayh, Birch. *One Heartbeat Away: Presidential Disability and Succession*. Indianapolis and New York: The Bobbs-Merrill Company, Inc., 1968.

Beeman, Richard. *Plain, Honest Men: The Making of the American Constitution*. New York: Random House Trade Paperbacks, 2009.

Berg, A. Scott. *Wilson*. New York: G.P. Putnam's Sons, 2013.

Best, Judith A. *The Choice of the People: Debating the Electoral College*. Lanham, Maryland: Rowman & Littlefield Publishers, Inc., 1996.

Blaine, James G. *Twenty Years of Congress: 1861–1881, Volume II*. Norwich, Connecticut: Henry Hill Publishing Company, 1886.

Bouverie, Tim. *Appeasement: Chamberlain, Hitler, Churchill, and the Road to War*. New York: Random House, 2019.

Brands, H.W. *Andrew Jackson: His Life and Times*. New York: Random House, 2005.

Brands, H.W. *Heirs of the Founders*, New York: Doubleday, 2018.

Brands, H.W. *Traitor to His Class: The Privileged Life and Radical Presidency of Franklin Delano Roosevelt*. New York: Doubleday, 2008.

Brands, H.W. *T.R.: The Last Romantic*. New York: Basic Books, 1997.

Brendon, Piers. *The Dark Valley: A Panorama of the 1930s*. London. Jonathan Cape, 2000.

Brown, Joshua M. "Stock Market Crash: Think 1938, not 2008." *Christian Science Monitor*, August 4, 2011.

"Bryan Begins Tour." *Boston Globe*, September 15, 1912.

Burns, James MacGregor. *Roosevelt: The Lion and the Fox*. New York: Harcourt, Brace, & World, Inc., 1956.

Burns, James MacGregor. *Roosevelt: The Soldier of Freedom*. New York: Harcourt, Brace, Jovanovich. 1970.

Chace, James. *1912: Wilson, Roosevelt, Taft, & Debs – The Election that Changed the Country*. New York: Simon & Schuster, 2004.

Chernow, Ron. *Grant*. New York: Penguin Press, 2017.

Chicago Daily Tribune (Chicago, Illinois), June 2, 1880.

Chronicling America: Historic American Newspapers. Library of Congress.

Clifford, Clark: *Counsel to the President: A Memoir*. New York: Doubleday, 1991.

Congressional Quarterly. "The Third-term Tradition in American Politics." *Editorial Research Reports*, Vol. 1 (1927).

Conner, L.R. "Third Term Becomes Basic Issue in Ohio; Splits Develop on War." *Washington Evening Star*. September 22, 1940.

Cook, James F. *Carl Vinson: Patriarch of the Armed Forces*. Macon, Georgia: Mercer University Press, 2004.

Coolidge, Calvin. *The Autobiography of Calvin Coolidge*. Plymouth, Vermont. The Calvin Coolidge Memorial Foundation, 1989 (original edition, 1929).

Cooper, John Milton. *Breaking the Heart of the World: Woodrow Wilson and the Fight for the League of Nations*. New York: Cambridge University Press, 2001.

Cordery, Stacy A. *Alice: Alice Roosevelt Longworth, from White House Princess to Washington Power Broker*. New York: Viking, 2007.

Crockett, David. A. "The Contemporary Presidency: 'An Excess of Refinement': Lame Duck Presidents in Constitutional and Historical Context, *Presidential Studies Quarterly*, Vol. 38, No. 4, December 2008.

Cronin, Thomas. *Inventing the American Presidency*. Lawrence, Kansas: University of Kansas Press, 1989.

"Curtain is Ready to Rise." *Cincinnati Enquirer*, August 5, 1912.

Daniels, Josephus. *The Wilson Era: Years of War and After: 1917–1923*. Chapel Hill, North Carolina: University of North Carolina Press, 1946.

Davis, Paul B. "The Future of Presidential Tenure." *Presidential Studies Quarterly*, Vol. 10, No. 3 (Summer 1980).

Dunn, Susan. *1940: FDR, Willkie, Lindbergh, Hitler – The Election Before the Storm.* New Haven: Yale University Press, 2013.

Dunn, Susan. *A Blueprint for War: FDR and the Hundred Days that Mobilized America.* New Haven: Yale University Press, 2018. Dunn, Susan. *Roosevelt's Purge: How FDR Fought to Change the Democratic Party.* Cambridge, Massachusetts: The Belknap Press of Harvard University, 2010.

Editorial Page of *The Detroit Times*, September 2, 1910.

"Editorials." *Northern Ohio Journal* (Painesville, Ohio), June 12, 1875.

Eisenhower, Dwight D. *At Ease: Stories I Tell to Friends. New York*: Doubleday, 1967.

Eisenhower, Dwight D. *Mandate for Change*, New York: Doubleday, 1963.

Eisenhower, Milton. *The President is Calling*. Garden City, New York: Doubleday & Company, Inc., 1974.

Farley, James A. *Jim Farley's Story: The Roosevelt Years*. New York: McGraw Hill Book Company, Inc., 1948.

Farrand, Max. *The Records of the Federal Convention of 1787, Volume II*. New Haven: Yale University Press, 1911.

Ferling, John. "Thomas Jefferson, Aaron Burr, and the Election of 1800." *Smithsonian Magazine*, November 1, 2004.

Ferrell, Robert H. *Choosing Truman: The Democratic Convention of 1944*. Columbia, Missouri: University of Missouri Press, 1994.

Flood, Charles Bracelen. *Grant and Sherman: The Friendship that Won the Civil War*. New York: Farrer, Strauss, and Giroux, 2005.

Fox, J.A. "Fourth Term Inquiries Parried by President with Bible Reference, "*Washington Evening Star,* Feb. 9, 1940.

"Franklin Roosevelt Wins Another Chance to be a Great Leader of a United People." *Life*. November 18, 1940.

"Franklin D, Roosevelt." *New York Times*, April 13, 1945.

Frist, William H. and J. Lee Annis, Jr. *Tennessee Senators 1911–2001*. Lanham, Maryland: Madison Books, 1999.

Fromkin, David. *In the Time of the Americans*, New York: Random House, 1995.

Fund, John. "Scrapping Term Limits Fits the 'Dictator Forever' Model." *National Review*. February 25, 2018.

Gellman, Irwin F. *The President and the Apprentice*. New Haven: Yale University Press, 2015.

"General Grant's Party." *The New York Herald*, March 4, 1875.

German, James C. Jr. "Taft, Roosevelt, and United States Steel, *The Historian,* Vol. 34, No. 2 (August 1972), pp. 598–613.

Gilbert, Robert. *The Tormented President: Calvin Coolidge, Death, and Clinical Depression*. Westport, Connecticut: Praeger, 2003.

Glad, Betty. *Charles Evans Hughes and the Illusions of Innocence*. Urbana, Illinois: University of Illinois Press, 1966.

Goodwin, Doris Kearns. *No Ordinary Time: Franklin and Eleanor Roosevelt: The Home Front in World War II*. New York: Simon & Schuster, 1994.

Goodwin, Doris Kearns. *The Bully Pulpit: Theodore Roosevelt, William Howard Taft, and the Golden Age of Journalism*. New York. Simon & Schuster, 2013.

Gould, Lewis. "Why TR Lost the Republican Nomination in 1912: What New Research Shows." www.historynewsnetwork.org.

"Grant and the Third Term." *The Andrew County Republican* (Savannah, Missouri), May 7, 1875.

"Grant and the Third Term." *The Daily Gazette* (Wilmington, Delaware) June 4, 1875.

"Grant's Campaign." *The Sun,* Oct. 16, 1880.

Grant, Julia Dent. *The Personal Memoirs of Julia Dent Grant,* reprint. New York: G.P. Putnam's Sons, 1975.

"Grant's Third Term Blunder." *The Louisiana Democrat* (Alexandria, Louisiana), June 16, 1875.

"Grant's Third-term Letter." *The Jasper Weekly Courier* (Jasper, Indiana), June 18, 1875.

Griffin, Gerald. "A New Voice in the Senate." *The Baltimore Sun,* Apr 11, 1937.

Grimes, Alan P. *Democracy and the Amendments to the Constitution.* Lanham, Maryland: University Press of America, 1987.

Haas, Lawrence. *Harry and Arthur: Truman, Vandenberg, and the Partnership that Created the Free World.* Lincoln, Nebraska: Potomac Books, 2016.

Hamilton, Nigel. *War and Peace: FDR's Final Odyssey D-Day to Yalta 1943–1945.* Boston: Houghton Mifflin Harcourt, 2019.

Hagerty, James A. "Willkie Declares New Deal 'Kidnaps' Democratic Party.' *New York Times*, October 15, 1940.

Hargreaves, Mary C. "Adams, John Quincy." *Encyclopedia of the American Presidency*, Volume I. New York: Simon & Schuster, 1994.

Harmsen, Peter. *Shanghai 1937: Stalingrad on the Yangtze.* Havertown, Pennsylvania: Casemate Publishers, 2013.

Hauptly, Denis J. *A Convention of Delegates: The Creation of the Constitution.* New York: Antheum, 1987.

Heidler, David S. and Jeanne T. Heidler. *Henry Clay: The Essential American.* New York: Random House, 2010.

Hennessey, M.E. "Roosevelt Plans Later Convention." *Boston Globe*, June 22, 1912.

Henry, John C. "Roosevelt Pledges New President After Third Term Ends, as Willkie Charges U.S. Way of Life Is In Peril." *Washington Evening Star*, November 3, 1940.

Hickok, Jr., Eugene W. "Pique Over Principle: Partisan Politics and the Twenty-second Amendment" in *Restoring the Presidency: Reconsidering the Twenty-second Amendment.* Washington, DC: The National Legal Center for the Public Interest, 1990.

Hitchcock, William. *The Age of Eisenhower.* New York: Simon & Schuster, 2018.

Hogue, Henry B. "Presidential Reorganization Authority: History, Recent Initiatives, and Options for Congress." Congressional Research Service, Report R42852 (2012).

Hoogenboom, Ari. *Rutherford B. Hayes: Warrior and President.* Lawrence, Kansas. University of Kansas Press, 1995.

Houck, David W. and Amos Kiewe. *FDR's Body Politics: The Rhetoric of Disability,* College Station. Texas: Texas A&M University Press, 2003.

Howard, James Q. "Duration of the Executive Term." *The Galaxy*, Vol. XVIII (1874).

Howe, Timothy O. "The Third Term." *The North American Review*, Vol. 130, No. 279 (February 1880).

Hull, Cordell. *The Memoirs of Cordell Hull*, Volume 1. New York: The MacMillan Company, 1948.

"Is Byrnes' Star Rising." *The Wilmington Morning Star* (Wilmington, NC), July 18, 1944.

Isaacson, Walter. *Benjamin Franklin: An American Life*. New York: Simon & Schuster, 2003.

Jackson, Robert H. *That Man: An Insider's Portrait of Franklin D. Roosevelt*. Oxford: Oxford University Press, 2003.

Jacobs, Travis B. "Dwight D. Eisenhower's Presidency of Columbia University." *Presidential Studies Quarterly*, Vol. 15, No. 3 (Summer 1985).

Jeffries, John W. *A Third Term for FDR: The Election of 1940*. Lawrence, Kansas: University of Kansas Press, 2017.

Johnson, Claudius O. *Borah of Idaho*. New York: Longman, Green, and Co., 1936.

Johnston, Richard Malcolm and William Hand Browne, *The Life of Alexander H. Stephens*, J.B. Lippincott & Co., 1878.

Jordan, David M. *FDR, Dewey, and the Election of 1944*. Bloomington, Indiana: Indiana University Press, 2011.

Kallenbach, Joseph E. "Constitutional Limitations on Re-eligibility of National and State Chief Executives." *American Political Science Review*, Vol. 26, No. 2 (June 1952).

Kaplan, Fred. *John Quincy Adams: American Visionary*. New York: HarperCollins Publishers, 2014.

Kazin, Michael. *A Godly Hero: The Life of William Jennings Bryan*. New York: Alfred A. Knopf, 2006.

Klarman, Michael J. *The Framers' Coup: The Making of the United States Constitution*. Oxford: Oxford University Press, 2018.

Korzi, Michael J. *Presidential Term Limits in American History: Power, Principles, and Politics*. College Station, Texas: Texas A&M University Press, 2011.

Korzi, Michael J. "Theorizing Presidential Tenure: The Difficult Case of FDR's Fourth Term." *Congress & the Presidency: A Journal of Capital Studies*, Vol. 35, No. 2 (2008), 39–64.

Kyvig, David E. "Everett Dirksen's Constitutional Charades." *Journal of the Illinois State Historical Society*, Vol. 25 (Spring 2002).

Lash, Joseph P. *Eleanor and Franklin*. New York: W.W. Norton and Company, 1971.

Laski, Harold. *The American Presidency: An Interpretation*. New York: Harper & Brothers Publishers, 1940.

Lawrence, David. "Middle West Gains Seen for Willkie." *Washington Evening Star,* October 22, 1940.

Lawrence, David. "President Places Decision on Party." *Washington Evening Star*, August 3, 1927.

Lawrence, W.H. "President Bars a 3d-Term Race Even If 'They Repeal' Ban on It." *New York Times*, January 31, 1957.

Lelyveld, Joseph. *His Final Battle: The Last Months of Franklin Roosevelt*. New York: Alfred A. Knopf, 2016.

Levin, Phyllis Lee. *Edith and Woodrow*. New York: Scribner, 2001.

Levitsky, Steven and Daniel Ziblatt, "Autocrats Love Emergencies." *New York Times*, January 12, 2019, p. SR4.

Levy, Leonard and Louis Fischer, eds. *Encyclopedia of the American Presidency*, Volume 3. New York: Simon & Schuster. 1994.

Lincoln, Gould. "Democrats Face Serious Battles." *Washington Evening Star,* July 16, 1944.

Lincoln, Gould. "Hughes Supports Coolidge for 1924." *Washington Evening Star*. May 21, 1927.

Lincoln, Gould. "Late Returns Boost Roosevelt's Lead." *Washington Evening Star,* November 6, 1940.

Lincoln, Gould. "President is Held Strongest GOP Possibility of 1928." *Washington Evening Star*, April 20, 1927.

Lincoln, Gould. "Republicans Hold President Still 1928 Possibility." *Washington Evening Star*, September 11, 1927.

Lincoln, Gould. "The Political Mill." *Washington Evening Star*, May 20, 1944.

Lincoln, Gould. "The Political Mill." *Washington Evening Star*, July 20, 1944.

Lincoln, Gould. "Truman Victory Ends Turbulent Chicago Session." *Washington Evening Star*, July 22, 1944.

Lingley, Charles R. "Public Opinion and the Third Term Tradition." *Texas Review*, Vol. 1, No. 4 (April 1916).

Link, Arthur. *Woodrow Wilson: Revolution, War, and Peace*. Wheeling, Illinois: Harlan, Davidson. Inc., 1979.

Lodge, Henry Cabot. *Alexander Hamilton*. New York: Houghton, Mifflin and Company, 1884.

Lodge, Henry Cabot. *The Senate and the League of Nations*. New York: Charles Scribner's Sons, 1925.

"Lonely Mr. Roosevelt." *Butler Weekly Tines* (Butler, Missouri), March 7, 1912.

Longworth, Alice Roosevelt. *Crowded Hours*. New York: Charles Scribner's Sons, 1933.

Madison, James. *The Debates in the Federal Convention of 1787 Which Framed the Constitution of the United States of America*. Buffalo, New York: Prometheus Books, 1987.

Maggs, Gregory A. "A Concise Guide to the Records of the Federal Constitutional Convention as a Source of the Original Meaning of the U.S. Constitution." *The George Washington Law Review*, Vol. 80 (2012), 1707.

Maney, Patrick. *Young Bob: A Biography of Robert M. LaFollette, Jr*. Madison, Wisconsin: Wisconsin Historical Society Press, 2003.

Marlow, James. "Truman Main Reason Ike Sought Presidency." *Gadsden Times*, August 4, 1959.

Martin, Douglas. "John Coolidge, Guardian of President's Legacy. Dies at 93." *New York Times,* June 4, 2000.

Martin, Philip. L. "Convention Ratification of Federal Constitutional Amendments." *Political Science Quarterly*, Vol. 82, No. 1 (March 1967).

McCabe, James D. *Our Martyred President: The Life and Public Services of President James A. Garfield*. Philadelphia: National Publishing Company, 1881.

McCullough, David. *John Adams*. New York: Simon & Schuster, 2001.

McCullough, David. *Truman*. New York: Simon & Schuster, 1992.

McKenna, Marian. *Borah*. Ann Arbor, Michigan: University of Michigan Press, 1961.

Meacham, Jon. *American Lion: Andrew Jackson in the White House*. New York: Random House, 2009.

Meacham, Jon. *Thomas Jefferson: The Art of Power*. New York: Random House, 2012.

Meijer, Hendrik. *Arthur Vandenberg: The Man in the Middle of the Twentieth Century*. Chicago: University of Chicago Press, 2017.

Merry, Robert W. *President McKinley: Architect of the American Century*. New York: Simon & Schuster, 2017.

Millard, Candace. *Destiny of the Republic: A Tale of Madness, Medicine, and the Murder of a President*. New York: Doubleday, 2011.

Miller, Nathan. FDR: An Intimate History. Garden City, New York: Doubleday & Company, 1983.

Moe, Richard. *Roosevelt's Second Act: The Election of 1940 and the Politics of War*. Oxford: Oxford University Press, 2013.

Morgan, Ted. *FDR: A Biography*. New York: Simon & Schuster, 1985.

Morris, Edmund. *Colonel Roosevelt*. New York: Random House, 2010.

Morris, Edmund. *Theodore Rex*, New York: Random House, 2001.

"Move Gains to Get Eisenhower Home." *New York Times*, March 12, 1953.

Molotsky, Irvin. "Reagan Wants End of Two-Term Limit." *New York Times*, November 28, 1987.

Neal, Steve. *Dark Horse: A Biography of Wendell Willkie*. Lawrence, Kansas: University of Kansas Press, 1984.

Neale, Thomas H. "Presidential and Vice-Presidential Terms and Tenure." Report RS20827 Congressional Research Service, February 26, 2001.

Neale, Thomas H. "Presidential Terms and Tenure: Perspectives and Proposals for Change." Report R40864, Congressional Research Service, October 19, 2009.

Nelson, Garrison. *John William McCormack*. New York: Bloomsbury Academic, 2017.

Nevins, Allan. *Grover Cleveland: A Study in Courage*. Newtown, Connecticut: American Political Biography Press, 1932.

"New Butt Letters Tell Taft History." *New York Times,* September 4, 1930.

"No Compromise with a Third Term." *New-York Tribune*, May 26, 1880

"No Third Term." *El Paso Herald* (El Paso, Tex.), February 13, 1912. "Of Course." *New York Times*, February 28, 1912.

Ohio: Special Dispatch to the *Chicago Tribune*." *Chicago Daily Tribune,* May 29, 1880.

Olson, Lynne. *Those Angry Days: Roosevelt, Lindbergh, and America's Fight Over World War II, 1939–1941*. New York: Random House, 2013.

"Opening the White House Doors for Teddy in Chicago." *The Detroit Times* (Detroit, Mich.), June 13, 1912.

"Oppose Third Term." *Washington Evening Star*, February 2, 1915, p. 4.

O'Toole, Patricia. *The Moralist: Woodrow Wilson and the World He Made*. New York: Simon & Schuster, 2018.

O'Toole, Patricia R. *When Trumpets Call: Theodore Roosevelt After the White House*. New York: Simon & Schuster, 2005.

Parmet, Herbert S. And Marie B, Hecht. *Never Again: A President Runs for a Third Term*. New York: The MacMillan Company, 1968.

Peabody, Bruce G. "George Washington, Presidential Term Limits, and the Problem of Reluctant Leadership." *Presidential Studies Quarterly*, Vol. 31, No. 3 (September 2001).

Perkins, Frances. *The Roosevelt I Knew*. New York: The Viking Press, 1946.

Peters, Charles. *Five Days in Philadelphia: The Amazing We Want Willkie Convention of 1940 and How it Freed FDR to Save the Western World.* New York: PublicAffairs, 2015.

Pietrusa, David. *TR's Last War*, Guilford, Connecticut: Globe Pequot, 2018.

"President Confuses Politicians by Employing Word 'Choose'; Out of Race, Associates Declare." *Washington Evening Star*, August 3, 1927.

"President Plans Forest Reserves." *American Falls Press* (American Falls, Idaho), February 5, 1910.

"President Shot at Buffalo Fair." *New York Times*, September 7, 1901.

"Promoting Reagan for a Third Term." *New York Times*, July 22, 1986.

Rabalais, Stephen. *General Fox Conner*. Philadelphia and Oxford: Casemate Publishers, 2017.

Reagan, Ronald W., et. al., *Restoring the Presidency: Reconsidering the Twenty-second Amendment.* Washington, DC: National Legal Center for the Public Interest, 1990.

Reedy, George. *The Twilight of the Presidency*. New York: The World Publishing Company, 1970.

"Refuses to Talk of a Third Term." *The Richmond Palladium and Sun-Telegram* (Richmond, Ind.), July 16, 1910.

Rehnquist, William H. *Centennial Crisis: The Disputed Election of 1876.* New York: Alfred A. Knopf, 2004.

Remini, Robert V. *The Life of Andrew Jackson*. New York: Harper & Row Publishers, 1988.

"Remove Monarchy Threat." *Spokane Daily Chronicle*, November 2, 1944.

"Republican Fight Looms on War Issue at the Convention." *New York Times*, June 23, 1940.

Robertson, David Brian. *The Original Compromise: What the Constitution's Framers Were Really Thinking.* New York: Oxford University Press, 2013.

Roll, David L. The Hopkins Touch: *Harry Hopkins and the Forging of the Alliance to Defeat Hitler.* Oxford: Oxford University Press, 2013.

"Roosevelt and Reciprocity Issue, *The Record-Democrat* (Wagoner, Oklahoma), October 17, 1912.

"Roosevelt Calls Committee's Act Morally a Crime." *Chicago Tribune*, June 9, 1912.

Roosevelt, Elliott and James Brough. *A Rendezvous with Destiny: The Roosevelts in the White House*. New York: G.P. Putnam's Sons, 1975.

Roosevelt, Elliott and James Brough. *An Untold Story: The Roosevelts of Hyde Park.* New York: G.P. Putnam's Sons, 1973. "Roosevelt Speaks at Osawatomie." *The Topeka State Journal* (Topeka, Kan.), August 31, 1910.

Roosevelt, Theodore. *The Autobiography of Theodore Roosevelt.* New York: Charles Scribner's Sons, 1913.

Roosevelt, Theodore and Henry Cabot Lodge. *Selections from the Correspondence between Theodore Roosevelt and Henry Cabot Lodge, 1884–1919,* Volume II. New York: Charles Scribner's Sons, 1925.

"Roosevelt Warns of Peril to Nation: Throng Acclaims His Fight for Right." *Chicago Tribune,* June 18, 1912.

"Roosevelt with Progressives." *Aberdeen Herald* (Aberdeen, Chehalis County, W.T.), September 1, 1910, p. 4.

"Root Wants Teddy Again." *The Hawaiian star* (Honolulu [Oahu]), October 29, 1910, p. 13.

Rosenman, Samuel. *Working with Roosevelt.* New York: Harper & Brothers, 1952.

"Russian Presidential Term Extended to Six Years." CNN.com, December 22, 2008.

Schlesinger, Arthur. *The Age of Roosevelt: The Crisis of the Old Order 1919–1933.* Boston: Houghton Mifflin Company, 1957.

Sebesteyn, Victor. *1946: The Making of the Modern World.* New York: Pantheon Books, 2014.

"Senate Declares Against Third Term by 56 to 26 Vote: LaFollette Resolution Adopted Viewing Departure from Precedent as 'Fraught with Peril'." *New York Times*, February 11, 1928.

"Senate Unit Clears a Bill to Repeal 2-Term Rule." *New York Herald Tribune*, September 2, 1959.

Shafer, Jack. "How the GOP Embraced the World and Then Turned Away." *Politico Magazine*, July 13, 2018.

Sherman, John, *John Sherman's Recollections of Forty Years in the House, Senate, and Cabinet: An Autobiography,* Volume 2. Chicago. The Werner Company, 1895.

Sherwood, Robert. *Roosevelt and Hopkins: An Intimate Story*. New York: Harper & Brothers, 1948.

Shlaes, Amity. *Coolidge.* New York: HarperCollins Publishers, 2011.

"Short Chats with the Editors." *The Durham Recorder* (Durham, N.C.), September 15, 1910, p. 4.

Sigel, Roberta S. and David J. Butler, "The Public and the No Third Term Tradition: Inquiry into Attitudes Toward Power, *Midwest Journal of Political Science*, Vol. 8. No. 1 (February 1964).

Smith, Gene. *When the Cheering Stopped: The Last Years of Woodrow Wilson.* New York: William Morrow and Company, 1964.

Smith, Kathryn. *The Gatekeeper: Missy LeHand, FDR, and the Untold Story of the Partnership that Defined a Presidency.* New York: Touchstone, 2016.

Smith, Richard Norton. *Thomas E. Dewey and His Times.* New York: Simon & Schuster, 1983.

"Something for Republicans: The Third Term Danger Still Imminent." *St. Paul Daily Globe,* October 30, 1880.

Stathis, Stephen W. "The Twenty-second Amendment: A Practical Remedy or a Partisan Maneuver." *Constitutional Commentary*, 1990.

Steil, Benn. *The Marshall Plan: Dawn of the Cold War,* New York: Simon & Schuster, 2018.

Stevenson, David. *1917: War, Peace, & Revolution*. Oxford: Oxford University Press, 2017.

Stimson, Henry L. and MacGeorge Bundy, *On Active Services in Peace and War*. New York: Harper Brothers, 1947.

"Taft in Youngstown, Roosevelt in Canton, End Strenuous Day." *Washington Evening Star*, May 15, 1912.

Taft, William Howard. *Our Chief Magistrate and His Powers*. New York: Columbia University Press, 1916.

"T.D. Garry, 'Voice of the Sewers' Who Backed FDR in '40 Dies." *New York Times*, July 3, 1976.

"Text of Willkie's Address at Rally in Syracuse." *New York Times*, October 15, 1940.

Thach, Charles Coleman. *The Creation of the Presidency, 1775–1789: A Study in Constitutional History*. Baltimore: Johns Hopkins Press, 1923.

"The Age of Taft." *Time*, January 20, 1947.

"The Anti-third Term League." *Washington Evening Star*, May 30, 1927.

"The Choice of a Candidate." *New York Times*, September 19, 1940.

"The Close of the Forty-third Congress." *New York Herald*, March 4, 1875.

"The Common Cause." *The Richmond palladium and Sun-Telegram* (Richmond, Ind.), September 5, 1910, p. 4.

The Federalist Papers, Mentor Books Edition. New York: Mentor Books, 1961.

"The Fight Up to Date." *Chicago Tribune*, June 24, 1912.

The Great Lesson of the Day." *The Hawaiian Star* (Honolulu [Oahu]), February 22, 1912. p. 4.

"The Greatest Issue of All: Roosevelt and the Third Term." *The Leon Reporter* (Leon, Iowa), March 7, 1912, p, 4.

"The Issue of Issues." *Brooklyn Daily Eagle,* November 3, 1912.

"The Nation: View from a Polling Booth." *Time,* November 1, 1948.

"The One Term Platform – Will Tilden Stand by Hayes?" *The New York Herald*, July 16, 1876.

"Theodore Roosevelt Dies Suddenly at Oyster Bay Home." *New York Times*, January 7, 1919.

"The Presidency." *The Indianapolis Leader*, May 22, 1880.

"The President Dead." *New York Times*, September 20, 1881.

"The Summary of the Reorganization Bill." *New York Times*, March 29, 1938.

"The Third Term." *Perry County Times*, October 10, 1912.

"The Third Term Finesse." *The Weekly Kansas Chief* (Troy, Kansas). January 8, 1880.

"The Unit Rule." *Chicago Daily Tribune*, June 2, 1880.

"Third-Term Fight Shelved by House." *New York Times*, February 6, 1912.

"To Kansas Republicans." *The Olathe Mirror*, September 26, 1912.

Truman, Harry S. *Years of Trial and Hope: 1946–1952*. Garden City, New York: Doubleday & Company, 1956.

"Truman, Taft Opponents Not Belittling Them." *Lewiston Evening Journal*, March 13, 1952.

Trussell, C.P. "President Defies Rain, Wind to Let New York See Him." *New York Times*, October 22, 1944.

Tully, Grace. *FDR: My Boss*. New York: Charles Scribner's Sons, 1949.

Tumulty, Joseph. *Woodrow Wilson as I Know Him*. Garden City, New York: Doubleday, Page & Company, 1921.

Vandenberg, Arthur H. *The Greatest American: Alexander Hamilton*. New York: G.P. Putnam's Sons, 1921.

Vile, John R. "The Critical Role of Committees at the U.S. Constitutional Convention of 1787." *The American Journal of Legal History*, Vol. 48, No. 2 (April. 2006).

"Wallace Gains as Balloting at Chicago Nears." *Washington Evening Star*, July 21, 1944.

Wapshott, Nicholas. *The Sphinx: Franklin Roosevelt, The Isolationists, and the Road to World War II*. New York: W.W. Norton, 2015.

Ward, Geoffrey C. Ward, *Closest Companion: The Unknown Story of the Intimate Friendship between Franklin Roosevelt and Margaret Suckley*. New York: Simon & Schuster, 1995.

Weiss, Nancy, *Farewell to the Party of Lincoln: Black Politics in the Age of FDR*. Princeton, New Jersey: Princeton University Press, 1983.

White, Ronald C. *American Ulysses: A Life of Ulysses S. Grant*. New York: Random House, 2016.

Whyte, Kenneth. *Hoover: An Extraordinary Life in Extraordinary Times*. New York: Alfred A. Knopf, 2017.

Wicker, Tom. "Six Years for the President." *New York Times*, June 26, 1983.

Wilcox, Francis O. "American Government and Politics: The Neutrality Fight in Congress: 1939." *The American Political Science Review*, Vol. 33, No. 5 (October 1939).

Wilkerson, Isabel. *The Warmth of Other Suns: The Epic Story of America's Great Migration*. New York: Random House, 2010.

"Will Grant Withdraw?" *Chicago Daily Tribune* (Chicago, Illinois), June 2, 1880.

Willkie Declares GOP Victory Is Vital to Nation's Welfare." *Washington Evening Star*, February 9, 1944.

"Willkie Funeral to be Tomorrow; Son Still at Sea." *New York Times*, October 9, 1944.

Willkie, Wendell L. "Roosevelt Should Run in 1940" *Look*. April 26, 1940.

Willis, Paul G. and George L. Willis. "The Politics of the Twenty-second Amendment. *The Western Political Science Quarterly*, Vol. 5, No. 3 (September 1952).

Winik, Jay. 1944: *FDR and the Year that Changed History*. New York: Simon & Schuster, 2015.

Wunderlin Jr., Clarence E., ed. *Papers of Senator Robert A. Taft, Volume 3, 1945–1948*. Kent, Ohio: Kent State University Press, 2001.

Index

About the Author

Martin B. Gold is an attorney, author, teacher, and speaker. A partner with Capitol Counsel, LLC, Gold has well over forty years of government and private practice experience related to Congress.

Gold served in several senior counsel roles at the United States Senate, and continues to advise Senators and Representatives on matters of congressional procedure and strategy. He is also on the Adjunct Faculty of George Washington University Graduate School of Political Management, where he teaches a course on "Advanced Legislative Procedures." Gold has lectured about American political institutions and politics to numerous domestic and international university audiences, foreign governments, as well as business and professional associations.

He is the author of eight books, each of which is centered on the U.S. Congress. His most recent are the fourth edition of *Senate Procedure and Practice*, and *A Legislative History of the Taiwan Relations Act: Bridging the Strait*. Both were published in 2017.

In 2000, Gold was elected to membership in the Cosmos Club of Washington. DC, for distinction in the field of public affairs. He lives in the capital with his wife, Celeste.